Scotland's Tourist A…

HOTELS AND GUEST HOUSES 2008

A castle hotel in the Highlands

Published by VisitScotland, 2007 Photography Paul Tomkins / VisitScotland / Scottish Viewpoint www.visitscotland.com 0845 22 55 121

Loch Awe and Kilchurn Castle, Argyll

WELCOME TO SCOTLAND

Once you've enjoyed a holiday in Scotland, it is easy to see why so many people from all over the world visit time and again. Scotland is a wonderful place for holidaymakers. From the briefest of breaks to annual vacations, Scotland has so much to offer that you'll never run out of options.

Flick through the pages of this guide and you'll immediately get a flavour of Scotland's diversity. You'll discover an inspiring array of fascinating places, each with its own unique attractions.

The best small country in the world

Though it's a relatively small country, Scotland is remarkably varied. You can climb mountains in the morning and still be on the beach in the afternoon. You can canoe across a remote loch and never see another soul all day long or you can sip coffee in a city centre pavement café and watch the whole world go by. You can get dressed up to the nines and go to a world premier on a balmy summer's evening or you can join in with some traditional folk songs round a welcoming log fire in a quaint little pub on a cold winter's night.

Because of its remarkable diversity, Scotland is a world-class holiday destination. No matter the season, there's always something happening, and when you've decided where you're going, you'll be spoiled for choice for somewhere special to stay.

A room with a view

From quiet country house hotels, to small family establishments to celebrated luxury resorts that are famed throughout the world, Scotland has everything the discerning traveller could ever want – and some of the most picturesque locations.

All over the country, you'll find that Scotland's hotel and guest house trade is booming and there will always be something to suit your taste and budget. So you can stay in an impressively grand traditional hotel with four poster beds and every luxury you could imagine or you could select a welcoming family-friendly establishment that's as comfortable on your pocket as it is for a good night's sleep.

You'll find inspirational, ultra-chic boutique hotels, cosy guest houses where you can really get to know your hosts and there are even places where the hotel itself is an attraction with spas and leisure complexes, golf courses, swimming pools and other sporting facilities.

And when you've found the ideal place, whether you select 5-star luxury or something a little more modest, you can always look forward to a warm welcome in a country that is renowned for its hospitality.

A warm welcome awaits

Nobody loves a good time like the Scots. Whether it's bringing in the New Year with a wee dram, swirling your partner at a ceilidh or enjoying a sumptuous dinner for two in an exclusive restaurant with a stunning view, unforgettable experiences are never far away.

There's always the chance that you'll meet some great folks – locals and other visitors – some of whom could well become friends for life. That's all just part of a visit to Scotland. As they say in the Gaelic tongue, *ceud mille failte* – 'a hundred thousand welcomes'. Come and enjoy our beautiful country.

A view towards Edinburgh Castle from Holyrood Park

Top left: A group of walkers near Glen Doll and Glen Clova, Angus Top right: Puffins on the Isle of Staffa, Inner Hebrides
Bottom: West Sands Beach, St Andrews, Fife

DON'T MISS

Walking

From the rolling hills in the south to the Angus Glens, to the mountainous north, Scotland is perfect for walkers whether it's a gentle stroll or a serious trek.

Beaches

Scotland's beaches are something special whether it's for a romantic stroll, or to try some surfing. Explore Fife's Blue Flag beaches or the breathtaking beaches in the Outer Hebrides.

Wildlife

From dolphins in the Moray Firth to capercaillie in the Highlands and seals and puffins on the coastline, you never know what you might spot.

Culture & Heritage

From the mysterious standing stones in Orkney and the Outer Hebrides to Burns Cottage and Rosslyn Chapel, traces of Scotland's history are never hard to find.

Ring of Brodgar, Orkney

Adventure

From rock climbing to white water rafting, you can do it all. Try Perthshire for some unusual adventure activities or the south of Scotland for some serious mountain biking.

Mountain biking in Glentress Forest, Scottish Borders

Shopping

From designer stores to unique boutiques, from Glasgow's swanky city centre to Edinburgh's eclectic Old Town, Scotland is a shopper's paradise with lots of hidden gems to uncover.

Victoria Street, Edinburgh

Golf

The country that gave the world the game of golf is still the best place to play it. Why not check out the historic courses in Ayrshire or Angus.

The Isle of Skye Golf Club

Castles

Wherever you are in Scotland you are never far from a great Scottish icon whether it's an impressive ruin or an imposing fortress, a fairytale castle or country estate.

Caerlaverock Castle, Dumfries and Galloway

Highland Games

From the famous Braemar Gathering in Aberdeenshire to the spectacular Cowal Highland Gathering in Argyll, hot foot it to a Highland Games for pipe bands, dancers, and tossing the caber.

Ballater Highland Games, Aberdeenshire

Events & Festivals

In Scotland there's so much going on with fabulous events and festivals throughout the year, wherever you choose to visit, from the biggest names to the quirky and traditional.

The Royal Mile during the Festival, Edinburgh

If you love food, get a taste of Scotland. A climate without extremes and the unspoilt environment provide the ideal conditions so Scotland's natural larder offers some of the best produce in the world. Scotland's coastal waters are home to an abundance of lobster, prawns, oysters and more, whilst the land produces world famous beef, lamb and game.

There's high quality food and drink on menus all over the country often cooked up by award-winning chefs in restaurants where the view is second to none. You'll find home cooking, fine dining, takeaways and tearooms. Whether you're looking for a family-friendly pub or a romantic Highland restaurant there's the perfect place to dine. And there's no better time to indulge than when you're on holiday!

Traditional fare

Haggis and whisky might be recognised as traditional Scottish fare but why not add cullen skink, clapshot, cranachan, and clootie dumpling to the list...discover the tastes that match such ancient names. Sample some local hospitality along with regional specialities such as the Selkirk Bannock or Arbroath Smokies. Or experience the freedom of eating fish and chips straight from the wrapper while breathing in the clear evening air.

Farmers' markets

Scotland is a land renowned for producing ingredients of the highest quality. You can handpick fresh local produce at farmers' markets in towns and cities across the country. Create your own culinary delights or learn from the masters at the world famous Nick Nairn Cook School in Stirling. Savour the aroma, excite your taste buds and experience the buzz of a farmers' market.

EATING AND DRINKING

Events

Scotland serves up a full calendar of food and drink festivals. Events like Taste of Edinburgh and Highland Feast are a must for foodies. Whisky fans can share their passion at the Islay Malt Whisky Festival, the Highland Whisky Festival, or the Spirit of Speyside Whisky Festival.

Tours and trails

If you're a lover of seafood spend some time exploring the rugged, unspoilt coastline of mid-Argyll following The Seafood Trail. Or if you fancy a wee dram visit the eight distilleries and cooperage on the world's only Malt Whisky Trail in Speyside. Look out for the new Scottish Café Trail for Scotland's best café experiences, and enjoy a cup of something lovely surrounded by amazing scenery.

EatScotland

EatScotland is a nationwide Quality Assurance Scheme from VisitScotland. The scheme includes all sectors of the catering industry from chip shops, pubs and takeaways to restaurants. A trained team of assessors carry out an incognito visit to assess quality, standards and ambience. Only those operators who meet the EatScotland quality standards are accredited to the scheme so look out for the logo to ensure you visit Scotland's best quality establishments.

The newly launched EatScotland Silver and Gold Award Scheme recognises outstanding standards, reflecting that an establishment offers an excellent eating out experience in Scotland.

www.eatscotland.com

Al fresco dining, Edinburgh

GREEN TOURISM

Scotland is a stunning destination and we want to make sure it stays that way. That's why we encourage all tourism operators including accommodation providers to take part in our Green Tourism Business Scheme. It means you're assured of a great quality stay at an establishment that's trying to minimise its impact on the environment.

VisitScotland rigorously assesses accommodation providers against measures as diverse as energy use, using local produce on menus, or promoting local wildlife walks or cycle hire. Environmentally responsible businesses can achieve Bronze, Silver or Gold awards, to acknowledge how much they are doing to help conserve the quality of Scotland's beautiful environment.

Look out for the Bronze, Silver and Gold Green Tourism logos throughout this guide to help you decide where to stay and do your bit to help protect our environment.

www.green-business.co.uk

Bronze
Green Tourism Award

Silver
Green Tourism Award

Gold
Green Tourism Award

Friendly and knowledgeable staff are able to answer your questions and give advice

TOURIST INFORMATION

Make the most of your stay in Scotland and call into a Tourist Information Centre wherever you go.

- There are over 100 Tourist Information Centres across Scotland.
- Knowledgeable and friendly staff are there to answer questions, give advice, and turn a good holiday into an unforgettable experience.
- Tell the staff what you're interested in doing and they'll suggest the best places to go.
- Staff can help you find and book accommodation anywhere in Scotland.
- Each centre has a wide stock of free guides and leaflets featuring local attractions and places of interest.
- Each centre also has an excellent range of maps, guide books, Scottish literature and books that you can buy.
- You can buy tickets for local and national events and book excursions, tours and travel.
- Most offer a splendid range of souvenirs and local crafts which make ideal gifts for you to take home for friends and family.
- Some centres also provide a bureau de change service and internet access.

VisitScotland, under the Scottish Tourist Board brand, administers the star grading schemes which assess the quality and standards of all types of tourist accommodation and visitor attractions from castles and historic houses to garden centres and arts venues. We grade around 80 per cent of the accommodation in Scotland and 90 per cent of the visitor attractions - so wherever you want to stay or visit, we've got it covered. The schemes are monitored all year round and reviewed once a year. We do the hard work so you can relax and enjoy your holiday.

The promise of the stars:

★
It is clean, tidy and an acceptable, if basic, standard

★★
It is a good, all round standard

★★★
It is a very good standard, with attention to detail in every area

★★★★
It is excellent – using high quality materials, good food (except self-catering) and friendly, professional service

★★★★★
An exceptional standard where presentation, ambience, food (except self-catering) and service are hard to fault.

IT'S WRITTEN IN THE STARS...

How does the system work?

Our advisors visit and assess establishments on up to 50 areas from quality, comfort and cleanliness to welcome, ambience and service. If an establishment scores less than 60 per cent it will not be graded. The same star scheme now runs in England and Wales, so you can follow the stars wherever you go.

Graded visitor attractions

Visitor attractions from castles and museums to leisure centres and tours are graded with 1-5 stars depending on their level of customer care. The focus is on the standard of hospitality and service as well as presentation, quality of shop or café (if there is one) and toilet facilities.

We want you to feel welcome

Walkers Welcome and Cyclists Welcome. Establishments that carry the symbols below pay particular attention to the specific needs of walkers and cyclists.

 Cyclists Welcome

 Walkers Welcome

There are similar schemes for Anglers, Bikers, Classic Cars, Golfers, Children and Ancestral Tourism. Check with establishment when booking.

Access all areas

The following symbols will help visitors with physical disabilities to decide whether accommodation is suitable.

 Unassisted wheelchair access

 Assisted wheelchair access

 Access for visitors with mobility difficulties

Further information:
Quality Assurance
Tel: 01463 723040
Fax: 01463 717244
Email: qainfo@visitscotland.com

We welcome your comments on star-awarded properties
Tel: 01463 723040
Fax: 01463 717244
Email: qa@visitscotland.com

The Glenfinnan Viaduct, Highlands

TRAVEL TO SCOTLAND

It's really easy to get to Scotland whether you choose to travel by car, train, plane, coach or ferry. And once you get here travel is easy as Scotland is a compact country.

By Air

Flying to Scotland couldn't be simpler with flight times from London, Dublin and Belfast only around one hour. There are airports at Edinburgh, Glasgow, Glasgow Prestwick, Aberdeen, Dundee and Inverness. The following airlines operate flights to Scotland (although not all airports) from within the UK and Ireland:

bmi
Tel: 0870 60 70 555
From Ireland: 1332 64 8181
flybmi.com

bmi baby
Tel: 0871 224 0224
From Ireland: 1 890 340 122
bmibaby.com

British Airways
Tel: 0870 850 9 850
From Ireland: 1890 626 747
ba.com

Eastern Airways
Tel: 08703 669 100
easternairways.com

easyJet
Tel: 0905 821 0905
From Ireland: 1890 923 922
easyjet.com

Flybe
Tel: 0871 522 6100
From Ireland: 1392 268 529
flybe.com

Ryanair
Tel: 0871 246 0000
From Ireland: 0818 30 30 30
ryanair.com

Air France
Tel: 0870 142 4343
airfrance.co.uk

Aer Arann
Tel: 0870 876 76 76
From Ireland: 0818 210 210
aerarann.com

Jet2
Tel: 0871 226 1737
From Ireland: 0818 200017
jet2.com

AirBerlin
Tel: 0871 5000 737
airberlin.com

Aer Lingus
Tel: 0870 876 5000
From Ireland: 0818 365 000
aerlingus.com

By Rail

Scotland has major rail stations in Aberdeen, Edinburgh Waverley and Edinburgh Haymarket, Glasgow Queen Street and Glasgow Central, Perth, Stirling, Dundee and Inverness. There are regular cross border railway services from England and Wales, and good city links. You could even travel on the First ScotRail Caledonian Sleeper overnight train service from London and wake up to the sights and sounds of Scotland.

First ScotRail
Tel: 08457 55 00 33
firstscotrail.com

Virgin Trains
Tel: 08457 222 333
virgintrains.co.uk

GNER
Tel: 08457 225 225
gner.co.uk

By Road

Scotland has an excellent road network from motorways and dual carriageway linking cities and major towns, to remote single-track roads with passing places to let others by. Whether you are coming in your own car from home or hiring a car once you get here, getting away from traffic jams and out onto Scotland's quiet roads can really put the fun back into driving. Branches of the following companies can be found throughout Scotland:

Arnold Clark
Tel: 0845 702 3946
arnoldclark.com/rental

Avis Rent A Car
Tel: 0870 606 0100
avis.co.uk

Budget
Tel: 08701 56 56 56
budget.co.uk

easyCar
Tel: 0906 333 3333
easycar.com

Enterprise Rent-A-Car
Tel: 0870 350 3000
enterprise.co.uk

Europcar
Tel: 0870 607 5000
europcarscotland.co.uk

Hertz
Tel: 08708 44 88 44
hertz.co.uk

National Car Rental
Tel: 0870 400 4560
nationalcar.com

Sixt rent a car
Tel: 0870 156 7567
sixt.co.uk

By Ferry

Scotland has over 130 inhabited islands so ferries are important. And whether you are coming from Ireland or trying to get to the outer islands, you might be in need of a ferry crossing. Ferries to and around the islands are regular and reliable and most carry vehicles. These companies all operate ferry services around Scotland:

Stena Line
Tel: 08705 204 204
stenaline.co.uk

P&O Irish Sea
Tel: 0870 24 24 777
poirishsea.com

Caledonian MacBrayne
Tel: 08705 650000
calmac.co.uk

Western Ferries
Tel: 01369 704 452
western-ferries.co.uk

Northlink Ferries
Tel: 08456 000 449
northlinkferries.co.uk

By Coach

Coach connections include express services to Scotland from all over the UK, and there is a good network of coach services once you get here too. You could even travel on the Postbus – a special feature of the Scottish mail service which carries fare-paying passengers along with the mail in rural areas where there is no other form of transport, bringing a new dimension to travel.

National Express
Tel: 08705 80 80 80
nationalexpress.com

City Link
Tel: 08705 50 50 50
citylink.co.uk

Postbus
Tel: 08457 740 740
royalmail.com/postbus

DRIVING DISTANCES

	ABERDEEN	BIRMINGHAM	CARDIFF	DOVER	DUMFRIES	DUNDEE	EDINBURGH	FORT WILLIAM	GLASGOW	HARWICH	HAWICK	HULL	INVERNESS	KYLE OF LOCHALSH	LONDON	MANCHESTER	NEWCASTLE	OBAN	PERTH	PRESTWICK	ROSYTH	STIRLING	STRANRAER	THURSO	TROON	ULLAPOOL
BIRMINGHAM	421 687																									
CARDIFF	529 851	113 182																								
DOVER	617 993	200 322	224 361																							
DUMFRIES	214 344	234 376	335 539	436 700																						
DUNDEE	71 114	357 575	465 749	553 890	149 240																					
EDINBURGH	131 210	290 467	398 641	486 782	80 128	62 99																				
FORT WILLIAM	161 258	396 637	504 811	592 952	179 288	123 197	138 221																			
GLASGOW	152 243	286 461	394 634	482 776	76 122	84 134	45 72	108 173																		
HARWICH	604 972	187 300	242 390	130 210	370 595	540 869	473 761	578 931	469 754																	
HAWICK	178 287	243 391	344 554	417 671	53 86	113 182	50 81	185 298	85 137	370 596																
HULL	387 619	137 221	251 405	255 411	205 330	318 509	255 408	384 614	275 440	214 346	206 331															
INVERNESS	118 189	446 717	553 890	641 1032	239 385	134 214	162 259	69 110	178 285	628 1011	209 337	444 710														
KYLE OF LOCHALSH	200 320	469 755	577 929	665 1070	253 407	179 286	207 331	76 122	184 294	652 1049	254 408	459 734	82 131													
LONDON	549 878	118 190	150 242	75 122	349 561	481 770	412 659	514 822	406 650	78 126	358 576	216 346	573 917	590 944												
MANCHESTER	345 556	93 150	201 324	281 453	157 252	281 453	214 345	320 515	210 338	268 431	166 267	95 154	370 595	393 633	201 322											
NEWCASTLE	244 390	208 336	323 519	350 563	91 147	175 280	112 179	267 427	159 254	309 498	64 102	148 237	274 438	343 549	288 461	147 237										
OBAN	190 304	385 620	493 794	581 935	168 270	121 194	125 200	50 80	96 154	568 914	175 281	371 594	112 180	125 200	502 803	309 498	310 496									
PERTH	86 139	348 560	449 723	550 884	128 205	21 34	43 69	104 166	64 104	484 778	96 155	319 513	114 183	158 254	463 744	271 436	152 245	94 151								
PRESTWICK	177 285	304 489	411 662	500 804	61 98	113 182	79 127	131 210	32 52	486 783	105 168	279 449	201 324	204 329	418 673	228 366	168 271	120 193	96 155							
ROSYTH	115 185	324 522	425 684	477 768	104 170	48 77	14 23	124 200	47 76	430 692	67 108	265 426	145 233	189 304	437 703	247 398	123 198	114 183	31 49	79 127						
STIRLING	120 193	313 503	414 666	514 823	92 149	55 89	38 61	97 157	29 47	448 722	87 141	284 456	145 234	172 277	427 688	236 379	143 231	87 140	37 60	61 99	26 42					
STRANRAER	241 386	297 478	404 651	489 787	71 115	172 275	133 213	196 314	89 142	475 765	125 202	284 454	265 424	272 435	415 664	224 358	161 259	172 277	149 240	54 87	131 211	114 611				
THURSO	234 374	555 893	663 1066	750 1208	348 560	250 400	278 445	183 293	293 469	737 1186	319 513	559 894	112 180	177 283	690 1104	499 798	391 626	233 373	221 311	355 500	254 409	252 406	382 183			
TROON	183 295	314 505	415 668	516 830	64 104	119 191	82 132	126 203	35 56	450 724	106 171	285 459	209 336	200 322	429 690	237 381	171 276	116 186	101 162	5 8	80 129	63 101	60 96	316 508		
ULLAPOOL	179 286	499 803	607 976	695 1118	293 472	194 310	222 355	119 190	238 381	681 1097	263 424	504 806	63 101	91 146	635 1016	444 710	335 536	169 270	168 270	255 411	199 320	199 320	128 205	327 523	263 423	
YORK	343 552	132 212	246 396	273 439	151 243	279 449	191 308	318 511	208 335	233 374	152 245	41 65	367 591	391 630	208 335	70 113	90 146	307 495	237 382	226 363	212 341	230 370	477 767	218 352	231 372	421 678

M KM

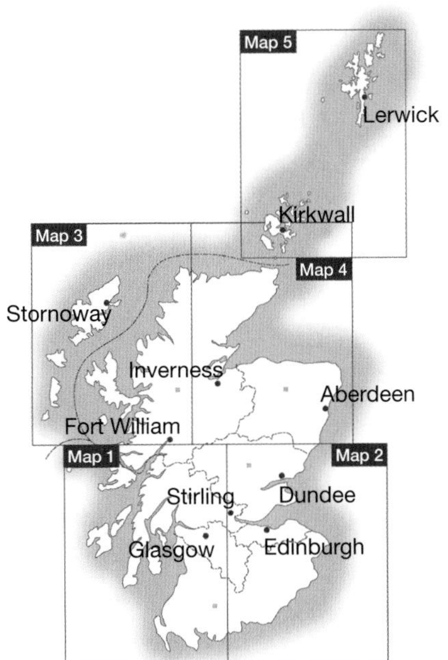
Map 5
Lerwick
Kirkwall
Map 3
Map 4
Stornoway
Inverness
Aberdeen
Fort William
Map 1
Map 2
Stirling
Dundee
Glasgow
Edinburgh

MAPS

These maps show locations of establishments appearing in the Main Advertising Section of this guide. For route planning and touring please use a current road atlas.

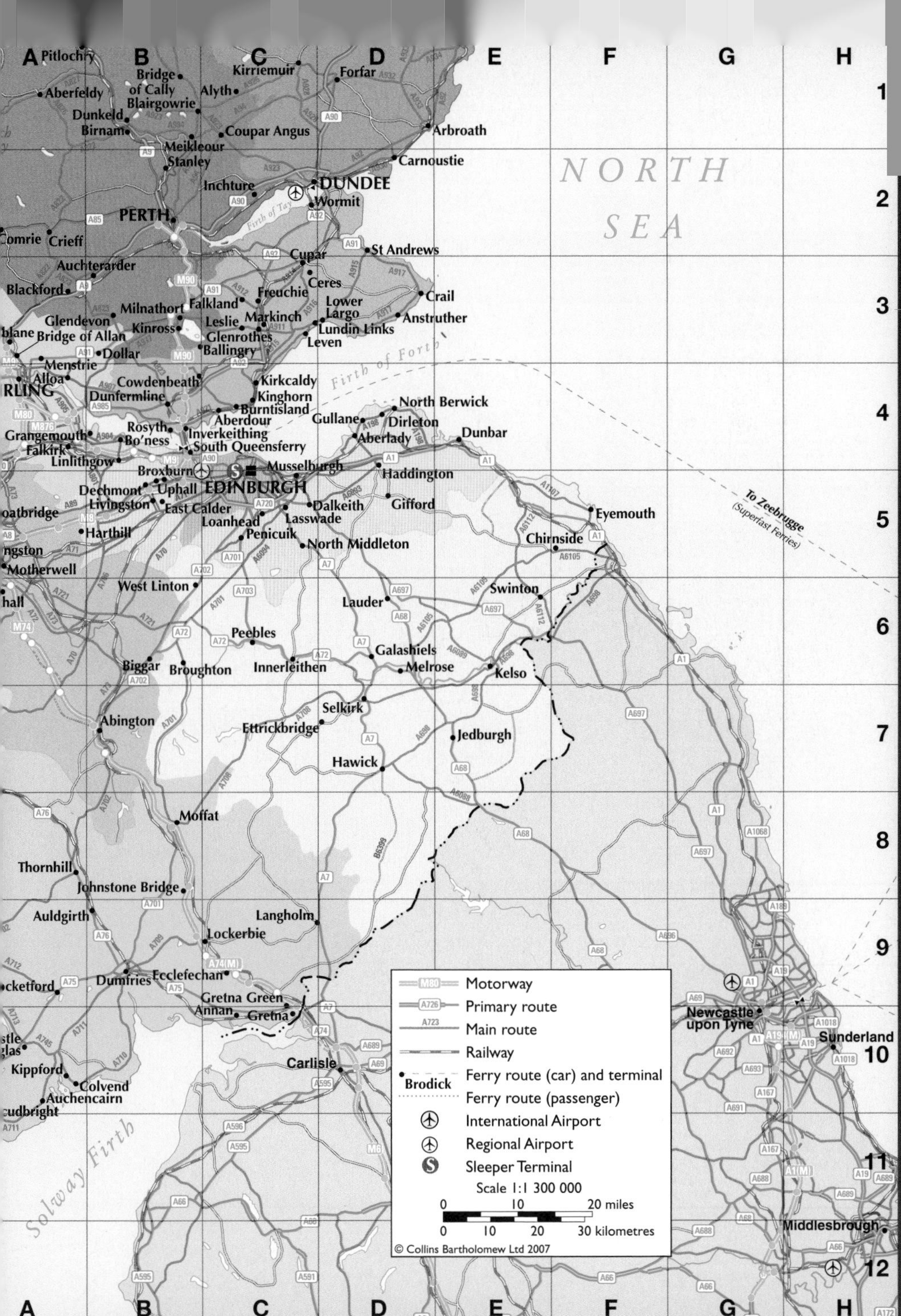

A B C D E F G H
1 2 3 4 5 6 7 8 9 10 11 12
NORTH SEA
Pitlochry
Aberfeldy
Bridge of Cally
Blairgowrie
Alyth
Kirriemuir
Forfar
Dunkeld
Birnam
Coupar Angus
Arbroath
Meikleour
Stanley
Carnoustie
Inchture
DUNDEE
Wormit
PERTH
Firth of Tay
Comrie
Crieff
St Andrews
Cupar
Auchterarder
Ceres
Blackford
Freuchie
Crail
Falkland
Lower Largo
Anstruther
Milnathort
Glendevon
Kinross
Leslie
Markinch
Lundin Links
Bridge of Allan
Glenrothes
Leven
Dollar
Ballingry
Menstrie
Firth of Forth
Alloa
Cowdenbeath
Kirkcaldy
Dunfermline
Kinghorn
Burntisland
North Berwick
Aberdour
Gullane
Dirleton
Rosyth
Inverkeithing
Grangemouth
Bo'ness
Aberlady
Dunbar
Falkirk
South Queensferry
Linlithgow
Musselburgh
Broxburn
Haddington
EDINBURGH
Dechmont
Uphall
Livingston
East Calder
Dalkeith
Gifford
Lasswade
Loanhead
Eyemouth
Harthill
Penicuik
Chirnside
Motherwell
North Middleton
To Zeebrugge
(Superfast Ferries)
West Linton
Swinton
Lauder
Peebles
Galashiels
Biggar
Broughton
Innerleithen
Melrose
Kelso
Selkirk
Abington
Ettrickbridge
Jedburgh
Hawick
Moffat
Thornhill
Johnstone Bridge
Auldgirth
Langholm
Lockerbie
Dumfries
Ecclefechan
Gretna Green
Annan
Gretna
Kippford
Colvend
Auchencairn
Carlisle
Solway Firth
Newcastle upon Tyne
Sunderland
Middlesbrough
Motorway
Primary route
Main route
Railway
Ferry route (car) and terminal
Brodick
Ferry route (passenger)
International Airport
Regional Airport
Sleeper Terminal
Scale 1:1 300 000
0 10 20 miles
0 10 20 30 kilometres
© Collins Bartholomew Ltd 2007

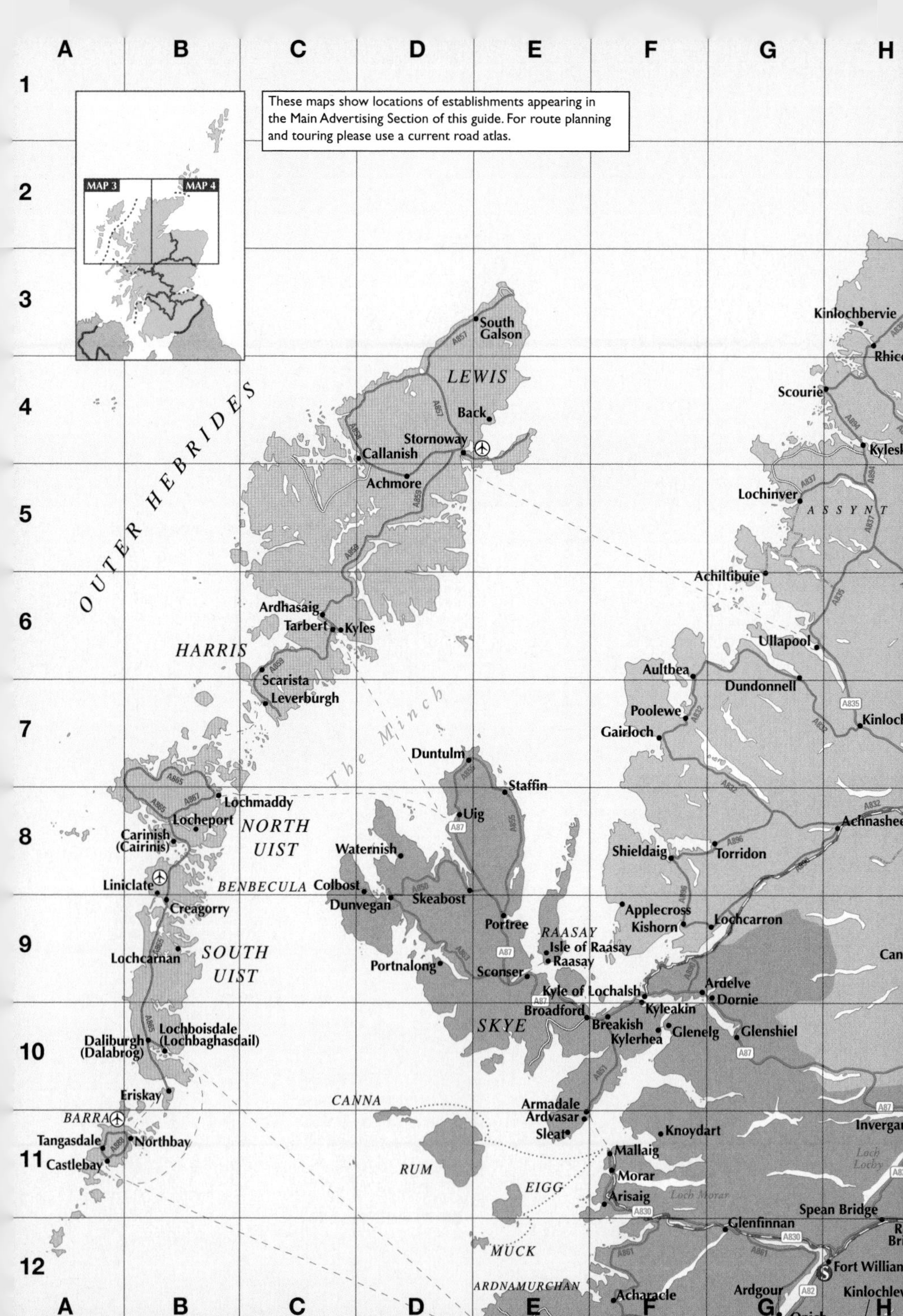

These maps show locations of establishments appearing in the Main Advertising Section of this guide. For route planning and touring please use a current road atlas.
MAP 3
MAP 4
OUTER HEBRIDES
LEWIS
South Galson
Back
Stornoway
Callanish
Achmore
HARRIS
Ardhasaig
Tarbert
Kyles
Scarista
Leverburgh
The Minch
Lochmaddy
Locheport
NORTH UIST
Carinish (Cairinis)
Liniclate
BENBECULA
Creagorry
SOUTH UIST
Lochcarnan
Lochboisdale (Lochbaghasdail)
Daliburgh (Dalabrog)
Eriskay
BARRA
Tangasdale
Northbay
Castlebay
Duntulm
Staffin
Uig
Waternish
Colbost
Dunvegan
Skeabost
Portree
RAASAY
Isle of Raasay
Raasay
Portnalong
Sconser
Kyle of Lochalsh
Broadford
Kyleakin
SKYE
Breakish
Kylerhea
Glenelg
CANNA
Armadale
Ardvasar
Sleat
Knoydart
Mallaig
Morar
RUM
EIGG
Arisaig
Loch Morar
MUCK
ARDNAMURCHAN
Acharacle
Kinlochbervie
Scourie
Lochinver
ASSYNT
Achiltibuie
Ullapool
Aultbea
Dundonnell
Poolewe
Gairloch
Shieldaig
Torridon
Achnasheen
Applecross
Kishorn
Lochcarron
Ardelve
Dornie
Glenshiel
Glenfinnan
Spean Bridge
Loch Lochy
Fort William
Ardgour
Onich
Kinlochleven

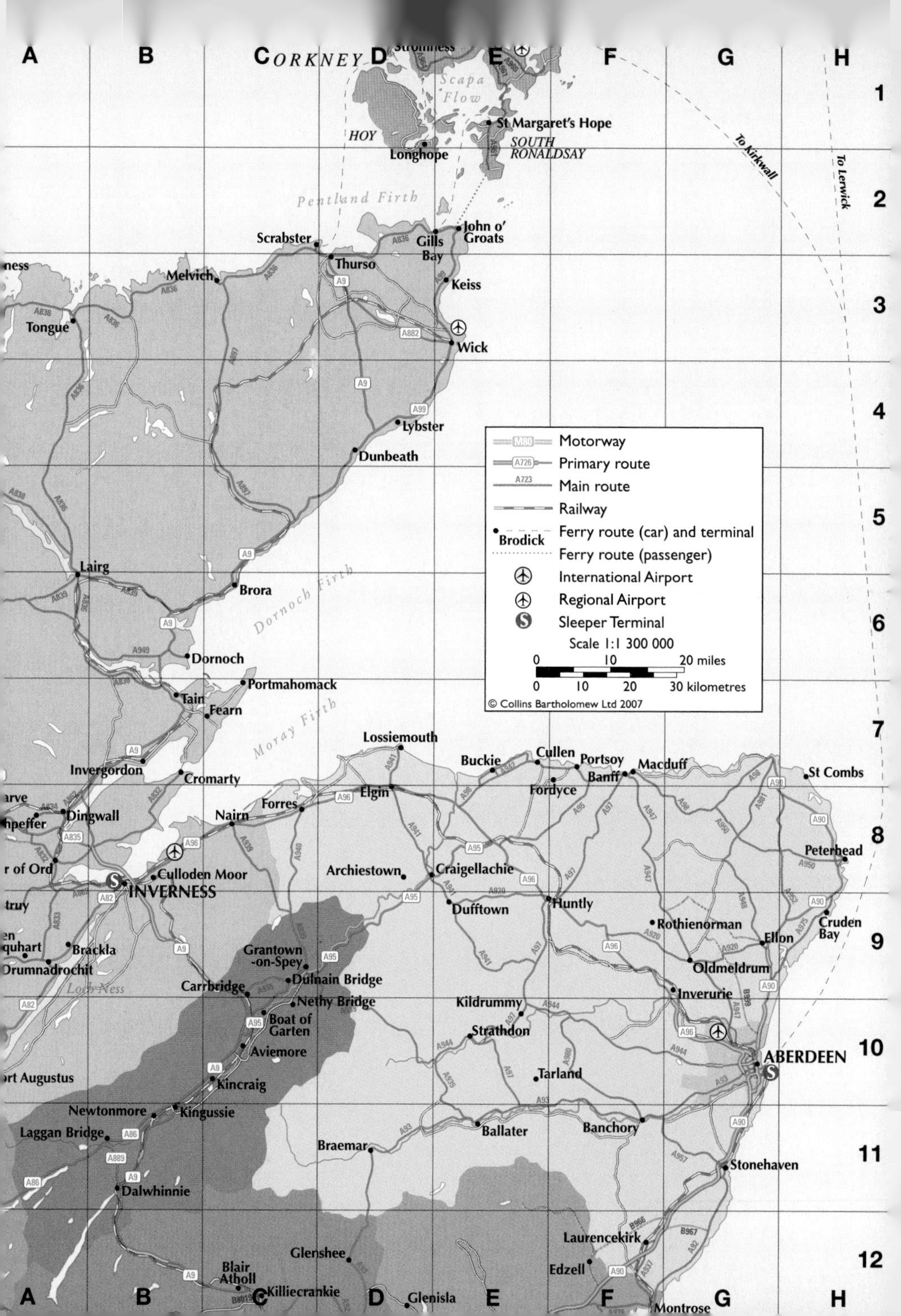

ORKNEY
Stromness
Scapa Flow
HOY
St Margaret's Hope
SOUTH RONALDSAY
Longhope
To Kirkwall
To Lerwick
Pentland Firth
John o' Groats
Gills Bay
Scrabster
Thurso
Melvich
Keiss
Tongue
Wick
Lybster
Dunbeath
Lairg
Brora
Dornoch Firth
Dornoch
Portmahomack
Tain
Fearn
Moray Firth
Lossiemouth
Invergordon
Cromarty
Buckie
Cullen
Portsoy
Banff
Macduff
Fordyce
St Combs
Elgin
Forres
Nairn
Dingwall
Peterhead
Culloden Moor
INVERNESS
Archiestown
Craigellachie
Dufftown
Huntly
Rothienorman
Cruden Bay
Ellon
Brackla
Drumnadrochit
Grantown-on-Spey
Oldmeldrum
Dulnain Bridge
Carrbridge
Loch Ness
Nethy Bridge
Kildrummy
Inverurie
Boat of Garten
Strathdon
Aviemore
ABERDEEN
Tarland
Kincraig
Newtonmore
Kingussie
Laggan Bridge
Ballater
Banchory
Braemar
Stonehaven
Dalwhinnie
Laurencekirk
Glenshee
Edzell
Blair Atholl
Killiecrankie
Glenisla
Montrose
Motorway
Primary route
Main route
Railway
Ferry route (car) and terminal
Brodick
Ferry route (passenger)
International Airport
Regional Airport
Sleeper Terminal
Scale 1:1 300 000
0 10 20 miles
0 10 20 30 kilometres
© Collins Bartholomew Ltd 2007

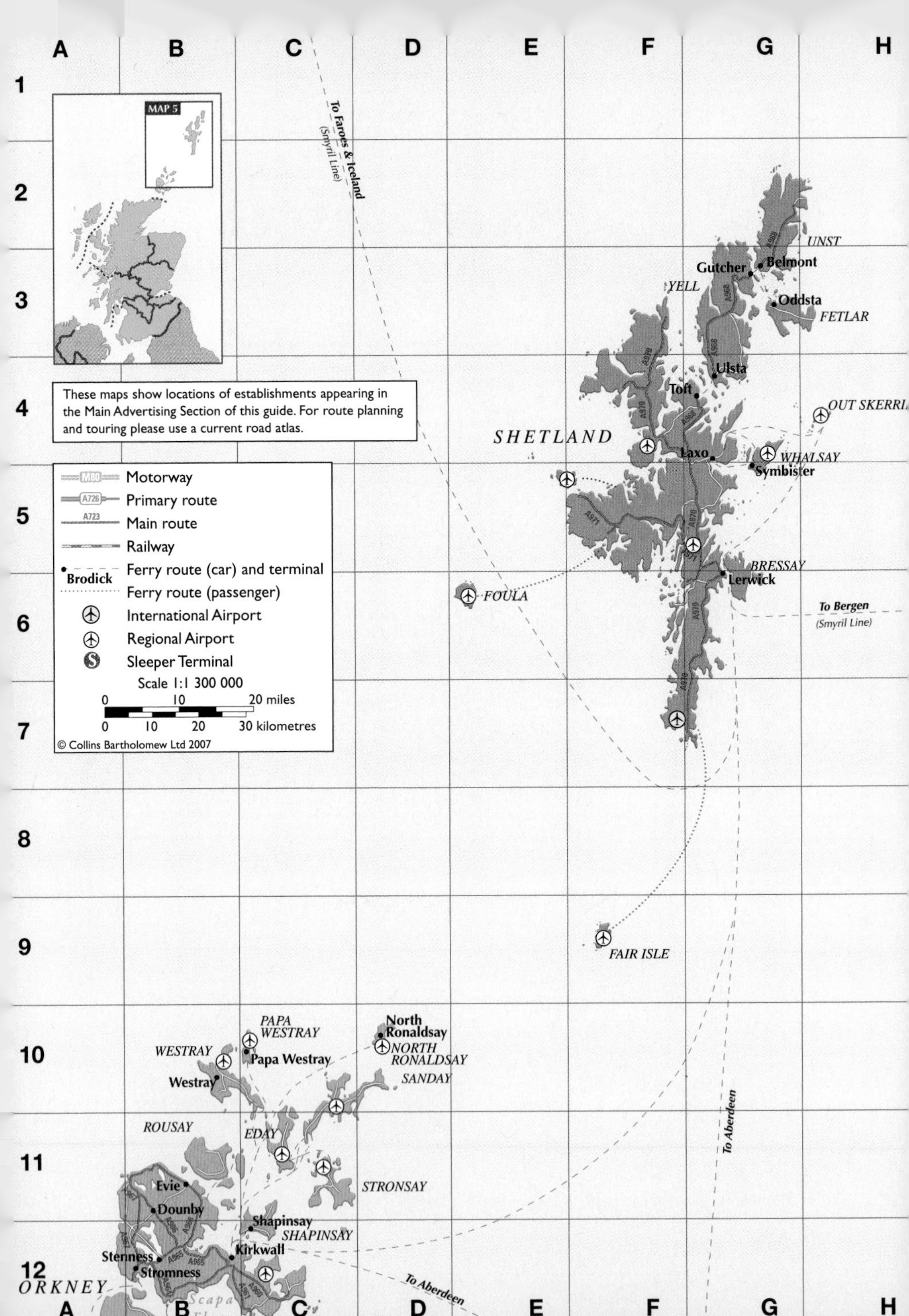

A
B
C
D
E
F
G
H
MAP 5
To Faroes & Iceland
(Smyril Line)
These maps show locations of establishments appearing in the Main Advertising Section of this guide. For route planning and touring please use a current road atlas.
Motorway
Primary route
Main route
Railway
Brodick
Ferry route (car) and terminal
Ferry route (passenger)
International Airport
Regional Airport
Sleeper Terminal
Scale 1:1 300 000
0 10 20 miles
0 10 20 30 kilometres
© Collins Bartholomew Ltd 2007
UNST
Gutcher
Belmont
YELL
Oddsta
FETLAR
Ulsta
Toft
OUT SKERRI
SHETLAND
Laxo
WHALSAY
Symbister
BRESSAY
Lerwick
FOULA
To Bergen
(Smyril Line)
FAIR ISLE
PAPA WESTRAY
North Ronaldsay
NORTH RONALDSAY
WESTRAY
Papa Westray
Westray
SANDAY
ROUSAY
EDAY
STRONSAY
Evie
Dounby
Shapinsay
SHAPINSAY
Kirkwall
Stenness
Stromness
ORKNEY
Scapa Flow
To Aberdeen

A hotel overlooking Loch Fyne, Argyll

ACCOMMODATION LISTINGS

- Hotel and guest house **accommodation listings** for all of Scotland.
- Establishments are listed **by location** in alphabetical order.
- At the back of the book there is a listing of **Accessible Accommodation** for visitors with mobility difficulties.
- For a full listing of all VisitScotland quality assured hotel and guest house accommodation see the **Directory** at the back.
- You will also find an **Index by location** which will tell you where to look if you already know where you want to go.
- Inside the back cover flap you will find a **key to the symbols**.

Kirriereoch Loch in Galloway Forest Park, Dumfries & Galloway

SOUTH OF SCOTLAND

Ayrshire & Arran, Dumfries & Galloway, Scottish Borders

No matter how many times you holiday in the Scottish Borders, Ayrshire & Arran or Dumfries & Galloway, you'll always find something new and interesting to do.

The proud heritage, distinct traditions and enthralling history of Scotland's most southerly places are sure to capture your imagination.

Across the south, the trail of an often bloody and turbulent past is easily followed from imposing castles to ruined abbeys. It's a story of battles and skirmishes from all out war to cattle rustling cross-border raids.

Living history

Though you'd be hard pushed to find a more peaceful part of the country these days, the legacy of these more unsettled times can still be experienced in many a Border town during the Common Ridings. Throughout the summer months hundreds of colourful riders on horseback commemorate the days when their ancestors risked their lives patrolling town boundaries and neighbouring villages.

The south is alive with history. Traquair House, near Innerleithen, is Scotland's oldest continuously inhabited house, dating back to 1107. In Selkirk the whole town is transformed in early December as locals step back to the days when Sir Walter Scott presided over the local courtroom, by partaking in the *Scott's Selkirk* celebrations.

Beautiful beaches

Southern Scotland isn't just about rolling hills and lush farmland, both coasts are well worth a visit. To the east you can see the rocky cliffs and picturesque harbours at St Abbs Head and Eyemouth, while over on the west, there are the beautiful Ayrshire beaches and more than 200 miles of the lovely Solway Coast to explore.

And off the Ayrshire coast is the Isle of Arran – one of Scotland's finest islands and everything a holidaymaker could want.

And in many ways that sums up all of southern Scotland. Whatever you like doing, you'll be spoiled for choice. So, for example, if you love angling, there's world-class salmon fishing on the Tweed. If golf's your game, Turnberry, Prestwick and Royal Troon are up with the best.

If you're a mountain biker, you won't find better than Glentress, one of the 7stanes mountain bike routes. Enjoy reading? Head for Wigtown, Scotland's National Book Town and home to more than 20 bookshops. Ice cream? Who can resist Cream o' Galloway at Gatehouse of Fleet?

If you're a gardener, you'll be inspired all year round by the flourishing collection of rare plants at the Logan Botanic Garden near Stranraer and Dawyck Botanic Garden near Peebles.

That's the South of Scotland. Bursting with brilliant places, waiting with a hearty Scottish welcome and ready to captivate you with a holiday experience you will never forget.

Galashiels Braw Lads' Gathering, Scottish Borders

What's On?

Easter in the Borders
23 March 2008
Events at Floors Castle, Traquair House, Paxton House, and Thirlestane Castle.

125th Melrose 7's Rugby Tournament
11 – 13 April 2008
www.melrose7s.com

burns an' a' that! Festival, Ayrshire
May 2008 (dates tbc)
www.visitscotland.com/burns

Newton Stewart Walking Festival
9 – 15 May 2008
Biggest walking festival in the south.
www.newtonstewartwalkfest.co.uk

Arran Wildlife Festival
14 – 21 May 2008
www.arranwildlife.co.uk

Spring Fling, Dumfries & Galloway
24 – 26 May 2008
Open art and craft studios.
www.spring-fling.co.uk

Border Common Ridings
June – August 2008

Kirkcudbright Jazz Festival
12-15 June 2008
Jazz lovers flock to the town.
www.kirkcudbrightjazzfestival.co.uk

Borders Book Festival, Melrose
19 – 22 June 2008
www.bordersbookfestival.org

Marymass, Irvine
14 – 25 August 2008
www.marymass.org

Ayr Gold Cup Festival
18 -20 September 2008
www.ayr-racecourse.co.uk

The Hairth World Music Festival, Carsphairn
19 – 21 September 2008
Equinox world music festival.
www.knockengorroch.org.uk

www.ayrshire-arran.com
www.visitdumfriesandgalloway.co.uk
www.visitscottishborders.com

MAP

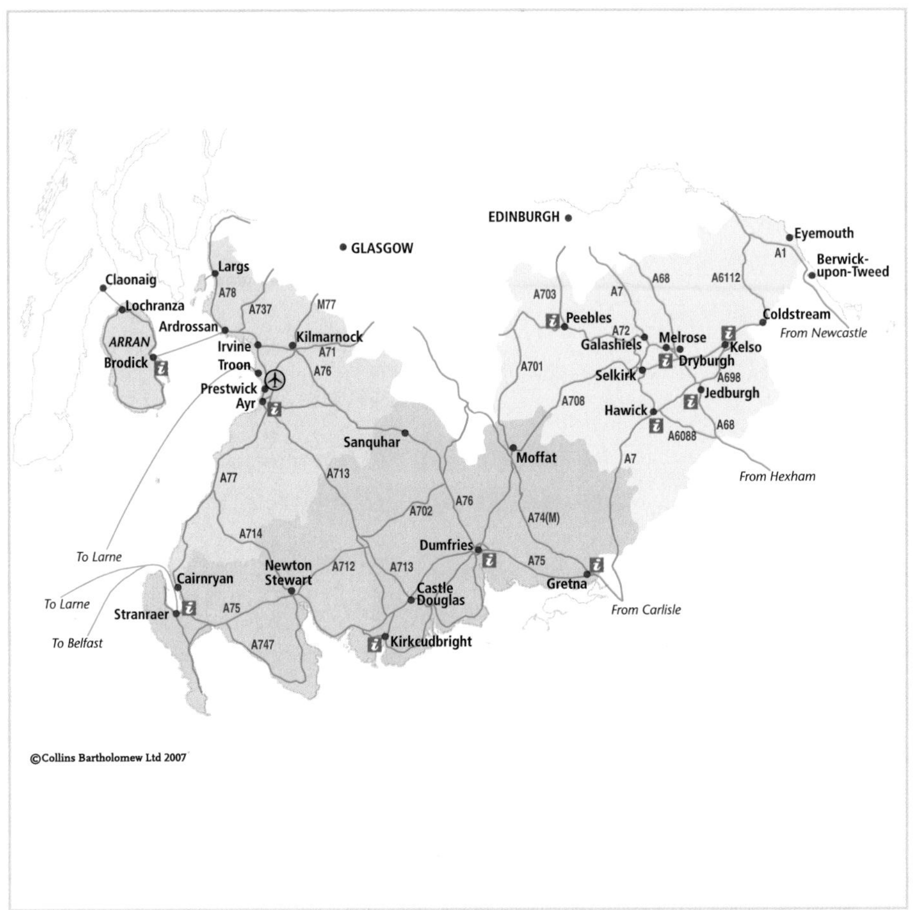
EDINBURGH
GLASGOW
Eyemouth
A1
Berwick-upon-Tweed
A68
A6112
A703
A7
Peebles
Coldstream
From Newcastle
A72
Galashiels
Melrose
Kelso
Dryburgh
A701
Selkirk
A698
Jedburgh
A708
Hawick
A68
A6088
Moffat
A7
From Hexham
A74(M)
A75
Gretna
From Carlisle
Largs
Claonaig
A78
Lochranza
A737
M77
Ardrossan
ARRAN
Irvine
Kilmarnock
A71
Brodick
Troon
A76
Prestwick
Ayr
Sanquhar
A713
A77
A76
A702
A714
Dumfries
To Larne
Newton Stewart
A712
A713
Cairnryan
Castle Douglas
To Larne
Stranraer
A75
To Belfast
A747
Kirkcudbright
©Collins Bartholomew Ltd 2007

TOURIST INFORMATION CENTRES

Ayrshire & Arran	
Ayr	22 Sandgate, Ayr KA7 1BW
Brodick	The Pier, Brodick, Isle of Arran KA27 8AU
Dumfries & Galloway	
Dumfries	64 Whitesands, Dumfries DG1 2RS
Gretna	Unit 10, Gretna Gateway Outlet Village, Glasgow Road, Gretna DG16 5GG
Kirkcudbright	Harbour Square, Kirkcudbright DG6 4HY
Stranraer	Burns House, 28 Harbour Street, Stranraer, Dumfries DG9 7RA
Scottish Borders	
Hawick	Drumlanrig's Tower, Tower Knowe, Hawick TD9 9EN
Jedburgh	Murray's Green, Jedburgh TD8 6BE
Kelso	Town House, The Square, Kelso TD5 7HF
Melrose	Abbey House, Abbey Street, Melrose TD6 9LG
Peebles	23 High Street, Peebles EH45 8AG

Make the most of your stay in Scotland and make your first stop the Tourist Information Centre wherever you go.

Knowledgeable and friendly staff can help you with information and advice; they can answer your questions, book accommodation and you can even pick up some souvenirs to take home for friends and family.

For information and ideas about exploring Scotland in advance of your trip, call our booking and information service or go to **www.visitscotland.com**

Call 0845 22 55 121

or if calling from outside the UK call
+44 (0) 1506 832 121

From Ireland call
1800 932 510

A £4 booking fee applies to telephone bookings of accommodation.

Glen Rosa, Isle of Arran

Ayrshire & Arran

Lying to the south of Glasgow, Ayrshire is a beautiful part of the world characterised by rolling green hills inland and sandy beaches round the coast.

There are some great places to visit whether you're heading to Ayr for the horse racing, touring round the country villages or jumping on the ferry at Ardrossan and sailing for Arran.

The Isle of Arran is an enchanted world that seems to pack everything that makes Scotland great into a space that's just 19 miles from top to bottom and 10 miles at its widest. There's a castle, a distillery, rugged mountains to the north, gentle hills to the south, pretty towns and villages, beaches, wildlife, fishing and seven golf courses.

Ayrshire is also Burns Country and the footsteps of Scotland's greatest ever poet can be traced all round the south. Born in Alloway, South Ayrshire in 1759, you can now visit Robert Burns' birthplace and learn about his life and see the sights that inspired him at the Burns National Heritage Park.

Burns Cottage, Alloway, Ayrshire

DON'T MISS

1. See what happens when you bring four of the world's best graffiti artists to Scotland and provide them with a castle as a canvas. This is exactly what the owners of **Kelburn Castle** did. Kelburn is the ancient home of the Earls of Glasgow and dates back to the 13th century. The **graffiti project** on the castle is a spectacular piece of artwork, surrounded by a beautiful country estate and wooded glen. There is plenty to interest all the family.

2. The island of **Great Cumbrae**, accessible via a 10-minute ferry crossing from Largs, has an undeniable charm and a fabulous setting on the Clyde with views towards Arran. The capital, Millport, is every inch the model Victorian resort, with its own museum and aquarium, as well as the Cathedral of the Isles, Europe's smallest cathedral. SportScotland National Centre Cumbrae is perfect for thrill seekers, while Country & Western fans will enjoy the week-long festival in late summer.

3. Opened in 1995, the **Isle of Arran Distillery** at Lochranza enjoys a spectacular location and is among the most recent to begin production in Scotland. The distillery has a visitor centre that offers fully guided tours, and the opportunity to pour your own bottle. Peat and artificial colourings aren't used in Arran whisky, which the distillers proudly claim offers 'the true spirit of nature'.

4. **Dean Castle** lies in Kilmarnock in East Ayrshire. Known for its astounding collection of medieval instruments and armoury, the Castle sits in a glorious country park. Dean Castle is a family favourite, with a pet corner, an adventure playground and many different woodland walks and cycle routes. Contact the Castle ahead of your visit to confirm seasonal opening hours for the Castle and its facilities.

5. For some crazy outdoor fun, head to **Loudoun Castle** in Galston – Scotland's No 1 Family Theme Park. Loudoun Castle is a terrific day out for younger kids with swashbuckling fun in the Pirates' Cove, and pony treks and tractor rides at McDougal's Farm. Open Easter – September.

6. One of the finest collections of Bronze Age **standing stones** in Scotland can be found at scenic **Machrie Moor**. Around seven separate rings of stones have been discovered on the moor, with many still undiscovered under the peat which now grows in the vicinity. Visit during the summer solstice for a truly atmospheric experience.

FOOD AND DRINK

www.eatscotland.com

7 With excellent **local produce** such as cheese, ale, honey, ice cream and chocolate made to the highest standard, the Ayrshire & Arran kitchen will delight the palate and ignite culinary creativity.

8 Being on the west coast, the **seafood** is delicious and could not be fresher. Take advantage of the opportunity to visit an up-market fish and chip shop or order the seafood at one of the excellent restaurants.

9 With such a range of natural and local ingredients to inspire, it is no wonder that Ayrshire & Arran has such fabulous **restaurants**. From Michelin Star and AA rosette winning restaurants to the best that gastro pubs have to offer, Ayrshire & Arran will satisfy the biggest gourmet's appetite.

GOLF

www.visitscotland.com/golf

10 Royal Troon and Turnberry Ailsa, found on the Ayrshire coastline, are two of the best **championship courses** on The Open circuit. The famous Prestwick golf course is also on the same stretch of coast. It was at Prestwick in 1860 where the first Open Championship was played. Although at that time it only attracted eight golfers, it was the beginning of competitive golf as we now know it.

11 It is not just championship courses that Ayrshire is famous for. It is the good value and spectacular play of some of the lesser renowned courses. The charm and challenge of **hidden gems** like Belleisle, Brodick, Rountenburn, Lochgreen and Largs, to name just a few, offer brilliant golf at a very reasonable price.

12 Scotland is not only the Home of Golf, it is the home of **links golf**, the original form of the game that had its beginnings in Scotland over 600 years ago. Ayrshire and Arran has some of the finest and most famous links golf courses in the world; Western Gailes, Glasgow Gailes, West Kilbride, Royal Troon, Prestwick, Prestwick St Nicholas, Turnberry Ailsa and Shiskine on the Isle of Arran are all part of the Great Scottish Links collection.

13 **The Open** returns to Ayrshire in 2009. It will see the world's best professional golfers flock to the legendary links of Turnberry to take on the greatest challenge in professional golf. If previous years are anything to go by, the competition will be fierce and the sun will be shining.

WALKS

www.visitscotland.com/walking

14 **The River Ayr Way** is the first source to sea path network, which follows the river from its source at Glenbuck to the sea at Ayr. Running through beautiful Ayrshire villages and countryside, the river is steeped in history and legend. With spectacular scenery and abundant wildlife it is enjoyable to walk the full 66 km / 40 mile route or just part of it.

15 Starting at Whiting Bay the 2-hour **Glenashdale Falls** walk shows off the impressive falls plummeting for about 140ft. This walk is also overflowing with history, featuring the remains of Whiting Bay Church, an Iron Age Hill Fort, and further out up a number of steps, the Giants' Graves – a group of Neolithic tombs. This easy-to-moderate walk has waymarkers and stays on footpaths and tracks.

16 As Arran's highest point, **Goatfell** is a challenging but enjoyable walk. There are two paths catering for different abilities, and those who make it to the summit may be rewarded with stunning views of Ayrshire, the Mull of Kintyre and Ireland. For the round trip from Brodick Country Park, allow around 5-6 hours.

17 **The Big Wood**, in Irvine Valley, offers a stunning one-hour walk, particularly in May when there is a virtual carpet of bluebells. Start at the A71 lay-by between Newmilns and Galston at the Hag Bridge. The walk itself gradually climbs through woodland until you reach the gate to Woodhead Farm. Tread the old Lime Road and descend gently down the 'Pit Brae' or follow the steep winding road through the Devil's Basin.

HISTORY

18 Robert Adam's fairytale **Culzean Castle**, perched on a clifftop overlooking Ailsa Craig and the Firth of Clyde, is a study in extravagance. A favourite of President Eisenhower, he was given his own apartment here by its previous owners, the Kennedys. Fans of military history should explore the Armoury, filled with antique pistols and swords. 565 acres of country park surround the Castle, with woodland walks, a walled garden and even a beach.

19 On January 25th 1759, Scotland's National Bard was born in the picturesque village of Alloway, a must for admirers of the man and his work. Here, you can visit **Burns Cottage** and a museum containing prized artefacts such as an original manuscript of Auld Lang Syne. Numerous surrounding sites, including the Brig O' Doon and Kirk Alloway, are familiar from Burns' epic poem Tam O'Shanter, which even has an entire visitor attraction dedicated to it.

20 The **Isle of Arran Heritage Museum** can be found on the main road at Rosaburn, just north of Brodick. The present group of buildings was once a working croft and smiddy, and include a farmhouse, cottage, bothy, milk house, laundry, stable, coach house and harness room. The fascinating exhibits reflect the social history, archaeology and geology of the island.

21 To visit **Dalgarven Mill**, and the Museum of Ayrshire Country Life and Costume, is to step back in time. The comprehensive exhibition of tools, machinery, horse and harness, churns, fire irons and furnishings, evokes a powerful sense of the past, which cannot fail to leave an impression. The costume collection is constantly changing, and demonstrates how fashion has evolved from 1780. The grind and splash of the wooden mill ensures the museum has an authentic ambience.

AYRSHIRE & ARRAN

23879 **Brodick, Isle of Arran** — **Map Ref: 1F7**

Scottish Tourist Board ★★★★ Guest House

Dunvegan House

Shore Road, Brodick, Isle of Arran, KA27 8AJ
Tel/Fax:01770 302811

9 rooms (3 downstairs)
8 en-suite, 1 priv.facilities
Open Jan-Dec excl Xmas/New Year
B&B per person, single from £40.00, double from £35.00. Evening meal £21.50.

48704 **Brodick, Isle of Arran** — **Map Ref: 1F7**

Scottish Tourist Board ★★ Small Hotel

Ormidale Hotel

Brodick, Isle of Arran, KA27 8BY
Tel:01770 302293 Fax:01770 302098
Email:reception@ormidale-hotel.co.uk
Web:www.ormidale-hotel.co.uk

7 rooms
All en-suite
Open Mar-Oct
B&B per person, single from £38.00, double from £38.00.

12337 **Lochranza, Isle of Arran** — **Map Ref: 1E6**

Scottish Tourist Board ★★★★ Guest House

Apple Lodge

Lochranza, Isle of Arran, KA27 8HJ
Tel/Fax:01770 830229

4 rooms
Open Jan-Dec
B&B per person single from £50.00, double from £36.00.

75918 **Whiting Bay, Isle of Arran** — **Map Ref: 1F7**

Scottish Tourist Board ★★ Guest House

Invermay

Shore Road, Whiting Bay, Isle of Arran, KA27 8PZ
Tel:01770 700431

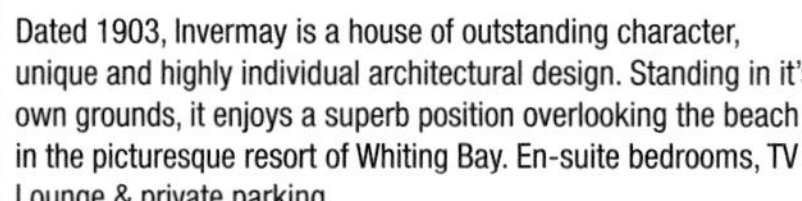

Dated 1903, Invermay is a house of outstanding character, unique and highly individual architectural design. Standing in it's own grounds, it enjoys a superb position overlooking the beach in the picturesque resort of Whiting Bay. En-suite bedrooms, TV Lounge & private parking.

7 rooms, Some en-suite. Open Jan-Dec. B&B per person, single from £50.00, double from £30.00.

14831 **Ayr** — **Map Ref: 1G7**

Scottish Tourist Board ★★★ Guest House

Belmont Guest House

15 Park Circus, Ayr, KA7 2DJ
Tel:01292 265588 Fax:01292 290303
Email:belmontguesthouse@btinternet.com
Web:www.belmontguesthouse.co.uk

5 rooms
All en-suite
Open Jan-Dec excl Xmas/New Year
B&B per person, single from £29.00, double/twin from £27.00 pppn, family from £27.00 pppn.

AYRSHIRE & ARRAN

25489 **Ayr** — **Map Ref: 1G7**

Fairfield House Hotel

12 Fairfield Road, Ayr, Ayrshire, KA7 2AS
Tel:01292 267461 Fax:01292 261456
Email:reservations@fairfield-hotel.demon.co.uk
Web:www.fairfieldhotel.co.uk

44 rooms
All en-suite
Open Jan-Dec
B&B per room, single from £79.00, double from £79.00.

60185 **Ayr** — **Map Ref: 1G7**

Scottish Tourist Board ★★★ Guest House

The Richmond

38 Park Circus, Ayr, KA7 2DL
Tel:01292 265153 Fax:01292 288816
Email:Richmond38@btinternet.com
Web:www.richmond-guest-house.co.uk

6 rooms
5 en-suite, 1 priv.facilities
Open Jan-Dec
B&B per person, single from £37.00, double from £29.00.

C £ V

63819 **Ayr** — **Map Ref: 1G7**

Scottish Tourist Board ★★★★ Hotel

Western House Hotel

2 Whitletts Road, Ayr, Ayrshire, KA9 0JE
Tel:0870 8505666
Email:sjardine@ayr-racecourse.co.uk
Web:www.ayr-racecourse.co.uk

49 rooms
All en-suite
Open Jan-Dec
B&B per person, single from £95.00, double from £55.00.

64306 **Largs, Ayrshire** — **Map Ref: 1F5**

Scottish Tourist Board ★★★ Hotel

Willowbank Hotel

96 Greenock Road, Largs, North Ayrshire, KA30 8PG
Tel:01475 672311 Fax:01475 689027
Email:iaincsmith@btconnect.com

30 rooms
All en-suite
Open Jan-Dec
B&B per person, single from £70.00, double from £50.00,
BB & Eve.Meal from £62.00.

C £ V

25804 **Prestwick, Ayrshire** — **Map Ref: 1G7**

Scottish Tourist Board ★★★ Guest House

Fernbank Guest House

213 Main Street, Prestwick, Ayrshire, KA9 1LH
Tel:01292 475027 Fax:01292 678944
Email:stay@fernbank.co.uk
Web:www.fernbank.co.uk

7 rooms
All en-suite
Open Jan-Dec excl Xmas/New Year
B&B per person, single from £25.00, double from £25.00.

C £ V

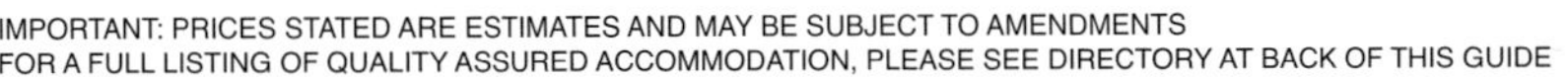

Loch Ken, Dumfries & Galloway

Dumfries & Galloway

Dumfries & Galloway, like Ayrshire, also has its Burns connections as the poet spent much of his adult life in the town of Dumfries. You can even visit Ellisland Farm where he lived for many years – it's now a popular visitor attraction dedicated to his life and works.

Burns found the natural beauty of this area inspiring and you'll be equally impressed. From the Galloway Forest Park to the Solway Coast, there are so many picturesque places to see.

There's a great deal of wildlife around too. You can spot rare birds like red kites which were re-introduced to the area a few years back and around the coast, you'll see waders and wildfowl of all shapes and sizes.

Not surprisingly, such a naturally beautiful area is also a big attraction for artists. Don't forget to pay a visit to the charming town of Kirkcudbright which has a thriving artistic community and its studios and galleries are filled with fine works.

Kirkcudbright

DON'T MISS

1 **Sweetheart Abbey** is a glorious ruin, set in pretty New Abbey, with a flamboyant architectural style which sets it apart from previous Cisterian constructions. Here you'll find the origins of the word sweetheart from the fascinating love story of Devorgilla de Balliol who kept her husband's heart close to her - even beyond the grave. Devorgilla and the heart are now buried together before the high altar. Be sure to pop in to the welcoming Abbey Cottage tearoom after your visit.

2 North of Thornhill, in the shadow of the glorious Lowther Hills, is **Drumlanrig Castle**. It was built in the 17th century as a home for the first Duke of Queensberry. Surrounded by its gardens, estate and country park, there is much to explore. Look out for the resident red squirrels.

3 **Ellisland Farm**, just north of Dumfries, is where Scotland's National Bard – Robert Burns - wrote the famous song Auld Lang Syne, sung all over the world at parties and new year celebrations. It is part of the **Burns Heritage Trail** which winds its way through Ayrshire to Dumfries incorporating many of the locations that inspired his finest poetry, as well as buildings where he lived and worked.

4 Painters, artists and craftsmen have flocked to this area for centuries, no place more so than **Kirkcudbright**, now known as the Artists' Town for its historic artistic heritage. With its pastel coloured houses and traditional working harbour it is no wonder that artists flock to the town. Whether or not you have artistic flair, soak up the inspirational views on drives along the scenic country roads that criss-cross this part of the region.

5 Bookshops line the streets of **Scotland's Book Town, Wigtown**. Spend an easy day browsing and burrowing your way through the shelves before stopping in a local coffee shop for refreshment. There are around 30 book-related businesses in this small community, which hosts a book fair in May and a literary festival in early autumn. Book fans will find it difficult to leave!

6 A fabulous array of bizarre and beautiful plants flourish outdoors in Scotland's most exotic garden – **Logan Botanic Garden**. Warmed by the North Atlantic Drift, the property – under the care of the Royal Botanic Garden, Edinburgh – brings a dash of colour to the Rhinns of Galloway. The range of sub-tropical species even includes a number of palm trees, meaning you may forget where you actually are!

1

6

FOOD AND DRINK

www.eatscotland.com

7 Robert Burns' favourite 'howff' (pub) - **The Globe Inn**, Dumfries – is a continuing favourite of 'Doonhamers' (Dumfries locals) and visitors alike. Dating from 1610, the Inn has many claims to fame including being home to the ghost of Anna Park, a servant girl, and the fact that it held the first ever Burns Supper back in 1819. Burns' chair is still in the bar, but if you sit on it you must recite a line from one of his poems or buy all the customers in the bar a drink. If you ask the staff, they will show you the bedroom he used during his time as an excise man. The Globe serves breakfasts and bar lunches.

8 **Bladnoch Distillery**, by Wigtown is Scotland's most southerly distillery, dating from 1817. Learn about the traditions of making whisky and enjoy the riverside and woodland walks nearby.

9 **The Linen Room** restaurant in Dumfries has been awarded a Michelin Rising Star award, Scottish Rural Chef of the Year and Which Guide's Scottish Restaurant of the Year. Chef Russell Robertson delights with his gourmet fine dining and tasty local produce.

10 The glass encased **Gallie Craig Coffee House** is part of a unique visitor facility at the Mull of Galloway. There are spectacular panoramic views from the coffee house and terrace, built into the cliffs at the most southerly point in Scotland.

WALKS

www.visitscotland.com/walking

11 The **Southern Upland Way**, Scotland's longest waymarked walking route, runs 212 miles from the west to the east coast, traversing some beautiful hill scenery. For those who simply want a taster, start at Portpatrick, on the Rhinns of Galloway, and head up the coast to **Killantringan Lighthouse**. Watch out for the seabirds that make their home here. Alternatively, try the 8-mile section between Clatteringshaws Loch and St Johns Town of Dalry on the edge of the forest park.

12 For those seeking a slightly longer walk, head west to **Galloway Forest Park** and enjoy the astoundingly scenic circuit of Loch Trool. You could be forgiven for thinking you'd arrived in the Highlands as you enter Glen Trool, situated a few miles north of Newton Stewart, just off the Girvan road. The full circuit of the loch is around 5 miles and should take about 3 hours in good conditions.

13 The pretty mill town of **Langholm**, situated between rolling hills in the valley of the River Esk, has an entire network of scenic waymarked walks which make it an ideal base for the eager rambler. Twelve hikes of varying difficulty, most beginning from the town centre, are detailed in a leaflet available locally. The town even has its own walking festival in early June.

14 **Burns Walk** starts at the foot of Devorgilla Bridge in Dumfries and follows the River Nith on a winding and northerly path. For a short while, you head out of town and start to climb the riverbank before passing under a railway bridge and two road bridges. If you choose to stick to the riverside, you'll climb up Dalscone Bank, walking among the impressive beech trees. You'll have Burns Walk signs along the route to follow which will take you back south to the bridge where you started. Allow 1½ hours.

WILDLIFE

www.visitscotland.com/wildlife

15 Once extinct in Scotland, the graceful red kite – identifiable by its swallow-like tail – has been successfully reintroduced into many areas, not least around Loch Ken in Galloway. Here, many local businesses and accommodation providers have grouped together to form the **Galloway Red Kite Trail**, almost guaranteeing a sighting of the bird – particularly at the Bellymack Farm feeding station, where up to 30 have been seen at once!

16 The Dumfries and Galloway **Wildlife Festival** is an annual event held over two weeks in early April. See some of the region's special wildlife and get up close and personal with a countryside ranger to help you. If you have never seen a red squirrel, red kite or badger – now is your chance. Experienced wildlife watchers and beginners should both find something of interest in the festival, and look out for a range of events for the whole family.

17 **Ospreys** are back in Galloway, and in the County Buildings in Wigtown there is a room dedicated to watching wildlife where you can see live CCTV coverage of the first ospreys to have nested in Galloway for over 100 years. Nesting ospreys can now also be seen via a live video link at Caerlaverock Wetland Centre. Get an unparalleled view of ospreys sitting on their eggs and bringing up their young, the male coming back with fish to share with the female and taking over nesting duties while she eats.

18 The long coastline of the Solway Firth welcomes over 40,000 wildfowl and 83,000 waders each winter making Dumfries and Galloway an ornithologists paradise, and places such as **WWT Caerlaverock** and **Mersehead Nature Reserve** make it easy to get close to flocks of thousands of barnacle geese which travel every year from Norway to winter on the wetlands of the Solway.

18

19

20

ACTIVITIES

19 Dumfries and Galloway is where **cycling** all began and there's still no better place to travel on two wheels with over 400 miles of signposted cycle routes and world class mountain biking at the 7stanes centres stretching across southern Scotland. This is where the bicycle was first invented and you'll even find the only museum in Scotland devoted to the history of cycling at Drumlanrig Castle.

20 At **Galloway Sailing Centre** on Loch Ken you can really learn something new with activities on offer including sailing, windsurfing, power boating, kayaking, canoeing, archery, quad biking, mountain biking and climbing.

21 No child will want to miss visiting **Cream o' Galloway** Visitor Centre in Gatehouse of Fleet. Even if you can tear them away from the amazing variety of scrumptious ice creams, they will still be attracted to the child-friendly nature trails and adventure playground, flying fox and play barn, or you can hire a cycle for them to ride in safety.

22 Explore some of Scotland's finest scenery in the heart of Dumfries and Galloway. There are three **National Scenic Areas** – The Nith Estuary, Fleet Valley and the East Stewartry Coast – making it a great part of the world for touring.

26856 **Auldgirth, Dumfriesshire** Map Ref: 2B9

Friars Carse Hotel

Auldgirth, Dumfriesshire, DG2 0SA
Tel:01387 740388
Email:fc@pofr.co.uk
Web:www.friarcarse.uk.com

Historical Scottish baronial house with close connections to Robert Burns, set in 45 acres of woodland, running down to the River Nith. Outdoor activities available to guests include private salmon fishing and a putting green. Shooting by arrangement. Variety of nearby golf courses. Non residents welcome for lunch, afternoon tea, dinner and drinks. Popular venue for weddings and functions. Small meeting facilities.

21 rooms, All en-suite. Open Jan-Dec. B&B per room, single from £99.00, double from £99.00.

13881 **Castle Douglas, Kirkcudbrightshire** Map Ref: 2A10

Balcary Bay Hotel

Shore Road, Auchencairn, by Castle Douglas
Kirkcudbrightshire, DG7 1QZ
Tel:01556 640217 Fax:01556 640272
Email:reservations@balcary-bay-hotel.co.uk
Web:www.balcary-bay-hotel.co.uk

Family-run country house in three acres of garden. A magnificent and peaceful setting on the shores of the bay. Ideal base for all leisure facilities or a relaxing holiday with warm hospitality, good food and wine.

AA ★★★

One of Scotland's Hotels of Distinction

★★★ COUNTRY HOUSE HOTEL

20 rooms.
All en-suite. Open Feb-Dec
B&B per person, single from £63.00, double from £56.00,
BB & Eve.Meal rates on request.

42687 **Castle Douglas, Kirkcudbrightshire** Map Ref: 2A10

Craigadam

Castle Douglas, Dumfries & Galloway, DG7 3HU
Tel/Fax:01556 650233
Email:inquiry@craigadam.com
Web:www.craigadam.com

7 rooms
All en-suite
Open Jan-Dec excl Xmas/New Year
B&B per person, single from £50.00, double from £40.00.

DUMFRIES & GALLOWAY

76361 **Castle Douglas, Kirkcudbrightshire** — **Map Ref: 2A10**

The Urr Valley Hotel

Ernespie Road, Castle Douglas, Kirkcudbrightshire, DG7 3JG
Tel:01556 502188 Fax:01556 504055
Email:info@urrvalleyhotel.co.uk
Web:www.urrvalleyhotel.co.uk

The Urr Valley is a long established Country House Hotel set in 14 acres of grounds with stunning views across the Galloway countryside. Ideal location for fishing and shooting, or enjoy the beaches, lochs and hills of northern Galloway.

19 rooms, All en-suite. Open Jan-Dec. B&B per person, single from £50.00, double from £38.50.

39005 **Dumfries** — **Map Ref: 2B9**

Moreig Hotel

67 Annan Road, Dumfries, DG1 3EG
Tel:01387 255524 Fax:01387 267105
Email:enquiries@moreighotel.co.uk
Web:www.moreighotel.co.uk

10 rooms
All en-suite
Open Jan-Dec
B&B per person, single from £55.00, double from £37.50, BB & Eve.Meal from £57.50.

68060 **Gretna Green, Dumfriesshire** — **Map Ref: 2C10**

Smiths at Gretna Green

Gretna Green, Dumfries & Galloway, DG16 5EA
Tel:01461 337007
Email:info@smithsgretnagreen.com
Web:www.smithsgretnagreen.com

50 rooms
All en-suite
Open Jan-Dec
B&B per room, single £115.00, double £135.00, executive £155.00, family £155.00, suite £360.00 and penthouse £490.00.

22691 **Johnstone Bridge, Dumfriesshire** — **Map Ref: 2B8**

Dinwoodie Lodge Hotel

Johnstone Bridge, by Lockerbie, Dumfriesshire, DG11 2SL
Tel/Fax:01576 470289
Email:dinwoodielodge@tinyworld.com
Web:www.dinwoodielodgehotel.co.uk

6 rooms
All en-suite
Open Jan-Dec
B&B per person, single from £47.50, double from £40.00.

28653

Kirkcudbright — Map Ref: 2A10

Gordon House Hotel

116 High Street, Kirkcudbright, Kirkcudbrightshire, DG6 4JQ
Tel:01557 330670
Email:mail@gordon-house-hotel.co.uk
Web:www.gordon-house-hotel.co.uk

Personally run small hotel, the listed building is situated in the old High Street of Kirkcudbright, a town steeped in history. Its situation on the estuary of the River Dee. All rooms ensuite. Popular restaurant. The emphasis on locally sourced and fresh produce.

8 rooms, All en-suite. Open Jan-Dec. B&B per person, single from £40.00, double from £35.00.

51167

Lockerbie, Dumfriesshire — Map Ref: 2C9

Ravenshill House Hotel

12 Dumfries Road, Lockerbie, Dumfriesshire,
DG11 2EF
Tel/Fax:01576 202882
Email:reservations@RavenshillHotelLockerbie.co.uk
Web:www.RavenshillHotelLockerbie.co.uk

A family run hotel set in 2.5 acres of garden in a quiet residential area, yet convenient for town centre and M6/M74. With a chef proprietor the hotel enjoys a reputation for good food, comfortable accommodation and friendly service. Weekend, short and golfing breaks.

8 rooms, Most en-suite. Open Jan-Dec. B&B per person, single from £48.00, double from £37.50, BB & Eve.Meal from £50.00.

12186

Moffat, Dumfriesshire — Map Ref: 2B8

Annandale Arms Hotel

High Street, Moffat, Dumfriesshire, DG10 9HF
Tel:01683 220013 Fax:01683 221395
Email:vs@annandalearmshotel.co.uk
Web:www.annandalearmshotel.co.uk

11 rooms
All en-suite
Open Jan-Dec excl Christmas & Boxing Day
B&B per person, single from £50.00, double from £40.00.

76925

Moffat, Dumfriesshire — Map Ref: 2B8

Scottish Tourist Board ★★★★ Guest House

Bridge House

Well Road, Moffat, Dumfrieshire, DG10 9JT
Tel:01683 220558
Email:info@bridgehousemoffat.co.uk
Web:www.bridgehousemoffat.co.uk

Licensed guest house, quiet location, private parking, beautiful views. Emphasis on your relaxation & enjoyment, freshly cooked dinners by international chef. Dinner by arrangement.

7 rooms, Open mid Feb-Dec. B&B per person, single £45.00, double from £32.50.

16754

Moffat, Dumfriesshire — Map Ref: 2B8

Scottish Tourist Board ★★★ Small Hotel

Buccleuch Arms Hotel

High Street, Moffat, Dumfriesshire, DG10 9ET
Tel:01683 220003 Fax:01683 221291
Email:enquiries@buccleucharmshotel.com
Web:www.buccleucharmshotel.com

14 rooms
All en-suite
Open Jan-Dec
B&B per person, single from £50.00, double from £40.00.

78223

Moffat, Dumfriesshire — Map Ref: 2B8

Scottish Tourist Board Awaiting Grading

The Stag Hotel

High Street, Moffat DG10 9HL
Tel:01683 220343 Fax:01683 220914
Email:sharon@visitthestaghotel.co.uk
Web:www.visitthestaghotel.co.uk

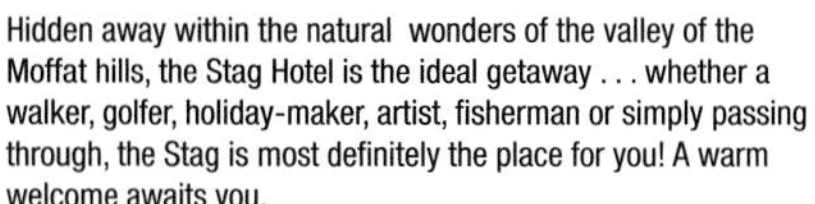

Hidden away within the natural wonders of the valley of the Moffat hills, the Stag Hotel is the ideal getaway . . . whether a walker, golfer, holiday-maker, artist, fisherman or simply passing through, the Stag is most definitely the place for you! A warm welcome awaits you.

7 rooms, All en-suite. Open Jan-Dec. B&B per person, single from £36.00, Double/Twin £32.00, Family £78.00 (room price)

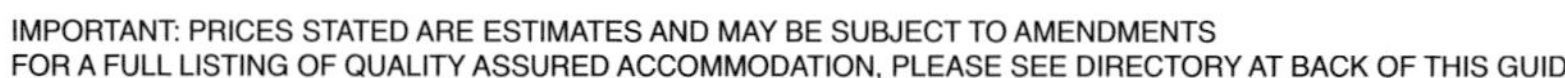

IMPORTANT: PRICES STATED ARE ESTIMATES AND MAY BE SUBJECT TO AMENDMENTS
FOR A FULL LISTING OF QUALITY ASSURED ACCOMMODATION, PLEASE SEE DIRECTORY AT BACK OF THIS GUIDE

13375 **by Moffat, Dumfriesshire** **Map Ref: 2B8**

Auchen Castle Hotel

Beattock, Moffat, Dumfriesshire, DG10 9SH
Tel:01683 300407 Fax:01683 300667
Email:reception@auchencastle.com
Web:www.auchencastleweddings.com

Auchen Castle hotel a building of local prominance and a perfect venue for that very special day or simply a romantic break. Also adjacent to main hotel, lodge accommodation on first floor level with access to hotel facilities. Set in 35 acres of mature grounds, all floors overlooking the trout Loch. Convenient for access to the M74 (and new M6) motorway.

25 rooms, All en-suite. Open Jan-Dec. Rates on application.

75976 **Newton Stewart, Wigtownshire** **Map Ref: 1G10**

The Bruce Hotel

88 Queen Street, Newton Stewart, Wigtownshire, DG8 6JL
Tel/Fax:01671 402294
Email:mail@thebrucehotel.com
Web:www.the-bruce-hotel.com

20 rooms
All en-suite
Open Jan-Dec
B&B per person, single from £45.00, double from £40.00.

63361 **Portpatrick, Wigtownshire** **Map Ref: 1F10**

The Waterfront Hotel & Bistro

North Crescent, Portpatrick, DG9 8SX
Tel:01776 810800 Fax:01776 810850
Email:waterfronthotel@aol.com
Web:www.waterfronthotel.co.uk

Dating originally from the 18th Century, this small hotel with popular bar and bistro, has been updated to give a contemporary style. Overlooking the picturesque harbour of Portpatrick, the bedrooms and ensuites are restricted in size but most are sea-facing. Ample free, street parking.

8 rooms, All en-suite. Open Jan-Dec. B&B per person, single from £65.00, double from £40.00, BB & Eve.Meal from £55.00.

38860 **Port William, Wigtownshire** **Map Ref: 1G11**

Monreith Arms Hotel

The Square, Port William, Dumfries & Galloway, DG8 9SE
Tel:01988 700232
Email:monreitharmshotel@supanet.com
Web:www.monreitharms.co.uk

10 rooms
All en-suite
Open Jan-Dec
Rates on application.

60606

Thornhill, Dumfriesshire **Map Ref: 2A8**

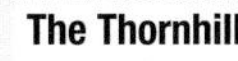

The Thornhill Inn

103-106 Drumlanrig Street, Thornhill, Dumfriesshire, DG3 5LU
Tel:01848 330326
Email:info@thornhillinn.co.uk
Web:www.thornhillinn.co.uk

Personally run former coaching Inn with friendly atmosphere. Situated in centre of Thornhill village, amidst scenic Nithsdale. Good base for touring. Popular with fishermen, walkers and golfers. Enjoys local reputation for good food. Mini bus available for those wishing to book group packages.

10 rooms, All en-suite. Open Jan-Dec. Room only per person, single from £45.00, double from £31.00.

Loch Trool, Dumfries and Galloway

Scott's View, Scottish Borders

Scottish Borders

There are many lovely towns to visit in the Scottish Borders and a lot of different things to see and do. Take the four great Borders Abbeys of Dryburgh, Kelso, Jedburgh and Melrose. They were founded by King David I in the 12th century and though each is in ruins, a strong impression of their former glory remains.

Hawick is the centre of the local textile industry and you can still pick up bargain knitwear, tartans and tweeds at the many outlets and mills in the area.

Abbotsford, the former home of Sir Walter Scott, is now a visitor attraction just west of Melrose and you can also visit the writer's old courtroom in Selkirk, preserved as it was in the 1800s when he presided over trials.

There's some great walking in the Borders too with over 1,500 miles of designated walking routes.

Abbotsford House, Melrose

DON'T MISS

1 Take the B6404 St Boswells to Kelso road and turn onto the B6356, signposted to Dryburgh Abbey. About 1 mile along this road there is a junction signposting **Scott's View** to the right. Drive for about 2 miles for panoramic views of the Eildon Hills and the Borders countryside stretching out before you. A good spot for a picnic!

2 **Traquair House**, near Innerleithen, dates back to the 12th century and is said to be the oldest continuously inhabited house in Scotland. When its Bear Gates were closed in 1745, it was decreed that they should not reopen until another Stuart took the throne. Watch out for the Medieval Fayre in May and the Summer Fair in August.

3 Walk the **Berwickshire Coastal Path** from Berwick to St Abbs. The sea cliffs along this path are the highest on the east coast of Britain. Look out for the family of seals in Eyemouth harbour!

4 The four great **Borders Abbeys** of Kelso, Melrose, Jedburgh and Dryburgh are a must see for any visitor to the area. Melrose Abbey is said to be the resting place of the casket containing the heart of King Robert the Bruce. Dryburgh is the buriel place of Field Marshall Earl Haig and Sir Walter Scott. All of the abbeys are under the care of Historic Scotland. Kelso is the most incomplete and has free access. At Melrose, Jedburgh and Dryburgh an admission charge applies.

5 **Floors Castle** in Kelso is the home of the Roxburghe family. It is the largest inhabited castle in Scotland and has 365 windows, one for every day of the year. The Castle, grounds, gardens and restaurant are open from Easter to October with The Terrace Restaurant, walled gardens, playground and garden centre open all year. The Castle also hosts an extensive events calendar.

2

3

4

FOOD AND DRINK

www.eatscotland.com

6 At **Giacopazzi's** in Eyemouth you can enjoy award-winning fresh fish and chips and home-made ice creams. Eat in or take them out and sit on the harbourside.

7 The **Selkirk Bannock** is a combination of bread dough, butter, fruit and sugar and is a Borders classic. Try a slice with butter or indulge in a whole one available from most bakeries.

8 **Jethart Snails** and **Hawick Balls** are minty sweeties sure to satisfy even the sweetest tooth. Available widely in the Jedburgh and Hawick areas.

9 To get a real flavour of the area sample some **local cuisine**. With many bars and restaurants to choose from, the Scottish Borders draw on the regional best of the land and sea and serve it in their own individual style. There are many fine food outlets and delicatessens where local food and produce abound, and farmers' markets are held regularly in Peebles and Kelso.

WALKS

www.visitscotland.com/walking

10 The life and progress of St Cuthbert provided the inspiration for the **St Cuthbert's Way** walking route. Starting in Melrose and ending on Holy Island (Lindisfarne) it passes through rolling farmland, river valleys, sheltered woods, hills and moorland culminating in The Holy Island Causeway, passable only at low tide. The full route is 100 km / 60 miles in length but it can be broken down into shorter stages.

11 The **Borders Abbeys Way** is a circular route linking the four great ruined abbeys in Kelso, Jedburgh, Dryburgh and Melrose. The full route is 105 km / 65 miles in length and can easily be broken down into stages.

12 The **Southern Upland Way** is Britain's first official coast to coast long distance footpath. It runs from Portpatrick in the west to Cockburnspath in the east, offering superb and varied walking opportunities. Of the total route 130 km / 82 miles is in the Scottish Borders passing through or near St Mary's Loch, Traquair, Yair, Galashiels, Melrose, Lauder, Longformacus and Abbey St Bathans.

13 The **John Buchan Way** is named after the writer and diplomat who had many associations with the Scottish Borders. The 22 km / 13 mile route takes you from Peebles to Broughton and ends at the John Buchan Centre which houses a collection of photographs, books and other memorabilia.

ACTIVITIES

14 Glentress and Innerleithen in the Tweed Valley, and Newcastleton to the south have a massive reputation for some of the best **mountain biking** in the UK and beyond. Glentress is probably the best biking centre in Britain, with brilliant trails of all grades, a top-notch cafe, a bike shop with bike hire, changing and showering facilities, and a great atmosphere. Innerleithen, situated just a few miles south east of Glentress, is quite different from its better-known sister - away from the hustle and bustle, it's a venue for the more experienced rider and home to the Traquair XC black run – not for the faint-hearted! All three centres are part of the 7Stanes – seven mountain biking centres of excellence across the south of Scotland.

15 The 'Freedom of the Fairways' is Scotland's best-selling **golf** pass. It offers access to 21 superb courses ranging from the coastal course at Eyemouth to St Boswells - winner of the award for 'most friendly' 9-hole course - to the championship Roxburghe and Cardrona courses. The Freedom of the Fairways scheme runs from April to October and both senior and junior passes are available.

16 **Touring** the Scottish Borders is an absolute pleasure with many miles of quiet roads and spectacular scenery. You can travel the full width and breadth of the region easily in a day taking in stunning lochs, rivers and moorland, gentle rolling farmland, historic attractions and picturesque coastline. The Scottish Borders also hosts many rallies and 'meets' from vintage cars to scooters and caravans to the Citroën 2CV World Rally (hosted at Floors Castle in 2005).

17 The Scottish Borders has everything for the angler. From the internationally famous salmon **fishing** on the River Tweed to the excellent sea trout fishing on its tributaries; from the rainbow trout in the local lochs to the wilder brown trout in the rivers; and from the coarse fishing of the lower Tweed to the sea fishing off the Berwickshire coast; there is plenty to choose from.

19

WILDLIFE

www.visitscotland.com/wildlife

18 The elusive, native **red squirrel** can still be found in pockets throughout the Scottish Borders. Try the following places to catch a glimpse - Paxton House, nr Berwick, Tweed Valley Forest Park and the Floors Castle Estate. Anywhere with plenty of trees and peace and quiet be sure to keep your eyes peeled!

19 The **Tweed Valley Osprey Watch** has two centres; Glentress and Kailzie Gardens. Both are open from Easter until mid-August and September respectively. You can see live camera action from an osprey nest within the Tweed Valley Forest Park. Follow the progress of the family, from nest building in spring to chicks hatching in May, to fledgings in August. Both centres have a variety of interpretive materials and volunteer guides. A small admission charge applies.

20 On the Berwickshire coast, **St Abbs Head** is a National Nature Reserve and a landmark site for birdwatchers and wildlife enthusiasts. Thousands of breeding seabirds can be seen between April and August and migrating birds in October. The scenery is stunning with wide-sweeping views from the lighthouse on 'The Head' north towards Edinburgh and the Fife coast and south towards Holy Island, Bamburgh and the Farne Islands. There are a number of waymarked trails around the reserve which all start from the car park and information centre.

19121 **Chirnside, by Duns, Berwickshire**  **Map Ref: 2F5**

Chirnside Hall Country House Hotel

Chirnside, By Duns, Berwickshire, TD11 3LD
Tel:01890 818219
Email:reception@chirnsidehallhotel.com
Web:www.chirnsidehallhotel.com

19c country mansion set in 5 acres of grounds, spacious en-suite bedrooms with magnificent views of the Cheviots. Open log fires. Emphasis on fine food, with innovative use of fresh Border produce.

10 rooms, All en-suite. Open Jan-Dec. Rates on application.

34079 **Galashiels, Selkirkshire** **Map Ref: 2D6**

Kingsknowes Hotel

Selkirk Road, Galashiels, Selkirkshire, TD1 3HY
Tel:01896 758375 Fax:01896 750377
Email:enquiries@kingsknowes.co.uk
Web:www.kingsknowes.co.uk

12 rooms
All en-suite
Open Jan-Dec
B&B per person, single from £65.00, double from £47.50.

28353 **by Hawick, Roxburghshire** **Map Ref: 2D7**

Glenteviot Park Hotel

Hassendeanburn, by Hawick, Roxburghshire, TD9 8RU
Tel:01450 870660 Fax:01450 870154
Email:enquiries@glenteviotpark.com
Web:www.glenteviotpark.com

Traditional country house hotel located in a rural estate between Hawick and Jedburgh with stunning views across the River Teviot. Luxurious accommodation, excellent cuisine and genuine hospitality are just some of the reasons why discerning guests return time and time again. Available to adult residents only, tranquillity and a sense of calm relaxation is ensured. Golf, walking, horse riding, fishing, cycling and other pursuits.

5 rooms, All en-suite. Open Jan-Dec. B&B per person, single £82.00, double from £55.00, BB & Eve.Meal from £85.00.

SCOTTISH BORDERS

59541 **Lauder, Berwickshire** **Map Ref: 2D6**

The Lodge, Carfraemill

Lauder, Berwickshire, TD2 6RA
Tel:01578 750750 Fax:01578 750751
Email:enquiries@carfraemill.co.uk
Web:www.carfraemill.co.uk

A former coaching Inn offering friendly hospitality and bistro/restaurant meals. Situated in rural Lauderdale at the junction of the A697/A68. Ideally situated for both Edinburgh and the Borders. Experienced in weddings, business meetings and corporate hospitality.

10 rooms, All en-suite. Open Jan-Dec. B&B per person, single from £60.00, double £40.00-45.00 per person.

78536 **Melrose, Roxburghshire** **Map Ref: 2D6**

Dryburgh Abbey Hotel

St Boswells, Melrose, Scottish Borders, TD6 0RQ
Tel:01835 822261 Fax:01835 823945
Email:enquiries@dryburgh.co.uk
Web:www.dryburgh.co.uk

Country house hotel on banks of River Tweed overlooked by 12c Dryburgh Abbey. Ideal base for fishing, shooting or exploring this historic area. Indoor pool, putting green and mountain bikes, trout rights on the Tweed.

38 rooms, All en-suite. Open Jan-Dec. B&B per person, single from £60.00, BB & Eve.Meal from £72.00 Single.

64076 **by Melrose, Roxburghshire** **Map Ref: 2D6**

Whitehouse

St Boswells, Roxburghshire, TD6 0ED
Tel:01573 460343
Email:whitehouse.tyrer@tiscali.co.uk
Web:www.aboutscotland.com/south/whitehouse.html

3 rooms
All en-suite
Open Jan-Dec
B&B per person, double from £47.00, BB & Eve.Meal from £74.00.

SCOTTISH BORDERS

49167 **Peebles** **Map Ref: 2C6**

Park Hotel

Innerleithen Road, Peebles, EH45 8BA
Tel:01721 720451 Fax:01721 723510
Email:reserve@parkhotelpeebles.co.uk
Web:www.parkhotelpeebles.co.uk

Quiet and comfortable, with extensive gardens and fine hill views. Ideal touring centre, and only 22 miles (35kms) from Edinburgh.

24 rooms, All en-suite. Open Jan-Dec. B&B per person, single from £59.50, double from £53.50.

49427 **Peebles** **Map Ref: 2C6**

Peebles Hotel Hydro

Innerleithen Road, Peebles, Peebles-shire, EH45 8LX
Tel:01721 720602
Email:reservations@peebleshotelhydro.co.uk
Web:www.peebleshotelhydro.co.uk

The Peebles Hotel Hydro is set within 30 acres in the stunning Scottish Borders, only 22 miles from Edinburgh. A resort in its own right, excellent leisure facilities, relaxing walks within the grounds, stunning views, elegant dining with inspired cuisine, combined with unrivalled service.

129 rooms, All en-suite. Open Jan-Dec. Rates on application.

49712 **Selkirk** **Map Ref: 2D7**

Philipburn Country House Hotel and Restaurant

Selkirk, Selkirkshire, TD7 5LS
Tel:01750 20747 Fax:01750 21690
Email:info@philipburnhousehotel.co.uk
Web:www.philipburnhousehotel.co.uk

Under new ownership, this fine country house is situated in the heart of the Scottish Borders. Bistro and fine dining options available. Self catering lodges also on site, with full access to hotel facilities including small outdoor pool.

12 rooms, All en-suite. Open Jan-Dec. B&B per person, single from £95.00, double from £55.00.

Jedburgh Abbey, Scottish Borders

Edinburgh skyline from Calton Hill

EDINBURGH AND THE LOTHIANS

Each year, more than four million visitors arrive in Scotland's capital and discover one of the finest cities in the world.

Whether you're partying at the biggest Hogmanay celebrations on Earth or taking your seat in the audience at the planet's largest arts festival, Edinburgh always offers more than you could ever hope to take in on one visit.

Streets steeped in history

No trip to Edinburgh is complete without a visit to the world famous Castle. Over a million people take to its ramparts every year. Many then set off down the Esplanade and onto the Royal Mile touching history with every step. During the Festival weeks, hundreds of acts perform on the Mile in an explosion of colour and sound, creating an exciting mêlée that changes every day.

Although the trappings of modern life are never far away in the shops, cafés and bars, the Old Town's fascinating history is impossible to ignore. Edinburgh's ghosts whisper in the closes: grave robbers and thieves rubbing shoulders with poets, philosophers, kings and queens – each conjured up and colourfully interpreted in the museums, exhibitions and visitor attractions you'll pass along the way.

A city of beauty

The city's rich history is matched by its beauty. Architecturally, Edinburgh is a stunning city. That beauty extends to its parks, gardens and wild places – don't miss the Royal Botanic Garden, the view from the top of majestic Arthur's Seat or the Water of Leith walkway which brings a touch of the countryside right into the city.

Edinburgh is also a city by the sea with a rapidly changing seafront. The busy port of Leith has been transformed in recent years and it boasts a wonderful selection of bars and restaurants.

Get out of town

Further out of town, there's much to explore. Take a trip down the coast to places like Aberlady, Gullane, Longniddry, Dirleton, North Berwick and Dunbar. Play golf on top-class courses, watch the seabirds on beautiful sandy beaches or go on a boat trip round the Bass Rock.

You could cycle for miles along the Union Canal towpath, visit Roslin Glen and the mysterious Rosslyn Chapel, head for Linlithgow and its ruined Palace or bet on a thrilling day out at the Musselburgh races.

So what is it you'd like to do on your visit to Edinburgh and the Lothians? And where would you like to stay? There's an ever expanding range to choose from. You can enjoy traditional 5-star luxury at the Balmoral, Sheraton or Caledonian or enjoy the boutique version at places like The Glasshouse, The Howard or Prestonfield House, or you can opt for something simpler – Edinburgh and the Lothians has everything from seaside guest houses to family-run country houses. Just flick through the pages ahead and you'll find your ideal selection.

Victoria Street, Edinburgh

What's On?

Dine Around Edinburgh
8 January – 4 February 2008
Excellent value fixed price meals at top Edinburgh restaurants.
www.eatscotland.com

Ceilidh Culture, Edinburgh
21 March – 13 April 2008
A vibrant celebration of traditional Scottish arts.
www.ceilidhculture.co.uk

Edinburgh International Science Festival
25 March – 5 April 2008
Quell the curiosity of inquiring minds.
www.sciencefestival.co.uk

Mary King's Ghost Fest, Edinburgh
May 2008 (dates TBC)
Explore Edinburgh's haunted places.
www.edinburghghostfest.com

Edinburgh Festival Fringe
3 – 25 August 2008
The largest arts festival on the planet.
www.edfringe.com

Edinburgh International Festival
10 – 31 August 2008
The very best of opera, theatre, music and dance.
www.eif.org.uk

Golden Oldies World Rugby Festival, Edinburgh
1 – 8 September 2008
The world's largest rugby festival for over-35s.
www.visitscotland.com/rugby

East Lothian Food & Drink Festival
September 2008 (dates TBC)
Food and entertainment for all ages.
www.foodanddrinkeastlothian.com

Edinburgh's Christmas
Late November – 24 December 2008
Edinburgh becomes a winter wonderland.
www.edinburghschristmas.com

www.edinburgh.org

DON'T MISS

1 Stroll down the **Royal Mile**, so-called due to its bookends of Edinburgh Castle at the top and the Palace of Holyroodhouse at the bottom. Browse through the wide range of quirky, independent gift shops. Upon reaching the Canongate, you will find the new Scottish Parliament building, with its striking contemporary architecture evident throughout.

2 Never a month passes without a major event or **festival** in Edinburgh, whether it be rugby in February and March, science in April, Children's Theatre in May, film in June, Jazz and Blues in July, or Christmas and Hogmanay in December. And of course, there's the world's largest international arts festival in August, taking in the Fringe, the International Festival, the Tattoo and the Book Festival. The city buzzes with excitement no matter what season you choose to come.

3 **The National Galleries of Scotland** offer a collection of some of the best Scottish and international artists in the world, housed in five galleries across Edinburgh. From Rembrandt and Monet, to Picasso and Bacon, there are also major touring exhibitions.

4 **Linlithgow Palace**, once an important royal residence and birthplace of Mary, Queen of Scots, is now a magnificent ruin. Set beside a loch, you can imagine what life must have been like in this vast palace with so many rooms, passages and stairways.

5 Within minutes of Edinburgh, you can stroll along the white sands of **East Lothian**, with only the sound of water lapping on the shore. Head for Gullane, Yellowcraig or North Berwick. The sheer expanses of beach are truly breathtaking.

6 Set amidst the beauty of Roslin Glen, the mysterious and magical **Rosslyn Chapel** is undoubtedly Scotland's most outstanding Gothic Church. According to Dan Brown's The Da Vinci Code, it is on the trail of the Holy Grail, which only adds to the intrigue.

2

4

5

6

FOOD AND DRINK

www.eatscotland.com

7 **Farmers' markets** are great ways to get the freshest quality local produce. Held every Saturday morning on Castle Terrace and the second and last Thursday of the month on Castle Street in Edinburgh, and the last Saturday of each month in Haddington in East Lothian, be sure to pop along early to pick up the very best supplies.

8 Set along the Union Canal, **The Bridge Inn**, to the west of Edinburgh, offers a great escape to the outdoors. With several child-friendly awards under its belt, it offers play areas and a children's menu.

9 For full-on romance, book ahead for a table at **The Witchery by the Castle** in Edinburgh. Its food, service and ambience consistently win awards. Located in a historic 16th century building at the gates of Edinburgh Castle, it aims to create a memorable and magical dining experience.

10 **Dine Around Edinburgh** is an initiative that allows you to experience some of Edinburgh's top restaurants at inexpensive prices. Held each January, over 25 eateries take place, from seafood to vegetarian, from the waterfront at Leith to all over the city centre.

HISTORY AND HERITAGE

11 With fantastic views over the Firth of Forth, the ship-shaped **Blackness Castle** looks almost poised to set sail, and has been used as a prison for much of its history. This was the impressive setting for Franco Zeffirelli's film of Hamlet starring Mel Gibson.

12 The **National Museum of Scotland** presents an impressive history of both our fascinating nation and that of our whole world. With a continuous programme of changing exhibitions you could happily spend the whole day here. Or why not go to the **Museum of Flight**, where you can discover the extraordinary story of our human ambition to take to the skies, and check out the Concorde Experience.

13 **The Royal Yacht *Britannia***, former floating home of the monarchy offers a superb visitor experience that will guide you through 40 years of royal life aboard, including private family quarters, the sick bay and the laundry!

14 The ruins of 14th century **Tantallon Castle** are perched on an East Lothian cliff top, just to the south east of North Berwick. From here, look out to the Bass Rock, the largest single island gannet colony.

SHOPPING

15 In **Princes Street**, Edinburgh has one of the most beautiful shopping streets in the country with the usual high street stores along one side while on the other, in the shelter of Edinburgh Castle, Princes Street Gardens provide a nearby escape. Check out nearby **George Street** for designer stores and unique boutiques.

16 **Multrees Walk** is located in the heart of the city and is headed by Harvey Nichols. This is the prestigious street that is a must-see on a shopping trip to the city. Locally known as The Walk, shops include Emporio Armani, Louis Vuitton, Calvin Klein Underwear and Reiss.

17 Surrounding the city centre, Edinburgh has a number of urban villages where you'll find **specialist shops**, from up-and-coming designers to crafts, jewellery, food and gifts. Try Bruntsfield, Stockbridge and Leith. In the centre, try Cockburn Street, Victoria Street, and the Royal Mile for something a bit different.

16

19

20

ACTIVITIES AND ATTRACTIONS

18 Edinburgh and the Lothians is a superb base for **golf**, whether you choose to play some of the city's fine courses or go east to the coast. Stay in the city for the challenges of Bruntsfield Links, Prestonfield or Duddingston. Or head to the Lothians for the perfect mixture of parkland and links courses, you can enjoy inspirational views across to Fife from some courses in East Lothian.

19 There is a fantastic range of **walks** and trails throughout scenic and historic countryside around Edinburgh and the Lothians. Through the heart of the city runs the Water of Leith where a peaceful path offers a handy escape from the vibrant centre. In East Lothian the stretch of beach from Gullane to Yellowcraig is perfect for a walk or a picnic. Or climb Arthur's Seat for a phenomenal view of the Scottish Lowlands.

20 The area is home to some of Scotland's most impressive visitor **attractions**. From interactive exhibits to wonders of the natural world, there is something for everyone. Head to the Scottish Seabird Centre in North Berwick or Edinburgh Zoo to see wildlife up close, travel back in time at Our Dynamic Earth, try rock climbing at Edinburgh International Climbing Arena or venture underground at The Real Mary King's Close.

21 With free entry to over 30 top attractions, free return airport and city centre bus transport, a free comprehensive guidebook as well as loads of exclusive offers, the **Edinburgh Pass** is the best way to discover all that Edinburgh has to offer. Buy a 1, 2 or 3 day Pass from www.edinburghpass.com or from one of the Tourist Information Centres in Edinburgh.

MAP

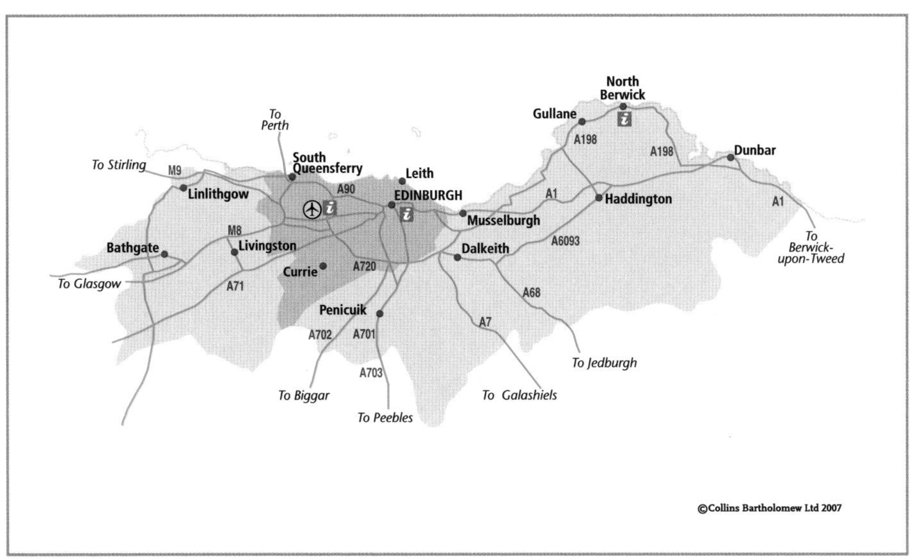

TOURIST INFORMATION CENTRES

Edinburgh & Lothians	
Edinburgh Airport	Main Concourse, Edinburgh International Airport, Edinburgh EH12 9DN
Edinburgh & Scotland Information Centre	Princes Mall, 3 Princes Street, Edinburgh EH2 2QP
North Berwick	1 Quality Street, North Berwick EH39 4HJ

Make the most of your stay in Scotland and make your first stop the Tourist Information Centre wherever you go.

Knowledgeable and friendly staff can help you with information and advice; they can answer your questions, book accommodation and you can even pick up some souvenirs to take home for friends and family.

For information and ideas about exploring Scotland in advance of your trip, call our booking and information service or go to **www.visitscotland.com**

Call 0845 22 55 121

or if calling from outside the UK call **+44 (0) 1506 832 121**

From Ireland call **1800 932 510**

A £4 booking fee applies to telephone bookings of accommodation.

14205

Broxburn, West Lothian — Map Ref: 2B5

Bankhead Farm

Dechmont, Broxburn, West Lothian, EH52 6NB
Tel:01506 811209 Fax:01506 811815
Email:bankheadbb@aol.com
Web:www.bankheadfarm.com

7 rooms
All en-suite
Open Jan-Dec excl Xmas
B&B per person, single from £40.00, double from £35.00.

55620

Dunbar, East Lothian — Map Ref: 2E4

Springfield Guest House

Belhaven Road, Dunbar, East Lothian, EH42 1NH
Tel:01368 862502
Email:smeed@tesco.net

5 rooms
Open Jan-Nov excl Xmas/New Year
B&B per person, single from £30.00, double from £25.00.

34321

Edinburgh — Map Ref: 2C5

Aaron Lodge Guest House

128 Old Dalkeith Road, Edinburgh, EH16 4SD
Tel:0131 664 2755 Fax:0131 672 2236
Email:dot@baigan.freeserve.co.uk
Web:www.aaronlodgeedinburgh.com

The truly luxurious Aaron Lodge was fully rebuilt and completed in June 2007. The rooms are furnished to an exacting standard, including 37in LCD televisions offering 120 channels including Sky Sports. There is ample resident only car parking and an abundance of local transport, with stops on our doorstep. The Lodge is central for all attractions including Edinburgh Castle, Holyrood Palace, Dynamic Earth and Royal Yacht Britannia as well as being only 15 minutes from the Airport! The owners Ted & Dot Baigan guarantee a relaxed and inviting atmosphere throughout your stay. Visit our website for further information - what you see is what you get!

Aaron Lodge Edinburgh

Tel: 0131 664 2755

9 rooms.
All ensuite. Open Jan-Dec
B&B per person single from £35.00, double from £22.50,
Family room available.

11183

Edinburgh — Map Ref: 2C5

Afton Guest House

1 Hartington Gardens, Edinburgh, EH10 4LD
Tel/Fax:0131 229 1019
Email:info@aftonguesthouse.co.uk
Web:www.aftonguesthouse.co.uk

7 rooms
Some en-suite
Open Jan-Dec
B&B per person, single from £25.00, double from £25.00.

10443

Edinburgh Map Ref: 2C5

A Haven Townhouse

180 Ferry Road, Edinburgh, EH6 4NS
Tel:0131 554 6559 Fax:0131 554 5252
Email:reservations@a-haven.co.uk
Web:www.a-haven.co.uk

14 rooms
All en-suite
Open Jan-Dec excl Xmas
B&B per person, single from £30.00, double from £30.00.

79278

Edinburgh Map Ref: 2C5

Albyn Townhouse

16 Hartington Gardens, off Bruntsfield Place, Edinburgh, EH10 4LD
Tel:0131 229 6459 Fax:0131 228 5807
Email:info@albyntownhouse.co.uk
Web:www.albyntownhouse.co.uk

The Albyn Townhouse is a beautiful Victorian three star guest-house, very quiet location, walkable from Edinburgh Old Town, Castle, major attractions & great restaurants. 4 parking spaces by arrangement.

10 rooms, All en-suite. Open Jan-Dec. B&B per person per night, from £30.00 in shared rooms.

11676

Edinburgh Map Ref: 2C5

Allison House

17 Mayfield Gardens, Edinburgh, EH9 2AX
Tel:0131 667 8049 Fax:0131 667 5001
Email:info@allisonhousehotel.com
Web:www.allisonhousehotel.com

11 rooms
10 en-suite
Open Jan-Dec
B&B per person, single from £40.00, double/twin from £30.00.

11691

Edinburgh Map Ref: 2C5

Alloway Guest House

96 Pilrig Street, Edinburgh, EH6 5AY
Tel:0131 554 1786
Email:davidgilfillan2@btinternet.com
Web:www.allowayguesthouse.co.uk

6 rooms
Some en-suite, 1 priv.facilities
Open Jan-Dec
B&B per person, single from £30.00, double/twin from £30.00.

11848 **Edinburgh** Map Ref: 2C5

AmarAgua Guest House

10 Kilmaurs Terrace, Edinburgh, Lothian, EH16 5DR
Tel:0131 667 6775
Email:reservations@amaragua.co.uk
Web:www.amaragua.co.uk

Comfortable Victorian residence. 10 minute bus ride to centre. Extensive breakfast selection. Free internet access. Unrestricted street parking. Please call for low season special offers, minimum 2 night stay.

6 rooms, All en-suite. Open Feb-Oct & Dec. B&B per person, single from £35.00, double from £33.00.

12535 **Edinburgh** Map Ref: 2C5

Ardenlee Guest House

9 Eyre Place, Edinburgh, EH3 5ES
Tel:0131 556 2838 Fax:0131 557 0937
Email:info@ardenlee.co.uk
Web:www.ardenlee.co.uk

Personally run terraced guest house, in New Town approximately 0.5 mile (1km) from Princes Street and city centre. Ideal touring base. Non-smoking house. Variety of shops and restaurants nearby. Most rooms en-suite.

9 rooms, Some en-suite. Open Jan-Dec. B&B per person, single from £27.50, double from £27.50.

12567 **Edinburgh** Map Ref: 2C5

Ardgarth Guest House

1 St Mary's Place, Portobello, Edinburgh, EH15 2QF
Tel:0131 669 3021 Fax:0131 468 1221
Email:stay@ardgarth.com
Web:www.ardgarth.com

9 rooms
Some en-suite
Open Jan-Dec excl Xmas
B&B per person, single from £20.00, double from £20.00.

12599 **Edinburgh** Map Ref: 2C5

Ardleigh Guest House

260 Ferry Road, Edinburgh, EH5 3AN
Tel:0131 552 1833 Fax:0131 552 4951
Email:info@ardleighhouse.com
Web:www.ardleighhouse.com

7 rooms
5 en-suite
Open all year
B&B per person, single from £25.00, double/twin from £22.50.

12613 **Edinburgh** Map Ref: 2C5

Ardmillan Hotel

9-10 Ardmillan Terrace, Edinburgh, EH11 2JW
Tel:0131 337 9588 Fax:0131 346 1895
Email:hotelardmillan@hotmail.com
Web:www.ardmillanhotel.com

10 rooms
Mostly en-suite
Open all year
B&B single from £39.00, double room from £59.00. Eve.meal 3 course from £10.00.

13135 **Edinburgh** Map Ref: 2C5

Ashgrove House

12 Osborne Terrace, Edinburgh, EH12 5HG
Tel:0131 337 5014 Fax:0131 313 5043
Email:info@theashgrovehouse.com
Web:www.theashgrovehouse.com

Family run guest house on main road leading into Edinburgh City, from the airport. Non smoking house, private parking, within easy walking distance to Princes Street and Murrayfield Stadium. Also close to Haymarket railway station.

7 rooms, Some en-suite. Open Jan-Dec. B&B per person, single £35.00-60.00, double £33.00-50.00.

77491 **Edinburgh** Map Ref: 2C5

Ballantrae-Albany Hotel

39/43 Albany Street, Edinburgh, EH1 3QY
Tel:0131 556 0397 Fax:0131 557 6633
Email:info@albanyhoteledinburgh.co.uk
Web:www.albanyhoteledinburgh.co.uk

Recently refurbished to an excellent standard, City Centre hotel within walking distance to Princes Street, George Street and all local tourist attractions. In an ideal location for business and pleasure.

22 rooms, Open Jan-Dec. B&B per room, single from £70.00, double from £90.00.

68710

Edinburgh — Map Ref: 2C5

Ballantrae Apartments

12 York Place, Edinburgh, Midlothian, EH1 3EP
Tel:0131 478 4748 Fax:0131 478 4749
Email:info@ballantraehotel.freeserve.co.uk

Recently refurbished to an excellent standard, these elegant Georgian city central apartments are an ideal base for business, shopping or exploring Edinburgh by foot. 3 out of 4 are very spacious and all with rooftop and sea views. Facilities in the Ballantrae Hotel (2 doors away) can be used. Porterage and private parking available.

4 apartments, Open Jan-Dec. Rates from £90.00-260.00.

71559

Edinburgh — Map Ref: 2C5

Ballantrae Hotel At The West End

6 Grosvenor Crescent, Edinburgh, Midlothian, EH12 5EP
Tel:0131 225 7033 Fax:0131 225 7044
Email:westend@ballantraehotel.co.uk
Web:www.ballantraehotel.co.uk

Well appointed victorian terraced house retaining many original features and set in a quiet residential area close to the city centre. Variety of restaurants close by. Within walking distance of Haymarket Station and public transport to the airport,

16 rooms, All en-suite. Open Jan-Dec. B&B per person, single from £55.00, double from £37.50.

14350

Edinburgh — Map Ref: 2C5

Barony House

23 Mayfield Gardens, Edinburgh, EH9 2BX
Tel/Fax:0131 667 5806
Email:booknow@baronyhouse.co.uk
Web:www.baronyhouse.co.uk

An impressive detached Victorian villa. Beautifully restored to a very high standard with decorative plasterwork and period cornices. Very comfortable spacious accommodation, all ensuite. Easy access to city centre via main bus route. Ample private parking.

9 rooms, All en-suite. Open Jan-Dec. B&B per room, double from £70.00.

14395 Edinburgh — Map Ref: 2C5

Barossa Guest House

21 Pilrig Street, Edinburgh, EH6 5AN
Tel:0131 554 3700

6 rooms
Some en-suite
Open Jan-Dec
B&B per person, double £27.00-45.00.

14914 Edinburgh — Map Ref: 2C5

Ben Craig House

3 Craigmillar Park, Edinburgh, EH16 5PG
Tel:0131 667 2593 Fax:0131 667 2125
Email:bencraighouse@hotmail.com
Web:www.bencraig-edinburgh.co.uk

8 rooms
All en-suite
Open Jan-Dec
B&B per person, single from £40.00, double from £25.00.

16696 Edinburgh — Map Ref: 2C5

Best Western Bruntsfield Hotel

69 Bruntsfield Place, Edinburgh, EH10 4HH
Tel:0131 229 1393 Fax:0131 229 5634
Email:reservations@thebruntsfield.co.uk
Web:www.thebruntsfield.co.uk

Overlooking a park close to the city centre, the Bruntsfield is a well appointed townhouse hotel with friendly, professional service. The 67 classic, superior and master bedrooms have sparkling bathrooms, free internet access and multi-channel TV. Bisque Brasserie offers modern Scottish cuisine in a contemporary and informal atmosphere. A relaxing lounge and stylish Bisque Bar add to the distinictive character of The Bruntsfield.

67 rooms, All en-suite. Open Jan-Dec excl Xmas. B&B per person per night, single from £75.00, double from £50.00.

34051 Edinburgh — Map Ref: 2C5

Best Western Kings Manor Hotel

100 Milton Road East, Edinburgh, EH15 2NP
Tel:0131 468 8003 Fax:0131 669 6650
Email:reservations@kingsmanor.com
Web:www.kingsmanor.com

95 rooms
All en-suite
Open Jan-Dec
B&B per person, single from £70.00, double from £45.00, BB & Eve.Meal from £65.00.

58265

Edinburgh Map Ref: 2C5

The Bonham

35 Drumsheugh Gardens, Edinburgh, EH3 7RN
Tel:0131 274 7400 Fax:0131 274 7405
Email:reserve@thebonham.com
Web:www.thebonham.com

The Bonham is the coolest hotel in Edinburgh, where you'll enjoy an uplifting contemporary ambience within the classic atmosphere of a Victorian town house. During your stay, experience Edinburgh's most timeless contemporary restaurant - Restaurant at the Bonham. You'll be tempted by distinct European-inspired food and enticed by provocative wines.

48 rooms, All en suite. Open Jan-Dec. B&B per room per night, single from £95.00-155.00, double from £110.00-350.00.

TV P C £ V

16323

Edinburgh Map Ref: 2C5

Briggend Guest House

19 Old Dalkeith Road, Edinburgh, EH16 4TE
Tel:0131 258 0810 Fax:0131 620 2873
Email:reservations@briggend.com
Web:www.briggend.com

Recently extended traditional cottage, now providing 4 ensuite bedrooms, all on ground level, on south side of city with very easy access to main routes, the new Edinburgh Royal Infirmary, Universities and many of the city's attractions. Also on main bus route.

4 rooms, All ensuite. Open Jan-Dec. B&B per person, single from £35.00, double from £22.50. Family room available.

TV P C £ V

77907

Edinburgh Map Ref: 2C5

The Broughton City Centre Hotel

37 Broughton Place, New Town, Edinburgh, Lothian, EH1 3RR
Tel:0131 558 9792 Fax:0131 558 9790
Email:broughton-hotel@hotmail.co.uk
also:info@broughton-hotel.com
Web:www.thebroughton.co.uk

6 rooms
All en suite
Open Jan-Dec
B&B per person, single from £40.00, double from £30.00.

TV P

18009

Edinburgh Map Ref: 2C5

Caravel Guest House

30 London Street, Edinburgh, EH3 6NA
Tel:0131 556 4444 Fax:0131 557 3615
Email:caravelguest@hotmail.com
Web:www.caravelhouse.co.uk

A warm welcome at this guest house with spacious, en-suite bedrooms. This Georgian house is situated in the heart of Edinburgh's New Town only a short distance from Princes Street and close to Waverley Station and the bus station.

11 rooms, Some en-suite. Open Jan-Dec. B&B per person, single from £30.00, double from £25.00.

18299

Edinburgh Map Ref: 2C5

Carrington Guest House

38 Pilrig Street, Edinburgh, EH6 5AL
Tel:0131 554 4769

7 rooms
Some en-suite
Open Feb-Nov
B&B per person, double £27.00-45.00.

18911

Edinburgh Map Ref: 2C5

Channings

12-16 South Learmonth Gardens, Edinburgh, EH4 1EZ
Tel:0131 274 7401 Fax:0131 274 7405
Email:reserve@channings.co.uk
Web:www.channings.co.uk

Channings is the friendliest hotel in Edinburgh, where you'll enjoy country-style tranquillity in a city setting and be charmed by our people. During your stay, experience great food and favoursome wine in a awrm and welcoming ambience in Channing's 2AA rosette restaurant.

41 rooms, All en suite. Open Jan-Dec. B&B per room per night, single from £85.00-140.00, double from £120.00-300.00.

18973

Edinburgh — Map Ref: 2C5

Charleston House Guest House

38 Minto Street, Edinburgh, EH9 2BS
Tel:0131 667 6589 Fax:0131 668 3800
Email:joan_wightman@hotmail.com
Web:www.charleston-house.co.uk

Traditional Georgian family home with many original features - circa 1826. Awarded prestigious Bronze Green Tourism plaque. Only 1- 1.5 miles from city centre. Excellent bus route, very frequent service. Within easy walking distance of various restaurants.

5 rooms, Some en-suite. Open Jan-Dec excl Xmas. B&B per person, single from £30.00, double from £25.00.

67259

Edinburgh — Map Ref: 2C5

Clan Walker Guest House

96 Dalkeith Road, Edinburgh, EH16 5AF
Tel:0131 667 1244
Email:enquiries@clanwalkerguesthouse.com
Web:www.clanwalkerguesthouse.com

Family run, stone built house. All bedrooms with en suite facilities. Situated on south side, approx 1.5 miles from city centre. Close to Royal Commonwealth Swimming Pool, Edinburgh University's Pollock Halls of Residence and Royal College of Surgeons.

6 rooms, All en-suite. B&B per person, twin/double £20.00-40.00. triple/family £20.00-40.00.

19507

Edinburgh — Map Ref: 2C5

Clarendon Hotel

25-33 Shandwick Place, Edinburgh, EH2 4RG
Tel:0131 229 1467 Fax:0131 229 7549
Email:res@clarendonhoteledi.co.uk
Web:www.clarendonhoteledi.co.uk

Situated in the heart of the city, approximately 20 yards from Edinburgh's famous Princes Street. Ideally situated for the city's financial district, tourist attractions, theatres, restaurants and the International Conference Centre (EICC), all within minutes walking distance. If arriving at Edinburgh International Airport, the Airport bus drops off and picks up opposite the hotel. Located between Waverley and Haymarket Railway stations, both within easy walking distance.

66 rooms, All en-suite. Open all year. B&B per person, single from £30.00, double from £25.00.

21723

Edinburgh Map Ref: 2C5

The Corstorphine Lodge

188 St Johns Road, Edinburgh, Lothians, EH12 8SG
Tel:0131 539 4237 Fax:0131 539 4945
Email:corsthouse@aol.com
Web:www.corstorphinehotels.co.uk

Pleasant Victorian house providing a warm welcome and excellent facilities. Close to city centre, Edinburgh airport, and all major attractions. On excellent frequent bus route. Off street parking. Extensive walled garden to rear for guests to use.

17 rooms, All en-suite. Open Jan-Dec. B&B per person, single from £29.00, double from £29.00.

TV P C £ V

21312

Edinburgh Map Ref: 2C5

Crioch Guest House

23 East Hermitage Place, Leith Links, Edinburgh
EH6 8AD
Tel:0131 554 5494 Fax:0870 706 6221
Email:welcome@crioch.com
Web:ww.crioch.com

Try Dora's famous full-cooked, continental or vegetarian breakfast. All rooms have ensuite shower or private bathroom, TV, radio alarm, welcome tray, hairdryer. Crioch overlooks the park of Leith Links, only a short walk from Leith's fine cafes, bars and restaurants, with the Royal Yacht Britannia nearby. Park your car for free, take a short bus journey to the city centre and enjoy Edinburgh's sights on foot. Wireless internet (Wi-Fi).

6 rooms, 5 en-suite. Open Jan-Dec. B&B per person, single from £27.50, double from £25.00.

TV C £ V

21722

Edinburgh Map Ref: 2C5

Cumberland Hotel

1-2 West Coates, Edinburgh, EH12 5JQ
Tel:0131 337 1198 Fax:0131 337 1022
Email:cumblhotel@aol.com
Web:www.corstorphinehotels.co.uk

Family run property in listed Victorian building. A short walk from the West End of the city centre. 10 - 15 min drive to the airport and Ingliston Highland Showground. Murrayfield Stadium within walking distance. The Cumberland offers a choice of continental, traditional or vegetarian breakfasts. There are several restaurants providing a variety of cuisine within easy walking distance of the property.

17 rooms, All en-suite. Open Jan-Dec. B&B per person, single £39.00-99.00, double £25.00-69.00 pppn.

TV P

22466 Edinburgh — Map Ref: 2C5

Dene Guest House

7 Eyre Place, off Dundas Street, Edinburgh
EH3 5ES
Tel:0131 556 2700 Fax:0131 557 9876
Email:deneguesthouse@yahoo.co.uk
Web:www.deneguesthouse.com

11 rooms
Some en-suite
Open Jan-Dec
B&B per person, single from £23.50, double from £23.50.

79350 Edinburgh — Map Ref: 2C5

Dunstane City Hotel

5 Hampton Terrace, Edinburgh, Lothian, EH12 5JD
Tel:0131 337 6169 Fax:0131 337 6060
Email:reservations@dunstanehotels.co.uk
Web:www.dunstanehotels.co.uk

Dunstane City Hotel is an elegant town house situated a short walk to Edinburgh City Centre with a bus stop for centre and airport right outside. The hotel has a free private car park and is ideal for business and leisure guests alike. Friendly staff are always on hand to help and ensure a truly memorable break.

15 rooms, Open Jan-Dec. B&B per person, single from £85.00, double from £44.00.

23861 Edinburgh — Map Ref: 2C5

Dunstane House Hotel

4 West Coates, Haymarket, Edinburgh, EH12 5JQ
Tel:0131 337 6169 Fax:0131 337 6060
Email:reservations@dunstanehousehotel.co.uk
Web:www.dunstanehotels.co.uk

Impressive Listed Victorian mansion retaining many original features enjoying imposing position within large grounds on the A8 airport road (major bus route). 10 mins walk from city centre. Close to Edinburgh Conference Centre, Murrayfield and Edinburgh Zoo. Private secluded car park. Unique lounge bar and restaurant themed on the Scottish Islands.

16 rooms, All en-suite. Open Jan-Dec. B&B per person, single from £75.00, double from £49.00, BB & Eve.Meal from £69.00.

23918

Edinburgh — Map Ref: 2C5

Duthus Lodge

5 West Coates, Edinburgh, EH12 5JG
Tel:0131 337 6876 Fax:0131 313 2264
Email:duthus.lodge@ukgateway.net
Web:www.duthuslodge.com

Magnificent detached sandstone building with attractive walled gardens. Ideal base for exploring Edinburgh. Close to the city centre, the conference centre, the zoo and Murrayfield stadium. Wireless connection in all bedrooms.

8 rooms, All en-suite. Open Jan-Dec. B&B per person, single £35.00-55.00, double £25.00-50.00.

50382

Edinburgh — Map Ref: 2C5

Edinburgh City Centre (Morrison St) Premier Travel Inn

1 Morrison Link, Edinburgh, EH3 8DN
Tel:0870 238 3319 Fax:0131 228 9836
Email:edinburghccmorrisonstpti@whitbread.com
Web:www.premiertravelinn.com

281 rooms
All en-suite
Open Jan-Dec
Rates on application.

24493

Edinburgh — Map Ref: 2C5

Edinburgh House

11 McDonald Road, Edinburgh, EH7 4LX
Tel/Fax:0131 556 3434
Web:www.edinburgh-house.co.uk

Small personally run guest house in a traditional tenement building approx 0.5 ml from Princes Street. Good bus service to city centre with all its amenities. Variety of restaurants nearby. Non-smoking house. French and Italian spoken.

4 rooms, All en-suite. Open Jan-Dec. B&B per person, double £30.00-55.00.

58833

Edinburgh — Map Ref: 2C5

The Edinburgh Residence

7 Rothesay Terrace, Edinburgh, EH3 7RY
Tel:0131 274 7403 Fax:0131 274 7405
Email:reserve@theedinburghresidence.com
Web:www.theedinburghresidence.com

The Edinburgh Residence is the most distinguished collection of luxury townhouse suites in Edinburgh, offering a refreshing alternative to a five star hotel where you will enjoy an experience to remember. Comprising three beautiful architectural Georgian townhouses and situated in Edinburgh's West End, close to both the city's financial district and main shopping area, The Edinburgh Residence enjoys a peaceful yet central location only 5 minutes walk from Edinburgh's main tourist attractions.

29 rooms, All en suite. Open Jan-Dec. B&B per person, single from £125.00-225.00, double from £150.00-410.00.

24812

Edinburgh — Map Ref: 2C5

Ellesmere Guest House

11 Glengyle Terrace, Edinburgh, EH3 9LN
Tel:0131 229 4823
Email:ruth@edinburghbandb.co.uk
Web:www.edinburghbandb.co.uk

4 rooms
All en-suite
Open Jan-Dec
B&B per person, single from £35.00, double from £35.00.

25545

Edinburgh — Map Ref: 2C5

Falcon Crest Guest House

70 South Trinity Road, Edinburgh, EH5 3NX
Tel/Fax:0131 552 5294
Email:manager@falconcrest.co.uk
Web:www.falconcrest.co.uk

6 rooms
Some en-suite
(1 single, 2 twin, 2 double, 1 family), from £18.00 Single, double from £18.00.

26652

Edinburgh — Map Ref: 2C5

Fountain Court Apartments

123 Grove Street & 228 Morrison Street, Edinburgh, EH3 8AA
Tel:0131 622 6677 Fax:0131 622 6679
Email:enq@fountaincourtapartments.com
Web:www.fountaincourtapartments.com

62 rooms
Open Jan-Dec
Rates on application.

75747

Edinburgh Map Ref: 2C5

Four Hill Street

4 Hill Street, Edinburgh, EH2 3JZ
Tel:0131 225 8884
Email:rooms@fourhillstreet.com
Web:www.fourhillstreet.com

Experience life in an 18th century townhouse - but with 21st century luxury! Open all year. Fantastic central location within walking distance of all city centre attractions and amenities.

Rooms to let, Jan-Dec., Rates on application.

26805

Edinburgh Map Ref: 2C5

Frederick House Hotel

42 Frederick Street, Edinburgh, EH2 1EX
Tel:0131 226 1999 Fax:0131 624 7064
Email:frederickhouse@ednet.co.uk
Web:www.townhousehotels.co.uk

Situated in the heart of Edinburgh close to all city centre amenities and with a wide variety of restaurants and bars in the immediate vicinity. Georgian building with all rooms to a high standard with en-suite facilities, fridges and modem points. Princes Street a short walk away. Breakfast available across the road at the award winning Rick's Bar/Restaurant. Street parking (metered).

45 rooms, All en-suite. Open Jan-Dec. B&B per person, single from £35.00, double from £25.00 per person subject to availability and season.

27602

Edinburgh Map Ref: 2C5

Gifford House

103 Dalkeith Road, Edinburgh, EH16 5AJ
Tel/Fax:0131 667 4688
Email:giffordhouse@btinternet.com
Web:www.giffordhousehotel.co.uk

7 rooms
All en-suite
Open Jan-Dec excl Xmas
B&B per person, single £35.00-75.00, double from £30.00-55.00.

27612

Edinburgh Map Ref: 2C5

Gildun Guest House

9 Spence Street, Edinburgh, EH16 5AG
Tel:0131 667 1368 Fax:0131 668 4989
Email:gildun.edin@btinternet.com
Web:www.gildun.co.uk

8 rooms
Some en-suite
Open Jan-Dec
B&B per person, single from £30.00, double from £30.00.

59071

Edinburgh Map Ref: 2C5

The Glasshouse

2 Greenside Place, Edinburgh, EH1 3AA
Tel:0131 525 8200
Email:resglasshouse@theetongroup.com
Web:http://www.theetoncollection.com

65 rooms
All en-suite
Open Jan-Dec
Room only per night, single/double from £275.00.

27974

Edinburgh Map Ref: 2C5

Glenalmond House

25 Mayfield Gardens, Edinburgh, EH9 2BX
Tel:0131 668 2392
Email:enquiries@glenalmondhouse.com
Web:www.glenalmondhouse.com

10 rooms
All en-suite
Open Jan-Dec
B&B per person, single from £40.00, double from £35.00.

C V

28302

Edinburgh Map Ref: 2C5

The Glenora

14 Rosebery Crescent, Edinburgh, EH12 5JY
Tel:0131 337 1186 Fax:0131 337 1119
Email:reservations@glenorahotel.co.uk
Web:www.glenorahotel.co.uk

Internet access in all bedrooms. Totally non-smoking.

11 rooms, Single from £40.00. double from £35.00. Telephones and modem points in rooms. Buffet & full cooked breakfasts. all entirely organic.

C V

28413

Edinburgh Map Ref: 2C5

The Globetrotter Inn Edinburgh Limited

Cramond Foreshore, Marine Drive, Edinburgh, Lothian, EH4 5EP
Tel:0131 336 1030 Fax:0131 336 0945
Email:edinburgh@globtrotterinns.com
Web:www.globetrotterinns.com

Discover a new concept in quality, affordable accommodation for independent travellers at the Globetrotter Inns. In a stunning unspoilt location on the shores of the Firth of Forth there is a mini-bus to and from the city from 6.30am to 11.00pm. Airport pick-ups are available by arrangement. Private car parking and coach parking.

382 rooms, Some en-suite. Open Jan-Dec. Rates on application.

29048

Edinburgh Map Ref: 2C5

Greenside Hotel

9 Royal Terrace, Edinburgh, EH7 5AB
Tel:0131 557 0121/0022 Fax:0131 557 0022
Email:greensidehotel@ednet.co.uk
Web:www.townhousehotels.co.uk

Personally run hotel in traditional Georgian terraced house. Quiet location, close to Princes Street and all amenities. 10 minutes walk from Waverley Station and Princes Street. Excellent selection of restaurants in immediate vicinity. Building of architectural interest.

16 rooms, All en-suite. Open Jan-Dec. B&B per person, single from £35.00, double from £25.00.

29146

Edinburgh Map Ref: 2C5

Grosvenor Gardens Hotel

1 Grosvenor Gardens, Edinburgh, EH12 5JU
Tel:0131 313 3415 Fax:0131 346 8732
Email:info@stayinedinburgh.com
Web:www.stayinedinburgh.com

10 rooms
All en-suite
B&B per person, single from £49.00-55.00
double from £30.00-75.00.

29383

Edinburgh Map Ref: 2C5

Halcyon Hotel

8 Royal Terrace, Edinburgh, EH7 5AB
Tel:0131 556 1033 Fax:0131 556 1383
Email:patricia@halcyon-hotel.com
Web:www.halcyon-hotel.com

14 rooms
Some en-suite
Open Jan-Dec
B&B per person, single from £54.00, double from £44.00.

29722

Edinburgh Map Ref: 2C5

Harvest Guest House

33, Straiton Place, Edinburgh, EH15 2BA
Tel:0131 657 3160 Fax:0131 468 7028
Email:sadol@blueyonder.co.uk
Web:www.edinburgh-bb.com

7 rooms
Some en-suite
Open Jan-Dec
B&B per person, single from £25.00, double from £20.00.

16770 Edinburgh Map Ref: 2C5

Haymarket Hotel

1-3 Coates Gardens, Edinburgh, Lothian, EH12 5LG
Tel:0131 337 1045 Fax:0131 313 0330
Email:ritchie@haymarket-hotel.co.uk
Web:www.haymarket-hotel.co.uk

Beautifully presented, family run, City Centre hotel consisting two fully modernised, charming, historical, 'B' listed Victorian townhouses where the emphasis is quality accommodation, impeccable service, friendly attentive staff and good food.

24 rooms, All en-suite. Open Jan-Dec. B&B per person, single from £47.50, double from £47.50.

41890 Edinburgh Map Ref: 2C5

Hotel Ibis Edinburgh

6 Hunter Square, Edinburgh, EH1 1QW
Tel:0131 240 7000
Web:www.ibishotel.com

Modern, recently built hotel situated just off the Royal Mile and only a short walk from Edinburgh Castle and Waverley railway station. No restaurant, but bar, 24 hour snack service and continental buffet breakfast are available. Discounted car parking is available nearby.

99 rooms, All en-suite. Open Jan-Dec. Room only rates, single from £69.00, double from £69.00.

59308 Edinburgh Map Ref: 2C5

The Howard

34 Great King Street, Edinburgh, EH3 6QH
Tel:0131 274 7402 Fax:0131 274 7405
Email:reserve@thehoward.com
Web:www.thehoward.com

The Howard is the most discreet 5-star hotel in Edinburgh - attention to detail together with the personal touch will ensure you feel special. 'Dining at The Atholl' is an experience full of decadent pleasures. You'll enjoy dinner, which will be meticulously prepared by our dedicated team of chefs, in this warm and exclusive Georgian setting. Alternatively, you can be served dinner in the comfort of your room.

17 rooms, All en-suite. Open Jan-Dec. B&B per room per night, single from £90.00-145.00, double from £165.00-395.00.

32014 **Edinburgh** Map Ref: 2C5

The Inverleith Hotel

5 Inverleith Terrace, Edinburgh, EH3 5NS
Tel:0131 556 2745 Fax:0131 557 0433
Email:info@inverleithhotel.co.uk
Web:www.inverleithhotel.co.uk

10 rooms
All en-suite
Open Jan-Dec
B&B per room, single from £55.00, double from £69.00.

33378 **Edinburgh** Map Ref: 2C5

Kariba Guest House

10 Granville Terrace, Edinburgh, EH10 4PQ
Tel:0131 229 3773 Fax:0131 229 4968
Email:karibaguesthouse@hotmail.com
Web:www.karibaguesthouse.co.uk

9 rooms
8 en-suite
Open Jan-Dec
B&B per person, single from £35.00, double £25.00-45.00.

33610 **Edinburgh** Map Ref: 2C5

Kenvie Guest House

16 Kilmaurs Road, Edinburgh, EH16 5DA
Tel:0131 668 1964 Fax:0131 668 1926
Email:dorothy@kenvie.co.uk
Web:www.kenvie.co.uk

A charming, comfortable, warm, friendly family run Victorian town house in a quiet residential street. Very close to bus routes and the city by-pass. We offer for your comfort, lots of caring touches including complimentary tea/coffee, colour TV, hairdryers and no-smoking rooms. En-suite available and vegetarians catered for. You are guranteed a warm welcome from Richard and Dorothy.

5 rooms, Some en-suite. Open Jan-Dec. B&B per person, single from £27.00, double from £25.00.

33763 **Edinburgh** Map Ref: 2C5

Kildonan Lodge Hotel

27 Craigmillar Park, Edinburgh, EH16 5PE
Tel:0131 667 2793 Fax:0131 667 9777
Email:info@kildonanlodgehotel.co.uk
Web:www.kildonanlodgehotel.co.uk

Elegant Victorian style hotel close to city centre well-known for its friendly country-style atmosphere. Offering individually designed en-suite bedrooms, free wireless internet access, private car parking, charming restaurant and honesty bar. Romatic four poster beds/spa baths available. Ideal retreat for business or leisure.

12 rooms, All en-suite. Open Jan-Dec. B&B per person, double from £39.00, 4 poster double from £49.00.

IMPORTANT: PRICES STATED ARE ESTIMATES AND MAY BE SUBJECT TO AMENDMENTS
FOR A FULL LISTING OF QUALITY ASSURED ACCOMMODATION, PLEASE SEE DIRECTORY AT BACK OF THIS GUIDE

79234

Edinburgh Map Ref: 2C5

Kingsburgh House

2 Corstorphine Road, Murrayfield, Edinburgh, Midlothian, EH12 6HN
Tel:0131 313 1679 Fax:0131 313 2283
Email:andrena.salter@btconnect.com

5 rooms
Open Jan-Dec
B&B per room, single from £80.00, double from £100.00.

34095

Edinburgh Map Ref: 2C5

Kingsview Guest House

28 Gilmore Place, Edinburgh, EH3 9NQ
Tel/Fax:0131 229 8004
Email:kingsviewguesthouse@talk21.com
Web:www.kingsviewguesthouse.com

City centre, family run since 1988. Smashing Scottish breakfast menu. Ideal base for the culture, vulture, shopaholic or disco diva. Our aim is to exceed your expectations. Warm welcome awaits.

9 rooms, All en-suite. Open Jan-Dec. B&B per person, double from £22.50.

70085

Edinburgh Map Ref: 2C5

The Laurels

320 Gilmerton Road, Edinburgh, Midlothian, EH17 7PR
Tel:0131 666 2229 Fax:0131 664 4400
Email:jill@laurelsguesthouse.net
Web:www.laurelsguesthouse.net

The Laurels Guest House is located in a quiet suburban setting only minutes from Edinburgh's bustling City Centre. Overlooking a private golf club to the front and playing fields to the rear, this lovingly restored late Victorian villa offers bed and breakfast facilities in purpose-built guest accommodation with private entrance.

5 rooms, All en-suite. Open Jan-Dec. B&B per person, double from £25.00.

59545

Edinburgh Map Ref: 2C5

The Lodge Hotel

6 Hampton Terrace, Edinburgh, EH12 5JD
Tel:0131 337 3682 Fax:0131 313 1700
Email:ritz@thelodgehotel.co.uk
Web:www.thelodgehotel.co.uk

Beautifully presented West End hotel, close to city centre attractions, shops, theatres, restaurants, galleries and conference centres. Tastefully appointed bedrooms. Private car park. Small private bar. Excellent public transport. Quiet individually styled hotel. Ideal central base for business or pleasure.

12 rooms, All en-suite. Open Jan-Dec. B&B per room, single from £60.00, double from £85.00.

38082

Edinburgh Map Ref: 2C5

Menzies Belford Hotel

69 Belford Road, Edinburgh, EH4 3DG
Tel:0131 332 2545 Fax:0131 332 3805
Email:belford@menzieshotels.co.uk
Web:www.bookmenzies.com

On the banks of the Water of Leith in a quiet secluded area, yet close to the city centre, the hotel offers the best of both worlds. The Forth Road Bridge and both of Edinburgh's main railway stations are only a short drive away and many of the city's local attractions, including the Dean Gallery and Princes Street are just a short walk from the hotel. Extensive private parking, which is free for all residents.

146 rooms, All en-suite. Open Jan-Dec. B&B per person, single from £72.50, double from £42.50 pppn.

38083

Edinburgh Map Ref: 2C5

Menzies Guest House

33 Leamington Terrace, Edinburgh, EH10 4JS
Tel/Fax:0131 229 4629
Email:menzies33@blueyonder.co.uk
Web:www.menzies-guesthouse.co.uk

7 rooms
Some en-suite
Open Jan-Dec
B&B (cooked vegetarian breakfast) per person, single from £15.00, double from £15.00.

49249

Edinburgh Map Ref: 2C5

Parliament House Hotel

15 Calton Hill, Edinburgh, EH1 3BJ
Tel:0131 478 4000 Fax:0131 478 4001
Email:info@parliamenthouse-hotel.co.uk
Web:www.parliamenthouse-hotel.co.uk

53 rooms
All en-suite
B&B per person, single from £60.00, double from £35.00.

50059

Edinburgh Map Ref: 2C5

The Point Hotel

34 Bread Street, Edinburgh, EH3 9AF
Tel:0131 221 5555 Fax:0131 221 9929
Email:reservations@point-hotel.co.uk
Web:www.point-hotel.co.uk

139 rooms
All en-suite
Open Jan-Dec
B&B per room, double from £70.00.

41380

Edinburgh Map Ref: 2C5

Prestonfield

Priestfield Road, Edinburgh, Lothian, EH16 5UT
Tel:0131 225 7800 Fax:0131 220 4392
Email:info@prestonfield.com
Web:www.prestonfield.com

Renowned by Tatler for 'Triple A-rated spoil me factor'. Edinburgh's most uniquely indulgent and distictive 5-Star hotel by far from Witchery creator James Thomson. 'Sheer glorious indulgence' - The Hotel Guru.

23 rooms and suites, All en-suite. Open Jan-Dec. Rates per room, from £225.00-275.00 incl. full breakfast and champagne.

73495

Edinburgh Map Ref: 2C5

Ravensdown Guest House

248 Ferry Road, Edinburgh, Midlothian, EH5 3AN
Tel:0131 552 5438
Email:david@ravensdownhouse.com
Web:www.ravensdownhouse.com

6 rooms
All en-suite
Open Jan-Dec
B&B per room, single from £50.00, double from £70.00.

52119

Edinburgh Map Ref: 2C5

Rosehall Hotel

101 Dalkeith Road, Newington, Edinburgh, EH16 5AJ
Tel/Fax:0131 667 9372
Email:info@rosehallhotel.co.uk
Web:www.rosehallhotel.co.uk

8 rooms
7 en-suite
Open Jan-Dec
B&B per person, single £30.00-65.00, double £25.00-50.00.

56130

Edinburgh Map Ref: 2C5

St Bernards Guest House

22 St Bernards Crescent, Edinburgh, EH4 1NS
Tel:0131 332 2339 Fax:0131 332 8842
Email:alexstbernards@aol.com

8 rooms
Some en-suite
Open Jan-Dec
B&B per person, single from £30.00, double from £25.00.

56103

Edinburgh Map Ref: 2C5

The St Valery

36 Coates Gardens, Edinburgh, EH12 5LE
Tel:0131 337 1893 Fax:0131 346 8529
Email:info@stvalery.co.uk
Web:www.stvalery.com

The St Valery Guest House is a New Town building situated in the heart of Edinburgh's West End and is a family run guest house recently refurbished to a high standard, but still retaining the charm, friendliness and personal touch of a small hotel. FREE Sky cable TV, DVD with CD player, direct dial telephone with modem access, FREE wi-fi Broadband access.

11 rooms, Some en-suite. Open Jan-Dec. B&B per person, single from £28.00-52.00, double from £28.00-52.00.

52861

Edinburgh Map Ref: 2C5

Sakura House

18 West Preston Street, Edinburgh, EH8 9PU
Tel/Fax:0131 668 1204

6 rooms
Some en-suite
Open Jan-Dec
B&B per person, single from £18.00, double from £18.00.

74684

Edinburgh Map Ref: 2C5

The Salisbury Hotel

43-45 Salisbury Road, Edinburgh, EH16 5AA
Tel/Fax:0131 667 1264
Email:enquiries@the-salisbury.co.uk
Web:www.the-salisbury.co.uk

Newly opened, 18 bedroom boutique Georgian townhouse with licensed bistro, lounge and walled gardens in central Edinburgh. Excellent Scottish food, uniquely stylish bedrooms and bathrooms, excellent value and quality service standards. Free parking.

18 rooms, Open Jan-Dec. B&B per person, single from £55.00, double from £35.00..

72168

Edinburgh Map Ref: 2C5

Salisbury Green Hotel Conference Centre

University of Edinburgh, Pollock Halls,
18 Holyrood Park Road, Edinburgh, EH16 5AY
Tel:0131 662 2000 Fax:0131 667 7271
Email:salisbury.green@ed.ac.uk
Web:www.salisburygreen.com

36 rooms
All en-suite
Open Jan-Dec
B&B per room from £79.00.

52940

Edinburgh Map Ref: 2C5

Sandaig Guest House

5 East Hermitage Place, Leith Links, Edinburgh
EH6 8AA
Tel:0131 554 7357 Fax:0131 467 6389
Email:info@sandaigguesthouse.co.uk
Web:www.sandaigguesthouse.co.uk

8 rooms
All en-suite
Open Jan-Dec
B&B per person, single from £35.00, double from £30.00.

54420

Edinburgh Map Ref: 2C5

Sheraton Grand Hotel & Spa, Edinburgh

1 Festival Square, Edinburgh, EH3 9SR
Tel:0131 229 9131 Fax:0131 221 9631
Email:grandedinburgh.sheraton@sheraton.com
Web:www.sheraton.com/grandedinburgh

This luxurious hotel is ideally situated in the heart of the city with magnificent views of Edinburgh Castle. Theatres, shops, restaurants and nightlife are within walking distance. Includes 2 outstanding restaurants and the award winning One Spa. Unsurpassed Scottish hospitality ensures a truly memorable stay at Edinburgh's most welcoming hotel.

260 rooms, All en-suite. Open Jan-Dec. B&B per person, from £135.00.

54428

Edinburgh Map Ref: 2C5

Sheridan Guest House

1 Bonnington Terrace, Edinburgh, EH6 4BP
Tel:0131 554 4107 Fax:0131 554 8494
Email:info@sheridanedinburgh.co.uk
Web:www.sheridanedinburgh.co.uk

8 rooms
Open Jan-Dec
B&B per person single from £35.00
double from £30.00, family from £28.00.

56377

Edinburgh Map Ref: 2C5

Star Villa

36 Gilmore Place, Edinburgh, EH3 9NQ
Tel/Fax:0131 229 4991
Email:starvillagh@hotmail.com
Web:www.starvillagh.com

Under new ownership, this family run guest house has been refurbished to a high standard offering comfortable and well appointed bedrooms. Very good breakfasts with a Scottish flair.

4 rooms, Some en-suite. Open Jan-Dec. B&B per person, single from £25.00, double from £25.00.

57628

Edinburgh — Map Ref: 2C5

Tania Guest House

19 Minto Street, Edinburgh, EH9 1RQ
Tel:0131 667 4144

6 rooms
Some en-suite
Open Jan-Dec excl Xmas
B&B per person, single from £20.00, double from £20.00.

71550

Edinburgh — Map Ref: 2C5

Ten Hill Place Hotel

10 Hill Place, Edinburgh, EH8 9DS
Tel:0131 662 2080 Fax:0131 662 2082
Email:reservations@tenhillplace.com
Web:www.tenhillplace.com

Tasteful accommodation immediately adjacent to the Surgeons Hall complex and within easy walking distance of the city centre and many of Edinburgh's main attractions.

78 rooms, All en-suite. Open Jan-Dec closed 23-26 Dec inclusive. B&B per person, single from £85.00, double from £47.50 per person.

60907

Edinburgh — Map Ref: 2C5

Thistle Edinburgh

107 Leith Street, Edinburgh, EH1 3SW
Tel:0870 3339153 Fax:0870 3339253
Email:edinburgh@thistle.co.uk
Web:www.thistle.com/edinburgh

139 rooms
All en-suite
Open Jan-Dec
B&B per person, single from £69.00, double from £49.00, BB & Eve.Meal from £69.00.

61057

Edinburgh — Map Ref: 2C5

Thrums Hotel

14-15 Minto Street, Edinburgh, EH9 1RQ
Tel:0131 667 5545 Fax:0131 6678707
Email:thrumshoteledinburgh@yahoo.co.uk
Web:www.thrumshotel.com

A warm welcome at this privately owned hotel on main bus route to city centre. Secure parking in private gardens. All bedrooms in annexe house are of period style retaining many original features including fireplaces and ornate plasterwork. Families welcome. Ground floor bedrooms available.

15 rooms, All en-suite. Open Jan-Dec. B&B per person, single from £70.00, double from £35.00.

62280

Edinburgh Map Ref: 2C5

The Turret Guest House

8 Kilmaurs Terrace, Edinburgh, EH16 5DR
Tel:0131 667 6704
Email:contact@turretguesthouse.co.uk
Web:www.turretguesthouse.co.uk

8 rooms
Some en-suite
Open Jan-Dec
B&B per room, single from £34.00, double from £56.00.

63311

Edinburgh Map Ref: 2C5

The Walton

79 Dundas Street, Edinburgh, EH3 6SD
Tel:0131 556 1137 Fax:0131 557 8367
Email:enquiries@waltonhotel.com
Web:www.waltonhotel.com

The Walton is a small privately run Bed & Breakfast and listed building in Edinburgh's Georgian new town. Located in the heart of the city. A short walk from Princes Street we are convenient for tourist attractions, city nightlife and business visitors alike. Off-street parking available.

10 rooms, All en-suite. Open Jan-Dec. B&B per person, single from £45.00, double from £39.50.

22032

by Edinburgh Map Ref: 2C5

Dalhousie Castle & Spa

Cockpen Road, Bonnyrigg, Edinburgh, Midlothian, EH19 3JB
Tel:01875 820153 Fax:01875 821936
Email:enquiries@dalhousiecastle.co.uk
Web:www.dalhousiecastle.co.uk

13c castle set in own parkland. Only 7 miles from the centre of Edinburgh. Orangery & Dungeon Restaurants. New Health Spa. Helipad. 5 bedrooms in lodge close to castle.

36 rooms, All en-suite. Open Jan-Dec. B&B per room, single from £110.00, double from £135.00.

34762 **nr Edinburgh** Map Ref: 2C5

The Laird & Dog Hotel

5 High Street, Lasswade, Midlothian, EH18 1NA
Tel:0131 663 9219
Web:www.lairdanddog.btinternet.co.uk

Old Coaching Inn (Est 1740) 1/2 mile from city by-pass with excellent bus service to Edinburgh. New conservatory restaurant, a la carte and bar meals, large car park, Olde World Bar and newly discovered historical well. All bedrooms ensuite.

10 rooms, All en-suite. Open Jan-Dec. B&B per person, single from £45.00, double from £32.50.

29119 **Gullane, East Lothian** Map Ref: 2D4

Greywalls

Muirfield, Gullane, East Lothian, EH31 2EG
Tel:01620 842144 Fax:01620 842241
Email:hotel@greywalls.co.uk
Web:www.greywalls.co.uk

23 rooms
All en-suite
B&B per person, single from £140.00, double from £150.00.

37175 **Haddington, East Lothian** Map Ref: 2D4

Maitlandfield House Hotel

24 Sidegate, Haddington, East Lothian, EH41 4BZ
Tel:01620 826513 Fax:01620 826713
Email:info@maitlandfieldhouse.co.uk
Web:www.maitlandfieldhouse.co.uk

25 rooms
All en-suite
Open Jan-Dec
B&B per person, single from £65.00, double from £47.50 pp, BB & Eve.Meal from £52.50.

58267 **Linlithgow, West Lothian** Map Ref: 2B4

The Bonsyde House Hotel

Bonsyde, By Linlithgow, West Lothian, EH49 7NU
Tel:01506 842229 Fax:01506 846233
Email:info@bonsyde.co.uk
Web:www.bonsydehouse.co.uk

8 rooms
All en-suite
Open Jan-Dec
B&B per room, single from £75.00, double from £75.00.

10594 **Loanhead, Midlothian** Map Ref: 2C5

Aaron Glen Guest House

7 Nivensknowe Road, Loanhead, Midlothian, EH20 9AU
Tel:0131 440 1293
Email:carolyn@aaronglen.com
Web:www.aaronglen.com

A warm welcome awaits at this family run guest house refurbished to a very high standard. Situated 5 miles from Edinburgh city centre with excellent bus service. Easy access to many historic sites including Roslyn Chapel. Large secured car park.

5 rooms, All en-suite. Open Jan-Dec. B&B per person, single from £40.00, double from £35.00.

47030 **North Berwick, East Lothian** Map Ref: 2D4

Nether Abbey Hotel

20 Dirleton Avenue, North Berwick, EH39 4BQ
Tel:01620 892802 Fax:01620 895298
Email:bookings@netherabbey.co.uk
Web:www.netherabbey.co.uk

12 rooms
All en-suite
Open Jan-Dec
B&B per person, single £65.00-100.00, double £45.00-70.00.

15812 **North Middleton, Midlothian** Map Ref: 2C5

Borthwick Castle Hotel

North Middleton, Gorebridge, Midlothian, EH23 4QY
Tel:01875 820514 Fax:01875 821702
Email:enquiries@borthwickcastle.co.uk
Web:www.borthwickcastle.co.uk

10 rooms
All en-suite
Open Mar-Jan excl Xmas/New Year
B&B per person, single from £80.00, double from £85.00.

16074 **Penicuik, Midlothian** Map Ref: 2C5

Braidwood Farm

Penicuik, Midlothian, EH26 9LP
Tel:01968 679959 Fax:01968 679805
Email:info@braidwoodfarm.co.uk
Web:www.braidwoodfarm.co.uk

Braidwood is an attractive modern farmhouse set in 240 acres on the edge of the Pentland hills only 10 miles from Edinburgh. Ideal base for visitors to both Edinburgh and the Borders. No children please.

4 rooms, All en-suite. Open Apr-Oct. B&B per person, single from £30.00, double from £30.00.

50527

South Queensferry, West Lothian Map Ref: 2B4

Priory Lodge

8 The Loan, South Queensferry, West Lothian
EH30 9NS
Tel:0131 331 4345 Fax:0131 331 4345
Email:calmyn@aol.com

Traditional Scottish hospitality in this friendly family run guest house located in the picturesque village of South Queensferry . Edinburgh city centre 7 miles: Airport/Royal Highland Exhibition grounds 3 miles. Priory Lodge is within walking distance of the village shops, variety of eating establishments, Forth Bridges and Dalmeny train station. Internet access available. Non-smoking establishment.

5 rooms, All en-suite. Open Jan-Dec. B&B per person, single from £50.00, double from £35.00.

36856

Uphall, West Lothian Map Ref: 2B5

Macdonald Houstoun House Hotel

Uphall, West Lothian, EH52 6JS
Tel:01506 853831

Early 17th century, this unique tower house offers 71 bedrooms with 21 in the original tower steading. Set in 20 acres of glorious gardens yet only 10 minutes from Edinburgh airport. New leisure club offers an extensive range of facilities together with informal steakhouse and floodlit tennis court. Log fires, 8 conference suites & award winning dining room.

71 rooms, All en-suite. Open Jan-Dec. B&B per room, single from £97.00, double from £126.00.

George Square, Glasgow

GREATER GLASGOW AND CLYDE VALLEY

Glasgow is a must-visit city. Stylish, flamboyant, confident and imaginative, Glasgow buzzes from early morning until late at night.

There's so much choice it's difficult to know where to start and even harder to know when to stop. And wherever you go in Scotland's largest city, you'll be overwhelmed by the irresistible friendliness of its inhabitants.

Shop 'til you drop

It's easy to get caught up in Glasgow's fast-moving social whirl – especially if you like shopping. Outside of London, there isn't a UK city that can touch Glasgow for quantity and quality.

If you're in need of retail therapy you'll revel in the elegance of Princes Square, the diversity of the Buchanan Galleries and the classy opulence of the Italian Centre in the chic Merchant City.

Glasgow is easily Scotland's most fashion-conscious city and its passion for all things stylish brings an exciting edge to its boutiques and malls.

That passion spills over into the cafés and bars, the boutique hotels, the restaurants, nightclubs, theatres and music venues. Glasgow nightlife is always exhilarating whether you're checking out the next hit band at King Tut's, watching ground-breaking theatre at Oran Mor or just sipping a pint in Ashton Lane.

Haute cuisine

Foodies love Glasgow too. From traditional afternoon tea at One Devonshire Gardens or the Willow Tearooms to every major culinary style in the world, Glasgow's restaurants have a rapidly growing international reputation.

Art for art's sake

Glasgow is an art lover's delight too. The impressive legacy of its most eminent architectural sons, Charles Rennie Mackintosh and Alexander 'Greek' Thomson can be seen in the city's streets and its galleries and museums host one of Europe's biggest collections of civic art. Don't miss Kelvingrove Art Gallery and Museum (recently restored at a cost of £27.9 million) or the Burrell Collection in Pollock Country Park.

Despite the endless hustle and bustle, peace and tranquillity are never far away. Glasgow is known as the 'dear green place' and there are over 70 parks and gardens in the city where you can escape for a while.

Beyond the city limits, you can trace the river back through the Clyde Valley all the way to the picturesque Falls of Clyde in Lanarkshire, just beside the immaculately preserved village of New Lanark which is a World Heritage site.

On the Clyde coast you can take a trip 'doon the watter' in the P.S. Waverley, the world's last sea-going paddle steamer. At Strathclyde Country Park near Hamilton and Mugdock Country Park near Milngavie you'll enjoy a wide range of outdoor activities including walking, cycling, horse riding, sailing, canoeing and much more.

Glasgow's maritime history can be explored at Braehead and Paisley is just a short journey away. Don't miss the impressive Paisley Abbey which dates back to 1163.

Whatever you choose to do, wherever you stay, a visit to Glasgow and Clyde Valley will be a revelation and you'll be very glad you came.

Kelvingrove Art Gallery and Museum, Glasgow

What's On?

Celtic Connections, Glasgow
16 January – 3 February 2008
Three weeks of the best in Celtic music from around the globe.
www.celticconnections.com

Magners Glasgow International Comedy Festival
6 - 23 March 2008
The largest comedy festival in the UK.
www.glasgowcomedyfestival.com

Paisley Beer Festival
28 April – 3 May 2008
Scotland's largest real ale festival, with well over 100 real ales on tap.
www.paisleybeerfestival.org.uk

West End Festival, Glasgow
13 – 29 June 2008
Arts festival celebrating the city's bohemian West End.
www.westendfestival.co.uk

World Pipe Band Championships and Piping Live: Glasgow International Piping Festival
11-17 August 2008
A week of piping events across Glasgow.
www.pipingfestival.co.uk

Gourmet Glasgow
August 2008 (dates TBC)
A month-long festival of food and drink.
www.gourmetglasgow.com

Kirkintilloch Canal Festival
August 2008 (dates TBC)
Two days of fun in the 'Canal Capital of Scotland'.
www.kirkintillochcanalfestival.org.uk

Classic Car Rally, Chatelherault Country Park
August 2008 (dates TBC)
Vintage and classic cars on display.
www.visitlanarkshire.com

Merchant City Festival, Glasgow
September 2008 (dates TBC)
Festival celebrating the cultural richness of the city's old commercial quarter.
www.merchantcityfestival.com

Glasgow's Hogmanay
31 December 2008 – 1 January 2009
Top bands, traditional music, DJs, and special guests.
www.winterfestglasgow.com

www.seeglasgow.com

DON'T MISS

1 **Kelvingrove Art Gallery and Museum** - Scotland's most visited museum - re-opened in 2006 following a three-year, £27.9 million restoration. It now has over 8,000 objects on display over three floors – 4,000 more than ever before. Old favourites and exciting new arrivals are waiting to welcome you. Forget everything you think you know about museums – Kelvingrove is different.

2 Step back in time at the 5-star, award-winning **New Lanark World Heritage Site**. The beautifully restored 18th century cotton mill village has a wonderful sense of space with plenty to keep the whole family amused. The ghost of mill-girl Annie McLeod tells you about her life in the village, then you can ride into the future in the new Millenium Experience to see how Harmony lives in the 23rd century. From here explore the Falls of Clyde Visitor Centre and Wildlife Reserve.

3 It's all about fun when you're on your holidays but what if at the same time, you could sneak in a bit of learning? **Glasgow Science Centre** has the answer. Easily accessible from Glasgow city centre by car, subway, train or bus, the Centre stands tall and instantly recognisable on the River Clyde. The interactive exhibits can keep not only the children entertained but the adults too and that's before you hit the IMAX cinema and the Scottish Power Planetarium.

4 Experience Glasgow's celebrated maritime history at **The Tall Ship**. A sight to behold, you can tour this beautiful vessel – the SV Glenlee – and discover life during its sea-faring days. Exhibitions on board tell the incredible story of its crew during four circumnavigations of the globe. On the quayside and in the Pumphouse Visitor Centre, discover more about the history of the Clyde and the Glasgow Harbour area.

5 Scotland's Centre for Architecture, Design and the City is suitably situated in the old Glasgow Herald Newspaper building which was design by Charles Rennie Mackintosh. Spanning six floors, **The Lighthouse** provides an unrivalled opportunity to experience architecture and design through a changing programme of exhibitions. The Lighthouse also contains the award winning Mackintosh Centre and Mackintosh Tower which offers stunning views of the city.

6 Charles Rennie Mackintosh designed the **Glasgow School of Art** in 1896. Today, over 100 years later, the Glasgow School of Art is still a working art school attracting talented students from all over the world. A tour will take you along the corridors of the School, through the Mackintosh Gallery and Furniture Gallery to finish in one of Mackintosh's most celebrated interiors, the Library. Along the way you will learn about Mackintosh's life and the history of the Glasgow School of Art.

2

3

FOOD AND DRINK

www.eatscotland.com

7 Arisaig Restaurant is a smartly presented restaurant and bar which offers some of the best Scottish cuisine. The menu is divided into "The Land" and "The Sea" with choices of the freshest of Scottish ingredients including haggis, Stornoway black pudding, Shetland monkfish, South Uist smoked salmon and Buccleuch beef, as well as long forgotten ingredients such as kale and cairgein. The food is served in a relaxed atmosphere with friendly service.

8 With a motto like "Think Global Eat Local" it is not surprising that the menu at Stravaigin has been built from diverse world influences while focusing on the best of Scottish ingredients. The result is a collection of eclectic and globe trotting dishes. Stravaigin is an excellent example of West End dining.

9 Michael Caine at ABode Glasgow is situated in the recently opened boutique hotel ABode, which itself is in an historic Edwardian building. The restaurant has recently received an EatScotland Gold Award which recognises outstanding standards in quality and service. This truly is an excellent dining experience with the modern menu utilising the best of Scotland's seasonal larder.

10 Uplawmoor Hotel & Restaurant is a relaxed and friendly establishment with professional and attentive service. Originally an old beamed barn, it has been tastefully converted and offers a cosy atmosphere and a choice of imaginative à la carte or seasonal table d'hote menus.

ACTIVITIES

11 Ten miles north of Glasgow is the 750-acre Mugdock Country Park. Embracing unspoiled countryside at the foot of the Campsie Fells, Mugdock offers a gentle introduction to hardy walkers starting out on the 96-mile West Highland Way. The less energetic can stay a while and enjoy horse riding, archery and orienteering, among other activities.

12 At Strathclyde Country Park you'll find 1,000 acres of mature woodlands, wetlands, wildlife refuges and open parkland surrounding Strathclyde Loch, with a variety of activities to try out from pedalos to water skiing, orienteering to mountain biking. A good starting point for exploring is the visitor centre. Keep an eye out for otters, roe deer and the other 150 species living in the park, which is also home to Scotland's first theme park, M & D's.

13 As you enter through the main doors of Xscape you can watch brave souls hanging from the ceiling as they have a go on the state of the art aerial adventure course. The Centre houses numerous outdoor shops, restaurants, bars, bowling, rock climbing and much more. However, without a doubt the piece-de-résistance is the incredible SnoZone which allows you to experience indoor skiing, snowboarding or sledging on the UK's biggest real snow slope.

14 Charles Rennie Mackintosh is considered the father of the 'Glasgow Style', with his motifs instantly recognisable to visitors. He was a true visionary who worked almost exclusively in the city. His legacy lives on and can be enjoyed with the help of a Mackintosh Trail ticket giving admission to all associated attractions in and around Glasgow including the School of Art, Scotland Street School House, House for an Art Lover and the Mackintosh Church.

SHOPPING

15 **Buchanan Street** is arguably one of the classiest major shopping thoroughfares in Britain. With a tempting mix of big high street names, alternative retailers and designer outlets, it's deservedly popular. **Buchanan Galleries** at the top of the street offers even more shopping opportunities.

16 Situated on Buchanan Street in the heart of Glasgow's shopping district, **Princes Square** is home to many of the world's best known lifestyle brands. A truly exquisite venue, Princes Square presents a sophisticated alternative to Scotland's high street and a stylish destination for both dining and drinking.

17 Visitors in search of the city's chic and modern side should head to the **Merchant City**. Beautiful Victorian buildings, many of them former tobacco warehouses, are now the place to be seen at weekends. Trawl through innovative boutiques in search of that must-have item.

18 With strong Italian heritage, it's only fitting that there should be somewhere to purchase the latest fashions from Milan. **The Italian Centre** may be easier on the eye than on the pocket, but it's ideal for a treat.

19 Glasgow is often complimented for its European flavour, and nowhere is this more in evidence than on **Byres Road**, with its fruit and veg stalls, butchers and fishmongers flanking hip record stores and clothing retailers. Head to the West End for some wonderful eateries in the mews lanes off Byres Road.

HERITAGE AND CULTURE

20 Take in a **football** match for 90 minutes you'll never forget. It would be an understatement to say that Glaswegians have a passion for the beautiful game, and Glasgow is the only city in the UK to support three 50,000+ capacity football stadiums. Situated within the national stadium, Hampden the Scottish Football Museum is an essential attraction for all football fans.

21 From Celtic Connections each January to the Miller Glasgow International Comedy Festival in March and Piping Live! in August, no matter when you arrive in Glasgow and Clyde Valley you'll find live performances, **events and festivals** and entertainment.

22 Situated within beautiful Bellahouston Park, the **House for an Art Lover** was inspired by Charles Rennie Mackintosh designs from 1901. The Art Lovers' Cafe and Shop house changing art exhibitions and visitors are entertained throughout the year with a programme of dinner concerts and afternoon music recitals.

23 **Chatelherault Country Park** hosts the magnificently restored hunting lodge and summer house built in 1732 by William Adam for the Duke of Hamilton. The 500-acre country park, set amongst ancient oaks along the Avon Water, boasts extensive woodland walks and a visitor centre with exhibitions on the area's history, wildlife, and also the story of Chatelherault itself.

MAP

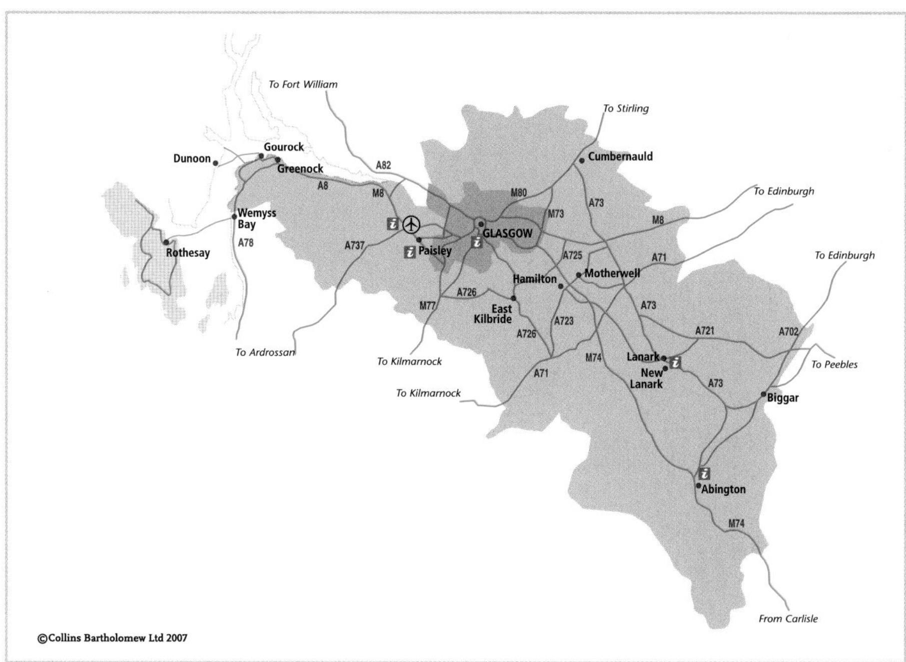

TOURIST INFORMATION CENTRES

Greater Glasgow & Clyde Valley	
Abington	Welcome Break, Motorway Service Area, Junction 13, M74 Abington ML12 6RG
Glasgow	11 George Square, Glasgow G2 1DY
Glasgow Airport	International Arrivals Hall, Glasgow International Airport, PA3 2ST
Lanark	Horsemarket, Ladyacre Road, Lanark ML11 7QL
Paisley	9A Gilmour Street, Paisley PA1 1DD

Make the most of your stay in Scotland and make your first stop the Tourist Information Centre wherever you go.

Knowledgeable and friendly staff can help you with information and advice; they can answer your questions, book accommodation and you can even pick up some souvenirs to take home for friends and family.

For information and ideas about exploring Scotland in advance of your trip, call our booking and information service or go to www.visitscotland.com

Call 0845 22 55 121

or if calling from outside the UK call
+44 (0) 1506 832 121

From Ireland call
1800 932 510

A £4 booking fee applies to telephone bookings of accommodation.

11097 Glasgow Map Ref: 1H5

Adelaides

209 Bath Street, Glasgow, G2 4HZ
Tel:0141 248 4970 Fax:0141 226 4247
Email:reservations@adelaides.co.uk
Web:www.adelaides.co.uk

Adelaide's is an unusual conversion of an 1877 church. The Guest House formed from some of the ancilliary accommodation comprises 8 individual rooms. Breakfast available. Centrally located near the Kings Theatre, 10 min walk from the main shopping and entertainment areas, on bus routes to most of Glasgow's tourist attractions and has a wide variety of restaurants in the vicinity. Parking nearby.

8 rooms, Most en-suite. Open Jan-Dec excl Xmas/New Year. B&B per person, single from £35.00, double from £30.00.

11443 Glasgow Map Ref: 1H5

Albion Hotel

405 North Woodside Road, Glasgow, G20 6NN
Tel:0141 339 8620 Fax:0141 334 8159
Email:albion@glasgowhotelsandapartments.co.uk
Web:www.glasgowhotelsandapartments.co.uk

17 rooms
All en-suite
Open Jan-Dec
B&B per room, single from £48.00, double from £61.00.

11842 Glasgow Map Ref: 1H5

Amadeus Guest House

411 North Woodside Road, Glasgow, G20 6NN
Tel:0141 339 8257 Fax:0141 339 8859
Email:alexandra@amadeusguesthouse.co.uk
Web:www.amadeusguesthouse.co.uk

Ideally located in the trendy West End of Glasgow, the Amadeus offers a comfortable B&B service with bright, airy and comfortable rooms. Enjoy our buffet breakfast to classical or jazzy music, and a friendly atmosphere.

9 rooms, Some en-suite. Open Jan-Dec. B&B per room, single from £24.00, double from £48.00.

11852 Glasgow Map Ref: 1H5

Ambassador Hotel

7 Kelvin Drive, Glasgow, G20 8QG
Tel:0141 946 1018 Fax:0141 945 5377
Email:
ambassador@glasgowhotelsandapartments.co.uk
Web:www.glasgowhotelsandapartments.co.uk

21 rooms
All en-suite
Open Jan-Dec
B&B per person, single £58.00-78.00, double per room £78.00, family per room £98.00.

14737 Glasgow — Map Ref: 1H5

Belgrave Guest House

2 Belgrave Terrace, Hillhead, Glasgow, G12 8JD
Tel:0141 337 1850 Fax:0141 337 1741
Email:belgraveglasgow@aol.com
Web:www.belgraveguesthouse.co.uk

11 rooms
Open Jan-Dec
B&B per person, single from £25.00, double from £20.00.

15838 Glasgow — Map Ref: 1H5

Bothwell Bridge Hotel

89 Main Street, Bothwell, Glasgow, G71 8EU
Tel:01698 852246 Fax:01698 854686
Email:enquiries@bothwellbridge-hotel.com
Web:www.bothwellbridge-hotel.com

Family run hotel, 9 miles (14kms) from Glasgow city centre and convenient for motorway. Business meeting rooms. Wireless Broadband available for conferences and guests rooms. Ample parking.

90 rooms, All en-suite. Open Jan-Dec. B&B per room, single from £60.00, double from £70.00.

58345 Glasgow — Map Ref: 1H5

Buchanan Hotel

185 Buchanan Street, Glasgow, G1 2JY
Tel:0141 332 7284 Fax:0141 3330635
Email:salesbuchanan@strathmorehotels.com
Web:www.strathmorehotels.com

Ideally situated in the heart of the city's shopping district, the hotel offers a great base for exploring the city and surrounding area. Queen St Station and Buchanan Underground nearby.

60 rooms, All en-suite. Open Jan-Dec. Rates on application.

17786 Glasgow — Map Ref: 1H5

Campanile Hotel Glasgow

Tunnel Street, Glasgow, G3 8HL
Tel:0141 287 7700 Fax:0141 287 7701
Email:glasgow@campanile.com
Web:www.campanile.com

106 rooms
All en-suite
Open Jan-Dec
B&B per person, double from £33.45.

18123 Glasgow Map Ref: 1H5

Carlton George Hotel

44 West George Street, Glasgow, G2 1DH
Tel:0141 353 6373 Fax:0141 353 6263
Email:george@carltonhotels.co.uk
Web:www.carltonhotels.co.uk

64 rooms
All en-suite
Open Jan-Dec
B&B per room, single from £100.00, double from £110.00.

25189 Glasgow Map Ref: 1H5

Euro Hostels

318 Clyde Street, Glasgow, G1 4NR
Tel:0141 222 2828 Fax:0141 222 2829
Email:info@euro-hostels.co.uk
Web:www.euro-hostels.co.uk

Glasgow's only City Centre hostel. Euro Hostel is located in the centre of Glasgow beside the River Clyde and offers en suite accommodation in twin, double and multiple bed dormitories. Well situated for exploring the city and close to major rail, road and air networks. Lively in-house bar.

364 rooms, All en-suite. Open Jan-Dec. B&B per person from £12.95 per night.

33519 Glasgow Map Ref: 1H5

Kelvin Hotel

15 Buckingham Terrace, Glasgow, G12 8EB
Tel:0141 339 7143 Fax:0141 339 5215
Email:enquiries@kelvinhotel.com
Web:www.kelvinhotel.com

Victorian terraced house in the West End. Close to the Kelvingrove Art Gallery and Museum, Botanical Gardens and Glasgow University. On main bus routes to city centre and five minutes walk from underground, restaurants and shops. Directions: Leave M8 at J17, follow Dumbarton A82 for one mile, Kelvin on right (tree-lined terrace).

21 rooms, Some en-suite. Open Jan-Dec. Room only rates, single from £28.00, double from £50.00.

66030

Glasgow Map Ref: 1H5

Kelvingrove Hotel

944 Sauchiehall Street, Glasgow, G3 7TH
Tel:0141 339 5011 Fax:0141 339 6566
Email:kelvingrove.hotel@business.ntl.com
Web:www.kelvingrovehotel.co.uk

A warm and welcoming family run hotel situated adjacent to Kelvingrove Park. Ideally situated close to main City attractions including the SECC, Science Centre, galleries and museums, famous parks and a variety of bars and restaurants. All 23 versatile and well-appointed rooms boast ensuite facilities, colour TVs, hospitality trays and a 24-hour reception service. Being on Sauchiehall Street, the hotel is conveniently located just 10 minutes walk from the City Centre and some of the best shopping in the UK.

22 rooms, All en-suite. Open Jan-Dec. B&B per person, single from £70.00, double from £40.00.

37231

Glasgow Map Ref: 1H5

The Malmaison

278 West George Street, Glasgow, G2 4LL
Tel:0141 5721000
Email:glasgow@malmaison.com
Web:www.malmaison.com

72 rooms
All en-suite
Open Jan-Dec
Room only rates, single from £119.00, double from £119.00.

67438

Glasgow Map Ref: 1H5

Newton House Hotel

248-252 Bath Street, Glasgow, G2 4JW
Tel:0141 332 1666 Fax:0141 332 7722
Email:info@newtonhotel.co.uk
Web:www.newtonhotel.co.uk

Newton House Hotel is a private family-run hotel central to all major attractions in the vibrant and exciting City of Glasgow, with Sauchiehall Street around the corner and a variety of restaurants a stones throw away.

19 rooms, Open Jan-Dec. Rates on application.

65795 Glasgow Map Ref: 1H5

Park Inn, Glasgow City Centre

2 Port Dundas Place, Glasgow, G2 3LB
Tel:0141 333 1500

A new and stylishly different experience in the centre of Glasgow. Ideally located for theatres and concert hall or for business and shopping. Hotel facilities include spa, gymnasium and award winning restaurants.

100 rooms, All en-suite. Open Jan-Dec. Room only rates, single from £109.00, double from £109.00.

53020 Glasgow Map Ref: 1H5

The Sandyford Hotel

904 Sauchiehall Street, Glasgow, G3 7TF
Tel:0141 334 0000 Fax:0141 337 1812
Email: info@sandyfordhotelglasgow.com
Web:www.sandyfordhotelglasgow.com

55 rooms
All en-suite
Open Jan-Dec excl Xmas
B&B per person, single from £32.00, double from £26.00.

60641 Glasgow Map Ref: 1H5

The Townhouse Hotel

21 Royal Crescent, Glasgow, G3 7SL
Tel:0141 332 9009
Email:townhousehotel@ukonline.co.uk
Web:www.hotelglasgow.com

19 rooms
Some en-suite
Open Jan-Dec
Rates on application.

62628 nr Glasgow Map Ref: 1H5

Uplawmoor Hotel

Neilston Road, Uplawmoor, Glasgow, G78 4AF
Tel:01505 850565 Fax:01505 850689
Email:info@uplawmoor.co.uk
Web:www.uplawmoor.co.uk

Small independently run Coaching Inn. 14 newly refurbished ensuite bedrooms, open fire, real ales, bar meals, 2AA rosette restaurant and genuine Scottish hospitality. Just 25 mins drive from city and airport. Gateway to Burns Country.

14 rooms, All en-suite. Open Jan-Dec excl Xmas/New Year. B&B per person, single from £55.00, double from £32.50.

15416

Harthill, by Shotts, Lanarkshire — Map Ref: 2A5

Blairmains Guest House

Harthill, Shotts, Lanarkshire, ML7 5TJ
Tel:01501 751278 Mob:07753 857150
Email:Heather@blairmains.freeserve.co.uk
Web:www.blairmains.co.uk

5 rooms
Some en-suite
Open Jan-Dec
B&B per person, single from £22.00, double from £20.00, BB & Eve.Meal from £27.50.

15882

Howwood, Renfrewshire — Map Ref: 1G5

Bowfield Hotel & Country Club

Howwood, Renfrewshire, PA9 1DZ
Tel:01505 705225 Fax:01505 705230
Email:enquiries@bowfieldhotel.co.uk
Web:www.bowfieldhotel.co.uk

A refreshingly different country retreat close to town and city attractions. A comprehensive leisure club with swimming pool and health & beauty spa and award winning restaurants.

23 rooms, All en-suite. Open Jan-Dec. B&B per person, single from £90.00, twin/double from £70.00.

23366

Paisley, Renfrewshire — Map Ref: 1H5

Dryesdale Guest House

37 Inchinnan Road, Paisley, Renfrewshire, PA3 2PR
Tel:0141 889 7178
Email:dd@paisley2001.freeserve.co.uk
Web:www.ga-taxis.co.uk/dryesdale.html

7 rooms
Open Jan-Dec
B&B per person, single from £25.00, double from £22.50.

Oban, Argyll

WEST HIGHLANDS AND ISLANDS, LOCH LOMOND, STIRLING AND TROSSACHS

Contrast is the word that best sums up an area that spans Scotland from the shores of the Forth in the east to the very tip of Tiree in the west. Here the Highlands meet the Lowlands and geography and cultures diverge.

For the visitor, the endlessly changing landscape means a rich and varied holiday experience.

There are rugged high mountains, spectacular freshwater lochs, fascinating islands and dramatic seascapes. You'll find pretty villages, mill towns and Scotland's newest city.

And you can discover the birthplace of the Scots nation and visit places that witnessed some of the most dramatic scenes in Scotland's history.

So where do you begin? In the east, the flat plain of the Forth Valley stretches up from the River Forth towards the little towns of the Hillfoots and the Ochil Hills behind.

You can visit Scotland's smallest county – Clackmannanshire, or the 'Wee County' as it is known. And while you're in the area, head for Dollar Glen and the magnificent Castle Campbell, once the Lowland stronghold of the Clan Campbell.

Moving to the Hillfoot towns you'll be tracing the roots of Scotland's textile industry which has thrived here for many years. Visit the Mill Trail Visitor Centre in Alva to learn the history of the local woollen industry.

New city, ancient history

Beyond Alva to the west lies Stirling – one of the most important places in Scottish history thanks to its strategically important location at the gateway to the Highlands.

Once, whoever controlled Stirling, controlled Scotland. Its impressive castle stands guard over all it surveys and was the capital for the Stewart Kings. No fewer than seven battle sites can be seen from the Castle ramparts – including Stirling Bridge, a scene of triumph for William Wallace and Bannockburn where Robert the Bruce led the Scots to victory in 1314.

A National Park on your doorstep

From Stirling, it is easy to take advantage of the natural treasures of Loch Lomond and The Trossachs National Park. And that means 20 Munros (mountains over 3,000ft) to climb, 50 rivers to fish, 22 lochs to sail and thousands of miles of road and track to cycle. And when you've had your fill of activities, head for Loch Lomond Shores for a wonderful cultural and retail experience.

A place in history

Further west still, the West Highlands and Islands are waiting to be explored. Follow the whisky trail round Islay and Jura. Or jump on a ferry at Gourock and explore The Cowal Peninsula with its sea lochs and deep forests.

You could also head for lovely Lochgilphead and beyond to Kilmartin where you can trace the very roots of the nation where the Scots arrived from Ireland in the 6th century.

Choosing a holiday destination in an area as diverse as this will always be difficult but the stunning array of hotels and guest houses will help. There are historical inns, grand hotels, intimate romantic country houses, and even restaurants with rooms so you're sure to find somewhere that will tempt you to return time and time again.

Port Ellen Distillery, Isle of Islay

What's On?

Lomond and Clyde Springfest, Helensburgh

26 April – 2 May 2008
A springtime festival with a touch of Japanese culture.
www.lomondclydespringfest.co.uk

Highlands and Islands Music and Dance Festival, Oban

1 – 4 May 2008
New events and competition classes every year, 2008 is the 25th anniversary.
www.obanfestival.org

Isle of Bute Jazz Festival

1 – 5 May 2008
A host of well-known names in Bute's annual jazz-fest.
www.butejazz.com

Big in Falkirk

3 – 4 May 2008
Scotland's National Street Arts Festival.
www.biginfalkirk.com

Stirling Highland Games

13 July 2008
A great Scottish day out for the whole family.
www.stirling-highland-games.co.uk

Loch Lomond Food and Drink Festival

September (dates TBC)
Enjoy fine food and drink from all over the region.
www.lochlomondfood anddrinkfestival.com

Cowalfest

3 – 12 October 2008
Scotland's largest combined walking and arts festival.
www.cowalfest.org

Tunnocks Tour of Mull Rally

10 – 12 October 2008
Enjoy the atmosphere at this annual car rally.
www.2300club.org

Aberfoyle Mushroom Festival

16 – 19 October 2008
A long weekend of fantasy, fungi, food and fun.
www.visitaberfoyle.com

www.visitscottishheartlands.com

MAP

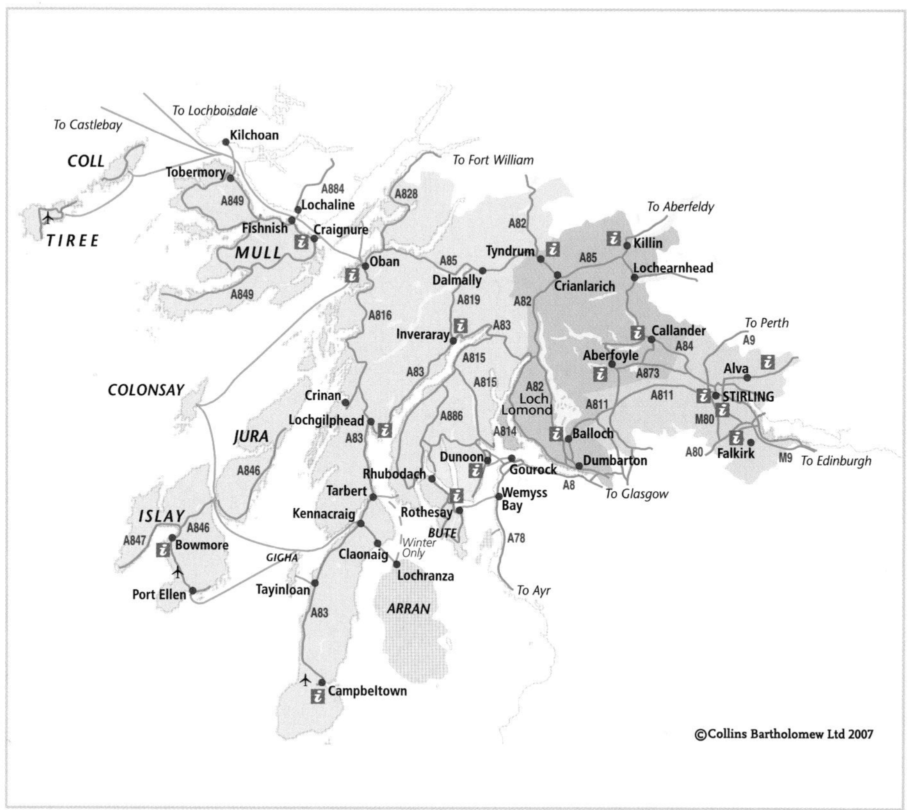
To Castlebay
To Lochboisdale
Kilchoan
COLL
Tobermory
TIREE
A849
A884
Lochaline
Fishnish
Craignure
MULL
A849
A828
To Fort William
Oban
A85
Dalmally
Tyndrum
A82
A85
Crianlarich
Killin
To Aberfeldy
Lochearnhead
A819
A816
Inveraray
A83
A82
Callander
A84
To Perth
A9
Aberfoyle
A873
Alva
A815
A815
A83
COLONSAY
Crinan
A82
Loch Lomond
A811
A811
STIRLING
M80
Lochgilphead
A83
JURA
A886
A814
Balloch
Falkirk
A80
M9
To Edinburgh
Dunoon
Gourock
Dumbarton
A846
Rhubodach
Tarbert
Wemyss Bay
A8
To Glasgow
ISLAY
A846
A847
Bowmore
Kennacraig
Rothesay
BUTE
A78
GIGHA
Claonaig
Winter Only
Lochranza
Port Ellen
Tayinloan
A83
ARRAN
To Ayr
Campbeltown
©Collins Bartholomew Ltd 2007

TOURIST INFORMATION CENTRES

West Highlands	
Bowmore	The Square, Bowmore, Isle of Islay PA43 7JP
Campbeltown	Mackinnon House, The Pier, Campbeltown PA28 6EF
Craignure	The Pier, Craignure, Isle of Mull PA65 6AY
Dunoon	7 Alexandra Parade, Dunoon, PA23 8AB
Inveraray	Front Street, Inveraray PA32 8UY
Lochgilphead	Lochnell Street, Lochgilphead PA31 8JL
Oban	Argyll Square, Oban PA34 4AR
Rothesay	Winter Gardens, Rothesay, Isle of Bute PA20 0AJ
Loch Lomond	
Aberfoyle	Trossachs Discovery Centre, Main Street, Aberfoyle FK8 3UQ
Callander	Rob Roy Centre, Ancaster Square, Callander FK17 8ED
Killin	Breadalbane Folklore Centre, Main Street, Killin FK21 8XE
Loch Lomond	National Park Gateway Centre, Loch Lomond Shores, Balloch G83 8QL
Tyndrum	Main Street, Tyndrum FK20 8RY
Stirling & Trossachs	
Alva	Mill Trail Visitor Centre, Alva FK12 5EN
Falkirk	2-4 Glebe Street, Falkirk FK1 1HU
Stirling (Dumbarton Rd)	41 Dumbarton Road, Stirling FK8 2LQ
Stirling (Pirnhall)	Motorway Service Area, Junction 9, M9

Make the most of your stay in Scotland and make your first stop the Tourist Information Centre wherever you go.

Knowledgeable and friendly staff can help you with information and advice; they can answer your questions, book accommodation and you can even pick up some souvenirs to take home for friends and family.

For information and ideas about exploring Scotland in advance of your trip, call our booking and information service or go to www.visitscotland.com

Call 0845 22 55 121

or if calling from outside the UK call +44 (0) 1506 832 121

From Ireland call 1800 932 510

A £4 booking fee applies to telephone bookings of accommodation.

Tobermory, Isle of Mull

West Highlands and Islands

Take a journey around some of Scotland's most magical isles and penisulas and savour the atmosphere of the rugged west coast. The attraction of island life is a powerful draw for visitors, and while there are parts of the mainland around Kintyre which feel more like island than mainland, if you're looking for the genuine island experience, you'll be spoiled for choice.

There are many islands to explore including Gigha, Jura, Islay and Colonsay. And no trip to these parts would be complete without visiting Oban, the gateway to the isles, from where boats make their way to and from the likes of Mull, Coll, Tiree and Iona.

Highlights are Islay for the whisky, Iona which is deeply spiritual, and Mull, where you can see colourful Tobermory (or Balamory as families with young children will recognise it). On your way to the isles stop off in Oban, its harbour is always bustling and the area around the port has a great selection of shops, bars and restaurants.

Isle of Jura, Inner Hebrides

DON'T MISS

1 Wherever you travel in this area, you're never far from a whisky distillery. Islay alone is home to eight working distilleries, producing world-famous whiskies such as Laphroaig and Bowmore, renowned for their peaty qualities. Here, you'll also find Kilchoman, a recently opened farm distillery. The neighbouring Isle of Jura manufactures its own popular malt, while Campbeltown on Kintyre now boasts two local whiskies, Springbank and Glengyle, the latter dating from only 2004. Facilities and opening hours vary.

2 Iona is a beautiful island with white beaches and turquoise sea. Situated off the western tip of the Ross of Mull, it is one of the world's foremost centres of Christian pilgrimage. Staffa is Iona's northerly neighbour where basalt lava has created some of Europe's most astonishing rock formations which are at their most impressive at Fingal's Cave.

3 Any trip which takes in the breathtaking Argyll coastline or Argyll's Atlantic Islands, known as Scotland's Sea Kingdom, promises a memorable experience. Negotiate the Gulf of Corryvreckan with its famous whirlpool and travel round Scarba while looking out for whales, dolphins, deer and eagles, or venture further to the remote Garvellachs. You can sail from Ardfern with Craignish Cruises, from Craobh Haven with Farsain Cruises or from Easdale with Seafari Adventures or Sealife Adventures.

4 Mount Stuart on the Isle of Bute was the ancestral home of the Marquess of Bute. Today it is a high quality, award-winning attraction featuring magnificent Victorian Gothic architecture and design together with contemporary craftsmanship. Mount Stuart is surrounded by 300 acres of gloriously maintained grounds and gardens.

5 Kilmartin Glen is home to a myriad of Neolithic and Bronze Age monuments, coupled with early Christian carved stones and ruined castles. South of Oban, this site was capital of the ancient Celtic kingdom of Dalriada, as evidenced at Dunadd Fort, where a footprint in the stone is thought to have featured in royal inauguration ceremonies.

6 The common characteristic of the Glorious Gardens of Argyll & Bute is their individuality. Each garden has a variety of terrain; many are mainly level with smooth paths, while some are steep and rocky. The Gardens range from informal woodland gardens to beautiful classic examples of 18th century design.

FOOD AND DRINK

www.eatscotland.com

7 The original Loch Fyne Oyster Bar and shop started in a small shed in the lay-by at the head of Loch Fyne in the early 1980s. In 1985 it moved into the old cow byre at Clachan Farm. It has been listed in the Good Food Guide every year since then.

8 At Chatters Restaurant in Dunoon the very best of Scottish produce is prepared and served in unique surroundings. If the weather is nice a meal can be enjoyed in the lovely garden and there are regular art exhibitions to enjoy. Chatters also has a great selection of wines and a heavenly pudding trolley.

9 The Seafood Trail takes you through some of the most spectacular coastal scenery Scotland has to offer, and enables seafood lovers to sample, share and enjoy seafood and shellfish from a wide variety of waterfront establishments.

10 For centuries the west coast of Scotland and whisky have been synonymous. The so-called Whisky Coast blends incredible Scottish scenery with the best single malt whisky for a truly unforgettable experience. Getting to and around the Whisky Coast is surprisingly easy for the independent traveller in search of stunning landscapes and the finest whiskies, as the area is well served by road, rail, air and ferry.

WILDLIFE

www.visitscotland.com/wildlife

11 There are numerous operators that offer sea trip safaris around the Oban and Mull area where you can spot majestic wildlife against a backdrop of spectacular scenery. The wildlife in this area is magnificent and you may well see the majestic sea eagle, golden eagle, or a range of seabirds along with seals, dolphins, porpoise and the occasional minke whale.

12 The extensive Argyll Forest Park offers a perfect introduction to Loch Lomond & The Trossachs National Park. Start at the Ardgartan Visitor Centre on the A83 at the north of Loch Long, where the Boathouse and Riverside walks provide options for pushchairs. You'll also find cycle paths, a play area and refreshments. With its spectacular mountains, glens, lochs and woodlands, many claim that Britain's first forest park is also the finest.

13 The islands of Islay and Jura are something of a mecca for wildlife lovers. With well over a hundred breeding bird species in summer, and some of Europe's largest populations of wintering wildfowl, they are a year round destination for ornithologists. Add to this some exceptional marine wildlife, including minke whales, common and bottlenose dolphins, basking sharks and literally thousands of seals, alongside some of Britain's best opportunities to spy otters, red deer and golden eagles, and you have a natural paradise. A particular highlight is the arrival of around 50,000 barnacle and white-fronted geese from the Arctic Circle each autumn.

14 Wildlife and Bird Watching safaris offer the chance to explore the remote areas of Mull with experienced guides to help you spot and learn about the wildlife which inhabits the island. This is your chance to see golden eagles, otters, harriers and merlin to name a few.

WALKS

www.visitscotland.com/walking

15 Lismore is a lovely location to get away from it all and is easy to reach by boat from Oban. The island is just 12 miles long and 1.5 miles at its widest point, and offers many interesting walks with spectacular views of the sea and mountains. Kerrera is a beautiful island where it is also possible to walk round the entire island although this walk is about 10 miles and will take some time.

16 The wonderfully unexplored Kintyre Peninsula boasts hidden coves, deserted beaches, tiny fishing communities, gentle hills, fabulous local produce and welcoming friendly people. Stretching from Tarbert to Southend, the waymarked Kintyre Way criss-crosses the peninsula, connecting communities and landscape, people and produce. At 89 miles long (142 kms), and with four to seven days worth of walking, there's serious hiking and gentle rambles, all of which bring home the beautiful reality that is Kintyre.

17 The West Island Way, which opened in September 2000, is the first long distance way-marked path on a Scottish island. It encompasses some of the best walking that the Isle of Bute has to offer and embraces a variety of landscapes.

18 The Cowal Way follows a route running the length of Argyll's Cowal Peninsula. It starts in the south west at Portavadie beside Loch Fyne, and finishes in the north east at Ardgartan by Loch Long, and involves walking on roads and on lochside, hill and woodland terrains. The waymarked route is 75 km / 47 miles in length and is divided into six shorter, more manageable sections.

VIEWS

19 Tiny Port Askaig on Islay is something of a ferry hub, serving Colonsay, the mainland and Jura. Its proximity to the last makes it an ideal location to view the Paps of Jura, three rounded mountains rising out of the sea to over 730m.

20 The village of Carradale on the eastern side of Kintyre makes an excellent base from which to explore the Peninsula. The delightful beach and harbour area offer stunning views over the Kilbrannan Sound to the dramatic hills of Arran.

21 One of Scotland's most romanticised stretches of water, the narrow straits known as the Kyles of Bute, more than live up to their reputation. The Kyles are best admired from the viewpoint on the A886 above Colintraive, where the view to their namesake island is truly awe-inspiring. Remember to bring along your picnic so you can really make the most of this view and open space.

22 The steep 10-minute climb from the centre of Oban to McCaig's Tower is well worth it for the view of Oban Bay, Kerrera and the Isle of Mull. The Tower was built by a local banker in the late 19th century in an effort to replicate Rome's Colosseum. The view of the town and the islands to the west is breathtaking.

WEST HIGHLANDS AND ISLANDS

35909

Arduaine, Argyll — Map Ref: 1E3

Loch Melfort Hotel

Arduaine, Argyll, PA34 4XG
Tel:01852 200233 Fax:01852 200214
Email:reception@lochmelfort.co.uk
Web:www.lochmelfort.co.uk

Family run hotel located 20 miles south from Oban in a magnificent location overlooking the Sound of Jura and many small islands. Spectacular views from all bedrooms, lounge and restaurant. Emphasis on local produce including seafood and enjoying an excellent reputation for home cooking and fresh produce. Arduaine Gardens adjacent with many other glorious gardens in the area. Pony trekking and watersports available. Some annexe bedrooms.

25 rooms, All en-suite. Open Jan-Dec. Rates on application.

56133

Kilchattan Bay, Isle of Bute — Map Ref: 1F6

St Blane's Hotel

Kilchattan Bay, Isle of Bute, PA20 9NW
Tel:01700 831224 Fax:01700 831381
Email:info@stblaneshotel.com
Web:www.stblaneshotel.com

10 rooms
All en-suite
Open Jan-Dec
B&B per person, single from £35.00, double from £30.00.

58066

Rothesay, Isle of Bute — Map Ref: 1F5

The Ardyne (Hotel and Restaurant)

38 Mountstuart Road, Rothesay, Isle of Bute, PA20 9EB
Tel:01700 502052 Fax:01700 505129
Email:ardyne.hotel@virgin.net
Web:www.theardynehotel.co.uk

Situated on the seafront with stunning views from the Lounge Bar, Dining room and many of the bedrooms. Excellent reputation for comfortable accommodation as well as for serving the best of Scottish fayre.

16 rooms, All en-suite. Open Jan-Dec. B&B per person, single from £37.50, double from £35.00, BB & Eve.Meal from £55.00. Special breaks available.

60161

Rothesay, Isle of Bute — Map Ref: 1F5

The Regent Hotel

23 Battery Place, Rothesay, Isle of Bute, PA20 9DU
Tel:01700 502006

6 rooms
Some en-suite
Open Jan-Dec
B&B per person, single from £27.50, double from £40.00.

17420 **Cairndow, Argyll** **Map Ref: 1F3**

Cairndow Stagecoach Inn

Cairndow, Argyll, PA26 8BN
Tel:01499 600286 Fax:01499 600220
Email:enq@cairndowinn.com
Web:www.cairndowinn.com

Across the 'Arrochar Alps' on Loch Fyne this historic coaching inn enjoys a delightful situation just off the A83. It is a haven of sparkling views, high mountains and magnificent woodlands and rivers.

We offer excellent accommodation in 18 en-suite bedrooms. Five new de-luxe rooms with stunning views over Loch Fyne. Conservatory restaurant and lounge meals served all day. Ideal centre for touring Western Highlands from Loch Lomond to Fort William.

Loch side beer garden, sauna, reduced golfing at Inveraray and tee times on Loch Lomond.

18 rooms.
All en-suite. Open Jan-Dec
B&B per person, single from £35.00, double from £30.00.

23869 **Carradale, Argyll** **Map Ref: 1E6**

Scottish Tourist Board ★★★★ Restaurant with Rooms

Dunvalanree

Portrigh Bay, Carradale, Argyll, PA28 6SE
Tel:01583 431226 Fax:01583 431339
Email:stay@dunvalanree.com
Web:www.dunvalanree.com

Traditional 1930's house with many original features in idyllic location overlooking Portrigh Bay with views to Arran. Refurbished to a high standard with rooms now ensuite. Eat Scotland Silver Award, AA Rosette and 2008 Good Food Guide. Fully licenced.

5 rooms, All en-suite. Open Jan-Dec. D.B&B per person, single from £75.00, double from £65.00.

WEST HIGHLANDS AND ISLANDS

12546

Colintraive, Argyll — Map Ref: 1F5

Colintraive Hotel

Colintraive, Argyll, PA22 3AS
Tel:01700 841207
Email:enquiries@colintraivehotel.com
Web:www.colintraivehotel.com

A former hunting lodge, fully refurbished to a high standard with stunning views over the Kyles of Bute. Cosy bar with log fire and excellent bar meals. Elegant à la carte restaurant using local produce & vegetables from our own garden. Period furniture & big leather chairs in coffee lounge. Beautiful spacious ensuite bedrooms. This family run hotel offers very high standards in relaxed informal surroundings. A great base for walking, sailing, cycling and fishing. Close to Bute ferry.

4 rooms, All en-suite. Open Jan-Dec. B&B per person, single from £45.00, double from £30.00.

20003

Coll, Isle of, Argyll — Map Ref: 1B1

Coll Hotel

Arinagour, Isle of Coll, Argyll, PA78 6SZ
Tel:01879 230334 Fax:01879 230317
Email:info@collhotel.com
Web:www.collhotel.com

6 rooms
All en-suite
Open Jan-Dec excl Xmas/New Year
B&B per person, single from £40.00, double from £40.00.

52032

Connel, Argyll — Map Ref: 1E2

Ronebhal Guest House

Connel, by Oban, Argyll, PA37 1PJ
Tel/Fax:01631 710310
Email:ronebhal@btinternet.com
Web:www.ronebhal.co.uk

5 rooms
Some en-suite
Open Mar-Oct
B&B per person, single £27.50-50.00, double £22.50-35.00.

75260

Dunoon, Argyll — Map Ref: 1F5

Scottish
TOURIST BOARD
★★★★
SMALL
HOTEL

Abbot's Brae Hotel

West Bay, Dunoon, Argyll, PA23 7QJ
Tel:01369 705021 Fax:01369 701191
Email:info@abbotsbrae.co.uk
Web:www.abbotsbrae.co.uk

A period house built in 1800s. Abbot's Brae commands excellent views over the 'Firth of Clyde' from its elevated site. All rooms individually decorated and retaining Victorian period features and offering a high standard of comfort and facility.

8 rooms, All en-suite. Open Jan-Dec. B&B per person, double from £54.00.

20912

Dunoon, Argyll **Map Ref: 1F5**

Craigen Hotel

85 Argyll Street, Dunoon, PA23 7DH
Tel:01369 702307

6 rooms
Some en-suite
Open Jan-Dec
Rates on application.

24981

Dunoon, Argyll **Map Ref: 1F5**

Enmore Hotel

Marine Parade, Kirn, Dunoon, Argyll, PA23 8HH
Tel:01369 702230 Fax:01369 702148
Email:enmorehotel@btinternet.com
Web:www.enmorehotel.co.uk

Beautifuly situated with open sea views. Small, comfortable hotel offering the very best in accomodation, cuisine and hospitaliy.

10 rooms, All ensuite. Open Jan-Dec. B&B per person, single from £65.00, double from £45.00, family from £60.00. Room Only rates per night, single from £65.00, double from £90.00, family from £120.00.

77829

Dunoon, Argyll **Map Ref: 1F5**

Mayfair Hotel

7 Clyde Street, Kirn, Dunoon, Argyll, PA23 8DX
Tel:01369 703803
Email:grayson.mayfair7@fsmail.net
Web:www.dunoonguesthouse.com

A friendly, family run establishment in a peaceful situation commanding magnificent views over the Firth of Clyde. Discounted rates for stays of 3 nights or more.

5 rooms, All en-suite. Open Jan-Dec. B&B per person from £26.00.

C £ V

60006

Dunoon, Argyll **Map Ref: 1F5**

Park Hotel

3 Glenmorag Avenue, Dunoon, Argyll, PA23 7LG
Tel:01369 702383
Email:info@parkhoteldunoon.co.uk
Web:www.parkhoteldunoon.co.uk

21 rooms
All en-suite
Open Jan-Dec
B&B per person, single from £40.00, double from £40.00.

77283

Glendaruel, Argyll Map Ref: 1F4

The Glendaruel Hotel

Clachan of Glendaruel, Argyll, PA22 3AA
Tel:01369 820274
Email:reception@glendaruel-hotel.co.uk
Web:www.glendaruel-hotel.co.uk

This seventeenth century coaching house is now a beautiful hotel at the heart of a community. It boasts nine stunning rooms, two lively bars and an elegant restaurant with a reputation for fine dining.

8 rooms, Open Jan-Dec. B&B per person, single from £35.00, double from £35.00.

48746

Innellan, by Dunoon, Argyll Map Ref: 1F5

The Osborne Hotel

44 Shore Road, Innellan, By Dunoon, Argyll, PA23 7TJ
Tel/Fax:01369 830445
Email:osbreservations@aol.com
Web:www.osbornehotel.net

4 rooms
All en-suite
Open Jan-Dec
B&B per person, single from £32.50, double from £32.50.

29549

Bowmore, Isle of Islay, Argyll Map Ref: 1C6

The Harbour Inn and Restaurant

Bowmore, Isle of Islay, Argyll, PA43 7JR
Tel:01496 810330 Fax:01496 810990
Email:info@harbour-inn.com
Web:www.harbour-inn.com

7 rooms
All en-suite
Open Jan-Dec
B&B per person, single from £65.00, double from £52.50.

C £ V

33246

Jura, Isle of, Argyll Map Ref: 1D4

Jura Hotel

Isle of Jura, Argyll, PA60 7XU
Tel:01496 820243 Fax:01496 820249
Email:jurahotel@aol.com
Web:www.jurahotel.co.uk

17 rooms
8 ensuite
Open Jan-Dec
B&B per person single from £40.00, double from £70.00 (room rate).

£ V

73781 **Kilfinan, Argyll** **Map Ref: 1E4**

Kilfinan Hotel

Kilfinan, Nr Tighnabruiach, Argyll, PA21 2EP
Tel:01700 821201 Fax:01700 821205
Email:info@kilfinan.com
Web:www.kilfinan.com

The Kilfinan Hotel, a former Coaching Inn, is located on the beautiful Cowal penisula and has been welcoming guests since before the 18th Century. All rooms ensuite. The hotel is a perfect all year round retreat. Very good walking country with spectacular views and lots of wildlife sightings.

9 rooms, All en-suite. Open Jan-Dec. Rates on application.

23237 **Dervaig, Isle of Mull, Argyll** **Map Ref: 1C1**

Druimnacroish

Dervaig, Isle of Mull, PA75 6QW
Tel:01688 400274
Web:www.druimnacroish.co.uk

Converted farm house and water mill set on a tranquil and secluded hillside in the north west of the island. Relaxed, friendly atmosphere, spacious accommodation, gardens, superb views from every room. Home made bread, wi-fi access. Private guest lounges and extensive conservatory with views across the glen. Well situated for Mull's many attractions including boat trips, walking and wildlife.

6 rooms, All en-suite. Open Mar-Nov. B&B per person, double/twin from £30.00.

77276 **Dervaig, Isle of Mull, Argyll** **Map Ref: 1C1**

Killoran House

Dervaig, Isle of Mull, PA75 6QR
Tel/Fax:01688 400362
Email:enquiries@killoranmull.co.uk
Web:www.killoranmull.co.uk

6 rooms
Open Jan-Dec
Rates on application.

17616 **by Dervaig, Isle of Mull, Argyll** **Map Ref: 1C1**

Scottish TOURIST BOARD ★★★ RESTAURANT WITH ROOMS

The Calgary Hotel

by Dervaig, Isle of Mull, Argyll, PA75 6QW
Tel:01688 400256
Email:calgary.hotel@virgin.net
Web:www.calgary.co.uk

9 rooms
All en-suite
Open Mar-Oct (weekends only in Nov)
B&B from £37.00-53.00. Dinner from £20.00-25.00 for 3 courses à la carte.

WEST HIGHLANDS AND ISLANDS

74718

Tobermory, Isle of Mull, Argyll — Map Ref: 1C1

Carnaburg

55 Main Street, Tobermory, Isle of Mull, PA75 6NT
Tel:01688 302479
Email:viven@carnaburg-tobermory.co.uk
Web:www.carnaburg-tobermory.co.uk

8 rooms
Some en-suite
Open Jan-Dec
B&B per person, single from £30.00, double from £22.00.

30309

Tobermory, Isle of Mull, Argyll — Map Ref: 1C1

Highland Cottage

Breadalbane Street, Tobermory, Isle of Mull,
PA75 6PD
Tel:01688 302030
Email:davidandjo@highlandcottage.co.uk
Web:www.highlandcottage.co.uk

Family-run 'country house in the town' hotel located in the heart of upper Tobermory in conservation area. Well appointed bedrooms themed after local islands and including 2 with 4 poster beds. Imaginative cuisine using fresh, local ingredients served in our attractive, homely, dining room. High level of personal attention from resident owners. 'AA 3 Red Stars, AA 2 Rosette'.

6 rooms, All en-suite. Open Mar-Nov. B&B per person, double from £75.00, BB & Eve.Meal from £117.50.

36109

North Connel, Argyll — Map Ref: 1E2

Lochnell Arms Hotel

North Connel, Argyll, PA37 1RP
Tel/Fax:01631 710239
Email:lochnellarms.co.uk
Web:www.lochnell.com

Traditional Highland family run hotel situated in a peaceful spot overlooking Loch Etive and the falls of Lora. Extensive home-cooked menu available.

10 rooms, All en-suite. Open Jan-Dec. B&B per person, single from £42.50, double from £85.00 (per room.)

67514

Oban, Argyll — Map Ref: 1E2

Alltavona

Corran Esplanade, Oban, Argyll, PA34 5AQ
Tel:01631 565067 Mob:07771 708301
Email:carol@alltavona.co.uk
Web:www.alltavona.co.uk

10 rooms
All en-suite
Open Jan-Dec
B&B per person, single from £30.00, double from £30.00.

14390 **Oban, Argyll** Map Ref: 1E2

The Barriemore

Corran Esplanade, Oban, Argyll, PA34 5AQ
Tel:01631 566356 Fax:01631 571084
Email:reception@barriemore-hotel.co.uk
Web:www.barriemore-hotel.co.uk

Delightfully restored Victorian detached villa overlooking Oban Bay offering the discerning holidaymaker a superior standard of style and comfort. Personally run by proprietors.

11 rooms, All en-suite. Open Feb-Dec. B&B per room, single from £45.00, double from £70.00.

20536 **Oban, Argyll** Map Ref: 1E2

Corriemar House

6 Corran Esplanade, Oban, Argyll, PA34 5AQ
Tel:01631 562476 Fax:01631 564339
Email:info@corriemarhouse.co.uk
Web:www.corriemarhouse.co.uk

14 rooms
13 en-suite, 1 priv.facilities
Open Jan-Dec
B&B per person, double £30.00-48.00. Queen sized deluxe rooms and 4 poster room available with seaviews.

68122 **Oban, Argyll** Map Ref: 1E2

Glenbervie Guest House

Dalriach Road, Oban, Argyll, PA34 5JD
Tel:01631 564770 Fax:01631 566723

Beautifully situated overlooking Oban Bay, commanding magnificent views. 2 minutes walk from town centre, promenade, harbour and amenities. Evening meal. Available by prior arrangement.

8 rooms, 6 en-suite. Open Feb-Dec excl Xmas/New Year. B&B per person, single from £28.00-35.00, double from £28.00-35.00 pp.

67995

Oban, Argyll — Map Ref: 1E2

Kathmore Guest House

Soroba Road, Oban, Argyll, PA34 4JF
Tel:01631 562104 Fax:01631 562104/570067
Email:wkathmore@aol.com
Web:www.kathmore.co.uk

Kathmore is a short walk to the town centre. Our rooms are tasteful and well appointed. Residence licence and comfortable lounge. Attractive decking area looking onto the garden. Ample private parking.

8 rooms, 7 en-suite. B&B per person, single £25.00-50.00, double/twin £23.50-35.00, family £60.00-80.00..

34047

Oban, Argyll — Map Ref: 1E2

Scottish TOURIST BOARD ★★★ SMALL HOTEL

Kings Knoll Hotel

Dunollie Road, Oban, PA34 5JH
Tel:01631 562536 Fax:01631 566101
Email:info@kingsknollhotel.co.uk
Web:www.kingsknollhotel.co.uk

15 rooms
Some en-suite
Open Feb-Dec
B&B per person, single from £25.00, double from £25.00, Room only double £50.00. BB & Eve.Meal from £38.00.

59608

Oban, Argyll — Map Ref: 1E2

Scottish TOURIST BOARD ★★★★ RESTAURANT WITH ROOMS

The Manor House

Gallanoch Road, Oban, Argyll, PA34 4LS
Tel:01631 562087 Fax:01631 563053
Email:info@manorhouseoban.com
Web:www.manorhouseoban.com

11 rooms
All en-suite
Open Jan-Dec excl Xmas
B&B per person, single from £65.00, double from £47.85 (low season).

68081

Oban, Argyll — Map Ref: 1E2

Scottish TOURIST BOARD ★★★ HOTEL

Royal Hotel

Argyll Square, Oban, Argyll, PA34 4BE
Tel:01631 563021
Email:salesroyaloban@strathmorehotels.com
Web:www.strathmorehotels.com

Imposing Victorian town centre hotel near to the water front. Easily accessible for ferry terminal, railway station and major roads.

91 rooms, All en-suite. Open Jan-Dec. B&B per person, single from £50.00, double from £45.00.

WEST HIGHLANDS AND ISLANDS

63546 **Oban, Argyll** **Map Ref: 1E2**

Wellpark House

Esplanade, Oban, Argyll, PA34 5AQ
Tel:01631 562948 Fax:01631 565808
Email:enquiries@wellparkhouse.co.uk
Web:www.wellparkhouse.co.uk

Family run establishment in a quiet position on the esplanade. Magnificent views over the bay to Isles of Kerrera and Mull.

19 rooms, All en-suite. Open Jan-Dec. B&B per person, single from £40.00, double from £35.00.

25591 **by Oban, Argyll** **Map Ref: 1E2**

Falls of Lora Hotel

Connel Ferry, by Oban, Argyll, PA37 1PB
Tel:01631 710483 Fax:01631 710694
Email:enquiries@fallsoflora.com
Web:www.fallsoflora.com

Oban 5 miles, only 2½ to 3 hours drive North-West of Glasgow/Edinburgh. Overlooking Loch Etive, this fine owner run Victorian Hotel with a modern extension. 30 rooms from special to inexpensive family. The super cocktail bar has an open log fire and over 100 brands of whisky. There is an attractive and comfortable bistro for evening meals - the menu is extensive and features local produce.

30 rooms, All en-suite. Open Feb-mid Dec. B&B per person, single from £39.50, double from £23.50.

11278 **Port Appin, Argyll** **Map Ref: 1E1**

The Airds Hotel

Port Appin, Appin, Argyll, PA38 4DF
Tel:01631 730236 Fax:01631 730535
Email:airds@aird-hotel.com
Web:www.airds-hotel.com

11 rooms
All en-suite
Open Jan-Dec
Room per night, full board from £255.00, half board from £245.00 per person.

79364 **Strachur, Argyll** **Map Ref: 1F3**

The Creggans Inn

Strachur, Argyll, PA27 8BX
Tel:01369 860279 Fax:01369 860637
Email:info@creggans-inn.co.uk
Web:www.creggans-inn.co.uk

14 rooms
All en-suite
Open Jan-Dec
B&B per person, single from £85.00, double from £65.00.

IMPORTANT: PRICES STATED ARE ESTIMATES AND MAY BE SUBJECT TO AMENDMENTS
FOR A FULL LISTING OF QUALITY ASSURED ACCOMMODATION, PLEASE SEE DIRECTORY AT BACK OF THIS GUIDE

Canoeing on Loch Lomond, Argyll

Loch Lomond and The Trossachs

Whatever road you take to the bonny banks of Loch Lomond, you'll arrive at one of the most picturesque places in all of Scotland. This vast National Park is, indeed, one of the most beautiful places in the world.

Towns like Callander, Balloch, Killin and Aberfoyle make a great base to explore different corners of the Park. And once you're there, you'll find so much to do from watersports to mountain climbing, angling to gentle strolls in stunning locations.

You can even integrate the sedate with the active – catch the SS Sir Walter Scott from the Trossachs Pier and cruise Loch Katrine to Stronachlachar, then enjoy the 13-mile shore hike back.

The Falls of Dochart, Killin

DON'T MISS

1 **Loch Lomond and The Trossachs National Park** has its Gateway Centre on the southern shore of the Loch in Balloch. From here and elsewhere on the Loch, boat trips offer visitors the chance to explore the largest body of freshwater in Britain. To the west, Argyll Forest Park provides secluded waymarked trails, while The Trossachs to the east have provided inspiration for poets and novelists throughout the centuries.

2 The main visitor centre of the **Queen Elizabeth Forest Park** is on the A821 north of Aberfoyle. An integral part of the National Park, it offers a host of walking, wildlife and photography opportunities from the foot of Loch Lomond to Strathyre Forest, north of Loch Lubnaig. Here, you'll find a multitude of waymarked paths, a forest shop, wildlife viewing station and Liz MacGregor's Coffee Shop.

3 The dramatic scenery of The Trossachs is said to be the inspiration behind Sir Walter Scott's 'The Lady of the Lake'. It is fitting then that the historic steamship which regularly sets sail on Loch Katrine is named after him. The **SS Sir Walter Scott** cruises up to Stronachlachar and will return you to the Trossachs Pier.

4 At **Go Ape!** in Aberfoyle, you can take to the trees and experience a new, exhilarating course of rope bridges, tarzan swings and zip slides (including the longest in the UK) up to 37 metres above the forest floor. Approximately three hours of fun and adventure await.

5 For a fun family day out, visit the **Scottish Wool Centre** in Aberfoyle, where you can enjoy a light-hearted look at 2,000 years of Scottish history portrayed by human and animal actors, plus spinning and weaving demonstrations. The live animal show features sheepdogs rounding up both sheep and Indian Runner Ducks, whilst younger visitors can enjoy the lambs and baby goats in springtime.

1

2

3

4

FOOD AND DRINK

www.eatscotland.com

6 Whilst touring around Loch Lomond, be sure to stop at the Coach House Coffee Shop in the conservation village of Luss. Accompany a bumper homemade scone with a Lomond Latte or a Clyde Cappuccino!

7 The Village Inn at Arrochar is a charming country inn on the edge of Loch Long. Offering traditional Scottish home-cooking, it proves to be a great favourite with walkers exploring the adjacent 'Arrochar Alps'.

8 The family-friendly Forth Inn at Aberfoyle is known for its good food and atmosphere. Its award-winning bar and restaurant are favourites with locals and visitors alike.

9 The Kilted Skirlie is a modern Scottish restaurant with a sense of theatre that caters for every taste and pocket at Loch Lomond Shores, combine your visit with a range of shopping and leisure experiences and watch the otters at Loch Lomond Aquarium.

HISTORY AND HERITAGE

10 The islands of Loch Lomond are home to many ancient ruins including a 7th century monastery and the remains of a former Victorian whisky distillery.

11 The Lake of Menteith is the only 'lake' in Scotland, all others being known as lochs. Sail from the Port of Menteith, off the A81 south of Callander, to the island that is home to Inchmahome Priory, an 18th century Augustinian monastery.

12 The historic village of Killin, with the spectacular Falls of Dochart, is the setting for the Breadalbane Folklore Centre which is housed in a beautifully restored mill with a working waterwheel. Dedicated to exploring the rich myths and legends prevalent in these parts, you can follow the stories of the local clans and learn about St Fillan and the arrival of Christianity in Scotland. Open April to October.

VIEWS

13 The beauty of **Loch Lomond** is undisputed but the finest vantage point is more open to debate. Everyone has their favourite spot and no doubt you will too. Take a cruise on the Loch itself from Luss, Balloch or Tarbet or head to Inversnaid on the west bank for more rugged views.

14 'The Dumpling' is the nickname for **Duncryne Hill**, a volcanic plug, situated just off the A811 at the east end of Gartocharn. At about 465ft high and accessible by a short steep path, it is an astounding vantage point overlooking Loch Lomond's islands.

15 **Conic Hill** is located just north of Balmaha on the B837. A 358m ascent, it offers superb views of Loch Lomond and its islands. From here, you can also see the dramatic changes to the landscape caused by the Highland Boundary Fault.

16 From the Stronachlachar junction on the Inversnaid road (B829), the wild landscape of **Loch Arklet** leads down towards Loch Lomond and its surrounding hills.

14

16

19

WALKS

www.visitscotland.com/walking

17 To walk along the shore of Loch Katrine start at the Trossachs Pier, approximately 25 minutes drive west of Callander (A821). You can walk as far as you like and retrace your steps, or take a cruise on Loch Katrine to Stronachlachar and then walk the 13-mile route back to where you started.

18 The village hall in Balquhidder is your starting point for one of Breadalbane's most glorious views. Head along the Kirkton Burn and upwards onto a forest road. Soon you'll reach **Creag an Tuirc** where you can absorb the beauty of Balquhidder Glen, Loch Voil and little Loch Doine. Including a short climb, this 2½ mile walk should take you about 2 hours.

19 **Rowardennan** (B837 from Drymen) on the eastern edge of Loch Lomond is a wonderful starting and finishing point for a gentle walk along the shores, following part of the famous West Highland Way.

65377 Aberfoyle, Stirlingshire Map Ref: 1H3

Forest Hills Hotel

Kinlochard, By Aberfoyle, Stirlingshire, FK8 3TL
Tel:08701 942105 Fax:01877 387307
Email:forest_hills@macdonald-hotels.co.uk
Web:www.foresthills-hotel.co.uk

Country house in 22 acres of grounds with magnificent views over Loch Ard. Extensive recreational facilities including watersports centre.

50 rooms, All en-suite. Open Jan-Dec. B&B per room, single from £80.00, double from £120.00.

58955 Aberfoyle, Stirlingshire Map Ref: 1H3

The Forth Inn

Main Street, Aberfoyle, Stirlingshire, FK8 3UQ
Tel:01877 382372
Email:reception@forthinn.com
Web:www.forthinn.com

Family run Inn set at the heart of the Scotland's 1st National Park. Known locally as 'A Taste of Aberfoyle' we are 'Inn keeping with Tradition and Good Food'. 6 en-suite bedrooms with Dinner Bed & Breakfast available. Ideal location for exploring the Trossachs and Loch Lomond. Magnificent Baronial Function suite for up to 120 guests.

6 rooms, All en-suite. Open Jan-Dec. B&B per person, single from £45.00, double from £30.00.

34694 Aberfoyle, Stirlingshire Map Ref: 1H3

Rob Roy Hotel

Aberfoyle, Stirlingshire, FK8 3UX
Tel:01877 382245 Fax:01877 382262

104 rooms
All en-suite
Open Jan-Dec
B&B per person, single from £30.00, double from £25.00, BB & Eve.Meal from £30.00.

12606

Ardlui, Argyll | Map Ref: 1G3

Ardlui Hotel

Ardlui, Loch Lomond, Argyll, G83 7EB
Tel:01301 704269/243 Fax:01301 704268
Email:info@ardlui.co.uk
Web:www.ardlui.co.uk

Former shooting lodge on A82 and on the banks of Loch Lomond with private gardens to shore. Caravan site adjacent. Moorings available. 1 hour from Glasgow or Oban & 1½ hours from Fort William via Glencoe.

10 rooms, All en-suite. Open Jan-Dec excl Xmas. B&B per person, single from £50.00, double from £37.50.

62979

Arrochar, Argyll | Map Ref: 1G3

Village Inn

Main Street, Arrochar, Dunbartonshire, G83 7AX
Tel:01301 702279 Fax:01301 707455
Email:villageinn@maclay.co.uk
Web:www.maclay.com/VillageInn.html

Traditional village inn of character, with beautiful views over Loch Long to Ben Arthur - The Cobbler. Creative Scottish menus, using only fresh produce. Real log fire. 5 Minutes drive to Loch Lomond. Two ground floor rooms in annexed accommodation.

14 rooms, All en-suite. Open Jan-Dec. B&B per person, single from £50.00, double from £37.50.

79026

Balloch, Dunbartonshire | Map Ref: 1G4

Gowanlea

Drymen Road, Balloch, Dunbartonshire, G83 8HS
Tel:01389 752456
Email:gowanlea@blueyonder.co.uk

4 rooms
Open Jan-Dec
B&B per person, single from £40.00, double from £30.00.

76335

Balloch, Dunbartonshire | Map Ref: 1G4

Time Out

24 Balloch Road, Balloch, Dunbartonshire, G83 8LE
Tel:01389 755859
Email:stay@timeoutbb.co.uk
Web:www.timeoutbb.co.uk

5 rooms
All en-suite
Open Jan-Dec
B&B per person, single from £35.00, double from £25.00.

60676 Balloch, Dunbartonshire Map Ref: 1G4

Tullie Inn

Balloch Road, Balloch, Dunbartonshire, G83 8SW
Tel:01389 752052 Fax:01389 711639
Email:tullieinn@maclay.co.uk
Web:www.maclay.com

Twelve bedroom inn on the lochside in Balloch. Newly refurbished to a high standard with all ammenities nearby. A wide choice of traditional Scottish and international cuisine served in our restaurant and lounge bar. Excellent service. Warm & friendly welcome.

12 rooms, All en-suite. Open Jan-Dec. Rates on application.

74811 Callander, Perthshire Map Ref: 1H3

Annfield Guest House

18 North Church Street, Callander, Perthshire, FK17 8EG
Tel:01877 330204
Email:reservations@annfieldguesthouse.co.uk
Web:www.annfieldguesthouse.co.uk

7 rooms
Most en-suite
Open Jan-Dec
B&B per person, single from £25.00, double from £25.00.

58697 Callander, Perthshire Map Ref: 1H3

The Crags Hotel

101 Main Street, Callander, Perthshire, FK17 8BQ
Tel:01877 330257 Fax:01877 339997
Email:nieto@btinternet.com
Web:www.cragshotel.co.uk

7 rooms
All en-suite
Open Jan-Dec
B&B per person, single from £32.50, double from £25.00.

50139 Callander, Perthshire Map Ref: 1H3

Poppies Hotel and Restaurant

Leny Road, Callander, Perthshire, FK17 8AL
Tel:01877 330329
Web:www.poppieshotel.com

One of the most charming family run small hotels in The Trossachs. Excellent restaurant, Camerons whisky bar. Garden seating. Car parking. Warm hospitality. Close to town centre and wonderful countryside.

9 rooms, All en-suite. Open end Jan-Dec. B&B per person, single from £45.00, double from £35.00, superior from £45.00. Special Breaks all year.

51756 Callander, Perthshire Map Ref: 1H3

Riverview Guest House

Leny Road, Callander, Perthshire, FK17 8AL
Tel:01877 330635 Fax:01877 339386
Email:drew@visitcallander.co.uk
Web:www.visitcallander.co.uk

Detached stone built Victorian house set in its own garden with private parking. Close to town centre, leisure complex and local amenities. Within easy walking distance of pleasant riverside park and cycle track. Ideal base for exploring the beautiful Trossachs.

5 rooms, All en-suite. Open Mar-Nov. B&B per person, single from £27.50, double from £25.00.

51999 Callander, Perthshire Map Ref: 1H3

Roman Camp Hotel

Main Street, Callander, Perthshire, FK17 8BG
Tel:01877 330003 Fax:01877 331533
Email:mail@romancamphotel.co.uk
Web:www.romancamphotel.co.uk

Dating from 1625 and reminiscent of a miniature chateau, with 20 acres of beautiful gardens bordering the River Teith.

14 rooms, All en-suite. Open Jan-Dec. Rates on application.

38491 Dumbarton Map Ref: 1G5

Milton Inn

Dumbarton Road, Milton, Dunbartonshire, G82 2DT
Tel:01389 761401 Fax:01389 768858
Email:hfilshie@aol.com
Web:www.miltoninn.co.uk

Friendly family run Inn on A82, 4 miles drive from the southern end of Loch Lomond and 8 miles from Glasgow Airport via the Erskine Bridge. Regular evening entertainment. Some annexe accommodation.

19 rooms, All en-suite. Open Jan-Dec. B&B per room, single from £63.80, double from £81.40.

70170

Helensburgh, Argyll — Map Ref: 1G4

Bellfield

199 East Clyde Street, Helensburgh, Dunbartonshire, G84 7AJ
Tel:01436 673361
Email:r.callaghan@virgin.net
Web:www.scotland2000.com/bellfield

3 rooms
All en-suite
Open Jan-Dec
B&B per person, single from £35.00, double from £30.00.

26217

Helensburgh, Argyll — Map Ref: 1G4

Sinclair House

91/93 Sinclair Street, Helensburgh, Argyll & Bute, G84 8TR
Tel:01436 676301/0800 1646301
Email:enquiries@sinclairhouse.com
Web:www.sinclairhouse.com

Sinclair House is located in Helensburgh town centre with views over the Clyde Estuary from the upper rooms (3 & 4). As such, we are close to numerous restaurants, bars, shops and Helensburgh Central Railway Station. We like to spoil our guests, providing mini-fridges, free wireless internet access, freeview receivers and DVD Players in all rooms with over 400 free DVD movies available. See our website for full details.

4 rooms, All en-suite. Open Jan-Dec. B&B per person, single from £55.00, double from £27.50.

75801

Lochearnhead, Perthshire — Map Ref: 1H2

Mansewood Country House

Lochearnhead, Stirlingshire, FK19 8NS
Tel:01567 830213
Email:stay@mansewoodcountryhouse.co.uk
Web:www.mansewoodcountryhouse.co.uk

This is a family owned run guest house where a warm welcome awaits you. Relaxed and friendly atmosphere, amenities include log/coal fire in both lounge and dining room and a cosy residents' bar where you can enjoy a 'wee dram' or pre-dinner drink. Beautiful scenery, sailing on the loch, fishing, walking, golf all available. A great base to tour The Trossachs & Highlands.

6 rooms, All en-suite. Open Jan-Dec. B&B per person, single from £38.00, double from £28.00.

20059

Luss, Argyll & Bute — Map Ref: 1G4

Colquhoun Arms Hotel

Luss,by Alexandria, Dunbartonshire, G83 8NY
Tel:01436 860282 Fax:01436 860309
Email:reservations@lochlomondarms.co.uk
Web:www.lochlomondarms.co.uk

The Colquhoun Arms Hotel is a traditional family run coaching inn once frequented by Queen Victoria. The hotel is located by Loch Lomond in the village of Luss, which was made famous due to the filming of the Scottish Soap Opera, Take The High Road. The hotel has a number of 4 poster beds and the bar stocks over 100 single malt whiskies. Along with home made pub grub, coal fire and live Scottish music in the summer months the hotel offers that true Scottish ambience. Also on the site there is a tea room/coffee shop.

19 rooms.
Open Jan-Dec. Room only, single from £35.00, double from £58.00.

45485

Luss, Argyll & Bute — Map Ref: 1G4

Culag Lochside Guest House

Luss, Loch Lomond, G83 8PD
Tel:01436 860248
Web:www.culag.info

Set right on the Loch side with spacious patios for sundowns and wonderful views across to Ben Lomond and the Islands. Only 1 mile north of Luss with its restaurants. Ideally placed for day trips to the West Coast, Stirling and Glasgow. On the cycle path.

10 rooms, All en-suite. Open Jan-Dec excl Xmas/New Year.
B&B per person, single from £45.00, double from £30.00.

36217

Luss, Argyll & Bute — Map Ref: 1G4

The Lodge on Loch Lomond

Luss, Dunbartonshire, G83 8NT
Tel:01436 860201
Email:res@loch-lomond.co.uk
Web:www.loch-lomond.co.uk

48 rooms
All en-suite
Open Jan-Dec
B&B per person double/twin from £45.00-£125.00.

21184

Strathyre, Perthshire   Map Ref: 1H3

Creagan House Restaurant with Accommodation

Strathyre, Callander, Perthshire, FK18 8ND
Tel:01877 384638 Fax:01877 384319
Email:eatandstay@creaganhouse.co.uk
Web:www.creaganhouse.co.uk

5 rooms
All en-suite
Open Mar-Jan
B&B per person, single from £70.00, double from £60.00, BB & Eve.Meal from £88.00.

Sunset on Loch Lomond

Stirling Castle at dusk

Stirling and Forth Valley

Stirling and Forth Valley has a huge range of tourist attractions but one recent addition to the list is proving extremely popular. Built to celebrate the new Millennium and opened in 2002, The Falkirk Wheel is a triumph of engineering. It's the world's only rotating boat lift and, standing an impressive 24 metres high, it has reconnected the Forth & Clyde Canal with the Union Canal.

Scotland's industrial heritage is well represented locally at The Bo'ness and Kinneil Steam Railway, Birkhill Fireclay Mine and Callendar House, while you can see traces of Scotland's woollen industry on the opposite shores of the Forth in Clackmannan.

Around Stirling history is everywhere. Don't miss Stirling Castle and the Wallace Monument but remember to leave enough time to take a walk round the town and enjoy a spot of shopping too.

Port Street, Stirling

DON'T MISS

1 **Stirling Castle**, undoubtedly one of the finest in Scotland, sits high on its volcanic rock towering over the stunning countryside known as 'Braveheart Country'. A favourite royal residence over the centuries and a key military stronghold, see the Great Hall, the Chapel Royal, and the Renaissance Palace. From the Castle esplanade the sites of no less than seven historic battles can be seen, as can the majestic National Wallace Monument built in tribute to William Wallace.

2 The world's only rotating boatlift, **The Falkirk Wheel**, was constructed in 2002 to link the Forth & Clyde and Union canals. It is now possible for boats to traverse Central Scotland by canal for the first time in more than 40 years. Learn about Scotland's canal network in the visitor centre or board a vessel to take a trip on the mechanical marvel itself.

3 Just a few miles north west of Stirling on the A84 you will find **Blair Drummond Safari Park**. Here you can drive through wild animal reserves and get close to lions and zebras, and a whole host of other animals. Or you can park and walk around the pet farm, see the only elephants in Scotland, watch a sea lion display, find out what it's like to hold a bird of prey and take a boat to Chimp Island. There is also an adventure play area, pedal boats for hire and for the more adventurous – the flying fox!

4 Formerly known as 'Castle Gloom', **Castle Campbell** is beautifully sited at the head of Dollar Glen, immediately north of Dollar. Sitting in lofty isolation and overlooked by the Ochil Hills, the Castle became the chief Lowland stronghold of the Campbell clan, upon whose members the successive titles of Earl, Marquis and Duke of Argyll were bestowed. There are excellent walks through Dollar Glen to enjoy too.

2

4

FOOD AND DRINK

www.eatscotland.com

5 While in Stirling be sure to stop at the Portcullis Restaurant. Situated right next to the historic Stirling Castle the Portcullis was built in 1787 to serve the community as a school for boys. Today it offers a warm welcome, superb food, and a range of ales and wines, all served in cosy surroundings, complete with a real log fire in the winter months.

6 The lovely Victorian spa town of Bridge of Allan is home to the Bridge of Allan Brewery where you can see how traditional Scottish handcrafted ales are produced and even have a free tasting session!

7 Harviestoun Country Hotel & Restaurant in Tillicoultry is the perfect place to stop, whether it is for lunch, high tea or an evening meal. The restored 18th century steading, with the backdrop of the stunning Ochil Hills, is the ideal setting for relaxing with good food and fine wine.

HISTORY AND HERITAGE

8 Built in tribute to Scotland's national hero Sir William Wallace, the National Wallace Monument, by Stirling, can be seen for miles around. The Monument exhibition tells of William Wallace's epic struggle for a free Scotland.

9 On the site of the original battlefield, the Bannockburn Heritage Centre on the southern outskirts of Stirling, tells the story of the greatest victory of Scotland's favourite monarch King Robert the Bruce. Walk the battlefield and then enjoy the audio-visual presentation in the Centre, recounting the battle. A re-enactment of the battle takes place over two days every September.

10 Open the door to Callendar House in Falkirk, and you open the door to 600 years of Scottish history. Journey through time from the days of the Jacobites to the advent of the railway, and don't forget to stop at the Georgian kitchens for some refreshments prepared using authentic Georgian recipes.

11 The Tower Trail takes you for a tour around the amazing houses of the people who built Clackmannanshire - the 'Wee County'. These buildings show the changing fashion in tower building and are a great survival of the heritage of medieval Scotland, built by the families who shaped the later industrial development of the county.

12 Situated by the banks of the River Teith, Doune Castle was once the ancestral home of the Earls of Moray. At one time occupied by the Jacobite troops, this castle can now be explored and makes a great picnic spot.

WALKS

www.visitscotland.com/walking

13 The Antonine Wall dates back to the 2nd century and once marked the northern frontier of the Roman Empire. Substantial lengths have been preserved and can still be seen at various sites around Falkirk. Follow the wall for a relaxing walk along the towpath on the north of the canal, taking you past the Falkirk Wheel to Bonnybridge.

14 Not far from Dollar where the A823 meets the A977 it's worth stopping to explore the delightful Rumbling Bridge, so named because of the continuous rumbling sound of the falls and the river below. The unusual double bridge spans a narrow gorge and you'll find a network of platforms and paths that take you over the river and deep into the gorge with spectacular views of waterfalls and swirling pools.

15 At the heart of Clackmannanshire's 300-acre Gartmorn Dam Country Park, visitors can enjoy a short walk with gentle gradients suitable for wheelchairs or pushchairs. Gartmorn Dam is the oldest man-made reservoir still in use in Scotland, and is a nature reserve which is the winter home of thousands of migratory ducks.

16 The Darn Walk from Bridge of Allan to Dunblane is a beautiful walk which can be enjoyed at any time of the year. Highlights include a scenic stretch alongside the River Allan and the cave which was Robert Louis Stevenson's inspiration for Ben Gunn's cave in Treasure Island. The walk can be completed in 1½ to 2 hours.

13

17

18

ATTRACTIONS

17 Savour the evocative sights, sounds and smells of a nostalgic railway journey aboard the Bo'ness & Kinneil Steam Train. Your journey will take you to the cavernous Birkhill Fireclay Mine where you can learn about the 300 year old fossils of giant tree ferns.

18 Plenty of fun, with laughs and thrills in equal measure, Stirling Old Town Jail presents life in an authentic Victorian prison. You'll see wardens, prisoners and governors, and might even meet the notorious hangman! When you're finished, head across to the Tolbooth, the former city jail. Today, it's a vibrant music and arts venue with a superb bistro and restaurant.

19 Just north of Stirling, Argaty Red Kites is Scotland's only red kite feeding station. After 130 years Scottish Natural Heritage and the RSPB have reintroduced these exciting, acrobatic birds to central Scotland. Spend a day and you can enjoy a guided walk or just watch the birds from the hide.

67139 Bridge of Allan, Stirlingshire Map Ref: 2A3

Knockhill Guest House

Bridge of Allan, Stirling, FK9 4ND
Tel/Fax:01786 833123
Email:info@knockhillguesthouse.co.uk
Web:www.knockhillguesthouse.co.uk

6 double/twin, all en-suite
Open Jan-Dec
Rates on application.

50773 Bridge of Allan, Stirlingshire Map Ref: 2A3

The Queen's Hotel

24 Henderson Street, Bridge of Allan, Stirlingshire, FK9 4HP
Tel:01786 833268 Fax:01786 831335
Email:info@queenshotelscotland.com

16 rooms
All en-suite
Open Jan-Dec
Rates on application.

30612 Dunblane, Perthshire Map Ref: 2A3

Dunblane Hydro

Perth Road, Dunblane, Perthshire, FK15 0HG
Tel:01786 822551
Email:sales@dunblanehydrohotel.com
Web:www.dunblanehydrohotel.com

Idyllically located, Dunblane Hydro provides an ideal setting for short-breaks. Unwind in our health & fitness club. Sample fine Scottish cuisine and most of all enjoy being away from it all.

206 rooms, All en-suite. Open Jan-Dec. B&B per person, single from £60.00, double from £80.00.

16573 Menstrie, Clackmannanshire Map Ref: 2A3

Broomhall Castle

Long Row, Menstrie, Clackmannanshire, FK11 7EA
Tel:01259 760396
Email:info@broomhallcastle.co.uk
Web:www.broomhallcastle.co.uk

Refurbished 19th Century Castle set in its own grounds offering comfortable accommodation. 5 miles from Stirling Castle and within 5 mins drive to Stirling University and Wallace Monument.

10 rooms, All en-suite. Open Jan-Dec. B&B per room, single from £95.00, double from £95.00.

29679 Stirling Map Ref: 2A4

Harviestoun Country Hotel & Restaurant

Dollar Road, Tillicoultry, Clackmannanshire
FK13 6PQ
Tel:01259 752522 Fax:01259 752523
Email:harviestounhotel@aol.com

A stunningly converted listed steading. Privately owned and managed, our rooms are ensuite with some on the ground floor. Lounge with open fire, coffees, and homebaking. Restaurant serving A-La-Carte lunches, dinners and high teas. Non-resident breakfast Saturday and Sunday only. Suitable for conferences or small, intimate weddings. Ideally situated for touring, golfing or business. 'AILLST Best Hotel 2004'.

11 rooms, All en-suite. Open Jan-Dec. B&B per person, single from £60.00, double from £40.00.

33982 Stirling Map Ref: 2A4

King Robert Hotel

Glasgow Road, Bannockburn, Stirling, FK7 0LJ
Tel:01786 811666 Fax:01786 811507
Email:info@kingroberthotel.co.uk
Web:www.ladyglen.co.uk

52 rooms
All ensuite
B&B per person, single £39.00-59.00, double/twin £24.50-44.50.

SS Sir Walter Scott sailing on Loch Katrine

The Queen's View, Perthshire

PERTHSHIRE, ANGUS AND DUNDEE AND THE KINGDOM OF FIFE

Scotland's heartlands are the perfect holiday destination in many ways. There's so much to discover in this part of the world that you're sure to find something that suits you perfectly. Golfing, fishing, walking, sightseeing, there's an abundance of choice and there are some wonderful places to stay.

How about staying at one of the great international resort hotels in St Andrews or at Gleneagles where the rich and famous relax? Or you could choose a charming hotel in a holiday town like Pitlochry or a contemporary hotel on Dundee's lively quayside.

Wherever you go, there will be something to inspire you. Fife has an enviable coastline with a number of perfect little harbour towns. Perthshire is unspoiled and magnificent, with some of Scotland's finest woodlands and stunning lochs and hills. And then there's Dundee – the area's largest city. There's always another fascinating place waiting to be explored.

This is a holiday destination that can be as active as you want it to be. For the outdoor enthusiast, there's anything from hill walking to whitewater rafting and pretty much everything in between. Anglers love the thrill of pursuing salmon and trout on some of the country's greatest river beats or heading out to sea where the catch can be bountiful.

Golfers love this area too – some of the world's finest courses are here from the home of golf at St Andrews to championship quality greats like Gleneagles and Carnoustie, host of last year's Open.

If wildlife's your thing, there are many wonderful sights to see. In the countryside of Perthshire and the Angus Glens there are ospreys, eagles, otters, red squirrels and deer. By the sea from Fife to Angus there are opportunities to spot a wide variety of seabirds – especially around the Montrose Basin which attracts thousands of migrant species.

You don't have to be escaping civilisation to enjoy these parts, however. There are towns and cities that you'll enjoy enormously, each with their own unique attractions. Perth has specialist shops and high street retailers. St Andrews is a fine university town with a fascinating history. Dunfermline was once the seat of Scotland's Kings while Dundee, the City of Discovery is enjoying something of a renaissance these days and is a great place for a big day out.

Church Square, St Andrews, Fife

Dundee Contemporary Arts Centre, Dundee

What's On?

Snowdrop Festival 2008
1 February – 16 March 2008
www.visitscotland.com/snowdrops

StAnza 2008, St Andrews
13 – 16 March 2008
www.stanzapoetry.org

Perth Festival of the Arts
22 May - 1 June 2008
www.perthfestival.co.uk

Angus Glens Walking Festival
29 May - 1 June 2008
www.angusanddundee.co.uk/walkingfestival

Dundee Blues Bonanza
27 - 29 June 2008
www.dundeebluesbonanza.co.uk

Game Conservancy Scottish Fair, Scone Palace
4 - 6 July 2008
www.scottishfair.com

The Big Tent 2008: Scotland's Festival of Stewardship, Falkland
26 – 27 July 2008
www.bigtentfestival.co.uk

Pittenweem Arts Festival
2 – 10 August 2008
www.pittenweemartsfestival.co.uk

Blair Castle International Horse Trials, Blair Atholl
21-24 August 2008
www.blairhorsetrials.co.uk

Dundee Flower and Food Festival, Camperdown Park
5 - 7 September 2008
www.dundeeflowerandfoodfestival.com

Angus and Dundee Roots Festival
6 -13 September 2008
www.tayroots.com

The Enchanted Forest, Faskally Wood, by Pitlochry
17 October – 2 November 2008
www.enchantedforest.org.uk

www.perthshire.co.uk
www.angusanddundee.co.uk
www.visitfife.com

All dates correct at time of publication. Please check before booking. VisitScotland cannot be held responsible for any inaccuracies.

MAP

From Braemar
From Inverness
From Aberdeen
A9
A93
A924
Queen's View
B846
Rannoch
Pitlochry
Kirkmichael
Brechin
A935
A90
Montrose
Kirriemuir
Forfar
A932
A933
A92
Aberfeldy
A926
A923
Blairgowrie
A827
Dunkeld
A826
A984
A94
A928
Arbroath
A9
A93
A94
A923
A92
DUNDEE
A90
From Crianlarich
A822
A85
PERTH
Crieff
A92
St Andrews
A9
A913
A91
Cupar
A91
A915
A822
Auchterarder
A916
East Neuk
A917
Crail
A9
A823
A91
A911
Glenrothes
Leven
From Stirling
Kinross
A92
M90
A92
A955
Kirkcaldy
From Belgium
Dunfermline
A921
Culross
A985
North Queensferry
From Glasgow
Rosyth
From Edinburgh
©Collins Bartholomew Ltd 2007

TOURIST INFORMATION CENTRES

Perthshire	
Aberfeldy	The Square, Aberfeldy PH15 2DD
Blairgowrie	26 Wellmeadow, Blairgowrie PH10 6AS
Crieff	High Street, Crieff PH7 3HU
Dunkeld	The Cross, Dunkeld PH8 0AN
Perth	Lower City Mills, West Mill Street, Perth PH1 5QP
Pitlochry	22 Atholl Road, Pitlochry PH16 5BX
Angus and Dundee	
Arbroath	Harbour Visitor Centre, Fishmarket Quay, Arbroath DD11 1PS
Brechin	Brechin Castle Centre, Haughmuir, Brechin DD9 6RL
Dundee	21 Castle Street, Dundee DD1 3AA
Fife	
Dunfermline	1 High Street, Dunfermline KY12 7DL
Kirkcaldy	The Merchant's House, 339 High Street, Kirkcaldy KY1 1JL
St Andrews	70 Market Street, St Andrews KY16 9NU

Make the most of your stay in Scotland and make your first stop the Tourist Information Centre wherever you go.

Knowledgeable and friendly staff can help you with information and advice; they can answer your questions, book accommodation and you can even pick up some souvenirs to take home for friends and family.

For information and ideas about exploring Scotland in advance of your trip, call our booking and information service or go to **www.visitscotland.com**

Call 0845 22 55 121

or if calling from outside the UK call **+44 (0) 1506 832 121**

From Ireland call **1800 932 510**

A £4 booking fee applies to telephone bookings of accommodation.

Scottish Crannog Centre, Kenmore, Loch Tay

Perthshire

Perthshire is one of the most strikingly picturesque parts of Scotland. It ranges from the wild and mountainous to sophisticated and cultured; from the wilderness of Rannoch Moor to the lap of luxury at the 5-star Gleneagles Hotel.

You can experience everything in Perthshire from traditional activities like golf, fishing and field sports to more recent innovations like sphereing and white water rafting. Whatever activities you pursue, it will be against a backdrop of spectacular scenery; high mountains, deep forests, sparkling lochs and wide rivers.

But you don't have to spend the day pushing yourself to the limits, a walk through Perthshire's wonderful woodlands may suffice. Or you could take a romantic stroll around the Birks of Aberfeldy, visit some of Britain's most colourful gardens, marvel at a reconstructed Iron Age crannog on Loch Tay or simply enjoy the Queen's View near Pitlochry.

The Famous Grouse Experience, Crieff

DON'T MISS

1 The **Scottish Crannog Centre** at Kenmore on Loch Tay is an authentic recreation of an ancient loch-dwelling. Imagine a round house in the middle of a loch with a thatched roof, on stilts. You can tour the Crannog to see how life used to be 2,600 years ago. Upon your return to shore, have a go at a variety of Iron Age crafts; see if you can grind the grain, drill through stone or make fire through wood friction.

2 **Scone Palace**, near Perth, was renowned as the traditional crowning palace of Scottish kings, as the capital of the Pictish kingdom and centre of the ancient Celtic Church. Nowadays, the great house and its beautiful accompanying grounds are home to the Earls of Mansfield, and offer an ideal day out.

3 **Blair Castle**, the stunningly situated ancient seat of the Dukes and Earls of Atholl, is a 5-star castle experience. The unmistakeable white façade is visible from the A9 just north of Blair Atholl. Dating back 740 years, the Castle has played a part in some of Scotland's most tumultuous events but today is a relaxing and fascinating place.

4 **The Famous Grouse Experience** is housed within Glenturret, Scotland's oldest malt whisky distillery. It is an interactive attraction where visitors can familiarise themselves with this renowned tipple and the brand that accompanies it! As well as a tour of the production areas, you can enjoy a unique audio-visual presentation which gives a grouse's eye view of Scotland.

5 Among its many other attractions, Perthshire – known as **Big Tree Country** - can boast some of the most remarkable trees and woodlands anywhere in Europe. Its forests, woods and country gardens offer an unsurpassed assortment of glorious greenery that is home to many different species of wildlife. Here you'll discover Europe's oldest tree in Fortingall Churchyard, the world's highest hedge and one of Britain's tallest trees at The Hermitage by Dunkeld.

6 Enjoy the renowned **Queen's View** by Loch Tummel. Although a favourite spot of Queen Victoria it was actually named after Isabella, wife of King Robert the Bruce. The viewpoint is well signposted from the A9 just north of Pitlochry and there is a fascinating visitor centre and café.

3

5

FOOD AND DRINK

www.eatscotland.com

7 Farmers' markets have seen something of resurgence in recent years in the UK and **Perth's Farmers' Market** is arguably the best know in Scotland. Taking place throughout the year on the first Saturday of each month, it is a showcase for local producers and growers. Look out for fish, meat and game, baked goods, fruit wines and liqueurs, honeys and preserves, fruit and vegetables, sweets and herbs.

8 The area around Blairgowrie is Europe's centre for soft fruit production and a particular feature of the area are the signs at farms inviting you to 'pick your own' strawberries, raspberries, gooseberries, redcurrants, and tayberries. Sample the local produce at **Cairn o' Mohr Wines** in Errol. A family-run business it produces truly unique Scottish fruit wines. Explore the winery and have a tasting session!

9 **Edradour Distillery** – Scotland's smallest malt whisky distillery - can be found in the Highland foothills just to the east of Pitlochry. Built in the early 19th century Edradour is the only remaining 'farm' distillery in Perthshire and sometimes it seems to have hardly changed in 170 years. Enjoy a guided tour and relax with a wee dram.

10 **Gloagburn Farm Shop and Restaurant** at Tibbermore near Perth is a rare gem of a food stop. A great menu is created from local produce, as much as possible reared or grown at the farm itself. The sandwiches and soup are superb and nutritious, or treat yourself to some of the mouth-watering cakes. Stock up on your way out at the farm shop.

9

11

12

WALKS

www.visitscotland.com/walking

11 The 63-mile circular **Cateran Trail**, through Perthshire and the Angus Glens, follows paths used by 15th century Caterans (cattle rustlers). Complete the whole route in a leisurely five days or enjoy a shorter section on a day's walk. Take in the soft contours of Strathardle on the Bridge of Cally to Kirkmichael section or head for the hills between Kirkmichael and the Spittal of Glenshee.

12 Revered in poetry by the national bard, Robert Burns, the **Birks of Aberfeldy** ('birks' being the old Scots for birch trees) line a short walk alongside the Moness Burn, reached from Aberfeldy town centre or a car park on the Crieff Road. A circular path leads to a beautiful waterfall, where birds and flowers are abundant.

13 **Killiecrankie**, just north of Pitlochry, is known for two reasons – the famous battle in 1689 and its status as a Site of Special Scientific Interest. The visitor centre has a seasonal interactive wildlife display and, together with the café and shop, makes for an interesting stop.

14 On the A9, 1 mile west of Dunkeld, you'll find **The Hermitage**. A beautiful walk along the banks of the River Braan takes you to the focal point, Ossian's Hall set in a picturesque gorge and overlooking Black Linn Falls. Ask the local rangers for advice or read the display panels as you pass amidst the huge Douglas Firs en route.

WILDLIFE

www.visitscotland.com/wildlife

15 **Loch Leven National Nature Reserve**, near Kinross, incorporates the largest loch in Lowland Scotland and is one of the most important sites for waterfowl in Britain. It attracts the largest concentration of breeding ducks in the UK, and many thousands of migratory ducks, geese and swans. Start your visit at RSPB Vane Farm which has excellent observation hides.

16 Visit **Loch of the Lowes** between April and August and there's every chance you'll encounter its famous nesting ospreys. The Scottish Wildlife Trust's visitor centre provides interpretation on the birds, which migrate to Scotland from their winter homes in West Africa. There are also telescopes and binoculars on hand to give you a better view. Between October and March, the nature reserve is worth visiting for the sheer numbers of wildfowl.

17 **Blair Castle Deer Park**, located in the grounds of Blair Castle, has a small herd of native red deer including an impressive stag. Red squirrels, a species now rare in many parts of Britain, are also a common sight in the woods around Atholl Estates. For a good chance of seeing one try the mile-long Red Squirrel Trail starting from Glen Tilt car park.

18 Each year between April and October an average of 5,400 salmon fight their way upstream and must by-pass the Hydro-Electric Dam at Pitlochry by travelling through the interconnected pools that form the **Pitlochry 'fish ladder'**. Witness it all at a very special attraction.

15

19

21

ADVENTURE

www.visitscotland.com/adventure

In this area you'll find over 35 different adventure activities! Here's a selection:

19 Perthshire is renowned for its stunning lochs and rivers, many of which are excellent for **white water rafting**. A truly unforgettable experience awaits you with a spectacular combination of rugged Highland scenery and the adrenaline rush of this activity. Get some friends together and go for it!

20 Perthshire is the only place in Scotland where you can try **sphereing**. It involves a huge 12ft inflatable ball which the willing participants strap themselves safely into and then take a wild and bouncy tumble down the hill. This one already has thrill seekers and outdoor enthusiasts queuing up!

21 Wet, wild and wonderful - **canyoning** is all this and more! Unleash your adrenaline streak as you swim through rapids, cliff jump into deep clear pools, abseil through waterfalls and slide down natural stone 'flumes'. This one is awesome and not to be missed!

22 If you enjoy wide-open spaces try a **microlight** flight for the nearest experience to flying like a bird. With the latest microlight technology, enjoy up to 60 miles of spectacular views and scenery in one hour. This is a great way to enjoy the Perthshire landscape as well as being the experience of a lifetime.

23 Try to imagine descending fast whitewater in a cross between a raft and an armchair armed with your wet suit, bouyancy aid, helmet, and hand and feet flippers ... the reality is **river bugging** and participants are called 'buggers' so strap in, sit back and go crazy!

26626 **Aberfeldy, Perthshire** Map Ref: 2A1

Fortingall Hotel

Fortingall, Aberfeldy, Perthshire, PH15 2NQ
Tel/Fax:01887 830367
Email:hotel@fortingallhotel.com
Web:www.fortingallhotel.com

Award-winning small country hotel set in the beautiful arts and crafts village of Fortingall. Boasting comfortable en-suite bedrooms and welcoming public rooms, it offers excellent cuisine using locally-sourced and Scottish produce in the elegant dining room or cosy public bar. With a wide range of activities on the doorstep, the hotel is a welcoming centre for touring, walking, fishing and field sports.

10 rooms, Room per night, single from £95.00, double £140.00-185.00.. Rates include breakfast..

38837 **Aberfeldy, Perthshire** Map Ref: 2A1

The Moness House Hotel & Country Club

Crieff Road, Aberfeldy, Perthshire, PH15 2DY
Tel:0870 4431460 Fax:0870 4431461
Email:info@moness.com
Web:www.moness.com

Former hunting lodge dating from 1758, situated in thirty five acres, on the south side of Aberfeldy. Onsite leisure centre, bar and restaurant, including indoor heated pool.

12 rooms, All en-suite. Open Jan-Dec. B&B per person, single £41.00-65.00, double £26.00-50.00, BB & Eve.Meal from £41.00-65.00.

C £ V

11828 **Alyth, Perthshire** Map Ref: 2C1

Alyth Hotel

6 Commercial Street, Alyth, Perthshire, PH11 8AT
Tel:01828 632447
Web:www.info@alythhotel.com

Traditional, family-run inn. Scottish food, music and a warm Scottish welcome. Specialist in golf, shooting and fishing packages.

10 rooms, All en-suite. Open Jan-Dec. Room only, single from £65.00, double from £65.00.

PERTHSHIRE

34851 Alyth, Perthshire Map Ref: 2C1

Lands of Loyal Hotel

Loyal Road, Alyth, Blairgowrie, PH11 8JQ
Tel:01828 633151 Fax:01828 633313
Email:info@landsofloyal.com
Web:www.landsofloyal.com

Country house with magnificent views of surrounding countryside. Central for many sports: walking, fishing, golf. Delicious food, fresh ingredients.

16 rooms, All en-suite. Open Jan-Dec. B&B per person, single from £82.50, double from £62.50 pp. BB & Eve.Meal from £90.50.

TV P C V

17405 Auchterarder, Perthshire Map Ref: 2B3

Cairn Lodge Hotel

Orchil Road, Auchterarder, Perthshire, PH3 1LX
Tel:01764 662634 Fax:01764 664866
Email:email@cairnlodge.co.uk
Web:www.cairnlodge.co.uk

Sitting proudly in beautiful gardens and fronted by Queen Victoria's Commemorative Jubilee Cairn, the Cairn Lodge neighbours the world famous Gleneagles complex on the edge of Auchterarder. Beautiful and luxuriously appointed en-suite accommodation, the elegant 'Capercaillie' à la carte restaurant and the new Jubilee Lounge, all add up to one of Perthshire's premier county house hotel and restaurants. B&B from £60.00 pppn. Short breaks: 3 nights for price of 2 subject to availability.

10 rooms.
All en-suite. B&B per person, single from £75.00, double from £60.00.

TV P C V

59091 Auchterarder, Perthshire Map Ref: 2B3

The Gleneagles Hotel

Auchterarder, Perthshire, PH3 1NF
Tel:01764 662231 Fax:01764 662134
Email:resort.sales@gleneagles.com
Web:www.gleneagles.com

232 rooms
All en-suite
Open Jan-Dec
B&B per room, double from £385.00.

TV P C V

15316

Blackford, Perthshire — Map Ref: 2A3

Blackford Hotel

Moray Street, Blackford, Perthshire, PH4 1QF
Tel:01764 682497 Fax:01764 682597
Email:info@blackfordhotel.co.uk
Web:www.blackfordhotel.co.uk

Former Coaching Inn, which dates back to the 1830's is situated in the charming village of Blackford, in the heart of Scotland and amidst the hill and rivers of Perthshire. A warm, cosy, friendly and privately run hotel which is ideally placed only 50 minutes from Edinburgh or Glasgow.

8 rooms, All en-suite. Open Jan-Dec. B&B per person, single from £37.50, double from £37.50.

13304

Blair Atholl, Perthshire — Map Ref: 4C12

Atholl Arms Hotel

Old North Road, Blair Atholl, by Pitlochry,
Perthshire, PH18 5SG
Tel:01796 481205
Email:info@athollarmshotel.co.uk
Web:www.athollarmshotel.co.uk

Scottish Baronial style Highland Hotel, in centre of Blair Atholl, close to castle. Offering traditional Scottish Hospitality and good base to tour the central highlands. Enjoy the Atholl experience all the year around.

31 rooms, All en-suite. B&B per room, single from £30.00-75.00. double/twin from £60.00-110.00.

11779

Blairgowrie, Perthshire — Map Ref: 2B1

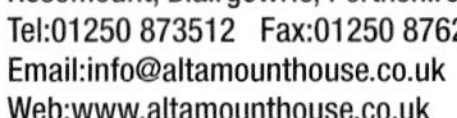

Altamount Country House Hotel

Rosemount, Blairgowrie, Perthshire, PH10 6JN
Tel:01250 873512 Fax:01250 876200
Email:info@altamounthouse.co.uk
Web:www.altamounthouse.co.uk

18 rooms
All en-suite
Open Jan-Dec
B&B per person, single from £60.00, double from £50.00.

12138 Blairgowrie, Perthshire Map Ref: 2B1

Angus Hotel

Wellmeadow, Blairgowrie, Perthshire, PH10 6NQ
Tel:01250 872455
Email:reservations@theangushotel.com
Web:www.theangushotel.com

Privately owned hotel situated in the centre of the country town of Blairgowrie. Excellent central base for exploring the area, whether to Perth and Dundee, or Braemar, Glamis and Balmoral. Great golf, fishing and activities available locally plus swimming pool, spa-bath, sauna, solarium and treatment room within hotel leisure complex.

89 rooms, All en-suite. Open Jan-Dec. B&B from £40.00, BB & Eve.Meal from £55.00.

16499 Blairgowrie, Perthshire Map Ref: 2B1

Broadmyre Motel

Carsie, Blairgowrie, Perthshire, PH10 6QW
Tel/Fax:01250 873262

5 rooms
Some en-suite
Open Jan-Dec
B&B per person, single from £17.00, double from £18.00, BB & Eve.Meal from £28.00.

52471 Blairgowrie, Perthshire Map Ref: 2B1

Royal Hotel

53 Allan Street, Blairgowrie, Perthshire, PH10 6AB
Tel:01250 872226 Fax:01250 875905
Email:visit@theroyalhotel.org.uk
Web:www.theroyalhotel.org.uk

27 rooms
All en-suite
Open Jan-Dec
B&B per person from £37.00.

72382 Bridge of Cally, Perthshire Map Ref: 2B1

Bridge of Cally Hotel

Bridge of Cally, Blairgowrie, Perthshire, PH10 7JJ
Tel:01250 886231
Email:enquiries@bridgeofcallyhotel.com
Web:www.bridgeofcallyhotel.com

"In the Heart of Northern Perthshire" and surrounded by some of Scotland's finest mountains, rivers, walks and scenery. The hotel offers a warm and friendly welcome, menus created from locally sourced ingredients, very comfortable accommodation and a truly relaxing experience.

18 rooms, All en-suite. Open Jan-Dec. B&B per person, single from £40.00, double from £35.00.

25760 **Crieff, Perthshire** Map Ref: 2A2

Fendoch Guest House

Sma' Glen, Crieff, Perthshire, PH7 3LW
Tel:01764 653446/655619 Fax:01764 653446
Email:bookings@fendoch.co.uk
Web:www.fendoch.co.uk

4 rooms
All en-suite
Open Jan-Dec
B&B per person, single from £23.00, double from £23.00, BB & Eve.Meal from £35.00.

33408 **Crieff, Perthshire** Map Ref: 2A2

Kingarth

Perth Road, Crieff, Perthshire, PH7 3EQ
Tel:01764 652060
Email:info@kingarthguesthouse.com
Web:www.kingarthguesthouse.com

Set in the heart of Scotland, in the bustling town of Crieff, Kingarth is a homely Victorian guest house set in mature gardens, with stunning views overlooking the Strathearn Vale and Ochil Hills. The house has a relaxed, comfortable atmosphere with a cosy residents' lounge, sunny conservatory and dining room. The letting rooms are in the garden wing of the house, and are all ground floor, ensuite and non-smoking. There is ample parking.

6 rooms, All en-suite. Open Jan-Dec. B&B per person, single from £30.00-35.00, double from £27.00.

23742 **Dunkeld, Perthshire** Map Ref: 2B1

Royal Dunkeld Hotel

Atholl Street, Dunkeld, PH8 0AR
Tel:01350 727322 Fax:01350 728989
Email:reservations@royaldunkeld.co.uk
Web:www.royaldunkeld.co.uk

Personally run, early 19c coaching inn, situated in centre of historic town of Dunkeld. Golfing breaks and fishing packages a speciality. Some annexe bedrooms.

34 rooms, All en-suite. Open Jan-Dec. B&B per person, single from £49.00, double from £34.00, BB & Eve.Meal from £52.00.

64913 **Glenshee, Perthshire** Map Ref: 4D12

Dalmunzie

Spittal of Glenshee, Blairgowrie, Perthshire
PH10 7QG
Tel:01250 885224 Fax:01250 885225
Email:reservations@dalmunzie.com
Web:www.dalmunzie.com

16 rooms
Open Dec 28-Nov 30
B&B per person, single from £63.00, double from £45.00, Dinner £30.00.

23522 **Kinloch Rannoch, Perthshire** Map Ref: 1H1

Dunalastair Hotel

The Square, Kinloch Rannoch, Perthshire, PH16 5PW
Tel:01882 632218 Fax:01882 632371
Email:stay@dunalastair.co.uk
Web:www.dunalastair.co.uk

28 rooms
All en-suite
Open all year round
B&B per person, single from £37.50, double from £37.50.

28960 **Kinross, Perthshire** Map Ref: 2B3

The Green Hotel

2 The Muirs, Kinross, KY13 8AS
Tel:01577 863467 Fax:01577 863180
Email:reservations@green-hotel.com
Web:www.green-hotel.com

Ideally located in central Scotland. This is one of Scotland's fine independently owned country house hotels. 46 spacious bedrooms equipped to the highest standard. The leisure complex has indoor pool, sauna, exercise facility and squash court plus a four sheet curling rink in season. The hotel has 2 '18 hole' golf courses and trout fishing can be arranged on nearby Loch Leven.

46 rooms, All en-suite. Open Jan-Dec. B&B per person, single from £95.00, double/twin from £85.00, BB & Eve.Meal from £75.00 pp sharing twin/double, min 2 night stay.

79591 **Kinross, Perthshire** Map Ref: 2B3

Kirklands Hotel

20 High Street, Kinross, Perthshire, KY13 8AN
Tel:01577 863313 Fax:01577 864440
Email:info@thekirklandshotel.com
Web:www.thekirklandshotel.com

This newly refurbished original coaching inn boasts 9 en-suite bedrooms. Enjoy the best of contemporary Scottish cuisine in our restaurant, or relax with a drink in front of one of our open fires.

9 rooms, All en-suite. Open Jan-Dec excl Xmas/New Year. B&B per person, single from £38.00, double/twin from £33.00.

76310 Kinross, Perthshire Map Ref: 2B3

Windlestrae Hotel

The Muirs, Kinross, Perthshire, KY13 8AS
Tel:01577 863217 Fax:01577 864733
Email:reservations@windlestraehotel.com
Web:www.windlestraehotel.com

The Windlestrae Hotel offers forty seven spacious bedrooms. Beautifully situated within landscaped gardens close to Loch Leven and to the hotel's two golf courses. Leisure Club facilities on site including a twenty metre indoor pool. Fine dining and weddings catered for, the hotel also having extensive conferencing facilities.

47 rooms, All en-suite. Open Jan-Dec. Rates on application.

11006 Loch Earn, Perthshire Map Ref: 1H2

Achray House Hotel & Lodges

St Fillans, Perthshire, PH6 2NF
Tel:01764 685231 Fax:01764 685320
Email:info@achray-house.co.uk
Web:www.achray-house.co.uk

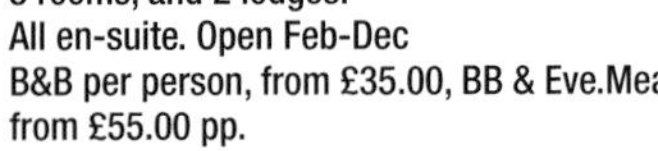

Relaxing, Walking, Golfing, Talking.Nestled in the tranquil village of St Fillans on the banks of Loch Earn inside the boundaries of the Loch Lomond and Trossachs National Park, Achray House is an ideal base to explore the treasures of Scotland. A warm welcome, relaxing atmosphere and beautiful scenery blend together to make a visit to the Achray House something to remember. The best of Scottish produce including local game, farming goods and seafood from the West Coast is used by Andrew Scott (owner/chef) and his team to prepare daily changing traditional dishes and those in the modern Scottish style.

AA ★★★

8 rooms, and 2 lodges.
All en-suite. Open Feb-Dec
B&B per person, from £35.00, BB & Eve.Meal from £55.00 pp.

26668

Loch Earn, Perthshire Map Ref: 1H2

The Four Seasons Hotel

St Fillans, Perthshire, PH6 2NF
Tel:01764 685333
info@thefourseasonshotel.co.uk
www.thefourseasonshotel.co.uk

The natural beauty of this location, looking down Loch Earn, is one of the most enviable settings in Scotland. The views are ever-changing, fresh colours of spring, light summer's evenings, spectacular sunsets, morning mists shrouding the loch and the snow covered Bens. Award winning fine dining restaurant serving Contemporary Scottish cuisine, at Two AA Red Rosettes, or informal bar meals, using the best ingredients sourced from Scotland's natural larder. Situated in Scotland's finest National Park we are well placed for touring, great variety of walking, thirty five golf courses and great cycle routes. Individually decorated lochview bedrooms and four poster rooms.

12 rooms.
All en-suite. Open Mar-Jan
B&B per person, single from £48.00, double from £48.00, BB & Eve.Meal from £77.00.

10981

Perth Map Ref: 2B2

Achnacarry Guest House

3 Pitcullen Crescent, Perth, PH2 7HT
Tel:01738 621421
Email:info@achnacarry.co.uk
Web:www.achnacarry.co.uk

4 rooms
All en-suite
Open Jan-Dec
B&B per person, single £30.00-40.00, double/twin £25.00-30.00 pp.

11010

Perth Map Ref: 2B2

Ackinnoull Guest House

5 Pitcullen Crescent, Perth, PH2 7HT
Tel:01738 634165
Web:www.ackinnoull.com

4 rooms
All en-suite
Open Jan-Dec
B&B per person, single from £25.00-30.00, double from £22.00-24.00.

12833

Perth Map Ref: 2B2

Arisaig Guest House

4 Pitcullen Crescent, Perth, PH2 7HT
Tel:01738 628240 Fax:01738 638521
Email:mail@arisaigonline.co.uk
Web:www.arisaigonline.co.uk

5 rooms
All en-suite
Open Jan-Dec
B&B per person, single from £30.00-35.00, double/twin £27.50-30.00.

IMPORTANT: PRICES STATED ARE ESTIMATES AND MAY BE SUBJECT TO AMENDMENTS
FOR A FULL LISTING OF QUALITY ASSURED ACCOMMODATION, PLEASE SEE DIRECTORY AT BACK OF THIS GUIDE

14653 Perth Map Ref: 2B2

Beechgrove Guest House

Dundee Road, Perth, PH2 7AQ
Tel/Fax:01738 636147
Email:beechgrove@btconnect.com
Web:www.smoothhound.co.uk/hotels/beechgr

Listed building, former manse (Rectory) set in extensive grounds. Peaceful, yet only a few minutes walk from the city centre. Close to local attractions e.g. Scone Palace, Branklyn Gardens, Blackwatch Museum, new Perth Concert Hall just over bridge. Many award winning restaurants closeby. GlenTurret Tourism award winner. Non-smoking establishment.

8 rooms, All en-suite. Open Jan-Dec. B&B per person, single from £40.00, double from £35.00. Non smoking establishment.

C £ V

36471 Perth Map Ref: 2B2

Best Western Queens Hotel

105 Leonard Street, Perth, Perthshire, PH2 8HB
Tel:01738 442222 Fax:01738 638496
Email:email@queensperth.co.uk
Web:www.symphonyhotels.co.uk

Privately owned and family run hotel ideally situated in city centre with ample free car-parking. High quality bedrooms, function and conference facilities. Leisure club including pool, jacuzzi, sauna, steam bath and gym. Free WIFI available.

51 rooms, All en-suite. Open Jan-Dec. B&B per person, single from £79.50, double from £49.50.

C £ V

25389 Perth Map Ref: 2B2

Scottish TOURIST BOARD ★★★ LODGE

Express by Holiday Inn

200 Dunkeld Road, Inveralmond, Perth, Perthshire, PH1 3AQ
Tel:01738 636666 Fax:01738 633363
Email:info@hiexpressperth.co.uk
Web:www.hiexpress.com/perthscotland

81 rooms
All en-suite
Open Jan-Dec
Rates on application.

78462 Perth — Map Ref: 2B2

Grampian Hotel

37 York Place, Perth, Perthshire, PH2 8EH
Tel:01738 621057 Fax:01738 445363
Email:reservations@grampianhotel.co.uk
Web:www.grampianhotel.co.uk

Family run hotel, situated in the centre of Perth five minutes walk from train station, cinema, theatre and leisure pool. All bedrooms en-suite with television and hospitality tray. Relax in our traditional lounge bar and restaurant serving lunches, high-teas and evening meals.

12 rooms, All en-suite. Open Jan-Dec. Single £55.00-£65.00 pp, Double/Twin £35.00-£55.00 pp, Executive Double £45.00-£65.00 pp

59770 Perth — Map Ref: 2B2

The New County Hotel

22-30 County Place, Perth, PH2 8EE
Tel:01738 623355 Fax:01738 628909
Email:enquiries@newcountyhotel.com
Web:www.newcountyhotel.com

23 rooms
All en suite
Rates on application

60259 Perth — Map Ref: 2B2

The Royal George

Tay Street, Perth, PH1 5LD
Tel:01738 624455
Web:www.theroyalgeorgehotel.co.uk

The Royal George Hotel, with its Royal Commission from Queen Victoria, overlooks the River Tay in the heart of historic Perth. Close to Scone Palace, Perth Racecourse, Black Watch Museum and Huntingtower Castle ensuring there is something for everyone. Offering charming accommodation for both the tourist and business visitor, a fine restaurant, conference and wedding facilities, and unspoilt views of the River Tay.100 metres from new Concert hall

43 rooms, All en-suite. Open Jan-Dec. Rates on application.

56942 Perth Map Ref: 2B2

Salutation Hotel

34 South Street, Perth, PH2 8PH
Tel:01738 630066 Fax:01738 633598
Email:salessalutation@stathmorehotels.com
Web:www.strathmorehotels.com

One of Scotlands oldest established hotels, recently modernised with a lift and accessible bedrooms. Ideally located in Perth with shops and local attractions nearby. An ideal base for exploring and touring Scotland.

84 rooms, All en-suite. Open Jan-Dec. B&B per person, single from £54.00, double from £46.00.

36470 Perth Map Ref: 2B2

Symphony Lovat Hotel

Glasgow Road, Perth, Perthshire, PH2 0LT
Tel:01738 636555 Fax:01738 643123
Email:enquiry@lovat.co.uk
Web:www.symphonyhotels.co.uk

Excellent location close to city centre with private free parking with facilities that include good quality bedrooms, function/conference rooms and large bar/restaurant.

30 rooms, All en-suite. Open Jan-Dec. B&B per person, single from £70.00, double from £45.00.

63893 Perth Map Ref: 2B2

Westview Bed & Breakfast

49 Dunkeld Road, Perth, PH1 5RP
Tel:01738 627787 Tel/Fax:01738 447790
Email:angiewestview@aol.com

4 rooms
3 en-suite
Open Jan-Dec
B&B per person, single from £30.00, double from £25.00, BB & Eve.Meal from £35.00.

64560 Perth Map Ref: 2B2

Woodlea Hotel

23 York Place, Perth, Perthshire, PH2 8EP
Tel/Fax:01738 621744
Email:info@woodleaperthuk.co.uk
Web:www.woodleaperthuk.co.uk

12 rooms
All en-suite
Open Jan-Dec
B&B per person, single from £36.00, double from £30.00.

10919

Pitlochry, Perthshire Map Ref: 2A1

Acarsaid Hotel and Lodge

8 Atholl Road, Pitlochry, Perthshire, PH16 5BX
Tel:01796 472389 Fax:01796 473952
Email:mail@mpmhotels.com
Web:www.acarsaidhotel.co.uk

Acarsaid Hotel and Lodge is an informal, relaxed, family run hotel. The hotel is located close to the centre of Pitlochry and has ample parking. Originally the hotel and lodge were large private homes, built in the late 19th century. Both houses have been extensively developed and now have an eclectic mix of traditional and contemporary, married with a fantastic modern approach to customer service. Food is uncomplicated and compiled with produce sourced as locally as possible.

29 rooms, All en-suite. Open Jan-Dec. B&B per person, single from £36.00, double from £34.00.

65011

Pitlochry, Perthshire Map Ref: 2A1

Atholl Palace Hotel

Pitlochry, Perthshire, PH16 5LY
Tel:01796 472400 Fax:01796 473036
Email:info@athollpalace.com
Web:www.athollpalace.com

90 rooms
All en-suite
Open Jan-Dec
B&B per person £64.00-92.00 single or double. BB & Eve.Meal £79.00-109.00 single or double.

21006

Pitlochry, Perthshire Map Ref: 2A1

Craigmhor Lodge

27 West Moulin Road, Pitlochry, Perthshire, PH16 5EF
Tel/Fax:01796 472123
Email:craigmhorlodge.co.uk
Web:www.craigmhorlodge.co.uk

Craigmhor Lodge is a spectacular Victorian House with tastefully furnished bedrooms and large public rooms. Set in its own grounds it has a fabulous setting with ample parking and wonderful views across the Tummel Valley. Breakfast at Craigmhor Lodge is a highlight - you may have a wonderful Continental Hamper in your bedroom or opt for our Full Scottish Breakfast in the Conservatory. New for 2008: The development of 12 deluxe bedroom suites with 6ft beds, flat screen TV's and wonderful furnishings and fabrics. Each room has an individual contemporary design using muted colours inspired from the textures and colours of the Perthshire countryside. Luxurious bathrooms have underfloor heating with free standing baths and walk in drench showers for the ultimate soak!

8 rooms.
All en-suite. Open Jan-Dec
B&B per person, single from £45.00, double from £30.00.

23616

Pitlochry, Perthshire — **Map Ref: 2A1**

Dundarach Hotel

Perth Road, Pitlochry, Perthshire, PH16 5DJ
Tel:01796 472862 Fax:01796 473024
Email:stb@dundarach.co.uk
Web:www.dundarach.co.uk

40 rooms
All en-suite
Open Feb-Dec excl Xmas/New Year
B&B per person, single from £30.00, double from £30.00.

25685

Pitlochry, Perthshire — **Map Ref: 2A1**

Fasganeoin Country House

Perth Road, Pitlochry, PH16 5DJ
Tel:01796 472387 Fax:01796 474285
Email:sabrina@fasganeoin.freeserve.co.uk
Web:www.fasganeoincountryhouse.co.uk

A long established family run country house with the accent on traditional values of hospitality and service. Dating from the 1870s and set in spacious, secluded gardens, it stands on the edge of town, close to the theatre. Food is available throughout the day in the form of light snacks, home baking and tasty theatre suppers.

8 rooms, 6 en-suite, 2 with priv.facilities. Open Apr-mid Oct. B&B per person, single from £28.00, en-suite double from £35.00, BB & Eve.Meal from £45.50.

59154

Pitlochry, Perthshire — **Map Ref: 2A1**

The Green Park Hotel

Clunie Bridge Road, Pitlochry, Perthshire,
PH16 5JY
Tel:01796 473248 Fax:01796 473520
Email:bookings@thegreenpark.co.uk
Web:www.thegreenpark.co.uk

Family run country house hotel enjoying spectacular views over Loch Faskally. Within strolling distance of the shops and a pleasant walk from the Festival Theatre, the hotel has become a well known landmark of the town. The hotel has a Red Rossette for food, reflecting the emphasis placed on the food served at the Green Park.

51 rooms, All en-suite. Open Jan-Dec. B&B per person, single from £42.00, double from £42.00, BB & Eve.Meal from £58.00.

34468 Pitlochry, Perthshire Map Ref: 2A1

Knockendarroch House Hotel

Higher Oakfield, Pitlochry, Perthshire, PH16 5HT
Tel:01796 473473 Fax:01796 474068
Email:bookings@knockendarroch.co.uk
Web:www.knockendarroch.co.uk

A grand Victorian mansion with stunning views in 1.5 acres of grounds in the heart of Pitlochry. Personal attention and a great location make this a perfect base for exploring Perthshire and the central Highlands.

12 rooms, All en-suite. Open Feb-Dec. BB & Eve.Meal from £50.00.

72825 Pitlochry, Perthshire Map Ref: 2A1

Loch Tummel Inn

Queens View, Strathtummel, Pitlochry, Perthshire, PH16 5RP
Tel/Fax:01882 634272
Email:info@lochtummelinn.co.uk
Web:www.lochtummelinn.co.uk

7 rooms
Open all year round
B&B per person, single £35.00-50.00, double/twin £65.00-95.00
Family £70.00-100.00.

66021 Pitlochry, Perthshire Map Ref: 2A1

Moulin Hotel

Moulin Hotel, 11-13 Kirkmichael Road, Pitlochry, Perthshire, PH16 5EW
Tel:01796 472196
Email:enquiries@moulinhotel.co.uk
Web:www.pitlochryhotels.co.uk/moulin

Former coaching Inn with wing dating back to 17th C. Quiet village square setting. Home brewed ales served to compliment the local malts. Log fires, extensive use of local fresh produce. 16 routed walks in the area. 6 local golf courses within a ½ hour drive.

16 rooms, All en-suite. Open Jan-Dec. Rates on application.

49840 Pitlochry, Perthshire Map Ref: 2A1

Pine Trees Hotel

Strathview Terrace, Pitlochry, Perthshire, PH16 5QR
Tel:01796 472121 Fax:01796 472460
Email:info@pinetreeshotel.co.uk
Web:www.pinetreeshotel.co.uk

20 rooms
All en-suite
Open Jan-Dec
B&B per person, single from £40.00, double from £40.00. Dinner from £21.50 per person.

IMPORTANT: PRICES STATED ARE ESTIMATES AND MAY BE SUBJECT TO AMENDMENTS
FOR A FULL LISTING OF QUALITY ASSURED ACCOMMODATION, PLEASE SEE DIRECTORY AT BACK OF THIS GUIDE

52160

Pitlochry, Perthshire — Map Ref: 2A1

Rosemount Hotel

12 Higher Oakfield, Pitlochry, PH16 5HT
Tel:01796 472302 Fax:01796 474216
Email:rosemounthotel@tiscali.co.uk
Web:www.scottishhotels.co.uk

A traditional stone-built villa enjoying beautiful views of Pitlochry to the North and South. Friendly, unobtrusive service and very clean. Frequently refurbished accommodation.

25 rooms, All en-suite. Open Jan-Dec. B&B per person, single from £32.00, double from £32.00, BB & Eve.Meal from £49.00.

61108

Pitlochry, Perthshire — Map Ref: 2A1

Tigh Na Cloich Hotel

Larchwood Road, Pitlochry, Perthshire, PH16 5AS
Tel:01796 472216
Email:tnchotel@lineone.net
Web:www.pitlochry-hotel.com

Small intimate hotel, centrally located with stunning views. Individually designed, comfortable and relaxing rooms. With an emphasis on a superior level of service to compliment our imaginative and contemporary cuisine.

9 rooms, All en-suite. Open Mar-Nov. B&B per person, single from £40.00, double from £34.00.

63524

Pitlochry, Perthshire — Map Ref: 2A1

The Well House

11 Toberargan Road, Pitlochry, Perthshire, PH16 5HG
Tel/Fax:01796 472239
Email:enquiries@wellhouseandarrochar.co.uk
Web:www.wellhouseandarrochar.co.uk

6 rooms
All en-suite
Open Feb-Nov
B&B per person, double from £25.00, BB & Eve.Meal from £44.00.

63551 Pitlochry, Perthshire Map Ref: 2A1

Wellwood House

13 West Moulin Road, Pitlochry, Perthshire, PH16 5EA
Tel:01796 474288 Fax:01796 474299
Email:booking@wellwoodhouse.com
Web:www.wellwoodhouse.com

A warm welcome from Maggi and Jim Tyrrell awaits you on arrival at our tastefully decorated, old Scottish Victorian mansion. We have an outstanding view down the Vale of Atholl, yet only a few minutes walk from the town centre restaurants. The house is set in two acres of secluded garden with a tree-lined drive and stream with varied wildlife. Enjoy a pre-dinner drink, or relax in the guest lounge after a night at the theatre. Our newly furnished, reasonably priced rooms are ensuite, hospitality tray and TV included. Once visited, you are sure to come back.

10 rooms, Open Jan-Dec. B&B per person, single from £40.00, double from £30.00.

River Tay, Aberfeldy

RRS Discovery at Discovery Point, Dundee

Angus and Dundee

The Angus and Dundee area boasts beautiful beaches and coastline – wonderful unspoiled stretches of sand which are, at times windswept and stormy but more frequently, warm and inviting, with the peace only occasionally shattered by the cries of the seabirds.

Dundee, you'll discover, has a proud maritime history. Captain Scott's polar research ship the RRS Discovery has returned to the city that built it and is now a top tourist attraction. The city's industrial past also features high on the tourist trail – don't miss the Verdant Works (a former winner of Europe's Top Industrial Museum award) where you can learn about the jute trade that was once a mainstay of the city's economy.

For a complete contrast to city life, explore the Angus Glens. There are five: Glen Isla, Glen Prosen, Glen Lethnot, Glen Clova and Glen Esk. Each has its own unique features but all of the Glens are exceptionally beautiful and wonderfully peaceful places to explore.

Lunan Bay, Angus

DON'T MISS

1 Perhaps Scotland's finest fairytale castle, **Glamis Castle** is famed for its Macbeth connections, as well as being the birthplace of the late Princess Margaret and childhood home of the late Queen Mother. Set against the backdrop of the Grampian Mountains, Glamis is an L-shaped castle built over 5-storeys in striking pink sandstone. The grounds host the Grand Scottish Proms the second week in August each year, complete with spectacular fireworks display.

2 Little more than half an hour's drive north of the bustling city of Dundee, a series of picturesque valleys runs north into the heart of the Grampians. Collectively known as the **Angus Glens**, they offer the perfect escape for those seeking a walk, a spot of wildlife watching, a scenic picnic or a pub lunch. Ranging from gentle and wooded (Glen Isla) to the truly awe-inspiring (Glen Clova and neighbouring Glen Doll), there is more to discover here than you can fit into a single trip.

3 Discover Dundee's polar past at **Discovery Point**. Step aboard Captain Scott's famous ship that took Scott and Shackleton to Antarctica in 1901 and come face to face with the heroes of the ice in the award-winning visitor centre.

4 Dundee is the perfect place for a city break, with great shopping, restaurants and nightlife. Spend a day in Dundee's vibrant and cool **Cultural Quarter** where you can indulge in speciality shopping at the Westport; visit Sensation Dundee's Science Centre which explores the world of the senses; take in a film or an exhibition at Dundee Contemporary Arts; visit Dundee's acclaimed Rep Theatre; and round it all off with a meal at one of the many restaurants and a drink at one of the area's contemporary bars.

5 For the chance to see bottlenose dolphins at close proximity, why not book a trip on one of the **River Tay Dolphin Trips**. If you prefer to stay on dry land the dolphins can sometimes be seen from Broughty Ferry Beach.

6 Angus was the heartland of the Picts, a warrior people who lived in Scotland around 2,000 years ago and left behind many intriguing monuments. **Pictavia**, in Brechin, provides a fascinating insight including hands-on exhibits and a themed play area for all the family. The small hamlet of **Aberlemno**, 6 miles north east of Forfar, is famous for its intricately sculptured Pictish cross-slab in the churchyard.

1

2

FOOD AND DRINK

www.eatscotland.com

7 The **But 'n Ben** in Auchmithie, just 5 miles north of Arbroath, is one of the best seafood restaurants in the area and serves as its speciality the 'smokie pancake'.

8 **Jute Café Bar** is situated on the ground floor of Dundee Contemporary Arts centre with panoramic river views. Its menu ranges widely, with the emphasis on informality, while the ambience goes from a relaxing morning coffee venue to a stylish evening hotspot. Eat, drink and enjoy yourself with freshly cooked dishes, everything from a light snack to a full meal.

9 **The Roundhouse Restaurant** at Lintrathen, by Kirriemuir, is an award-winning restaurant offering innovative modern menus using Angus and Perthshire produce in a peaceful rural setting. The chef is a former Master Chef of Great Britain, whose specialities include local Angus beef and game.

10 No visit to the area would be complete without stopping off to pick up some of the area's best local produce to take home. **Milton Haugh Farm Shop** specialises in the freshest seasonal potatoes, own-reared beef and free range chickens. The Corn Kist Coffee Shop also serves up some delicious home made meals and tempting treats.

11

13

14

WALKS

www.visitscotland.com/walking

11 Scenic **Glen Doll** is one of the famous Angus Glens, north of Dundee. Follow one of the waymarked forest walks from the car park, or more ambitious hikers can take any of three rights of way leading over the surrounding hills into the neighbouring valleys of Glen Shee and Royal Deeside.

12 Situated five miles north west of Carnoustie, **Crombie Country Park** covers 100 hectares of mixed woodland around a picturesque reservoir. There are great opportunities for wildlife watching including butterflies, water and woodland birds.

13 **Seaton Cliffs Nature Trail** is a self guided trail which goes from Arbroath into Sites of Special Scientific Interest, and the sea cliffs are spectacular. There are 15 interpretative points of interest and a wide variety of seabird species can be seen including puffins, guillemots, razorbill and eider duck to name but a few. Allow approximately 2 hours and 30 minutes.

14 If you want to get out and about in the fresh air, see some of what Dundee has to offer, and get fit at the same time, why not try out one of the themed **Dundee city centre walks** in the Dundee Walking Guide available from the Tourist Information Centre. The trails include buildings of historical significance, examples of both 19th and 20th century architecture, plus explorations of Dundee's maritime and industrial heritage, and along the routes you will pass many of Dundee's visitor attractions where you can take a break.

GOLF

www.visitscotland.com/golf

15 If you want to experience the very best in Scottish golf, a visit to the **Carnoustie Championship Course** is a must. Venue for the 2007 Open Golf Championship, the course has been deemed the 'toughest links course in the world'.

16 **Montrose Medal Golf Course**, established in 1562, is the fifth oldest golf course in the world with a traditional links layout.

17 **Downfield Golf Club** is an attractive parkland course that has played host to many golfing tournaments and has an excellent reputation as a challenging course.

18 **Kirriemuir Golf Course** is a gem of a parkland course designed by the renowned James Braid. Look out for the notorious oak tree at the 18th!

15

19

20

21

HISTORY AND HERITAGE

19 **JM Barrie's Birthplace** at Kirriemuir has been carefully restored to reflect how it might have looked in the 1860s. The exhibition next door details the life and work of this hugely talented and celebrated author, famous for writing Peter Pan.

20 In 1178 William the Lion founded the now ruined Tironensian monastery that is **Arbroath Abbey**, near the harbour in Arbroath. The Abbey is famously associated with the Declaration of Arbroath, signed here in 1320, which asserted Scotland's independence from England. An adjacent visitor centre tells the building's story.

21 **Edzell Castle** is an elegant 16th century residence with tower house that was home to the Lindsays. The beautiful walled garden was created by Sir David Lindsay in 1604 and features an astonishing architectural framework. The 'Pleasance' is a delightful formal garden with walls decorated with sculptured stone panels, flower boxes and niches for nesting birds.

57760 Dundee, Angus Map Ref: 2C2

Taychreggan Hotel

4 Ellieslea Road, Broughty Ferry, Dundee, Angus, DD5 1JG
Tel:01382 778626
Email:enquiries@taychreggan-hotel.co.uk
Web:www.taychreggan-hotel.co.uk

You may supply a short description for insertion here - no more than 30 words.

10 rooms, All en-suite. Open Jan-Dec. B&B per person, single from £45.00, double from £35.00.

49086 Edzell, Angus Map Ref: 4F12

Panmure Arms Hotel

52 High Street, Edzell, Angus, DD9 7TA
Tel:01356 648950 Fax:01356 648000
Email:david@panmurearmshotel.co.uk
Web:www.panmurearmshotel.co.uk

16 rooms
All en-suite
Open Jan-Dec excl Xmas. New Year
B&B per person, single from £47.50, double from £35.00.

15031 Montrose, Angus Map Ref: 4F12

Best Western Links Hotel

Mid Links, Montrose, Angus, DD10 8RL
Tel:01674 671000 Fax:01674 672698
Email:reception@linkshotel.com
Web:www.bw-linkshotel.co.uk

Set on the historic Mid Links, the Links is a lovely hotel. It has a central location close to the town centre and is within walking distance of the 5th oldest golf course in the world and Montrose beach with three miles of golden sand. This former Edwardian townhouse offers quality and individually designed bedrooms and the food and service is highly recommended.

25 rooms, All en-suite. Open Jan-Dec. B&B £39.00 per person per night sharing.

The golf course at Aberdour, Fife

Kingdom of Fife

If you're a golfer, the ancient Kingdom of Fife will be a powerful draw. Every serious golfer wants to play the Old Course at St Andrews at least once in a lifetime and, thanks to a public allocation of rounds each day, you can. There are also over 40 other fabulous courses in Fife to put your game to the test.

For keen walkers, one of the great ways to explore Fife is on foot. The Fife Coastal Path takes in some truly delightful places and you'll get to relax on some of the best beaches in the country – with four Fife beaches achieving the top standard Blue Flag status in 2007.

Fife's seaside communities have their roots in fishing and the North Sea herring fleet used to land its catch in the East Neuk's ports. The harbour's still busy at Anstruther but the halcyon days of deep sea fishing have been consigned to the fascinating exhibitions in the Scottish Fisheries Museum in the town.

Dunfermline Abbey, Fife

DON'T MISS

1 A prosperous university town and Mecca for golfers from across the planet, **St Andrews** is one of Scotland's top attractions. Situated above two of the country's finest sandy beaches, there is a real medieval feel to the town's cobbled streets and closes, reinforced by the presence of a ruined cathedral dating from 1180 and a castle founded around 1200. Notwithstanding the many golf courses to pick from, you may also wish to visit the local Aquarium or Botanic Garden.

2 **Dunfermline's** royal and monastic past dominates the town. This former capital of Scotland, birthplace of James I and Charles I, boasts a royal palace, a 12th century abbey and is the final resting place of King Robert the Bruce and eleven other Scottish Kings and Queens. King Malcolm Canmore established his court after the death of Macbeth at the now ruined fortified tower in the heart of "The Glen" – the extensive and picturesque Pittencrieff Park – gifted to the people of Dunfermline by local philanthropist Andrew Carnegie.

3 Travel through the quaint fishing villages of the **East Neuk** of Fife and you travel back through time. This corner of Fife is filled with traditional cottages with red pantile roofs and crow-stepped gable ends which appear unchanged from a bygone age. Fishing boats lie at rest in the harbours following the bustle of unloading their catch. Between communities lie unspoilt stretches of sandy beach, perfect for walks and picnics. Visit Pittenweem for art, Crail for crafts or Anstruther for a trip to the Isle of May, followed by some of Britain's finest fish and chips.

4 To wander through the narrow cobbled streets of the **Royal Burgh of Culross** is to experience life from a past time. Meander through the cobbled streets skirting the shoreline of the Firth of Forth, overlooked by the red pantiled roofs of the harled whitewashed cottages. Now in the care of the National Trust for Scotland – this is without doubt the finest and most complete example of a 17th and 18th century Scottish town.

1

3

4

FOOD AND DRINK

www.eatscotland.com

5 **The Inn at Lathones**, near St Andrews, is a coaching inn with a history stretching back 400 years. The restaurant here continues to welcome travellers with a tempting menu featuring the best of local produce transformed into à la carte gourmet delights.

6 The renowned **Peat Inn**, 3 miles from Cupar, offers top quality modern Scottish cuisine. Only the very best of local produce is used and dishes are prepared with great skill and flair. A mouth-watering wine list is available and visitors wishing to sleep off a hearty meal can stay over in the indulgent 5-star accommodation.

7 **Balbirnie House**, a Georgian mansion set in its own 416-acre country estate, is recognised as one of Scotland's finest Grade A listed historic houses. Dining in either the Orangery or the Balbirnie Bistro provides a delightful way to experience the natural larder that Scotland has to offer and both have built up a deserved reputation as two of the best restaurants in Fife.

8 **Cardoon** at Best Western Keavil House offers a varied menu of light dishes to modern Scottish dishes using locally sourced, quality food, which is served in a relaxed and stylish setting. Experience mouth-watering food and excellent service in this award-winning restaurant – one of Fife's dining gems.

7

9

10

BEACHES AND GOLF

9 Fife boasts some of Scotland's finest and cleanest sandy **beaches**, great for peaceful strolls or quiet contemplation. The area is home to four of Scotland's five Blue Flag award-winning strands at Aberdour, Burntisland, Elie, and West Sands, St Andrews – each offering magnificent views and wonderful experiences.

10 Recognised worldwide as the Home of Golf – the **Old Course** in St Andrews is where it all began and it still remains a real test for today's champions. To play on these hallowed fairways and greens is a dream come true for the golfing fan and an experience which will not be forgotten.

11 As well as the iconic Old Course – the small peninsula of the Kingdom of Fife boasts over 40 other wonderful **golf courses** each offering something different for the visiting golfer. Try the testing challenges of the Open Qualifying courses or an enjoyable, relaxing game, links or parkland, 9 or 18 hole – golf is a way of life in the Kingdom of Fife and there is something for everyone.

12 The sand dunes and beach at the mouth of the Tay estuary are one of the fastest growing parts of Scotland and home to **Tentsmuir** – one of Scotland's National Nature Reserves. This dynamic coastline is important for waders and wildfowl, common and grey seals, ducks and seaduck, and colourful butterflies that light up the grassland and dunes in summer. It is truly one of Scotland's most magical coastlines and well worth a visit.

WALKING AND WILDLIFE

13 Stretching around much of Fife's coastline from the Royal Burgh of Culross to the Tay Bridge, the **Fife Coastal Path** can be experienced in short bite-sized walks or as a long distance route to bring your senses to life. Listen to the seabirds soaring above the waves, smell the salt sea air and savour the sea breezes on this wonderful stretch of coast.

14 The **Isle of May**, accessible via the May Princess from Anstruther in spring and summer, provides nesting sites for 200,000 seabirds, including over 100,000 puffins between May and July alone. In autumn, thousands of grey seals come ashore here to pup.

15 Dominating the skyline of central Fife, the **Lomond Hills** are one of the area's most popular walking destinations. The regional park which encompasses the hills extends over 65 square miles and provides ample opportunity for both moderate and more challenging walking experiences with spectacular vistas over the surrounding countryside.

16 The **Scottish Deer Centre**, near Cupar, allows visitors to spot nine species of deer in over 55 acres of scenic parkland as well as its very own pack of wolves. There are daily falconry displays featuring native Scottish species, a range of shops and a cosy café.

16

18

19

HERITAGE AND GARDENS

17 The **Scottish Fisheries Museum** in Anstruther is a multi-award winning national museum which tells the story of Scottish fishing and whaling from the earliest times to the present – bringing the sea-faring heritage of the people of the Fife coast to life.

18 The **Royal Palace of Falkland** was the countryside residence of Stuart Kings and Queens when they hunted deer and wild boar in the forests of Fife, and was a favourite childhood playground of Mary, Queen of Scots. The Palace was built in the 1500s by James IV and James V, replacing an earlier castle from the 12th century. The current spacious garden, dating from the mid-20th century, houses the original Royal Tennis Court – the oldest in Britain still in use – built in 1539.

19 **Cambo Gardens** is a romantic 'Secret Garden' nestled on the coast between St Andrews and the East Neuk of Fife. Created around Cambo Burn the garden boasts everything from spectacular snowdrops to glowing autumn borders, a wild array of woodland plants and animals, waterfalls and rose-clad wrought-iron bridges. This truly is a plantsman's paradise.

20 **Aberdour Castle** was built by the Douglas family in the 13th century and has been added to throughout the centuries to create a wonderful mix of styles. Situated in the delightful village of the same name, Aberdour Castle boasts fine interior painted ceilings, galleries, a beehive shaped doocot as well as a delightful walled garden only recently uncovered.

75438 **Aberdour, Fife** Map Ref: 2C4

The Woodside Hotel

High Street, Aberdour, Fife, KY3 0SW
Tel:01383 860328 Fax:01383 860920
Email:reception@thewoodsidehotel.co.uk
Web:www.thewoodsidehotel.co.uk

Hotel situated in centre of Aberdour and within easy reach of the motorway, Edinburgh & St Andrews. Direct rail link to Edinburgh. Many golf courses within easy reach. Two minute walk to Aberdour Castle, close to Fife coastal walk and blue flag beach nearby. Unique stained glass and mahogany ceiling from RMS Orontes (1902-1925) now fitted in the clipper bar.

20 rooms, All en-suite. Open Jan-Dec. B&B per person, single from £70.00, and £42.00 per person sharing double room.

60455 **Anstruther, Fife** Map Ref: 2D3

The Spindrift

Pittenween Road, Anstruther, Fife, KY10 3DT
Tel/Fax:01333 310573
Email:info@thespindrift.co.uk
Web:www.thespindrift.co.uk

Stone built Victorian house with wealth of original features, set in fishing village. Short walk from town centre. Ideal touring base. Non smoking. Private parking. Evening meal by arrangement.

8 rooms, 7 en-suite, 1 priv.facilities. Open Feb-Dec. B&B per person, single from £40.00, double from £30.00, Eve.Meal from £20.00.

76705 **Ceres, Fife** Map Ref: 2C3

Meldrums Hotel

56 Main Street, Ceres, Fife, KY15 5NA
Tel:01334 828286 Fax:01334 828795
Email:meldrumshotel@btconnect.com
Web:www.meldrumshotel.co.uk

7 rooms
All en-suite
Open Jan-Dec
B&B per person, single from £48.00, double from £37.50.

17390 **Crail, Fife** Map Ref: 2D3

Caiplie House

53 High Street, Crail, Fife, KY10 3RA
Tel:01333 450564
Email:mail@caipliehouse.com
Web:www.caipliehouse.co.uk

6 rooms
En-suite
Open Jan-Dec
B&B per person, single from £35.00, double from £30.00, BB & Eve.Meal from £42.00.

33438

Dunfermline, Fife — Map Ref: 2B4

Best Western Keavil House Hotel

Crossford, Fife, KY12 8QW
Tel:01383 736258 Fax:01383 621600
Email:reservations@keavilhouse.co.uk
Web:www.keavilhouse.co.uk

Historic country house, including extensive leisure facilities, is set in 12 acres of grounds and gardens, making it an ideal location for relaxing. The hotel offers an award winning restaurant. Within easy reach of Edinburgh - only 25 minutes by train.

47 rooms, B&B per person single from £55.00, double from £55.00. family rooms from £65.00 per adult. Four poster rooms from £75.00 per person..

19522

Dunfermline, Fife — Map Ref: 2B4

Clarke Cottage Guest House

139 Halbeath Road, Dunfermline, Fife, KY11 4LA
Tel:01383 735935 Fax:01383 623767
Email:clarkecottage@ukonline.co.uk
Web:www.clarkecottageguesthouse.co.uk

9 rooms
All en-suite
Open Jan-Dec
B&B per person, single £33.00, double/twin £26.00.

22219

Dunfermline, Fife — Map Ref: 2B4

Davaar House Hotel

126 Grieve Street, Dunfermline, Fife, KY12 8DW
Tel:01383 721886 Fax:01383 623633
Email:enquiries@davaar-house-hotel.com
Web:www.davaar-house-hotel.com

Jim and Doreen extend a warm welcome. Experience Davaar's special atmosphere and enjoy the hospitality comfortable rooms and excellent food. Central location for golfing, walking, touring and enjoying a relaxing break.

10 rooms, All en-suite. Open Jan-Dec excl Xmas/New Year. B&B per person, single from £45.00, double/twin from £40.00.

68058

Dunfermline, Fife — Map Ref: 2B4

Express By Holiday Inn Dunfermline

Halbeath, Dunfermline, Fife, KY11 8DY
Tel:01383 748220 Fax:01383 748221
Email:info@hiexpressdunfermline.co.uk
Web:www.hiexpress.co.uk/dunfermline

82 rooms
All en-suite
Open Jan-Dec
Rates on application.

27355 Dunfermline, Fife Map Ref: 2B4

Scottish Tourist Board ★★★★ HOTEL

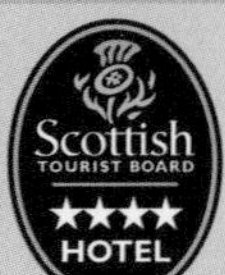

Garvock House Hotel

St Johns Drive, Dunfermline, KY12 7TU
Tel:01383 621067 Fax:01383 621168
Email:sales@garvock.co.uk
Web:www.garvock.co.uk

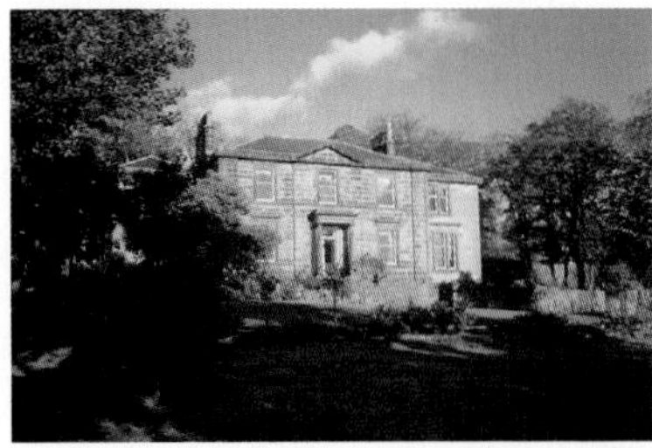

A restored Georgian house set in its own grounds close to Dunfermline town centre. Spacious non-smoking rooms with many thoughtful touches to ensure a comfortable & relaxing stay for all. Comfortable lounges & elegant dining room with good old-fashioned service. Weddings & functions catered for.

26 rooms, All en-suite. Open Jan-Dec. B&B per person, single from £70.00, double from £47.50.

49441 Dunfermline, Fife Map Ref: 2B4

Scottish Tourist Board ★★★ HOTEL

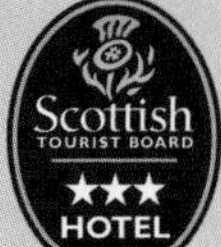

King Malcolm Hotel

Queensferry Road, Dunfermline, Fife, KY11 8DS
Tel:01383 722611
Email:info@kingmalcolm-hotel-dunfermline.com
Web:www.peelhotels.co.uk

48 rooms
All en-suite
Open Jan-Dec
Room only rates, double from £47.50.

49892 Dunfermline, Fife Map Ref: 2B4

Scottish Tourist Board ★★★ HOTEL

Pitbauchlie House Hotel

Aberdour Road, Dunfermline, KY11 4PB
Tel:01383 722282 Fax:01383 620738
Email:info@pitbauchlie.com
Web:www.pitbauchlie.com

50 rooms
All en-suite
Open Jan-Dec
B&B per person, single from £85.00, double from £51.50.

68045 Dunfermline, Fife Map Ref: 2B4

Scottish Tourist Board ★★★ SMALL HOTEL

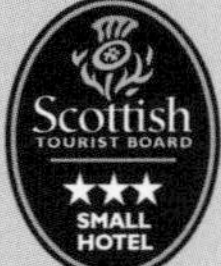

Rooms at 29 Bruce Street

29-35 Bruce Street, Dunfermline, Fife, KY12 7AG
Tel:01383 840041
Email:stay@29brucestreet.co.uk
Web:www.29brucestreet.co.uk

17 rooms
All en-suite
Open Jan-Dec
B&B per person from £47.50.

36274 Freuchie, Fife Map Ref: 2C3

Scottish Tourist Board ★★★ HOTEL

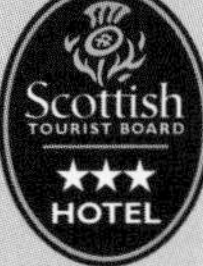

Lomond Hills Hotel and Leisure Centre

Parliament Square, Freuchie, Cupar, Fife, KY15 7EY
Tel:01337 857329 Fax:01337 858180
Email:reception@lomondhillshotel.com
Web:www.lomondhillshotel.com

24 rooms
All en-suite
Open Jan-Dec
B&B per person, single from £59.95, double from £39.95.

73135 Glenrothes, Fife — Map Ref: 2C3

The Gilvenbank Hotel

Huntsmans Road, Glenrothes, Fife, KY7 6NT
Tel:01592 742077 Fax:01592 748152
Email:enquiries@gilvenbankhotel.co.uk
Web:www.gilvenbankhotel.co.uk

19 rooms
All en-suite
Open Jan-Dec
Room only per person, single from £49.95, double from £49.95.

79438 Kinghorn, Fife — Map Ref: 2C4

Bay Hotel

Burntisland Road, Kinghorn, Fife, KY3 9YE
Tel:01592 892222 Fax:01592 892206
Email:info@pettycur.co.uk

Simply Breathtaking Stunning new hotel standing in an area of natural beauty with breathtaking views across the River Forth to Edinburgh and beyond. The adjacent Bay Leisure centre includes a swimming pool, sauna, steam room, jacuzzi and multi gym. And a soft play area for the children with bouncy castle. Our beautifully furnished restaurant offers the ultimate dining experience from delicious snacks to fine a la carte dining, complemented by fine wines and excellent service. Our popular night club, Images, for all guests who wish to enjoy a wide variety of live cabaret entertainment including carbaret, dance, traditional Scottish nights and theme nights.

27 rooms.
Open Jan-Dec. Rates on application.

17588 Leven, Fife — Map Ref: 2C3

Caledonian Hotel

81 High Street, Leven, Fife, KY8 4NG
Tel:01333 424101 Fax:01333 421241
Email:reservations@thecaledonianhotel-leven.co.uk
Web:www.thecaledonianhotel-leven.co.uk

24 rooms
Open Jan-Dec
B&B per person, single from £40.00, double from £25.00.

75627 Lundin Links, Fife — Map Ref: 2C3

Lundin Links Hotel

Leven Road, Lundin Links, Fife, KY8 6AP
Tel:01333 320207
Email:info@lundin-links-hotel.co.uk
Web:www.lundin-links-hotel.co.uk

21 rooms
All en-suite
Open Jan-Dec
Rates on application.

21018 St Andrews, Fife Map Ref: 2D2

Craigmore Guest House

3 Murray Park, St Andrews, Fife, KY16 9AW
Tel:01334 472142 Fax:01334 477963
Email:jim.williamson@virgin.net
Web:www.standrewscraigmore.com

7 rooms
All en-suite
Open Jan-Dec
B&B per person, single from £50.00, double from £38.00.

75013 St Andrews, Fife Map Ref: 2D2

Greyfriars Hotel

129 North Street, St Andrews, Fife, KY16 9AG
Tel:01334 474906 Fax:01334 472442
Email:stay@greyfriarshotel.com
Web:www.greyfriarshotel.com

20 rooms
All en-suite
Open Jan-Dec
B&B per person, single from £65.00, double from £60.00.

36865 St Andrews, Fife Map Ref: 2D2

Macdonald Rusacks Hotel

Pilmour Links, St Andrews, Fife, KY16 9JQ
Tel:0870 4008128 Fax:01334 477896
Email:general.russacks@macdonald-hotels.com
Web:www.macdonald-hotels.com

68 rooms
All en-suite
Open Jan-Dec
B&B per person, single from £71.00, double from £85.00, Dinner B&B from £96.00.

20248 St Andrews, Fife Map Ref: 2D2

New Hall, University of St Andrews

North Haugh, St Andrews, Fife,
KY16 9XW
Tel:01334 467000 Fax:01334 467001
Email:new.hall@st-andrews.ac.uk
Web:www.discoverstandrews.com

New Hall offers comfortable en-suite facilities, excellent value and a friendly service. New Hall is located within easy walking distance of the beach, golf courses and the historic town centre and is ideal for golfers, families, short breaks and holidays. All bedrooms have double beds, TVs and tea and coffee making facilities.

100 rooms, All en-suite. Open Jun-Sep. B&B per person, single from £49.50, double from £36.00. Evening meals available.

48257 St Andrews, Fife Map Ref: 2D2

Old Course Hotel, Golf Resort & Spa

St Andrews, Fife, KY16 9SP
Tel:01334 474371 Fax:01334 477668
Email:reservations@oldcoursehotel.co.uk
Web:www.oldcoursehotel.co.uk

Overlooking the famous 17th Fairway, the Old Course Hotel Golf Resort & Spa blends the elegant with the strikingly modern. Enjoy superb cuisine and international atmosphere in the resort's many restaurants and bars. The hotel also boasts its own championship 18 hole course, The Dukes, and newly refurbished Kohler Waters Spa. Cot available.

144 rooms, All en-suite. Open Jan-Dec. B&B per person, single from £195.00, double from £225.00, BB & Eve.Meal from £145.00 (sharing).

52628 St Andrews, Fife Map Ref: 2D2

Rufflets Country House Hotel

Strathkinness Low Road, St Andrews, Fife, KY16 9TX
Tel:01334 472594 Fax:01334 478703
Email:reservations@rufflets.co.uk
Web:www.rufflets.co.uk

Country house with relaxing ambience, set in 10 acres of beautiful gardens. Fresh seasonal produce served in the restaurant. 1.5 miles (3kms) from golf courses and coast. Small Luxury Hotels Of The World Member.

25 rooms, All en-suite. Open Jan-Dec. B&B per person, single from £135.00, double from £105.00, BB & Eve.Meal from £140.00.

55697 St Andrews, Fife Map Ref: 2D2

Fairmont St Andrews, Scotland

St Andrews, Fife, KY16 8PN
Tel:01334 837000 Fax:01334 471115
Email:standrews.scotland@fairmont.com
Web:www.fairmont.com

Fairmont St Andrews, Scotland sits proudly amidst the rugged coastal landscape of the East of Scotland, while commanding spectacular views of the bay's golden beaches and medieval St Andrews skyline. A luxurious 5 star hotel with 209 generous guest rooms, an array of dining options, a revitalising spa, a dedicated conference centre and, of course, two championship golf courses.

209 rooms, All en-suite. Open Jan-Dec. B&B per room, double from £170.00, BB & Eve.Meal from £215.00.

55694 St Andrews, Fife Map Ref: 2D2

St Andrews Golf Hotel

40 The Scores, St Andrews, Fife, KY16 9AS
Tel:01334 472611 Fax:01334 472188
Email:reception@standrews-golf.co.uk
Web:www.standrews-golf.co.uk

Situated just a 9 iron from the first tee of the Old Course, this recently refurbished, boutique hotel offers true Scottish hospitality with a personal touch along with the ideal location to both relax and explore St Andrews. Breathtaking views over St Andrews Links and Bay can be taken in from some of the beautiful bedrooms and our award winning restaurant 'number forty'. Number forty bar and terrace offers a dining experience with a difference, alfresco when the weather allows. Within an hours drive of many Scottish Championship courses, as the name suggests, arranging golfing holidays is our speciality.

22 rooms.
All en-suite. Open Jan-Dec
B&B per person, single £145.00, standard £100.00, superior £130.00, junior suite £160.00. BB & Eve.Meal single £160.00, standard £140.00, superior £160.00, junior suite £170.00.

77060 St Andrews, Fife Map Ref: 2D2

West Bar & Kitchen

170 South Street, St Andrews, Fife, KY16 9EG
Tel:01334 473186 Fax:01334 479732
Email:westport@maclay.co.uk
Web:www.maclay.com

4 rooms
All en-suite
Open Jan-Dec
Rates on application.

64810 St Andrews, Fife Map Ref: 2D2

Scottish Tourist Board ★★★ Guest House

Yorkston Guest House

68-70 Argyle Street, St Andrews, Fife, KY16 9BU
Tel:01334 472019 Fax:01334 470351
Email:yorkstonhouse@aol.com
Web:www.yorkstonguesthouse.co.uk

Privately owned guest house with several spacious family rooms situated close to West Port and town centre with easy access to golf course, shops, restaurants and cafe bars.

10 rooms, Most en-suite. Open Mar-Dec. B&B per person, single from £40.00, double from £38.00.

59338

by St Andrews, Fife   Map Ref: 2D2

The Inn At Lathones

By Largoward, St Andrews, Fife, KY9 1JE
Tel:01334 840494 Fax:01334 840694
Email:Lathones@theinn.co.uk
Web:www.theinn.co.uk

21 rooms
All en-suite
B&B per person, single from £120.00, double from £90.00.

The Royal and Ancient Clubhouse, St Andrews

Crail, Fife

Fyvie Castle, Aberdeenshire

ABERDEEN AND GRAMPIAN HIGHLANDS

Scotland's Castle and Whisky Country

Silvery grey it may be but the 'Granite City' of Aberdeen has won more awards for its floral displays than any other city in the UK.

In 2006 it scooped a unique hat-trick, winning Scotland in Bloom for the 39th consecutive year and adding the British and International equivalents.

With 45 parks in the city and a celebrated Winter Garden at Duthie Park, Aberdeen is always in bloom and every season brings further floral flights of fancy.

A seaside city

But then, Aberdeen is a city of acute contrasts. It's an important port with links to the fishing and oil industries, it's a thriving cultural centre with a stylish selection of galleries, museums, restaurants, nightclubs and bars.

It has a busy central shopping area yet just a short distance away there's a brilliant beach complete with funfair.

The many fascinations of the Aberdeenshire coastline extend beyond the city and there are miles of golden, sandy beaches and towering cliffs to explore. All along the coast you'll find captivating harbour towns like Stonehaven, Peterhead, Fraserburgh, Banff and Macduff and quaint little places like the stunning Pennan, a former smugglers' town at the foot of a cliff.

Castles and whisky galore

Some great trails have been laid out for visitors to follow including the intriguing Castle Trail. There are over 350 castles in Aberdeen and Grampian

Highlands and they come in all shapes and sizes from fairytale castles to crumbling ruins and even royal holiday homes.

And speaking of royalty, the Deeside towns of Banchory, Ballater and Braemar have all enjoyed many decades of royal patronage, the annual highlight of which is the Braemar Gathering in September.

You may also want to take the Malt Whisky Trail which features 8 famous distilleries and a cooperage in Moray. Each tells the story of 'the water of life' in its own distinctive way and if you happen to stagger off the trail at any point, there are another 42 distilleries to discover in the Speyside area.

Alongside the whisky, there are other delights that will soon have you raising your glass – music, song and, of course, fine food. Aberdeen and Grampian Highlands is Scotland's natural larder. Beautiful Aberdeen Angus beef, sumptuous seafood, fabulous fruit and vegetables – all come fresh to the table, prepared by the finest chefs. There's even a festival to celebrate –Taste of Grampian, held annually in June at Inverurie.

So where would you like to stay in Aberdeen and Grampian Highlands? There's a lot of choice – historical baronial mansions, elegant country houses, Victorian townhouses, seaside guest houses – just take your pick!

Dunnottar Castle, Aberdeenshire

What's On?

Burning of the Clavie, Burghead
11 January 2008
A fire festival commemorating the old New Year.

Aberdeen Jazz Festival
5 – 9 March 2008
Live jazz events with local and international artists.
www.jazzaberdeen.com

Spirit of Speyside Whisky Festival
1 – 5 May 2008
Whisky takes centre stage.
www.spiritofspeyside.com

Word Festival, Aberdeen
9 – 11 May 2008
One of the most popular literary events in Scotland.

Taste of Grampian, Inverurie
7 June 2008
A 1-day food and drink festival.
www.tasteofgrampian.co.uk

Aberdeen Highland Games
15 June 2008
A rich programme of events and competitions.
www.aberdeenhighlandgames.com

Turriff Show
3 – 4 August 2008
The largest 2-day agricultural show in Scotland.
www.turriffshow.org

Braemar Gathering
6 September 2008
The biggest Highland Games attended by the Royal Family.
www.braemargathering.org

City of Aberdeen Hogmanay Street Party
31 December 2008
Featuring a programme of live music.

Stonehaven Fireball Festival
31 December 2008
A spectacular winter fire festival to bring in the New Year.

www.aberdeen-grampian.com

DON'T MISS

1 The railway originally came to Ballater in 1866, when Deeside Railway built its terminus here. In its heyday, many famous people – including the Tsar of Russia – used **Ballater Station**. Today, the building has been lovingly restored and hosts an exhibition on its amazing history.

2 Scotland's Castle Trail winds its way between some of Scotland's finest fairytale homes and fortresses including **Crathes Castle**. Built in the second half of the 16th century, Crathes Castle is a splendid example of the tower house style of the time, and retains many of its original interior features. Perhaps the best reason to visit, however, is the 1½ hectare walled garden, complete with herbaceous borders and a stunning array of unusual plants. Crathes can be found 3 miles east of the town of Banchory.

3 Found in homes and bars around the globe, Glenfiddich is the world's favourite single malt Scotch whisky. Discover the history of the **Glenfiddich Distillery**, owned and managed by the fifth generation of the Grant family, learn how whisky is produced and at the end of your visit enjoy a dram of Glenfiddich in the Glenfiddich Bar. A journey to the home of Glenfiddich makes you appreciate each mouthful even more.

4 **Aberdeen's beachfront** is a family paradise. Take a walk along the 2 miles of soft sandy beach and discover a range of attractions on offer for all the family, as well as a mix of restaurants old and new.

5 The **Art Gallery** is one of Aberdeen's most popular tourist attractions and offers a fantastic day out for art lovers and novices alike with paintings ranging from Victorian to Scottish, Impressionist to 20th century British.

6 For the ultimate opportunity to 'get back to nature' take a **wildlife tour** - North 58° Sea Adventures, Troup Tours, Moray Diving and Gemini Explorer are just some of the boat operators offering the chance to spot dolphins, porpoise, seabirds and seals in stunning surroundings and if you don't have seafaring legs you can experience the fascinating wildlife of the Cairngorms National Park with WalkDeeside and Glenlivet Wildlife.

2

5

6

7

FOOD AND DRINK

www.eatscotland.com

7 The **Malt Whisky Trail** incorporates eight distilleries and the Speyside Cooperage. This is an excellent way to find out all about Scotland's National Drink. Indeed, two annual celebrations of whisky take place each year at the **Spirit of Speyside Whisky Festival** in late April/early May and the Autumn Speyside Whisky Festival in late September. Fine malts such as Glenlivet and Glenfiddich can be savoured as well as kilt-making demonstrations and tours of nearby distilleries.

8 While in the area ensure you try **Cullen Skink** – a thick soup made with smoked haddock. This local speciality is sure to warm you up before setting off to explore the coastal village of Cullen.

9 **The Laird's Kitchen** at Delgatie Castle in Turriff was voted 17th best place to have afternoon tea in Britain – a pretty little restaurant serving good food with local produce. The carrot cake is legendary and has been written about in books and magazine articles all over the world.

10 Based in Huntly is the renowned **Dean's of Huntly** factory, complete with a shop offering all your favourite varieties of shortbread and much more in which to indulge. Ideal for stocking up or for purchasing gifts to take home!

8 & 11

12

13

ACTIVITIES

11 **Cullen – Logie Head – Findlater Castle – Sandend** – This unspoilt coastline boasts cliffs and bays interspersed with traditional fishing villages. The walk from Cullen to the quaint village of Sandend arrives at a beautiful sandy bay – Sandside beach – and, just beyond it, Findlater Castle, an ancient ruined fortress built on a narrow promontory. The first stage of the walk is along good paths with sections of beach but the second half is less developed, so may be less manageable for some. Allow 3 hours for the full 4-mile route.

12 Where better to experience true Scottish **golf** than on the variety of fairways in Aberdeen and Grampian Highlands. You can choose from 25 links courses from the traditional Royal Aberdeen (6th oldest golf course in the world), Cruden Bay, Murcar and Moray Old to the amazing Cullen, Stonehaven, Royal Tarlair and Fraserburgh. There are more than 70 golf courses to get on 'par' with.

13 The sea, the lochs, the rivers. Why not hook up with a **water sports** company like the Surf and Watersports Club to bag a few new activities or have a go at Kite Land Boarding with Synergy Kite Sports – all the fun of surfing but without getting wet!

14 If you enjoy your **snow sports** nothing can quite match the thrill and breathtaking exhilaration of swooping down a snowy slope at the Glenshee Ski Centre. Or how about buggy riding in the Lecht Ski Resort (trust us, this activity has to be sampled to be believed!).

HISTORY AND HERITAGE

15 Braemar's Highland Games - **The Braemar Gathering** – are held on the first Saturday of September each year, and are notable for the scale and for their unique chieftain, none other than Her Majesty The Queen. Royalty is always in attendance, watching tossing the caber, Highland dancing, and piping.

16 Scottish home of the Royal Family since the mid-19th century, **Balmoral Castle** is a grand granite pile set amidst spectacular scenery. Seasonal opening hours allow visitors to see the ballroom – the Castle's largest room - and an audio-visual presentation provides the history of the Castle since it was purchased for Queen Victoria by Prince Albert. Visit some more of Queen Victoria's favourite spots on the **Victorian Heritage Trail**.

17 Designed to bring the past to life, award-winning **Archaeolink Prehistory Park** near the village of Insch allows you to travel 10,000 years in one day! With hands-on activities and guided tours there's plenty to interest all ages.

18 Step back in time through the last millennium on Scotland's only **Castle Trail**. In all 13 properties make up the trail, from fairytale Craigievar Castle to ruined Kildrummy Castle, from the distinctive turrets of Castle Fraser to the star-shaped ramparts of Corgarff Castle.

15

16

WALKS

www.visitscotland.com/walking

19 Allow around 2 hours for an enjoyable circular walk in Cairngorms National Park starting from Braemar village. Take the A93 to Glenshee for ½ mile, and then follow signs for **'Queen's Drive'** and 'Lion's Face'. The track will take you through birch woodland, passing a small lochan on the left, and returns to the village.

20 The **Burghead to Hopeman** coastal walk will take you between two peaceful villages on the coast of Moray, past several quiet sandy beaches with views across the Moray Firth. You can start at either end, and shops, food and drink are available in either village. The path follows the track of a long disused and removed railway line. You can return by the same path or follow another alongside the shore. Allow 3 - 3½ hours for the 4 mile route.

21 **Cambus O' May Forest**, near Ballater, welcomes walkers of all abilities. Areas of native Scots pine and a variety of classic Scottish wildlife, such as red squirrels and crossbills, make for a pleasant stroll. There are a number of paths, some offering spectacular views of the Dee Valley below.

22 From the Bennachie Centre near Chapel of Garioch, a fabulous array of woodland walks are available through **Bennachie Forest**, most offering an opportunity to view sculptures and wildlife from the path. Red squirrels, roe deer and crossbills are present in good numbers, while any of Bennachie's summits offer sightings of moorland species such as grouse, pippets and buzzards.

MAP

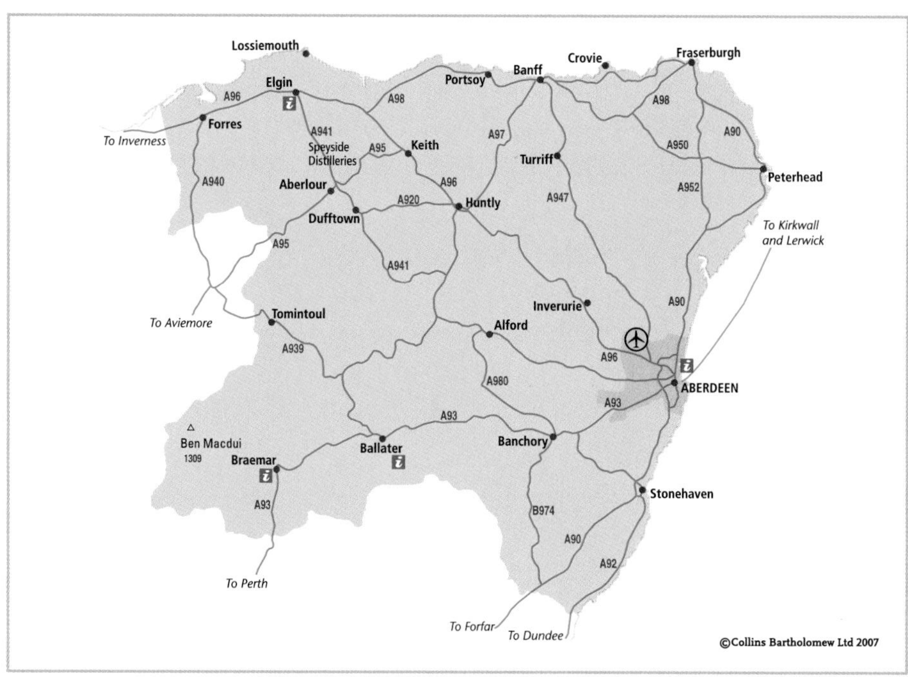

TOURIST INFORMATION CENTRES

Aberdeen and Grampian Highlands	
Aberdeen Visitor Centre	23 Union Street, Aberdeen KY12 7DL
Ballater	The Old Royal Station, Station Square, Ballater AB35 5QB
Braemar	Unit 3, The Mews, Mar Road, Braemar AB35 5YL
Elgin	17 High Street, Elgin IV30 1EG

Make the most of your stay in Scotland and make your first stop the Tourist Information Centre wherever you go.

Knowledgeable and friendly staff can help you with information and advice; they can answer your questions, book accommodation and you can even pick up some souvenirs to take home for friends and family.

For information and ideas about exploring Scotland in advance of your trip, call our booking and information service or go to **www.visitscotland.com**

Call 0845 22 55 121

or if calling from outside the UK call **+44 (0) 1506 832 121**

From Ireland call **1800 932 510**

A £4 booking fee applies to telephone bookings of accommodation.

58314 Aberdeen Map Ref: 4G10

Brentwood Hotel

101 Crown Street, Aberdeen, AB11 6HH
Tel:01224 595440 Fax:01224 571593
Email:reservations@brentwood-hotel.co.uk
Web:www.brentwood-hotel.co.uk

65 rooms
All en-suite
Open Jan-Dec excl Xmas/New Year
B&B per person, single £43.00-89.00, double £33.00-49.00

20936 Aberdeen Map Ref: 4G10

Craighaar Hotel

Waterton Road, Bucksburn, Aberdeen, AB21 9HS
Tel:01224 712275 Fax:01224 716362
Email:info@craighaar.co.uk
Web:www.craighaarhotel.com

55 rooms
All en-suite
Open Jan-Dec excl Xmas
B&B per person, single from £45.00, double from £32.50.

26933 Aberdeen Map Ref: 4G10

Furain Guest House

92 North Deeside Road, Peterculter, Aberdeen, AB14 0QN
Tel:01224 732189 Fax:01224 739070
Email:furain@btinternet.com

Late Victorian house built of red granite. Family run. Convenient for town, Royal Deeside and the Castle Trail. Private car parking. Dinner available on Wednesday, Friday and Saturday.

8 rooms, All en-suite. Open Jan-Dec excl Xmas/New Year. B&B per person, single from £37.00, double from £26.00.

59622 Aberdeen Map Ref: 4G10

Marcliffe Hotel and Spa

North Deeside Road, Pitfodels, Aberdeen, AB15 9YA
Tel:01224 861000 Fax:01224 868860
Email:stewart@marcliffe.com
Web:www.marcliffe.com

The Marcliffe Hotel and Spa is the country house hotel in the city, providing all modern business facilities in 11 acres of wooded grounds.

42 rooms including 7 suites, All en-suite. Open Jan-Dec. B&B per room, single from £150.00, double from £160.00.

49044 Aberdeen — Map Ref: 4G10

Palm Court Hotel

81 Seafield Road, Aberdeen, AB15 7YX
Tel:01224 310351 Fax:01224 312707
Email:palmcourt@G1group.com

This fully refurbished and extended hotel has a modern and contemporary feel throughout. With a stylish restaurant and popular whisky bar it is situated in a quiet residential area in West End of city. Convenient for city bypass, airport 10 miles (16kms).

23 rooms, All en-suite. Open Jan-Dec. B&B per room, single from £85.00, double from £95.00.

52465 Aberdeen — Map Ref: 4G10

Scottish
TOURIST BOARD
★★
HOTEL

Royal Hotel

1-3 Bath Street, Aberdeen, AB11 6BJ
Tel:01224 585152 Fax:01224 583900
Email:info@royalhotel.uk.com
Web:www.royalhotel.uk.com

42 rooms
All en-suite
Open Jan-Dec
B&B per person, single from £50.00, double from £31.00.

54826 Aberdeen — Map Ref: 4G10

Scottish
TOURIST BOARD
★★★★
SERVICED APARTMENT

Skene House HotelSuites

96 Rosemount Viaduct, Aberdeen, AB25 1NX
Tel:01224 645971 Fax:01224 626866
Email:rosemount@skene-house.co.uk
Web:www.skene-house.co.uk

188 one-three bedroom suites
En-suite
Open Jan-Dec
Rates from £29.50 pppn based upon 6 sharing a 3 bed suite.

34041 Aberdeen — Map Ref: 4G10

University of Aberdeen, King's Hall

College Bounds, Aberdeen, AB24 3TT
Tel:01224 273444 Fax:01224 276246
Email:accommodation@abdn.ac.uk
Web:www.abdn.ac.uk/kingshall

Modern, hotel style accommodation located in the heart of historic Old Aberdeen. Rooms - available from June 2008 - are alll ensuite and include a plasma TV, hairdryer, telephone and trouser press. Breakfast is served in the adjacent Zeste restaurant. Free access to leisure facilities.

65 rooms, All en-suite. Open from Jun, excl Xmas/New Year. B&B per room, single from £53.50, twin from £80.50.

48319

nr Aberdeen — Map Ref: 4G10

Old Mill Inn

South Deeside Road, Maryculter, Aberdeen, AB12 5FX
Tel:01224 733212 Fax:01224 732884
Email:info@oldmillinn.co.uk
Web:www.oldmillinn.co.uk

7 rooms
All en-suite
Open Jan-Dec
B&B per person, single from £59.00, double from £34.50.

56854

nr Aberdeen — Map Ref: 4G10

Strathburn Hotel

Burghmuir Drive, Inverurie, Aberdeenshire,
AB51 4GY
Tel:01467 624422 Fax:01467 625133
Email:strathburn@btconnect.com

Modern hotel and restaurant with friendly atmosphere, overlooking Strathburn Park in Inverurie. Personally run.

27 rooms, All en-suite. Open 3 Jan-Dec 31. B&B per person, single from £65.00, double from £45.00, BB & Eve.Meal from £65.00.

17716

Ballater, Aberdeenshire — Map Ref: 4E11

Cambus O'May Hotel

nr Ballater, Aberdeenshire, AB35 5SE
Tel/Fax:013397 55428
Email:mckechnie@cambusomay.freeserve.co.uk
Web:www.cambusomayhotel.co.uk

Family owned and traditionally run country house hotel dating from the 1870's set amongst its own grounds, 4 miles from Ballater. Very popular with many regular guests. Quality freshly prepared food making use of local produce with the menu changing daily.

12 rooms, All en-suite. Open Jan-Dec. B&B per person, single from £35.00, double from £35.00.

22416 Ballater, Aberdeenshire — Map Ref: 4E11

Deeside Hotel

Braemar Road, Ballater, Aberdeenshire, AB35 5RQ
Tel:013397 55420 Fax:013397 55357
Email:deesidehotel@btconnect.com
Web:www.deesidehotel.co.uk

'Heartily recommended' in the Good Hotel Guide 2008, the Deeside Hotel is a Victorian house set in an acre of grounds. Fresh food prepared daily with emphasis on locally sourced, free-range produce, complemeted by good wines, malt whiskies and real ale. Log fires in winter, sunny conservatory/ gardens in summer.

10 rooms, All en-suite. Open Jan-Dec. B&B per person, double from £45.00.

73409 Ballater, Aberdeenshire — Map Ref: 4E11

Glenernan Guest House

37 Braemar Road, Ballater, Aberdeenshire, AB35 5RQ
Tel:013397 53111 Fax:013397 53288
Email:enquiries@glenernanguesthouse.com
Web:www.glenernanguesthouse.com

7 rooms
All en-suite
Open Jan-Dec
B&B per person, single from £35.00, double/twin from £25.00.

28644 Ballater, Aberdeenshire — Map Ref: 4E11

The Gordon Guest House

Station Square, Ballater, Aberdeenshire, AB35 5QB
Tel:013397 55996

5 rooms
All en-suite
Open Jan-Dec
B&B per person, single from £30.00-60.00, double from £25.00-65.00.

35851 by Ballater, Aberdeenshire — Map Ref: 4E11

Loch Kinord Hotel

Ballater Road, Dinnet, Royal Deeside,
Aberdeenshire, AB34 5JY
Tel:013398 85229 Fax:013398 87007
Email:stay@lochkinord.com
Web:www.lochkinord.com

Under the enthusiastic new ownership of Jenny and Andrew Cox the hotel has undergone public areas refurbishment featuring some 4 poster bedrooms with all modern facilities. Situated in the centre of this small village it makes a great base for exploring Royal Deeside, skiing, walking, and playing golf. Non-residents very welcome and popular in the area for excellent food from their AA rosette restaurant.

21 rooms, All en-suite. Open Jan-Dec. B&B per person, single from £30.00, double from £30.00, BB & Eve.Meal from £49.50.

16913 Banchory, Aberdeenshire — Map Ref: 4F11

The Burnett Arms Hotel

25 High Street, Banchory, Aberdeenshire, AB31 5TD
Tel:01330 824944 Fax:01330 825553
Email:theburnett@btconnect.com

16 rooms
All en-suite
Open Jan-Dec
B&B per person, single £67.00-82.00, double £42.00-51.00.

35133 by Banchory, Aberdeenshire — Map Ref: 4F11

Learney Arms Hotel

The Square, Torphins, Kincardineshire, AB31 4GP
Tel:01339 882202 Fax:01339 882123
Email:sales@learneyarmshotel.com
Web:www.learneyarmshotel.com

12 rooms
En-suite rooms available
Open Jan-Dec
Rates on application.

16019 Braemar, Aberdeenshire — Map Ref: 4D11

Braemar Lodge Hotel

Glenshee Road, Braemar, Aberdeenshire, AB35 5YQ
Tel:013397 41627
Email:info@braemarlodge.co.uk
Web:www.braemarlodge.co.uk

7 rooms
All en-suite
Open Jan-Dec
B&B per person, single from £45.00. double from £45.00.

59874 Braemar, Aberdeenshire — Map Ref: 4D11

Callater Lodge Guest House

9 Glenshee Road, Braemar, Aberdeenshire, AB35 5YQ
Tel:013397 41275
Email:laura2@hotel-braemar.co.uk
Web:www.hotel-braemar.co.uk

6 rooms
All en-suite
Open Jan-Oct
B&B per person, single from £32.00, double from £30.00.

33838 Cruden Bay, Aberdeenshire — Map Ref: 4H9

Kilmarnock Arms Hotel

Bridge Street, Cruden Bay, by Peterhead, AB42 0HD
Tel:01779 812213 Fax:01779 812153
Email:reception@kilmarnockarms.com
Web:www.kilmarnockarms.com

Traditional Victorian village hotel, providing comfortable and recently upgraded accommodation for business travellers, golfers and families. Many activities available in the area - walking, birdwatching, historic houses and much more. All rooms have satellite television, whilst wireless access to the internet is available as well.

14 rooms, All en-suite. Open Jan-Dec excl Xmas/New Year.
B&B per person, single from £45.00, double from £35.00.

IMPORTANT: PRICES STATED ARE ESTIMATES AND MAY BE SUBJECT TO AMENDMENTS
FOR A FULL LISTING OF QUALITY ASSURED ACCOMMODATION, PLEASE SEE DIRECTORY AT BACK OF THIS GUIDE

57634 Dufftown, Banffshire — Map Ref: 4E9

Tannochbrae Guest House & Restaurant

22 Fife Street, Dufftown, Banffshire, AB55 4AL
Tel:01340 820541 Fax:01340 820922
Email:info@tannochbrae.co.uk
Web:www.tannochbrae.co.uk

6 rooms
All en-suite
Open Jan-Dec
B&B per person, single from £45.00, double from £34.00.

73753 Forres, Moray — Map Ref: 4C8

Cluny Bank Hotel

St Leonards Road, Forres, Morayshire, IV36 1DW
Tel:01309 674304 Fax:01309 671400
Email:info@clunybankhotel.co.uk
Web:www.clunybankhotel.co.uk

8 rooms
All en-suite
Open Jan-Dec
B&B per room, single from £75.00, double from £88.00.

25148 Inverurie, Aberdeenshire — Map Ref: 4G9

Grant Arms Hotel

Monymusk, Inverurie, Aberdeenshire, AB51 7HJ
Tel:01467 651226 Fax:01467 651250
Email:ag@monymusk.com
Web:www.fishingthefly.co.uk

Formerly an 18th Century Coaching Inn. The Grant Arms is full of traditional charm. Accommodation more recently refurbished to a high standard. There being six rooms in the main building and a further six in courtyard annexe to rear, including one room suitable for the less able bodied guest.

12 rooms, All en-suite. Open Jan-Dec. B&B per room, single from £77.00, double from £88.00.

49952 by Inverurie, Aberdeenshire — Map Ref: 4G9

Pittodrie House Hotel

Chapel of Garioch, by Inverurie, Aberdeen
AB51 5HS
Tel:01467 681744 Fax:01467 681648
Email:pittodrie@macdonald-hotels.co.uk
Web:www.macdonald-hotels.co.uk/Pittodrie

Country house dating from 1480 on large estate. Mixed arable, forestry and hill land with interesting walks. Open fires, billiards, squash, clay pigeon shooting and 4x4 off road driving.

27 rooms, Some en-suite. Open Jan-Dec. B&B per person, single from £75.00, double from £60.00, BB & Eve.Meal from £75.00 pp.

54834 Lossiemouth, Moray — Map Ref: 4D7

Skerry Brae Hotel

Stotfield Road, Lossiemouth, Moray, IV31 6QS
Tel:01343 812040
Email:info@skerrybrae.co.uk
Web:www.skerrybrae.co.uk

19 rooms
All en-suite
Open Jan-Dec
B&B from £40.00.

74238 Macduff, Aberdeenshire — Map Ref: 4F7

Knowes Hotel

78 Market Street, Macduff, Banffshire, AB44 1LL
Tel/Fax:01261 832152
Email:info@knoweshotel.co.uk
Web:www.knoweshotel.co.uk

5 rooms, 4 en-suite (3 dbl, 1 twin), 1 single with priv.facilities.
B&B per room, single from £30.00, double from £65.00.

60159 Oldmeldrum, Aberdeenshire — Map Ref: 4G9

The Redgarth

Kirk Brae, Oldmeldrum, Aberdeenshire, AB51 0DJ
Tel:01651 872353

Family run inn offering varied menu including vegetarian choices using fresh local produce. Range of cask ales available. Large comfortable rooms with panoramic views.

3 rooms, All en-suite. Open Jan-Dec excl Xmas/New Year. B&B per person, single from £65.00, double from £42.50.

C £ V

18278 Peterhead, Aberdeenshire — Map Ref: 4H8

Carrick Guest House

16 Merchant Street, Peterhead, Aberdeenshire, AB42 1DU
Tel:01779 470610
Email:carrickpeterhead@aol.com

6 rooms
All en-suite
Open Jan-Dec excl Xmas/New Year
B&B per person, single from £25.00, double from £22.00.

V

52263 Rothienorman, Aberdeenshire — Map Ref: 4F9

Rothie Inn

Main Street, Rothienorman, Aberdeenshire, AB51 8UD
Tel:01651 821206
Email:rothieinn@fsmail.net

2 rooms
All en-suite
Open Jan-Dec excl Xmas/New Year
B&B per person, single from £30.00, double from £25.00.

C £ V

78269 St Combs, by Fraserburgh, Aberdeenshire Map Ref: 4H7

The Tufted Duck Hotel

Corsekelly Place, St Combs, Fraserburgh, Aberdeenshire, AB43 8ZS
Tel:01346 582481
Email:reception@tufteddoughotel.co.uk
Web:www.tufteddoughotel.co.uk

Resting above the historic Buchan coastline our hotel has a warm and peaceful ambience. With eleven attractive and comfortable bedrooms and a restaurant renowned in the area for its excellent cuisine, we are the ideal base for all types of holiday stays.

12 rooms, All en-suite. Open Jan-Dec. B&B per room, single from £65.00, double from £75.00.

60406 Stonehaven Map Ref: 4G11

The Ship Inn

5 Shore Head, Stonehaven, Aberdeen-Shire, AB39 2JY
Tel:01569 762 617
Email:enquiries@shipinnstonehaven.com
Web:www.shipinnstonehaven.co.uk

Inn dating back to 1771. Overlooking the local picturesque harbour of Stonehaven with open views to see and cliffs beyond. All rooms recently refurbished. Five of which have sea views. Restaurant - The Captain's Table, serving local produce and specialising in fish.

6 rooms, All en-suite. Open Jan-Dec. B&B per room, single from £50.00, double from £75.00.

20057 Strathdon, Aberdeenshire Map Ref: 4E10

The Colquhonnie House Hotel

Strathdon, Aberdeenshire, AB36 8UN
Tel:01975 651210 Fax:01975 651398
Email:info@thecolquhonniehotel.co.uk
Web:www.thecolquhonniehotel.co.uk

8 rooms
All en-suite
Open Jan-Dec
B&B per room, single from £41.00, double from £83.00.

C £ V

Aberdeen City Centre

Glen Coe, Highlands

THE HIGHLANDS AND SKYE

If you're searching for tranquillity and a more balanced perspective, you'll find that life in the Highlands moves at a refreshingly relaxed pace.

Stirringly beautiful and dramatically wild, it's hard not to be moved by the rugged majesty of the mountainous north. It's the stuff of picture postcards and coffee table books and views that will be etched in your memory forever.

Unspoiled beauty

There are so many places you have to experience: the eerie silence of Glen Coe; the arctic wilderness of the Cairngorms; the deep mysteries of Loch Ness; the wild flat lands of the Flow Country; the astonishing beauty of Glen Affric; and the golden beaches of the west coast where you can gaze out to the Atlantic and never meet a soul all day.

In this great, unspoiled, natural environment, wildlife flourishes. You'll see red squirrels and tiny goldcrests in the trees, otters chasing fish in fast flowing rivers, deer coming down from the hill to the forest edge, dolphins and whales off the coast, ospreys and eagles soaring overhead.

A natural playground

And this great natural playground is yours to share. Climbers, walkers, mountain bikers, skiers and hunters take to the hills. Surfers, sailors, canoeists and fishermen enjoy the beaches, rivers and lochs.

If it's adrenaline-filled adventure you're after you can try sports like sphereing, canyoning and white water rafting. Whatever outdoor activity you like to pursue, you'll find experienced, professional experts on hand to ensure you enjoy it to the full.

Highland hospitality

And once you've had enough exercise and fresh air, you can be assured of some fine Highland hospitality, whether you're staying in a tiny village, a pretty town, a thriving activity centre like Aviemore or in the rapidly expanding city of Inverness.

In the pubs and hotels, restaurants and other venues around the community, you'll find music and laughter, perhaps a riotous ceilidh in full fling and unforgettable nights of eating and drinking into the wee small hours.

Back to your roots

Highlanders know how to enjoy life and they're always keen to welcome visitors – especially those who are tracing their Scottish roots. Every year people come to discover the traditional homeland of their clan, learn about their history and walk in their ancestors' footsteps over battlefields like Culloden where the Jacobite army made its last stand.

You could follow Bonnie Prince Charlie over the sea to Skye whether it's by boat or by bridge. You can even take a glass bottom boat trip around the island and watch the sea life below.

Wherever you decide to go, the Highlands and Skye will cast a spell on you and it will be a holiday you will remember for as long as you live.

Portree, Isle of Skye

What's On?

O'Neill Highland Open, Thurso
25 April – 1 May 2008
One of the most progressive events in competitive surfing.
www.oneilleurope.com/highlandopen

Fèis an Eilein – The Skye Festival, Sleat
15 – 25 July 2008
An 11-day festival of traditional music, theatre and film.
www.feisaneilein.com

Tulloch Inverness Highland Games
19 – 20 July 2008
Clan gathering and heavyweight competition in Inverness.
www.invernesshighlandgames.com

Inverness Highland Tattoo
21 – 26 July 2008
Previewing artists from the Edinburgh International Tattoo.
www.tattooinverness.org.uk

Rock Ness, Dores, Loch Ness
7 – 8 June 2008
The only music event with its own monster.
www.rockness.co.uk

Belladrum Tartan Heart Festival, nr Inverness
8 – 9 August 2008
Open air, family-friendly traditional music festival.
www.tartanheartfestival.co.uk

UCI Mountain Bike World Cup, Fort William
7 – 8 June 2008
Voted best event on the tour 2 years running.
www.fortwilliamworldcup.co.uk

Highland Feast
26 September – 12 October 2008
A series of unique culinary and gastronomic events.
www.highlandfeast.co.uk

www.visithighlands.com

All dates correct at time of publication. Please check before booking. VisitScotland cannot be held responsible for any inaccuracies.

MAP

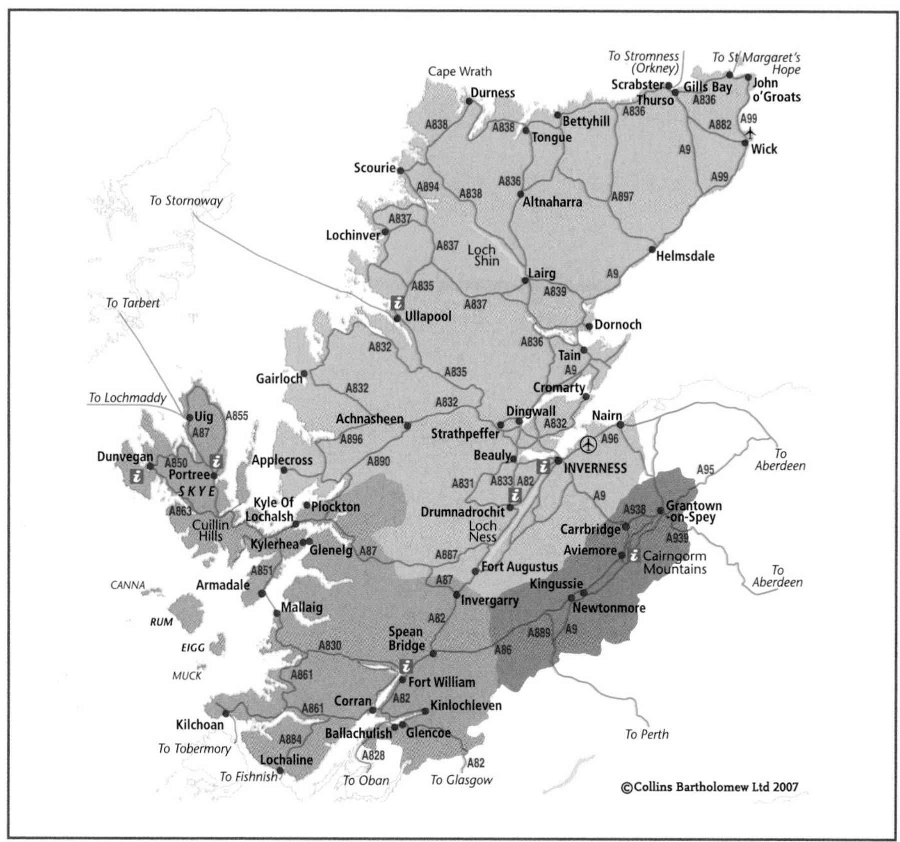
To Stromness (Orkney)
To St Margaret's Hope
Cape Wrath
Durness
Scrabster
Gills Bay
John o'Groats
Thurso
Bettyhill
Tongue
Wick
Scourie
Altnaharra
To Stornoway
Lochinver
Loch Shin
Helmsdale
Lairg
To Tarbert
Ullapool
Dornoch
Tain
Gairloch
Cromarty
To Lochmaddy
Uig
Achnasheen
Dingwall
Nairn
Strathpeffer
Dunvegan
Portree
SKYE
Applecross
Beauly
INVERNESS
To Aberdeen
Kyle Of Lochalsh
Plockton
Drumnadrochit
Loch Ness
Grantown -on-Spey
Carrbridge
Cuillin Hills
Kylerhea
Glenelg
Aviemore
Cairngorm Mountains
Fort Augustus
To Aberdeen
CANNA
Armadale
Kingussie
Invergarry
Mallaig
Newtonmore
RUM
EIGG
Spean Bridge
MUCK
Fort William
Corran
Kinlochleven
Kilchoan
Ballachulish
Glencoe
To Perth
To Tobermory
Lochaline
To Fishnish
To Oban
To Glasgow
A838
A836
A882
A99
A9
A894
A897
A837
A835
A839
A832
A855
A87
A850
A896
A890
A831
A833
A82
A96
A95
A863
A938
A939
A851
A887
A889
A86
A830
A861
A884
A828
©Collins Bartholomew Ltd 2007

TOURIST INFORMATION CENTRES

Northern Highlands, Inverness, Loch Ness and Nairn	
Drumnadrochit	The Car Park, Drumnadrochit, Inverness-shire IV63 6TX
Inverness	Castle Wynd, Inverness IV2 3BJ
Ullapool	6 Argyle Street, Ullapool, Ross-shire IV26 2UB
Fort William and Lochaber, Skye and Lochalsh	
Dunvegan	2 Lochside, Dunvegan, Isle of Skye IV55 8WB
Fort William	15 High Street, Fort William PH33 6DH
Portree	Bayfield Road, Portree, Isle of Skye IV51 9EL
Aviemore and the Cairngorms	
Aviemore	Grampian Road, Aviemore PH22 1PP

Make the most of your stay in Scotland and make your first stop the Tourist Information Centre wherever you go.

Knowledgeable and friendly staff can help you with information and advice; they can answer your questions, book accommodation and you can even pick up some souvenirs to take home for friends and family.

For information and ideas about exploring Scotland in advance of your trip, call our booking and information service or go to **www.visitscotland.com**

Call 0845 22 55 121

or if calling from outside the UK call
+44 (0) 1506 832 121

From Ireland call
1800 932 510

A £4 booking fee applies to telephone bookings of accommodation.

Loch Maree, Highlands

Northern Highlands, Inverness, Loch Ness and Nairn

Scotland's most northerly mainland territory is characterised by its mountainous, unspoiled wild places and its stunning coastline.

Within this great wilderness, there are places where nature has been tamed to dramatic effect – the celebrated Inverewe Gardens being an unmissable spot on the west coast.

Equally essential on the itinerary of any Highland visitor is Loch Ness, Britain's deepest and most mysterious freshwater expanse. Take a tour by boat and stare into its impenetrably dark waters and while you're there, don't miss the sprawling ruin of Urquhart Castle which never fails to impress.

There are many fine towns and villages to visit – Ullapool, Autlbea, Lochinver and Kinlochbervie to the west, Thurso, John O'Groats, Wick, Dornoch, Strathpeffer and Nairn on the eastern side.

You should also take some time to explore the rapidly growing city of Inverness, capital of the Highlands and a thriving, modern city with lots of attractions.

Footbridge over the River Ness, Inverness

DON'T MISS

1 Accessible by boat from Tarbet, just north of Scourie, **Handa Island** is home to one of Britain's biggest seabird colonies during spring and early summer. Under the care of the Scottish Wildlife Trust, there are few better – or more beautiful – sites to spot guillemots, razorbills and puffins, among a myriad of other species.

2 **Culloden Battlefield** is the site of the last major battle fought on mainland Britain in 1746. Bonnie Prince Charlie's Jacobite troops were defeated here by the Duke of Cumberland and the Hanoverian government forces. The new visitor centre – opened in 2007 – features a battle immersion cinema and handheld multi-lingual audio devices to bring the battle to life.

3 Not only is there a wealth of wildlife on land, but also in the waters nearby. The Beauly, Moray and Cromarty Firths all play host to **bottlenose dolphins** – the North Sea's only resident group. A number of boat trips departing from Nairn, Inverness or Cromarty can take you out to see them without disturbing their habitat – look out for members of the Dolphin Space Programme, accredited operators conducting cruises of high quality with low environmental impact.

4 Perhaps the most spectacularly scenic of all Scottish lochs, **Loch Maree** greets unsuspecting visitors travelling north-west on the A832 between Inverness and Gairloch. Bounded by the imposing masses of Beinn Eighe to the west and Slioch to the east, the loch's shores play host to a wealth of wildlife, as well as fragments of ancient Caledonian pinewood.

5 One of the largest castles in Scotland, the ruins of **Urquhart Castle** lie on the banks of Loch Ness, near Drumnadrochit. Blown up in 1692 to prevent Jacobite occupation, this 5-star visitor attraction has a fascinating interactive visitor centre which depicts the story of the castle's turbulent history. Explore the ruins of the castle, before visiting the on-site café where you will be rewarded with breathtaking views of Loch Ness.

6 At **Learnie Red Rock Trails** an exciting mix of short well made uphills and challenging fast downhill sections make for a great day's mountain biking on the Black Isle with fantastic views of the Moray Firth. Situated in woodland on the A832 between Rosemarkie and Cromarty this attraction will fill your adrenaline needs.

5

6

FOOD AND DRINK

www.eatscotland.com

7 In the attractive fishing settlement of Achiltibuie, the Summer Isles Hotel boasts an astounding menu and even better views. Enjoy the local seafood while the sun sets over its namesake islands. Five miles north, the Smokehouse allows you to see delicious fish being cured and gives you the chance to purchase it afterwards.

8 Highland Feast, an annual food and drink festival held in late September/early October, is a celebration of the fantastic produce and culinary skills present in the local area and beyond.

9 Fresh, local ingredients are combined to make the Falls of Shin Visitor Centre the ultimate place to stop for lunch. See salmon leap on the magnificent waterfall as you tuck in. There is also a children's playground so you can fill up while the kids are kept entertained.

10 On the A82 near Inverness, at Moniack Castle Wineries, see how a selection of 9 wines and liqueurs and 22 marmalades, preserves and sauces are made from the best of natural Highland ingredients. Tour the fermenting room, filtering processes, bottling and labelling, then pass through the cellars to the kitchen and watch the cooking of the preserves and sauces.

10

12

13

GOLF

www.visitscotland.com/golf

11 Gairloch Golf Course is superbly situated above a sandy bay beside the road into Gairloch. This 9-hole links course is one of the Highland's best kept secrets. Take your time soaking up the views towards Skye. Arrange tee times in advance to guarantee a round.

12 Durness Golf Course, surrounded by stunning coastal scenery, is notorious for its 9th hole, which requires players to clear the Atlantic Ocean! Check with the secretary in advance to ensure a round is possible.

13 Considered one of the finest links courses in the world, Royal Dornoch Golf Course is situated on public land in its namesake royal burgh, 45 miles north of Inverness. Play on the course about which Tom Watson famously remarked 'the most fun I've ever had on a golf course'.

14 A traditional Scottish links course, Brora Golf Course offers a challenge for all abilities. Situated on the northeast coast, 20 minutes drive from Dornoch, this 18-hole favourite is perfect for the discerning golfer looking to experience a course steeped in tradition.

OUTSTANDING VIEWS

15 A classic view of Loch Ness is to be savoured from the beach at the village of Dores, at the quieter side of the Loch to the south. Look out for Nessie, or at the very least, the resident Nessie spotter!

16 Round the bay from Lochinver, a minor road allows fantastic views back towards the community and the incredible sugar loaf of Suilven rising up in the background.

17 Near John o'Groats see a dramatic coastline where thousands of seabirds nest in vast colonies. A walk across the clifftop fields will reward you with a stunning view south to Thirle Door and the Stacks of Duncansby. The first is a rocky arch, the second a group of large jagged sea stacks. This is a spot you will want to savour, with a view that varies as you move along the clifftop path and bring into play different alignments of the stacks and arch.

18 The Corrieshalloch Gorge National Nature Reserve, south-east of Ullapool, comprises a box canyon dropping 200ft to the river below. Adding to the drama are the spectacular Falls of Measach, best seen from the viewing platform to the north.

WALKS

www.visitscotland.com/walking

19 Reelig Glen is a short walk through spectacular old conifer and broad-leaved trees on easy paths with short gentle gradients, making it a suitable walk for almost anyone. Approximately 10 minutes from Inverness, take the A862 west towards Beauly and after 8 miles, turn left onto the minor road signposted to Reelig and Moniack and continue for 1 mile – follow the Forestry Commission sign and look out for one of Britain's tallest trees named Dughall Mor.

20 Gentle walking or cycling awaits through an extensive network of formal and informal trails at Culbin Forest between Nairn and Forres. Forest trails, guided walks and a badger hide are among the many attractions of this forest, which hosts a variety of plant, animal and bird life.

21 Take the minor B869 road to Storr lighthouse, from which a 3-hour circular walk leads to a spectacular rock-stack – the Old Man of Stoer - surrounded by jaw-dropping cliff scenery. The path is clear throughout, and offers views to the Assynt mountains in the south, and to Lewis and Harris many miles to the west.

22 The Caithness and Sutherland Walking Festival, held in May, consists of themed walks led by local guides. These interesting walks explore archaeology, history and wildlife and are a great way to learn more about the surrounding area.

35155 Achnasheen, Ross-shire Map Ref: 3H8

Ledgowan Lodge Hotel

Ledgowan, Achnasheen, Ross-shire, IV22 2EJ
Tel:01445 720252
Web:www.ledgowanlodge.co.uk

A country house hotel in the heart of the Highlands, amongst some of the most amazing scenery, with access to many areas of interest. We have cosy log fires and candle lit rooms.

12 rooms, All en-suite. Open Jan-Dec. Rates on application.

77137 Brackla, Loch Ness-side, Inverness-shire Map Ref: 4A9

Loch Ness Clansman Hotel

Brackla, Loch Ness-side, Inverness-shire, IV3 8LA
Tel:01456 450326 Fax:01456 450845
Email:info@lochnessview.com
Web:www.lochnessview.com

The ONLY hotel situated on the banks of Loch Ness. Fully refurbished, our facilities include deluxe bedrooms overlooking the loch at excellent rates. The 'Observation Lounge Bar' and restaurant have stunning views over the loch to the hills beyond. Local Scottish produce. Idyllic setting. 9m Inverness, 4m Drumnadrochit (A82). Great touring base. Boat trips all year.

26 rooms, All en-suite. Open Jan-Dec excl Xmas/New Year. B&B per person, single from £49.00, double from £34.50.

34115 by Dingwall, Ross-shire Map Ref: 4A8

Kinkell Country House

Easter Kinkell, by Conon Bridge, Ross-shire, IV7 8HY
Tel:01349 861270 Fax:01349 865902

8 rooms
All en-suite
Open Jan-Dec
Rates on application.

22964 Dornoch, Sutherland Map Ref: 4B6

Dornoch Castle Hotel

Castle Street, Dornoch, Sutherland, IV25 3SD
Tel:01862 810216

24 rooms
All en-suite
Open Jan-Dec
Rates on application.

79343 Durness, Sutherland Map Ref: 4A3

Wild Orchid Guest House

Durine, Durness, Sutherland, IV27 4PN
Tel:01971 511280
Email:wildorchidguesthouse@hotmail.co.uk
Web:www.wildorchidguesthouse.co.uk

6 rooms
Open Jan-Dec
Rates on application.

75829 Fearn, Ross-shire Map Ref: 4C7

Fearn Hotel

Hill of Fearn, Fearn, Ross-shire, IV20 1TJ
Tel:01862 832234
Email:fearnhotel@yahoo.co.uk

6 rooms
Some en-suite
Open Jan-Dec
B&B per person, single from £35.00, double from £35.00.

17592 Fort Augustus, Inverness-shire Map Ref: 4A10

Caledonian Hotel

Fort Augustus, Inverness-shire, PH32 4BQ
Tel:01320 366256 Fax:08717 145639
Email:hotel@thecaledonianhotel.com
Web:www.thecaledonianhotel.com

10 rooms
All en-suite
Open Easter-Nov
B&B per person, single from £45.00, double from £35.00, BB & Eve.Meal from £52.50.

28370 Glen Urquhart, Inverness-shire Map Ref: 4A9

Glenurquhart House

Glenurquhart, Drumnadrochit, Inverness-shire, IV63 6TJ
Tel:01456 476234 Fax:01456 476286
Email:carol@glenurquhartlodges.co.uk

Situated in a scenic location overlooking Loch Meiklie. Attractions nearby include Loch Ness, Glen Affric for hill-walking, loch and river fishing, and pony trekking. Restaurant using freshly prepared produce. At the end of your day relax in our comfortable lounge by the log fires.

6 rooms, Some en-suite. Open Mar-Nov. B&B per person, single from £40.00, double from £40.00, BB & Eve.Meal from £55.00.

28180 Invergarry, Inverness-shire Map Ref: 3H11

Glengarry Castle Hotel

Invergarry, Inverness-shire, PH35 4HW
Tel:01809 501254 Fax:01809 501207
Email:castle@glengarry.net
Web:www.glengarry.net

Country House Hotel privately owned and personally run by the MacCallum family for over 40 years. Situated in the heart of the Great Glen, this is a perfect centre for touring both the West Coast and Inverness/Loch Ness area. Magnificently situated in 60 acres of wooded grounds overlooking Loch Oich. Recently refurbished, 5 rooms with 4 poster beds, all rooms have ensuite bathrooms, TV, radio and telephone. Private tennis court, trout and pike fishing in Loch Oich. Children and dogs welcome. For brochure please contact Mr D MacCallum.

26 rooms.
All en-suite. Open mid Mar-mid Nov
B&B per person, single from £70.00, double from £52.00.

33956 Invergordon, Ross-shire Map Ref: 4B7

Kincraig House Hotel

Invergordon, Ross-shire, IV18 0LF
Tel:01349 852587 Fax:01349 852193
Email:info@kincraig-house-hotel.co.uk
Web:www.kincraig-house-hotel.co.uk

Kincraig House Hotel offers 15 en-suite rooms, a number of which are newly created Premier and Executive rooms, A refurbished a'la Carte Restaurant and bar and a spacious oak panelled lounge offer superb character and comfort.

15 rooms, All en-suite. Open Jan-Dec. B&B per person, single from £55.00, double from £45.00, BB & Eve.Meal from £68.00.

11992 Inverness Map Ref: 4B8

Anchor and Chain

Coulmore Bay, North Kessock, Inverness-shire, IV1 3XB
Tel:01463 731313
Web:www.anchorandchainhotel.co.uk

10 rooms
All en-suite
Open Jan-Dec
B&B per room, single from £40.00, double from £65.00. Special deals available for short breaks.

13974 Inverness Map Ref: 4B8

Ballifeary Guest House

10 Ballifeary Road, Inverness, IV3 5PJ
Tel:01463 235572 Fax:01463 717583
Email:william.gilbert@btconnect.com
Web:www.ballifearyhousehotel.co.uk

6 rooms
All en-suite
Open Jan-Dec excl Xmas
B&B per person, single from £40.00, double from £35.00.

18524 Inverness Map Ref: 4B8

Castle View Guest House

2A Ness Walk, Inverness, IV3 5NE
Tel/Fax:01463 241443
Email:jmunro4161@aol.com
Web:www.castleviewinverness.co.uk

6 rooms
Some en-suite
Open Jan-Dec
B&B per person, single from £26.00, double/twin from £24.00.

21689 Inverness Map Ref: 4B8

Culloden House Hotel

Milton of Culloden, Inverness, IV1 2NZ
Tel:01463 790461
Email:info@cullodenhouse.co.uk
Web:www.cullodenhouse.co.uk

Elegant, historic Georgian mansion built in the Palladian style dating from 1788, offering high standard of service, cuisine and ambience. Set in 40 acres of grounds. Conference facilities.

28 rooms, All en-suite. Open Jan-Dec. Rates on application.

23340 Inverness Map Ref: 4B8

Drumossie Hotel

Old Perth Road, Inverness, Inverness-shire, IV2 5BE
Tel:01463 236451 Fax:01463 712858
Email:stay@drumossiehotel.co.uk
Web:www.drumossiehotel.co.uk

Luxury hotel standing in its own grounds 3 miles (5kms) South of Inverness with easy access to A9. Ideal for touring. Facilities for meetings and conferences. 44 Newly refurbished bedrooms all ensuite.

44 rooms, All en-suite. Open Jan-Dec. B&B per person, single from £150.00, double from £80.00.

72450 Inverness Map Ref: 4B8

Dunain Park Hotel

Inverness, IV3 8JN
Tel:01463 230512 Fax:01463 224532
Email:dunainparkhotel@btinternet.com
Web:www.dunainparkhotel.co.uk

Dunain Park is a personally run small country house hotel set in six acres of beautiful landscaped gardens, offering a very high standard of comfort and friendly efficient service. Our award winning restaurant takes pride in its use of our wonderful Highland produce, with an extensive range of wines and over 200 whiskies.

13 rooms, Incl. suites four-posters and half-testers. B&B per person from £99.00, D,B&B from £125.00.

60443 Inverness Map Ref: 4B8

Express by Holiday Inn

Stoneyfield, Inverness, IV2 7PA
Tel:01463 732700 Fax:01463 732732

94 rooms
All en-suite
Open Jan-Dec
Rates on application.

28283 Inverness Map Ref: 4B8

Glenmoriston Town House

20 Ness Bank, Inverness, Inverness-shire, IV2 4SF
Tel:01463 223777
Email:reception@glenmoristontownhouse.com
Web:www.glenmoristontownhouse.com

Located in a peaceful setting overlooking the River ness, close to the city centre. Most bedrooms fitted with CD/DVD players,wireless internet. Award winning Abstract restaurant specialising in modern French Cuisine using the best Scottish produce. Also available Contrast brasserie open 7 days a week for lunch and dinner.

30 rooms, All en-suite. Open Jan-Dec. B&B per room, single from £85.00, double from £120.00.

31988 Inverness Map Ref: 4B8

Inverglen

7 Abertarff Road, Inverness, IV2 3NW
Tel:01463 236281 Fax:01463 712902
Email:inverglen@globalnet.co.uk
Web:www.inverglenguesthouse.co.uk

Detached villa situated in quiet residential area. Walking distance from town centre, railway station and restaurants. Relaxing atmosphere. Ample private parking.

5 rooms, All en-suite. Open Jan-Dec. B&B per person, single from £33.00, double from £28.00.

47694 Inverness Map Ref: 4B8

Kessock Hotel

North Kessock, Ross-shire, IV1 1XN
Tel:01463 731208
Email:nkhtl@gloddnet.co.uk

6 rooms
All en-suite
Open Jan-Dec
B&B per room, single from £60.00, double from £95.00.

65094 Inverness Map Ref: 4B8

Kingsmills Hotel, Inverness

Culcabock Road, Inverness, IV2 3LP
Tel:01463 257100 Fax:01463 712984
Email:info@kingsmillshotel.com
Web:www.kingsmillshotel.com

Original manor house dating back to the 18th century set in 4 acres of gardens. Leisure club with indoor swimming pool, jacuzzi, sauna, steam room, exercise room, hairdresser, beauty treatments. Choice of 2 restaurants. 1 mile (2kms) from city centre, 7 miles (11kms) from airport.

82 rooms, All en-suite. Open Jan-Dec. B&B per person from £55.00.

35931 Inverness Map Ref: 4B8

Loch Ness House Hotel

Glenurquhart Road, Inverness, Inverness-shire, IV3 8JL
Tel:01463 231248
Email:lnhhchris@aol.com

22 rooms
All en-suite
Open Jan-Dec
B&B per room, single from £80.00, double from £80.00.

36871 Inverness Map Ref: 4B8

MacDougall Clansman Hotel

103 Church Street, Inverness, IV1 1ES
Tel/Fax:01463 713702
Email:macdougallhotel@aol.com
Web:www.invernesscentrehotel.co.uk

Family-run hotel in convenient town centre location, close to Rail & Bus stations, Tourist Information Centre and all shops. On street parking and limited private parking available. French, German and Spanish spoken. Most rooms non-smoking.

14 rooms, All en-suite. Open Jan-Dec. B&B per room, single from £38.00, double from £58.00.

70379 Inverness Map Ref: 4B8

Strathness Guest House

4 Ardross Terrace, Inverness, IV3 5NQ
Tel:01463 232765 Fax:01463 332970
Email:info@strathnesshouse.com
Web:www.strathnesshouse.co.uk

12 rooms
Open all year
B&B per person, single from £45.00, double from £35.00.

63970 Inverness Map Ref: 4B8

Whinpark Guest House

17 Ardross Street, Inverness, Inverness-shire, IV3 5NS
Tel/Fax:01463 232549
Email:info@whinparkhotel.com
Web:www.whinparkhotel.co.uk

13 rooms
All en-suite
Open Jan-Dec
B&B per person, single from £30.00-50.00, double/twin from £25.00-39.00.

64396 Inverness Map Ref: 4B8

Winston Guest House

10 Ardross Terrace, Inverness, Inverness-shire, IV3 5NQ
Tel:01463 234477 Fax:01463 235001
Email:info@whinparkhotel.com

18 rooms
All en-suite
Open Jan-Dec
B&B per person, double/twin from £25.00-39.00.

54083 John O'Groats, Caithness Map Ref: 4E2

Seaview Hotel

John O'Groats, Caithness, KW1 4YR
Tel/Fax:01955 611220
Email:seaviewhotel@barbox.net
Web:www.johnogroats-seaviewhotel.co.uk

10 rooms
9 en-suite
Open Jan-Dec
B&B per person, single from £35.00, double from £30.00, BB & Eve.Meal from £40.00.

48851 by Lairg, Sutherland Map Ref: 4A6

The Overscaig House Hotel

Loch Shin, Sutherland, IV27 4NY
Tel:01549 431203 Fax:01549 431210
Email:visits@overscaig.com
Web:www.overscaig.com

Located on the banks of Loch Shin, the Overscraig is an ideal base to explore all the attractions of the Northern Highlands. Hill walking, bird watching, fishing available. A warm highland welcome awaits.

8 rooms, All ensuite with bath & shower. Open Apr-Oct. B&B per person £44.00 per night, family room £128.00 per night incl breakfast. Discounts for longer stays.

66454 Lochinver, Sutherland Map Ref: 3G5

Inver Lodge Hotel

Lochinver, Sutherland, IV27 4LU
Tel:01571 844496 Fax:01571 844395
Email:stay@inverlodge.com
Web:www.inverlodge.com

Opened in 1988 and refurbished in 2001 the hotel combines modern facilities and comforts with the traditional ambience of a Highland Lodge. Our foreground is Lochinver Bay & The Western Sea, our backdrop the great peaks of Sutherland: Canisp & Suliven. Amidst the dramatic coastline can be found clear white sandy beaches. All bedrooms are ensuite and sea facing with many facilities to make your stay comfortable and memorable. Making the most of locally landed fish and shellfish, the Scottish beef, lamb & game our restaurant offers high standards in cuisine & service, complemented with a fine selection of wines. Salmon and trout fishing can also be arranged.

20 rooms.
All en-suite. Open Apr-Oct
B&B per person, single from £130.00, double from £100.00, BB & Eve.Meal from £100.00.

50075 Lochinver, Sutherland Map Ref: 3G5

Polcraig Guest House

Lochinver, Sutherland, IV27 4LD
Tel/Fax:01571 844429
Email:cathelmac@aol.com
Web:www.smoothhound.co.uk/hotels/polcraig.html

6 rooms
All en-suite
Open Jan-Dec
B&B per person, single from £30.00, double from £30.00.

15127 Melvich, Sutherland Map Ref: 4C3

Bighouse Lodge

Melvich, by Thurso, Sutherland, KW14 7YJ
Tel/Fax:01641 531207
Email:info@bighouseestate.com
Web:www.bighouseestate.com

Stunningly located at the mouth of the Halladale river, and surrounded by water on 3 sides. A charming, warm and welcoming Scottish country house which is very well appointed.

11 rooms, All en-suite. Open all year. B&B per person, from £79.50.

48572 Muir of Ord, Ross-shire Map Ref: 4A8

Ord House Hotel

Muir of Ord, Ross-shire, IV6 7UH
Tel/Fax:01463 870492
Email:admin@ord-house.co.uk
Web:www.ord-house.co.uk

10 rooms
All en-suite
Open May-Oct
B&B per person single from £40.00, BB & Eve.Meal from £66.00.

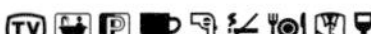

13519 Nairn Map Ref: 4C8

Aurora Hotel

2 Academy Street, Nairn, Nairn-shire, IV12 4RJ
Tel:01667 453551 Fax:01667 456577
Email:aurorahotelnairn@aol.com

10 rooms
All en-suite
Open Jan-Dec
B&B per person from £37.50.

73794 Nairn Map Ref: 4C8

Braeval Hotel

Crescent Road, Nairn, Inverness-shire, IV12 4NB
Tel:01667 452341 Fax:01667 456063
Email:info@braevalhotel.co.uk
Web:www.braevalhotel.co.uk

Comfortable family run hotel refurbished 2007. Beach location with magnificent sea views. Close to harbour, leisure facilities and town centre. Excellent fine-dining restaurant and bar meals by award-winning Chef.

10 rooms, Open Jan-Dec. B&B per room, single from £40.00, double from £80.00.

19579 Nairn — Map Ref: 4C8

Claymore House Hotel

Seabank Road, Nairn, IV12 4EY
Tel:01667 453731 Fax:01667 455290
Email:claymorehouse@btconnect.com
Web:www.claymorehousehotel.com

13 rooms
All en-suite
Open Jan-Dec
B&B per person, single from £47.50, double from £47.50, BB & Eve.Meal from £59.50.

32033 Nairn — Map Ref: 4C8

Invernairne Guest House

Thurlow Road, Nairn, Inverness-shire, IV12 4EZ
Tel:01667 452039 Fax:01667 456760
Email:info@invernairne.com
Web:www.invernairne.com

9 rooms
All en-suite
Open Mar-Nov plus New Year
B&B per person, single from £39.50, double from £37.50.

50130 Poolewe, Ross-shire — Map Ref: 3F7

Poolewe Hotel

Main Street, Poolewe, IV22 2JX
Tel:01445 781241
Email:info@poolewehotel.co.uk
Web:www.poolewehotel.co.uk

9 rooms
All en-suite
Open Jan-Dec
B&B per person, single from £42.00, double from £39.50, BB & Eve.Meal from £59.50.

51541 Rhiconich, Sutherland — Map Ref: 3H3

Rhiconich Hotel

Rhiconich, Sutherland, IV27 4RN
Tel:01971 521224 Fax:01971 521732
Email:rhiconichhotel@aol.com
Web:www.rhiconichhotel.co.uk

11 rooms
All en-suite
Open Jan-Dec closed Xmas/New Year
B&B per person, single from £40.00, double from £39.50.

24356 Scourie, Sutherland — Map Ref: 3H4

Eddrachilles Hotel

Badcall Bay, Scourie, Sutherland, IV27 4TH
Tel:01971 502080 Fax:01971 502477
Email:enq@eddrachilles.com
Web:www.eddrachilles.com

Magnificently situated overlooking the islands of Eddrachillis Bay, this 200 year old building has been carefully refurbished, providing modern comfortable bedrooms but retaining the charm and character of older times. Fully licensed with an extensive wine list, cooking concentrates on traditional style benefiting from high quality local produce, commended by Taste of Scotland. Close to Handa Island bird sanctuary. Deer, seals, otters and badgers can be seen in and around the hotel grounds.

11 rooms, All en-suite. Open Mar-Oct.

49965 Scourie, Sutherland — Map Ref: 3H4

Scourie Hotel

Scourie, Sutherland, IV27 4SX
Tel:01971 502396 Fax:01971 502423
Email:patrick@scourie-hotel.co.uk
Web:www.scourie-hotel.co.uk

20 rooms
All en-suite
Open Apr-Oct
B&B per person, single from £38.00, double from £35.00 per person.

20630 Strathpeffer, Ross-shire — Map Ref: 4A8

Coul House Hotel

Contin, By Strathpeffer, Ross-shire, IV14 9ES
Tel:01997 421487 Fax:01997 421945
Email:stay@coulhousehotel.com
Web:www.coulhousehotel.com

Secluded country house with forest walks and pitch & putt course in the grounds. The hotel is enjoying a growing reputation for quality food and good hospitality.

21 rooms, All en-suite. Open Jan-Dec. B&B per person, single from £89.00, double from £59.50.

19846 Struy, by Beauly, Inverness-shire — Map Ref: 4A9

Cnoc Hotel

Struy, By Beauly, Inverness-shire, IV4 7JU
Tel:01463 761 264 Fax:01463 761 207
Email:cnochotel@talk21.com

7 rooms
All en-suite
Open Jan-Dec
B&B per person, single from £55.00, double from £42.50.

49173 Thurso, Caithness — Map Ref: 4D3

Park Hotel

Thurso, KW14 8RE
Tel:01847 893251 Fax:01847 804044
Email:reception@parkhotelthurso.co.uk
Web:www.parkhotelthurso.co.uk

21 rooms
All en-suite
Open Jan-Dec excl New Year
B&B per person, single from £45.00, double from £38.00. Reduced rates off season.

68291 Thurso, Caithness — Map Ref: 4D3

Pentland Lodge House

Granville Street, Thurso, Caithness, KW14 7LG
Tel:01847 8611206
Email:sandys@fwi.co.uk

8 rooms
All en-suite
Open Jan-Dec
B&B per person, single from £45.00, double from £40.00.

56405 Thurso, Caithness Map Ref: 4D3

Station Hotel and Apartments

54-58 Princes Street, Thurso, Caithness, KW14 7DH
Tel:01847 892003 Fax:01847 891820
Email:stationhotel@lineone.net
Web:www.stationthurso.co.uk

30 rooms and 2 selfcatering apartments
All en-suite
Open Jan-Dec
B&B per person, single from £45.00, double from £30.00.

58200 Tongue, Sutherland Map Ref: 4A3

Ben Loyal Hotel

Main Street, Tongue, Sutherland, IV27 4XE
Tel:01847 611216 Fax:01847 611212
Email:stay@benloyal.co.uk
Web:www.benloyal.co.uk

11 rooms
All en-suite
Open Mar-Dec
B&B per person, single from £35.00, double from £35.00.

66585 Tongue, Sutherland Map Ref: 4A3

Borgie Lodge Hotel

Skerray, By Tongue, Sutherland, KW14 7TH
Tel:01641 521332
Email:info@borgielodgehotel.co.uk
Web:www.borgielodgehotel.co.uk

A former hunting lodge in a quiet and peaceful location. Dinner menu changes daily but features local and homegrown produce when available. Excellent countryside for walking, fishing, stalking, photography or simply relaxing.

8 rooms, Some en-suite. Open Jan-Dec. B&B per room, single from £50.00, double from £80.00.

79169 Tongue, Sutherland Map Ref: 4A3

Tongue Hotel

Tongue, Sutherland, IV27 4XD
Tel:01847 611206 Fax:01847 611345
Email:info@tonguehotel.co.uk
Web:www.tonguehotel.co.uk

Duke of Sutherland's former hunting lodge. Set overlooking the beautiful Kyle of Tongue. A hotel full of character, offering a warm reception, excellent local produce, fine wines and interesting malts.

19 rooms, Open from Mar2008 - all year excl Xmas. Rates on application..

12714 Ullapool, Ross-shire Map Ref: 3G6

Ardvreck House

North Road, Morefield, Ullapool, IV26 2TH
Tel:01854 612028 Fax:01854 613000
Email:ardvreck@btinternet.com
Web:www.smoothhound.co.uk/hotels/ardvreck.html

Guest house set amidst some of the best hillwalking country and breathtaking scenery in Scotland. Elevated country position overlooking Ullapool and Lochbroom. Spacious, well appointed rooms most with spectacular sea view, all with ensuite shower room, T.V and tea/coffee facility. Residents lounge available at all times. Local facilities include a leisure centre, swimming pool, sauna, golf course, fishing and museum.

10 rooms, All en-suite. Open Mar-Nov. B&B per person, single from £30.00, double from £30.00.

23205 Ullapool, Ross-shire Map Ref: 3G6

Dromnan Guest House

Garve Road, Ullapool, Ross-shire, IV26 2SX
Tel:01854 612333
Email:info@dromnan.com
Web:www.dromnan.com

7 rooms
All en-suite
Open Jan-Dec
B&B per person, single £30.00-40.00, double £30.00-35.00.

Elgol, Loch Scavaig, Isle of Skye

Fort William, Lochaber, Skye and Lochalsh

Fort William is often referred to as the 'Outdoor Capital of the UK'. It has been host to the Mountain Biking World Championships, it's next door to Ben Nevis, Scotland's highest mountain, and the surrounding area provides a bewildering range of opportunities to enjoy the outdoors.

The local scenery is quite stunning. From the towering beauty of Glen Coe to the breathtaking views across Loch Duich from Castle Stalker to the wild isolation of Ardnamurchan Point, there are hundreds of amazing places to visit.

Why not take in some of the finest coastal and hill scenery on what is considered one of the Great Railway Journeys of the World. Travel the length of the legendary Road to the Isles on the Jacobite Steam Train from Fort William to Mallaig. Take in such sites as the Caledonian Canal, the Glenfinnan Viaduct and the glorious coastline of Arisaig and Morar, and when you reach Mallaig you'll be able to see the jagged peaks of the Cuillin Mountains on the Isle of Skye.

The turbulent history and majestic scenery of Skye and Lochalsh make the area one of Scotland's most romantic destinations. From the delightfully situated Eilean Donan Castle and the picture-postcard village of Plockton to the soaring craggy heights of the Cuillin and the eerie pinnacles of the Trotternish, the area is sure to leave an imprint on your heart.

DON'T MISS

1. One of the most picturesque – and most photographed – castles in Scotland, **Eilean Donan Castle**, sits on an island in Loch Duich, beside the tiny village of Dornie. Stroll across the causeway that links it to the shore and explore it for yourself. For a panoramic view, follow the path from the village which leads up to the Carr Brae viewpoint.

2. Take a boat trip from Elgol to isolated and inspiring **Loch Coruisk**. You will get up close to Britain's most dramatic landscapes, while your local guide will make sure you don't miss out on seeing the local wildlife – including the famous seal colony on the banks of the Loch.

3. Accessible only by boat from Mallaig or via a very long walk from Kinlochhourn, **Knoydart** is recognised as the remotest part of mainland Britain and is perfect for the adventurous. One of the best hiking spots in the country, there are also options for wildlife watching, canoeing and fishing, amongst other activities organised by operators in the area. The scenery is outstanding and will leave a lasting impression.

4. Familiar to fans of the film Local Hero, and every bit as stunning in reality, **Camusdarach Beach** is one of a string of exquisite beaches along the shoreline between Arisaig and Morar. While away a few hours picnicking with the breathtaking backdrop of the Small Isles rising sheer out of the sea in front of you. For an alternative, try the Silver Sands of Morar to the north.

5. To travel the whole length of the legendary Road to the Isles, hop aboard the **Jacobite Steam Train**. This steam engine runs between Fort William and Mallaig throughout the summer months and takes in some truly impressive sites such as Neptune's Staircase, the Glenfinnan Viaduct and the glorious coastline of Arisaig and Morar. Regarded as one of the Great Railway Journeys of the World, this is a must while in the area, especially for Harry Potter fans who will recognise it from the movies.

6. The biggest indoor ice climbing facility in the world, **The Ice Factor**, is situated in a former aluminium works in Kinlochleven. With rock climbing walls, a gym, sauna, and plunge pool, this is a great day out for the activity enthusiast or indeed, the whole family. As the National Centre for Indoor Ice Climbing, experts can try out new techniques whilst novices can get to grips with the basics in a safe and secure environment.

4

6

FOOD AND DRINK

www.eatscotland.com

7 The **Three Chimneys** restaurant is known far and wide as one of the most romantic eateries in the land. The candlelit crofter's cottage on the shores of Loch Dunvegan, voted 28th in Restaurant Magazine's 'definitive list' of the World's Top 50 Restaurants, is an idyllic setting for a proposal, a honeymoon or any special occasion. Book ahead to ensure your table.

8 Mallaig is the place to go if you're looking for fresh, locally-caught seafood in the area. **The Cabin** has a good value menu, and does a mean fish and chips.

9 **Crannog** at the Waterfront in Fort William serves the very best in seafood. Be sure to give their speciality a try – the langoustine fresh from Loch Linnhe!

10 For an AA rosette dinner, seek out **Russell's Restaurant**, Smiddy House in Spean Bridge. Innovation and flair are deftly applied to a fine range of local produce.

7

11

13

WALKS

www.visitscotland.com/walking

11 **Glen Finnan** - From the Glenfinnan Visitor Centre car park, follow the Mallaig road across a bridge and then look out for a sign pointing towards Glenfinnan Lodge. From here continue up the Glen where kids will be impressed by the famous viaduct, featured in the Harry Potter films. An easy 5½-mile route, taking in most of this scenic glen, can be completed in roughly 2 hours.

12 **Morar to Loch Morar and Mallaig** - This is a walk you can enjoy without the hassle of taking the car. The starting and finishing points are both adjacent to train stations, so check out www.firstscotrail.com to ensure you're onboard! Set off from Morar station and walk south, taking a left turn onto the minor road along Loch Morar's north shore. Keep a look out for Nessie's cousin 'Morag' who supposedly occupies this loch. Continue along, as the road becomes a path, before arriving in Tarbet. Here, a boat departs daily at 3.30 pm throughout the summer to take you back via Loch Nevis to the connecting train at Mallaig. Allow 6 hours for the walk.

13 **Glen Coe** is one of the most popular hiking destinations in Scotland with the likes of Allt Coire for more experienced hikers and, for the less experienced walker, places like the Lost Valley to seek out. From the car parks on the A82, the path takes you across the bridge over the River Coe towards the triple buttresses known as the Three Sisters. Turn right after the bridge and follow the trail upwards. After a couple of miles you'll reach the false summit marking the edge of the hidden basin where the MacDonald clan used to hide their cattle in times of attack.

14 For a longer more challenging walk, drive 6 miles north from Portree on the Isle of Skye, where you will find a car park. A path leads through woodland onto a steep climb to an area of geological formations. There are then a number of paths that can be followed to the base of the **Old Man of Storr**. Along the way you can enjoy good views across the Sound of Raasay. This walk should take in excess of 3 hours.

OUTSTANDING VIEWS

15 Quite apart from the rock formations, it is well worth the hike to Storr for the views of the western seaboard. The mountains and sea lochs of **Wester Ross** are perhaps more reminiscent of Norway than Scotland.

16 From Rannoch Moor on the A82, the twin peaks of **Buachaille Etive Mor** and Buachaille Etive Beag spectacularly mark the entrance to Glen Coe. Appearing like steep-sided pyramids they stand sentinel on the moor, offering a glimpse of the wild landscape just around the corner.

17 There are many classic views of the **Cuillin Ridge**. However, for sheer drama, few views in all of Scotland compare with the sight of Sgurr Nan Gillean rearing up behind Sligachan Bridge, or the full mountain range rising almost sheer from Loch Scavaig, opposite the tiny village of Elgol, west of Broadford.

18 To see the **Five Sisters of Kintail** from Ratagan Pass, take the Glenelg road from Shiel Bridge on the A87. As you rise up towards Mam Ratagan, about a mile along, take a look back over Loch Duich, framed by the majestic peaks of Kintail. Simply stunning.

15

16

18

HERITAGE

19 **Dunvegan Castle**, the stronghold of the MacLeod chiefs for nearly 800 years, remains their home today. Although it still has the atmosphere of a family home it is open to the public so that you can share in the unique possessions of beauty and interest. Highland cattle roam around the estate, making you feel that you've well and truly reached the Scottish Highlands!

20 Kilmuir, home of the **Skye Museum of Island Life**, comprises a group of seven thatched-roof cottages depicting past life on Skye, including items used by Bonnie Prince Charlie and Flora MacDonald.

21 For a full interpretation of this amazing setting, head to the **Glencoe Visitor Centre** on the A82, 17 miles south of Fort William. Particularly eco-friendly, this centre provides a great viewing platform, as well as an interactive exhibit for kids of all ages where you can find out how it feels to climb on ice!

22 **The West Highland Museum** is to be found in Fort William and houses a collection of artefacts that dates from Mesolithic times to the modern day. All elements of society are included, from crofters to soldiers and princes to clergy.

17304 **Ardelve, by Dornie, Ross-shire** Map Ref: 3F9

Caberfeidh House

Caberfeidh House, Upper Ardelve, by Kyle of Lochalsh, Ross-shire, IV40 8DY
Tel:01599 555293
Email:info@caberfeidh.plus.com
Web:www.caberfeidh.plus.com

6 rooms
Some en-suite
Open Jan-Dec
Rates on application.

73699 **Ballachulish, Argyll** Map Ref: 1F1

Craiglinnhe House

Lettermore, Ballachulish, Argyll, PH49 4JD
Tel:01855 811270
Email:info@craiglinnhe.co.uk
Web:www.craiglinnhe.co.uk

Lochside Victorian villa amid spectacular mountain scenery offering period charm with modern comfort. Warm, friendly atmosphere, good food and wine. Ideal base for exploring the Western Highlands.

5 rooms, All en-suite. Open Mar-Jan. B&B per person, double from £28.00, BB & Eve.Meal from £45.50.

36649 **Ballachulish, Argyll** Map Ref: 1F1

Lyn Leven Guest House

Ballachulish, Argyll, PH49 4JP
Tel:01855 811392 Fax:01855 811600
Email:macleodcilla@aol.com
Web:www.lynleven.co.uk

Family-run award winning guest house with the freedom and comfort of a hotel at guest house prices, situated on the shores of Loch Leven - Glencoe 1 mile. Magnificent scenery with spectacular views of Glencoe and Mamore Hills. All bedrooms ensuite. Colour TV, tea-making. Ideal for all types of countryside activities. Restricted licence. Private parking. AA Selected 4 Diamonds.

8 rooms.
All en-suite. Open Jan-Dec excl Xmas
B&B per person, double from £25.00-32.00.BB & Eve.Meal from £35.00, 7 days DBB from £238.00 pp.

22958 Dornie, by Kyle of Lochalsh, Ross-shire Map Ref: 3G9

Dornie Hotel

Francis Street, Dornie, Ross-shire, IV40 8DT
Tel:01599 555205 Fax:01599 555429
Email:dorniehotel@hotmail.co.uk
Web:www.dornie-hotel.co.uk

Occupying one of the most scenic areas in Scotland, this family run 13 bedroom hotel is situated in the village of Dornie, & is only a short walk from the magnificent Eilean Donan Castle. Rooms are well equipped & the hotel offers an excellent selection of modern cuisine specializing in local seafood. Castle weddings attractively catered for. We look forward to welcoming you to a relaxing & peaceful stay.

13 rooms, Some en-suite. Open Jan-Dec. B&B per person, single £25.00-37.50, double £25.00-37.50.

TV P C £ V

24651 Dornie, by Kyle of Lochalsh, Ross-shire Map Ref: 3G9

Eilean A-Cheo

Dornie, by Kyle of Lochalsh, Ross-shire, IV40 8DY
Tel:01599 555485
Email:stay@scothighland.com
Web:www.scothighland.com

5 rooms
All en-suite
Open Jan-Dec
B&B per person, single from £26.00, double from £18.00, triple from £20.00.

TV P £ V

11536 Fort William, Inverness-shire Map Ref: 3H12

Alexandra Hotel

The Parade, Fort William, Inverness-shire, PH33 6AZ
Tel:01397 702241 Fax:01397 705554

Large traditional hotel fully modernised, situated in town centre. Some rooms with views of the surrounding hills and lochside.

93 rooms, All en-suite. Open Jan-Dec. B&B per room, single from £59.00, double from £99.00.

TV P C £ V

38485 Fort William, Inverness-shire Map Ref: 3H12

Ben Nevis Hotel & Leisure Club

North Road, Fort William, Inverness-shire, PH33 6TG
Tel:01397 702331 Fax:01397 700321
Email:bennevismanager@strathmorehotels.com

On the A82 facing Ben Nevis, this hotel with its own grounds and modern leisure club is about 1ml (2km) from the town centre.

119 rooms, All en-suite. Open Jan-Dec. Rates on application.

19453 Fort William, Inverness-shire Map Ref: 3H12

Clan MacDuff Hotel

Achintore Road, Fort William, Inverness-shire, PH33 6RW.
Tel:01397 702341 Fax:01397 706174
Email:reception@clanmacduff.co.uk
Web:www.clanmacduff.co.uk

Situated overlooking Loch Linnhe, yet only two miles south of Fort William on the A82. Close to Ben Nevis and Glencoe. Our friendly helpful staff will soon put you at ease so you can enjoy the magnificent views from the restaurant or lounges of Loch Linnhe and the mountains beyond. This is an ideal base for touring the Highlands. Traditional restaurant menu or delicious bar meals complemented by our wine list & numerous malt whiskies. We have a large selection of bedroom types to suit most requirements, all are ensuite with TV, radio, hairdryer, hospitality tray etc. Ample parking in large car park. This friendly family managed hotel is dedicated to providing good quality and value hospitality.

42 rooms.
All en-suite. Open Apr-Nov
B&B per person, single from £37.50, double from £27.50,
BB & Eve.Meal from £42.50.

21541 Fort William, Inverness-shire Map Ref: 3H12

Cruachan Hotel

Achintore Road, Fort William, Inverness-shire, PH33 6RQ
Tel:01397 702022 Fax:01397 702239
Email:reservations@cruachan-hotel.co.uk

57 rooms
Open Jan-Dec
B&B per person, single from £25.00, double from £22.00 per person.

22781 Fort William, Inverness-shire Map Ref: 3H12

Distillery Guest House

Nevis Bridge, Fort William, Inverness-shire,
PH33 6LR
Tel:01397 700103 Fax:01397 702980
Email:disthouse@aol.com

Distillery house at old Glenlochy Distillery in Fort William beside A82, road to the Isles. Situated at the entrance to Glen Nevis short distance from the town centre. Distillery House has been upgraded to high standards. Set in the extensive grounds of the Glenlochy Distillery with views over the River Nevis. All bedrooms are ensuite with TV, and hospitality tray. Non smoking establishment.

8 rooms, All en-suite. Open Jan-Dec. B&B per person, single from £22.50, double from £22.50.

28243 Fort William, Inverness-shire Map Ref: 3H12

Glenlochy Guest House

Nevis Bridge, Fort William, Inverness-shire, PH33 6LP
Tel:01397 702909
Email:glenlochy1@aol.com
Web:www.glenlochyguesthouse.co.uk

Detached house with garden situated at Nevis Bridge, midway between Ben Nevis and the town centre. 0.5 miles (1km) to railway station. 1 annexe room.

10 rooms, All en-suite. Open Jan-Dec. B&B per person, single £25.00-50.00, double £25.00-38.00.

68003 Fort William, Inverness-shire Map Ref: 3H12

Lawriestone Guest House

Achintore Road, Fort William, Inverness-shire, PH33 6RQ
Tel/Fax:01397 700777
Email:susan@lawriestone.co.uk
Web:www.lawriestone.co.uk

A warm welcome awaits you at Lawriestone. Our main concern is your comfort and well being. The beautifully furnished rooms are all en-suite with colour TV and tea/coffee making etc. At breakfast a varied selection, including Scottish or vegetarian breakfasts, is available. Come and experience our hospitality and our beautiful location by Loch Linnhe and surrounding hills. Walking, fishing, golf, skiing etc are available locally.

5 rooms, All en-suite. Open Jan-Dec excl Xmas/New Year. B&B per person, double £30.00-45.00.

35490 Fort William, Inverness-shire Map Ref: 3H12

Lime Tree An Ealdhain

Achintore Road, Fort William, Inverness-shire, PH33 6RQ
Tel/Fax:01397 701806
Email:info@limetreefortwilliam.co.uk
Web:www.limetreefortwilliam.co.uk

View: Dine: Stay: Centre of Fort William overlooking Loch Linnhe set in its own private gardens. Award winning Art Gallery, Restaurant and Small Hotel. Nine rooms all ensuite, open fires, drying rooms, comfy lounges. Some rooms with air conditioning. Open all year round. Seasonal packages. 4 Star Arts Venue also applicable.

9 rooms, All en-suite. Open Jan-Dec, seasonal packages. B&B per person, single from £60.00, double from £40.00.

35986 Fort William, Inverness-shire Map Ref: 3H12

Lochan Cottage Guest House

Lochyside, Fort William, Inverness-shire, PH33 7NX
Tel:01397 702695
Email:lochanco@btopenworld.com
Web:www.fortwilliam-guesthouse.co.uk

6 rooms
All en-suite
Open Jan-Dec
B&B per person, double from £26.00.

37294 Fort William, Inverness-shire Map Ref: 3H12

Mansefield Guest House

Corpach, Fort William, Inverness-shire, PH33 7LT
Tel:01397 772262
Email:mansefield@btinternet.com
Web:www.fortwilliamaccommodation.com

6 rooms
All en-suite
Open Jan-Dec
B&B per person, single from £24.00, double from £24.00, BB & Eve.Meal from £35.00.

63632 Fort William, Inverness-shire Map Ref: 3H12

West End Hotel

Achintore Road, Fort William, PH33 6ED
Tel:01397 702614 Fax:01397 706279
Email:welcome@westend-hotel.co.uk
Web:www.westend-hotel.co.uk

Family run hotel in the centre of Fort William overlooking Loch Linnhe. Ideal base for touring the West Highlands.

51 rooms, All en-suite. Open Feb-Dec excl Xmas/New Year. B&B per person, single from £35.00, double from £25.00.

48335 by Fort William, Inverness-shire Map Ref: 3H12

Old Pines Hotel & Restaurant

Spean Bridge, by Fort William, PH34 4EG
Tel:01397 712324
Email:enquiries@oldpines.co.uk
Web:www.oldpines.co.uk

A unique blend of relaxed informality and excellent food. All rooms ensuite with TV/DVD. Light lunches and five course evening meals. Children welcome.

8 rooms, All en-suite. Open Jan-Dec..

66920 nr Fort William, Inverness-shire Map Ref: 3H12

The Tailrace Inn

Riverside Road, Kinlochleven, Argyll, PH50 4QH
Tel:01855 831777 Fax:01855 831291
Email:tailrace@btconnect.com
Web:www.tailraceinn.co.uk

6 rooms
All en-suite
Open Jan-Dec
B&B per person, single from £40.00, double from £30.00 pp.

19383 Glencoe, Argyll Map Ref: 1F1

Clachaig Inn

Glencoe, Argyll, PH49 4HX
Tel:01855 811252 Fax:01855 812030
Email:inn@clachaig.com
Web:www.clachaig.com

Located in the heart of Glencoe with stunning mountain views and a great Highland atmosphere. The Inn offers upgraded ensuite accommodation, an imaginative all day menu and an unrivalled selection of cask ales and malt whiskies. Recent winners Best Pub in Scotland. An outdoor Inn for outdoor folk. Open all year.

23 rooms, All en-suite. B&B from £34.00-40.00 per person per night..

36849 Glencoe, Argyll Map Ref: 1F1

MacDonald Hotel

Fort William Road, Kinlochleven, Argyll, PH50 4QL
Tel:01855 831539 Fax:01855 831416
Email:enquiries@macdonaldhotel.co.uk
Web:www.macdonaldhotel.co.uk

A modern, yet traditional, hotel set beside a tidal creek at the head of Loch Leven. Mid-way between Glen Nevis and Glencoe at the foot of the Mamores, the Macdonald Hotel is the perfect base to enjoy the best of West Highland walking or touring. Personally managed by John, Lynn and team who pride themselves on providing a relaxed, informal, environment and the very best of Highland foods from fresh local produce.

10 rooms, All en-suite. Open Jan-Dec. B&B per person, single from £40.00, double from £28.00, BB & Eve.Meal from £40.00.

TV P C V

53242 Glencoe, Argyll Map Ref: 1F1

Scorrybreac Guest House

Glencoe, Argyll, PH49 4HT
Tel:01855 811354
Email:info@scorrybreac.co.uk
Web:www.scorrybreac.co.uk

6 rooms
5 en-suite
Open Jan-Dec
B&B per person, single from £30.00, double/twin from £23.00

TV P £ V

56833 Glencoe, Argyll Map Ref: 1F1

Strathassynt Guest House

Loan Fern, Ballachulish, Argyll, PH49 4JB
Tel:01855 811261 Fax:01855 811914
Email:info@strathassynt.com
Web:www.strathassynt.com

6 rooms
All en-suite
Open Jan-Dec
B&B per person, single from £25.00, double from £20.00.

TV P C £ V

50489 Glenfinnan, Inverness-shire Map Ref: 3G12

The Princes' House Hotel

Glenfinnan, Inverness-shire, PH37 4LT
Tel:01397 722246 Fax:01397 722323
Email:princeshouse@glenfinnan.co.uk
Web:www.glenfinnan.co.uk

9 rooms
All en-suite
Open Mar-Dec excl Xmas and 1wk Oct
B&B per person, single from £49.00, double from £37.00.

TV P C £ V

34181 Glenshiel, by Kyle of Lochalsh, Ross-shire Map Ref: 3G10

Kintail Lodge Hotel

Glenshiel, Ross-shire, IV40 8HL
Tel:01599 511275 Fax:01599 511226
Email:reception@kintaillodgehotel.co.uk
Web:www.kintaillodgehotel.co.uk

Early Victorian former shooting lodge on shores of Loch Duich at the foot of Five Sisters of Kintail. Ideal touring and hill walking centre. Conservatory restaurant and bar open to non-residents.

12 rooms, All en-suite. Open Jan-Dec. B&B per person, single from £38.00, double from £38.00, BB & Eve.Meal from £65.00.

23031 Knoydart, Inverness-shire Map Ref: 3F11

Doune-Knoydart

Doune, Knoydart, Mallaig, Inverness-shire, PH41 4PU
Tel:01687 462667 Fax:08700 940428
Email:martin@doune-knoydart.co.uk
Web:www.doune-knoydart.co.uk

Remote and unique holiday setting on the western tip of Knoydart. Spectacular low and high level walking. Delicious home cooking, a warm welcome and total relaxation. Mountains, sea, boat trips, and wildlife.

3 Family rooms, Open Apr-Sep. £70.00 per person per night full board. Discounts for children..

63661 Mallaig, Inverness-shire Map Ref: 3F11

West Highland Hotel

Mallaig, Inverness-shire, PH41 4QZ
Tel:01687 462210 Fax:01687 462130
Email:westhighland.hotel@virgin.net
Web:www.westhighlandhotel.co.uk

40 rooms
All en-suite
Open Apr-Nov
B&B per person, single from £40.00, double from £35.00, BB & Eve.Meal from £50.00.

50965 Raasay, Isle of, Ross-shire Map Ref: 3E9

Isle of Raasay Hotel

Raasay, Kyle of Lochalsh, Ross-shire, IV40 8PB
Tel/Fax:01478 660222
Web:www.isleofraasayhotel.co.uk

Family run hotel, peacefully situated on the Isle of Raasay, just a short ferry crossing from 'Mainland' Skye. The island is just 14 miles long and 5 miles wide, but provides much to offer the visitor - a rich mix of heritage, flora, fauna, geology and archaeology, or just peace and quiet.

12 rooms, All en-suite. Open Jan-Dec. B&B per person, single from £40.00, double from £35.00.

TV C V

79444 Roy Bridge, Inverness-shire Map Ref: 3H12

Glenspean Lodge Hotel

Roy Bridge, Inverness-shire, PH31 4AW
Tel:01397 712223 Fax:01397 712660
Email:reservations@glenspeanlodge.co.uk
Web:www.glenspeanlodge.com

Glenspean Lodge is a beautiful, old, fully refurbished hunting lodge situated amongst the rolling hillside of the Scottish Highlands. An oasis of peace and tranquillity with 17 bedrooms, all en-suite, offering tea and coffee making facilities, hairdryers and complimentary toiletries, satellite TV and Wi-Fi.

17 rooms, All en-suite, Open Jan-Dec. Rates on application.

12706 Ardvasar, Sleat, Isle of Skye, Inverness-shire Map Ref: 3E11

Ardvasar Hotel

Ardvasar, Isle of Skye, IV45 8RS
Tel:01471 844223
Email:richard@ardvasar-hotel.demon.co.uk
Web:www.ardvasarhotel.com

This historic 19th Century Inn has fine views across the sea to Mallaig. Well established reputation for good food.

9 rooms, All en-suite. Open Jan-Dec. B&B per person, single from £70.00, double from £45.00.

TV C V

61034 Colbost, by Dunvegan, Isle of Skye, Inverness-shire Map Ref: 3D9

The Three Chimneys and The House Over-By

Colbost, by Dunvegan, Isle of Skye, IV55 8ZT
Tel:01470 511258
Email:eatandstay@threechimneys.co.uk
Web:www.threechimneys.co.uk

Candlelit crofters cottage restaurant in a remote and beautiful corner of Skye, with six well-appointed bedroom suites adjacent. Overlooking the sea, with the misty isles of the Outer Hebrides on the horizon.

6 rooms, All en-suite. Open Jan-Dec. B&B per room, single from £260.00, double from £260.00.

23820 Dunvegan, Isle of Skye, Inverness-shire Map Ref: 3D9

Dunorin House Hotel

2 Herebost, Dunvegan, Isle of Skye, Inverness-shire, IV55 8GZ
Tel:01470 521488

10 rooms
All en-suite
Open Jan-Dec
B&B per person, single from £45.00, double from £45.00.

67994 Dunvegan, Isle of Skye, Inverness-shire Map Ref: 3D9

Dunvegan Hotel

Main Street, Dunvegan, Isle of Skye, IV55 8WA
Tel/Fax:+44 (0)1470 521497
Email:enquiries@hoteldunvegan.co.uk
Web:www.hoteldunvegan.co.uk

Friendly family run hotel offers cosy, en-suite accommodation. Enjoy home-cooked food in our cosy lounge bar or loch view restaurant. Regular live music in our Cellar Bar. Lunches daily from 12.30, evening meals from 5.30pm.

6 rooms, 3 dbl, 2 twn, 1 fam, 2 bunkrooms, All en-suite. Open Feb-Dec. Room only per person, single from £60.00, double from £49.50.

11735 Portree, Isle of Skye, Inverness-shire Map Ref: 3E9

Almondbank

Viewfield Road, Portree, Isle of Skye, IV51 9EU
Tel:01478 612696 Fax:01478 613114
Email:j.n.almondbank@btconnect.com

4 rooms
Some en-suite
Open Jan-Dec
B&B per person, single from £35.00, double from £35.00.

21631 Portree, Isle of Skye, Inverness-shire Map Ref: 3E9

Cuillin Hills Hotel

Portree, Isle of Skye, IV51 9QU
Tel:01478 612003 Fax:01478 613092
Email:info@cuillinhills-hotel-skye.co.uk
Web:www.cuillinhills-hotel-skye.co.uk

19th century former hunting lodge, set in 15 acres of grounds overlooking Portree Bay, with views towards the Cuillin Hills. Friendly staff, and an emphasis on good food, with a choice of formal or informal dining. Facilities available for conferences, functions and weddings. Open all year.

27 rooms, All en-suite. Open Jan-Dec. B&B per person, single from £55.00, double from £55.00, BB & Eve.Meal from £89.00.

52112 Portree, Isle of Skye, Inverness-shire Map Ref: 3E9

Rosedale Hotel

Beaumont Crescent, Portree, Isle of Skye, IV51 9DB
Tel:01478 613131 Fax:01478 612531
Email:rosedalehotelsky@aol.com
Web:www.rosedalehotelskye.co.uk

Very comfortable and unusual family run hotel imaginatively created from former fishermens houses dating back to the reign of William IV. Award winning cuisine in an outstanding waterside location.

18 rooms, All en-suite. Open Mar-Nov. B&B per person, single from £30.00, double from £30.00, BB & Eve.Meal from £56.00.

52487 Portree, Isle of Skye, Inverness-shire Map Ref: 3E9

Royal Hotel

Bank Street, Portree, Isle of Skye, Inverness-shire, IV51 9BU
Tel:01478 61 2525
Email:info@royal-hotel-skye.com
Web:www.royal-hotel-skye.com

Family run hotel in central position, looking out over Portree Bay. All rooms ensuite, open all year. Regular live traditional entertainment. Nearby leisure and fitness centre available for hotel guests.

21 rooms, All en-suite. Open Jan-Dec. B&B per room, single from £99.00, double from £99.00.

67064 Sleat, Isle of Skye, Inverness-shire Map Ref: 3E11

Duisdale House Hotel

Isle Ornsay, Sleat, Isle of Skye, IV43 8QW
Tel:01471 833202
Email:info@duisdale.com
Web:www.duisdale.com

Former hunting lodge now a stylish, contemporary hotel on the romantic Isle of Skye. Each bedroom is unique in décor and layout. Rich, bold colours, feature and four-poster beds and striking modern fabrics are complimented by the original features of the building and the panoramic views over the sea. The elegant lounge with chandeliers and blazing log fire is complete with sumptuous sofas and tasteful art. The restaurant is candle-lit and atmospheric. À la carte menus contain Skye langoustines, scallops, Scotch beef and venison. Carefully selected wines and a malt whisky selection that comes highly recommended, complete the picture. Exclusive daily sailing trips from May to September.

17 rooms.
All en-suite. Open Jan-Dec
Bed & Breakfast from £130.00 per room per night for a small double.

61518 Sleat, Isle of Skye, Inverness-shire Map Ref: 3E11

Toravaig House Hotel

Knock Bay, Sleat, Isle of Skye, IV44 8RE
Tel:0845 055 1117
Email:info@skyehotel.co.uk
Web:www.skyehotel.co.uk

Scottish Island Hotel of the Year 2007 – *Hotel Review Scotland*

Most Excellence Service UK 2006 – *Conde Naste Johansen's*

Excellence in Tourism Award 2006 – VisitScotland

"A Gem in the Hebrides". Romantic, boutique hotel on the Isle of Skye, set in large garden enjoying fine views over the sea. Nine unique bedrooms – feature beds, Sky TV, telephone, en-suite bathrooms complete with fluffy bath towels and luxury toiletries. Mouthwatering menus created using fresh local produce, seafood, lamb, beef and venison. Intimate candle-lit evenings relaxing by the fire in the cozy lounge enjoying fine wines and malt whiskies. Exclusive daily sailing trips available from May to September.

9 rooms.
All en-suite. Open Jan-Dec
Rates: Dinner, Bed & Breakfast from £220.00 per room per night.

26324 Staffin, Isle of Skye, Inverness-shire Map Ref: 3E8

Flodigarry Country House Hotel

Flodigarry, Staffin, Isle of Skye, IV51 9HZ
Tel:01470 552203 Fax:01470 552301
Email:info@flodigarry.co.uk
Web:www.flodigarry.co.uk

Family run Flodigarry for that well earned break. Dramatic views, private grounds, welcome dram and piper. Home grown produce, home baking, fantastic food, log fires, walks and sea fishing fun.

18 rooms, All en-suite. Open Feb-Dec. B&B per person per night from £40.00.

20535 Spean Bridge, Inverness-shire Map Ref: 3H12

Corriegour Lodge Hotel

Loch Lochy, by Spean Bridge, Inverness-shire
PH34 4EA
Tel:01397 712685 Fax:01397 712696
Email:info@corriegour-lodge-hotel.com
Web:www.corriegour-lodge-hotel.com

'Better food than the top London restaurants and a view to die for.' – THE MIRROR. This former Victorian hunting lodge enjoys the very finest setting in 'The Great Glen'. Dine in our Loch View Conservatory, enjoying the very best Scottish cuisine, fresh seafood, Aberdeen Angus, homemade breads and puddings, extensive selection of wines and malt whiskies. Our emphasis is on your total relaxation and comfort. Log fires and big comfy sofas. Come and be cushioned from the stresses of everyday life. Walking, scenery, skiing, history. Private beach and fishing school. Special Spring/Autumn breaks available.

12 rooms.
All en-suite. Open Feb-Nov & New Year
B&B per person, single £79.00-89.00, double £79.00-89.00. BB & Eve.Meal from £95.00-125.00 pp.

A sailing lesson on Loch Morlich with a view to the Cairngorms

Aviemore and the Cairngorms

If you love the outdoor life, you'll be impressed by the many activities on offer around Aviemore and the Cairngorms.

For watersports including canoeing, sailing and windsurfing, head for Loch Insh or Loch Morlich. Mountaineers will find the Cairngorm range is always a challenge while more leisurely walkers can ramble to their heart's content in places like Glenmore Forest Park, Rothiemurchus Estate, Inshriach Forest, Craigellachie National Nature Reserve, Glenlivet Estate and many other wonderful places. Pop in to a local Tourist Information Centre for advice.

And while you're travelling round you'll see so much wildlife, crossbills, crested tits, capercaillie, red squirrels and pine martens in the forests, hare, ptarmigan, dotterel and snow buntings on the peaks.

You can cycle too – try Laggan Wolftrax for top mountain biking action and you can ski in the winter at CairnGorm Mountain and The Lecht.

There are also lots of opportunities for golfing – and fishing, of course. You can even take a steam train trip from Aviemore to Boat of Garten and Broomhill or you can scale mighty Cairn Gorm on the funicular railway.

Pony trekking near Aviemore

DON'T MISS

1 The **Cairngorms National Park** offers many events and activities throughout the year which are suitable for all ages and abilities. Visitor centres and ranger bases have leaflets, guides and trail maps to help you make the most of your time in the Park, and Tourist Information Centres throughout the area will be able to provide you with local information on events, attractions and activities.

2 At the heart of the beautiful Cairngorms National Park is the **CairnGorm Mountain Railway**. It takes eight minutes from bottom to top, where an interactive exhibition tells the history and ecology of the surrounding area and you can see some stunning panoramic views of the National Park. Have a bite to eat and take in the view stretching from the Cairngorm plateau to the Monadhliath Mountains and beyond.

3 Spend the day at **Landmark Forest Heritage Park** in Carrbridge and follow the Tree Top Trails, the Red Squirrel Trail or the Timber Trails complete with fire tower! See a steam powered sawmill and explore Microworld (a hands-on exhibition). Cap it all off with a ride on the spectacular Wildwater Coaster. There's plenty to keep everyone – young and old – amused.

4 Step back in time to the **Highland Folk Museum** with sites in Kingussie and Newtonmore, where you can experience over 400 years of Highland life. Re-constructions of an 18th century Highland township and 20th century working croft can be seen at Newtonmore. Both locations have programmes of live demonstrations and activities where you can see traditional skills and crafts in action.

5 Take to the water at **Loch Morlich** or **Loch Insh** and try your hand at sailing, canoeing, windsurfing or rowing in picturesque surroundings. Both centres offer a range of hire options from ½ hour sessions to full days, or if you're complete beginners, try the 1½ -2 hour introductory courses.

6 Drive amongst wolves, bison and Highland cattle roaming free at the **Highland Wildlife Park** in Kincraig. Featuring a number of different habitats, you can see the amazing variety of animals found in present day Scotland and also many of the animals that inhabited our countryside in years gone by. Each day, at breakfast time – that's 10am for the animals at the park – your car can follow the patrol vehicle as the warden hands out food.

3

5

FOOD AND DRINK

www.eatscotland.com

7 At **The Old Bridge Inn**, on the outskirts of Aviemore, the staff are friendly and the service is excellent. A selection of meat, game and fish awaits and all dishes are cooked simply and with flair. The dining room adjacent to the bar area allows more formal and romantic dining with its open fire, and the puddings are all home-made and vary from day to day.

8 At the Speyside Heather Centre, near Dulnain Bridge, **The Clootie Dumpling** restaurant has established a reputation for delicious hot meals and home baking. It offers the perfect opportunity to sample its namesake. This traditional and versatile pudding can be enjoyed in a variety of different ways from sweet to savoury. The recipe has a mixture of spices, carrots, apple, raisins and more, all mixed together in a 'cloot' (muslin cloth), steamed for hours and served with accompaniments.

9 Dine at **Craggan Mill** in the picturesque water mill near Grantown-on-Spey. Fine dining in a relaxed environment offers you the choice of bistro lunch or à la carte evening meal – all prepared from local, seasonal produce. Local artists exhibit paintings for view and sale within the restaurant and gallery.

10 Stylish and creative food at **The Boat Hotel** in Boat of Garten is presented in an intimate and restful atmosphere. Seasonal menus and a hand-picked wine list ensure you experience classic Scottish fayre.

8

13

14

ACTIVITIES

11 Take a step back in time and travel by steam engine. The **Strathspey Railway** runs from Aviemore to Broomhill (also known as Glenbogle from the TV series Monarch of the Glen) and affords beautiful views of the Cairngorms from the carriage window. To make the trip really special, you can even have afternoon tea on board.

12 **Insh Marshes Bird Reserve** is a birdwatching paradise! Around half of all British Goldeneyes nest at Inch Marshes in spring. You're also likely to see lapwings, redshanks and curlews, as well as oystercatchers, snipe and wigeon. In winter, the marshes host flocks of whooper swans and greylag geese. Roe deer, wildcats, otters and foxes may all be seen along the edges of the marshes.

13 Just outside Aviemore and Kincraig is **Alvie Stables**, a great place to try pony trekking. With hundreds of acres of National Park to ride through, the scenery will keep you engrossed.

14 The **Laggan WolfTrax** centre near Newtonmore, offers purpose built mountain bike trails with a range of options from the fun park to the double black route! Base Camp MTB provides bike hire so you don't even have to take your own, and also hires out safety equipment like knee pads to prevent any unwanted injuries! Suitable from 10 years old.

WALKS

www.visitscotland.com/walking

15 Follow the circular walk in upper **Glen Feshie** (from Kincraig on the B970) to the ruins of the bothy where Landseer did preliminary sketches for his Monarch of the Glen painting. The views over the Spey Valley are stunning and you may even spot red deer. The old bridge and adjacent falls offer the perfect picnic spot in fine weather.

16 **Glenmore Forest Park** has a range of walks from all-ability trails suitable for pushchairs, to longer walks through beautiful woodland which open out to give fantastic views of the Cairngorm Mountains. The visitor centre provides an audio-visual presentation plus café, toilets and shop.

17 There are a variety of waymarked trails throughout the **Rothiemurchus Estate**, with maps available from the visitor centre. The Estate is teeming with Highland wildlife, including the red squirrel and the rare capercaillie, with guided tours available courtesy of Scottish Natural Heritage. Free tours on Tuesdays.

18 The 5½ mile walk from **Aviemore to Boat of Garten** incorporates part of the Speyside Way. The walk goes through heather moors and woodland and gives great views of the Cairngorm Mountains. If you're too tired to walk back, then take the return trip on the Strathspey Steam Railway.

ATTRACTIONS

19 The **Cairngorm Reindeer Centre** is home to the only reindeer herd in the country and you can encounter the animals grazing in their natural environment. During the guided visits you can wander freely among the reindeer, stroking and feeding them. These friendly deer are a delight to all ages and, if you feel especially fond of one, you might be able to adopt it!

21 The **Macdonald Aviemore Highland Resort**, located in the heart of the town, offers guests accommodation and activity packages throughout the summer. For non-guests access to the fantastic swimming pool, toddlers' pool, wave machine and giant flume can be a great way to spend a rainy day.

22 Join in the working day of a Highland shepherd and his dogs at Working Sheepdogs, **Leault Farm**, Kincraig. As well as seeing sheepdog demonstrations you can help to shear a sheep and bottle feed the orphaned lambs or make new friends with the farm's collie puppies.

17434 **Aviemore, Inverness-shire** Map Ref: 4C10

Cairngorm Guest House

Grampian Road, Aviemore, Inverness-shire, PH22 1RP
Tel:01479 810630
Email:conns@lineone.net
Web:www.cairngormguesthouse.com

12 rooms
All en-suite
Open Jan-Dec
B&B per person, single from £30.00, double from £25.00.

17439 **Aviemore, Inverness-shire** Map Ref: 4C10

Cairngorm Hotel

Grampian Road, Aviemore, PH22 1PE
Tel:01479 810233 Fax:01479 810791
Email:reception@cairngorm.com
Web:www.cairngorm.com

31 rooms
All en-suite
Open Jan-Dec
B&B per person, single from £47.50, double from £37.50.

51158 **Aviemore, Inverness-shire** Map Ref: 4C10

Ravenscraig Guest House

Grampian Road, Aviemore, Inverness-shire, PH22 1RP
Tel:01479 810278 Fax:01479 810210
Email:info@aviemoreonline.com
Web:www.aviemoreonline.com

12 rooms
All en-suite
Open Jan-Dec
B&B per person, single from £30.00, double from £30.00.

78833 **Boat of Garten, Inverness-shire** Map Ref: 4C10

The Boat Hotel

Boat of Garten, Inverness-shire, PH24 3BH
Tel:01479 831258 Fax:01479 831414
Email:info@boathotel.co.uk
Web:www.boathotel.co.uk

Located in the heart of the Cairngorm National Park, a moments walk from the Spey River, the Boat Hotel offers Highland scenery and rural tranquillity at the foot of the Cairngorm mountains. The hotel has a traditional Bistro restaurant and an award-winning 2 AA rosette restaurant, using only the finest of local and seasonal ingredients.

26 rooms, All en-suite. Open Feb-5 Jan. B&B per person, single from £84.50, double from £64.50, BB & Eve.Meal from £89.50.

29887 **Boat of Garten, Inverness-shire** Map Ref: 4C10

Heathbank House

Drumuillie Road, Boat of Garten, Inverness-shire, PH24 3BD
Tel:01479 831234
Email:enquiries@heathbankhotel.co.uk
Web:www.heathbankhotel.co.uk

6 rooms
All en-suite
Open Jan-Dec
B&B per person, double from £26.00.

38931 **Boat of Garten, Inverness-shire** Map Ref: 4C10

Moorfield House

Deshar Road, Boat of Garten, Inverness-shire,
PH24 3BN
Tel:01479 831646
Email:enquiries@moorfieldhouse.com
Web:www.moorfieldhouse.com

6 rooms
All en-suite
Open Dec-Nov excl Xmas
B&B per person, single from £40.00, double from £33.00.

17400 **Carrbridge, Inverness-shire** Map Ref: 4C9

The Cairn Hotel

Main Road, Carrbridge, Inverness-shire, PH23 3AS
Tel:01479 841212 Fax:01479 841362
Email:info@cairnhotel.co.uk
Web:www.cairnhotel.co.uk

7 rooms
Most en-suite
Open Jan-Dec
B&B per person from £26.00.

22083 **Carrbridge, Inverness-shire** Map Ref: 4C9

Dalrachney Lodge Hotel

Carrbridge, Inverness-shire, PH23 3AT
Tel: 01479 841252 Fax: 01479 841383
Email: dalrachney@aol.com
Web: www.dalrachney.co.uk

Victorian former hunting lodge, with many antique and period furnishings, set in 16 acres of peaceful surroundings. Cuisine using local produce.

10 rooms, 9 en-suite, 1 priv.facilities. Open Jan-Dec. B&B per person, single from £50.00, double from £35.00, BB & Eve.Meal from £45.00.

77411 **Dulnain Bridge, by Grantown-on-Spey, Inverness-shire** Map Ref: 4C9

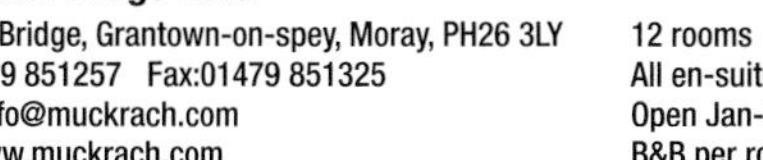

Muckrach Lodge Hotel

Dulnain Bridge, Grantown-on-spey, Moray, PH26 3LY
Tel:01479 851257 Fax:01479 851325
Email:info@muckrach.com
Web:www.muckrach.com

12 rooms
All en-suite
Open Jan-Dec
B&B per room, single from £95.00, double from £140.00.

11944

Grantown-on-Spey, Moray Map Ref: 4C9

An Cala Guest House

Woodlands Terrace, Grantown on Spey, Moray, PH26 3JU
Tel:01479 873293
Email:ancala@globalnet.co.uk
Web:www.ancala.info

An Cala is a fine traditional Victorian villa in a peaceful residential area in easy walking distance of the town centre. Val and Keith have lovingly restored the house to its original splendour. Intricate cornices, a magnificent kingsize mahogany 4 poster bed from Castle Grant and mahogany dining tables all contribute to a very comfortable, relaxing stay with friendly hospitable hosts. (all double beds are kingsize or superking.)

4 rooms, Open Jan-Dec. B&B per person, single from £50.00, double from £32.00, family from £30.00. Room rate, single from £50.00, double from £64.00, triple from £80.00..

79435

Grantown-on-Spey, Moray Map Ref: 4C9

Ravenscourt House Hotel

Seafield Avenue, Grantown-on-Spey, Morayshire, PH26 3JG
Tel:01479 872286 Fax:05601 162846
Email:info@ravenscourthouse.co.uk
Web:www.ravenscourthouse.co.uk

Friendly family run hotel offering two resident lounges, a conservatory restaurant, and a selection of twin, double and family bedrooms. Wi-Fi internet access and Satellite television available in bedrooms.

8 rooms, Open Jan-Dec. B&B per person, double from £35.00.

77326

Kingussie, Inverness-shire Map Ref: 4B11

Allt Gynack Guest House

Gynack Villa, 1 High Street, Kingussie, Inverness-shire, PH21 1HS
Tel:01540 661081
Email:alltgynack@tiscali.co.uk
Web:www.alltgynack.com

5 rooms
Some en-suite
Open Jan-Dec
B&B per person, from £24.00.

74655

Kingussie, Inverness-shire Map Ref: 4B11

Arden House

Newtonmore Road, Kingussie, Inverness-shire, PH21 1HE
Tel/Fax:01540 661369
Email:ardenhouse1@btconnect.com
Web:www.arden-house.info

Just one of the many fantastic comments taken from our guest book. 'had a great time, lovely food, room, comfortable bed and made very welcome' Mr and Mrs Murphy, Paisley.

5 rooms, All en-suite. Open all year round. B&B per person from £27.00.

17444

Kingussie, Inverness-shire Map Ref: 4B11

Duke of Gordon Hotel

Kingussie, Inverness-shire, PH21 1HE
Tel:01540 661302 Fax:01540 661989
Email:info@dukeofgordonhotel.co.uk
Web:www.dukeofgordonhotel.co.uk

Victorian hotel on main street with golf and fishing available locally in summer and skiing in winter. Facilities may vary depending on season.

66 rooms, All en-suite. Open Jan-Dec. B&B per person from £58.00. BB & Eve.Meal from £68.00.

53252

Kingussie, Inverness-shire Map Ref: 4B11

The Scot House Hotel

Newtonmore Road, Kingussie, Inverness-shire, PH21 1HE
Tel:01540 661351 Fax:01540 661111
Email:enquiries@scothouse.com
Web:www.scothouse.com

Originally built in 1884 as a Church Manse and now a family owned Small Hotel. Popular Bar for meals and drinks and Restaurant has a growing good reputation. Small meetings and weddings are also accommodated.

9 rooms, All en-suite. Open Jan-Dec. B&B per person, single from £39.00, double from £29.00.

38809 Laggan Bridge, by Newtonmore, Inverness-shire Map Ref: 4B11

Monadhliath Hotel

Laggan Bridge, nr Newtonmore, Inverness-shire
PH20 1BT
Tel/Fax:01528 544276
Email:monadhliath@lagganbridge.com

8 rooms
All en-suite
Open Feb-Dec
B&B per person, single from £20.00, double from £20.00, BB & Eve.Meal from £29.50.

47084 Nethy Bridge, Inverness-shire Map Ref: 4C10

Nethybridge Hotel

Nethybridge, Inverness-shire, PH25 3DP
Tel:01479 821203 Fax:01479 821686
Email:salesnethybridge@strathmorehotels.com
Web:www.strathmorehotels.com

Victorian building of character recently upgraded, situated in Highland village and ideally situated for the amenities of Strathspey.

69 rooms, All en-suite. Open Jan-Dec. B&B per person, single from £45.00, double from £90.00, Evening meal from £21.95.

11819 Newtonmore, Inverness-shire Map Ref: 4B11

Alvey House

Golf Course Road, Newtonmore, Inverness-shire,
PH20 1AT
Tel:01540 673260 Fax:01540 673003
Email:enquiries@alveyhouse.co.uk
Web:www.alveyhouse.co.uk

6 rooms
All en-suite
Open Jan-Dec
single from £22.50, double from £22.50, BB & Eve.Meal from £40.00.

73443 Newtonmore, Inverness-shire Map Ref: 4B11

Coig Na Shee

Fort William Road, Newtonmore, Inverness-shire, PH20 1DG
Tel:01540 670109
Email:stay@coignashee.co.uk
Web:www.coignashee.co.uk

A stunning Edwardian lodge within large grounds. An ideal base to explore the Highlands. Relax in your luxury room, in peaceful surroundings. Bring your 'bike, boots and books'.

5 rooms, All en-suite. Open Jan-Dec. B&B per person, single from £35.00, double from £25.00.

Cairngorms

Stornoway, Isle of Lewis, Outer Hebrides

THE OUTER ISLANDS

Outer Hebrides, Orkney, Shetland

There's something very special about island holidays and Scotland has so many wonderful islands to explore.

On an island holiday, you can leave all the stresses and strains of mainland life far behind. You don't have to settle for just one destination either – try a bit of island hopping, there's a lot of choice.

A different pace

At Scotland's western edge, the Outer Hebrides look out to the Atlantic swell and life moves at a relaxed pace. In this last Gaelic stronghold, a warm welcome awaits.

You can get there by ferry from Oban or Uig on Skye or by plane. Fly to Barra and you'll land on the beach at low tide!

Lewis is the largest of the Outer Hebrides with a busy town at Stornoway and historical sites like the standing stones at Calanais stretching back over 3,000 years. It's distinctly different from the more mountainous Harris. Don't forget to visit the traditional weavers making the wonderful Harris Tweed.

The Uists, Benbecula, Eriskay and Barra are all well worth a visit too and each has its own attractions.

Life at the crossroads

Island life can also be experienced in Scotland's two great northern archipelagos. Some 70 islands make up Orkney with 17 inhabited. Shetland, at the crossroads where the Atlantic meets the North Sea, has over 100 islands and is home to around 22,000 people and well over a million seabirds.

In Orkney, you can see the oldest houses in northern Europe at Papa Westray, dating back to 3800 BC.

The influence of the Vikings is everywhere. Orcadians spoke Old Norse until the mid 1700s and the ancient Viking Parliament used to meet at Scalloway in Shetland.

These parts enjoy long summer days and at midsummer it never really gets dark. You can even play midnight golf in the 'Simmer Dim'.

In winter, the nights are long but the islanders have perfected the art of indoor life. Musicians fill the bars and community halls and there always seems to be something to celebrate.

Two great unmissable events are the winter fire festival of Up Helly Aa at Lerwick and the Ba' in Kirkwall, Orkney where up to 400 players take to the streets for a great rough and tumble that is somewhere between football, rugby and all-out war.

Have a wild time

Orkney and Shetland are a joy for wildlife watchers. There are millions of birds to observe as well as otters, seals, dolphins and whales. Being surrounded by sea, angling, yachting, sea kayaking, cruising and diving are readily available.

Wherever you decide to experience island life, remember that island holidays are a popular choice and while there's a surprisingly good selection of small hotels and guest houses in the outer isles, it makes sense to book your accommodation well in advance.

Eshaness, Shetland

What's On?

Up Helly Aa, Shetland
29 January 2008
In Lerwick they burn a Viking galley at this fire festival.

Orkney Jazz Weekend
25 – 27 April 2008
A weekend of jazz with local and visiting performers.
www.stromnesshotel.com

Shetland Folk Festival
1 – 4 May 2008
Every year sees another eclectic line-up.
www.shetlandfolkfestival.com

Orkney Folk Festival
22 – 25 May 2008
The best in modern and traditional folk music.
www.orkneyfolkfestival.com

Johnsmas Foy, Shetland
19 – 29 June 2008
The Festival of the Sea.
www.johnsmasfoy.co.uk

St Magnus Festival, Orkney
20 – 25 June 2008
Midsummer celebration of the Arts.
www.stmagnusfestival.com

Lewis Golf Week, Stornoway
5 – 12 July 2008
A week of golf at Stornoway Golf Club.

Taransay Fiddle Week
14 – 18 July 2008
Learn new skills from leading fiddlers.

Hebridean Celtic Festival
16 – 19 July 2008
Biggest homecoming party of the year.
www.hebceltfest.com

Harris Arts Festival
4 – 9 August 2008
Celebrate arts and crafts on the island.

Orkney International Science Festival
4 – 10 September 2008
A kaleidoscopic mix of insights, ideas and activities.
www.oisf.org

Accordion and Fiddle Festival, Shetland
9 -13 October 2008
Musicians from all over the world perform.

www.visithebrides.com
www.visitorkney.com
www.visitshetland.com

All dates correct at time of publication. Please check before booking. VisitScotland cannot be held responsible for any inaccuracies.

DON'T MISS

1 The peace and tranquillity found here, blended with the vibrant nature of the people and their language, has been a true inspiration to many, demonstrated in the islands' crafts, music and culture. Arts venues such as **An Lanntair** in Stornoway and **Taigh Chearsabhagh** in Uist often attract internationally renowned performers and artists.

2 The 5,000 year old **Calanais Standing Stones** on the west side of Lewis are one of the most famous landmarks in the Outer Hebrides. These mystical stones are unique in their cross-shaped layout which has caused endless fascinating debate.

3 **Seallam!** Visitor Centre in Northton at the southern end of Harris presents a variety of fascinating exhibitions on the history and natural environment of the Hebrides. There is also a tea and coffee bar and a small craft shop.

4 The area around **Loch Druidibeg** on South Uist is a National Nature Reserve with many different habitats including freshwater, brackish lagoon, dune, machair, peatland and scrub woodland. The loch itself has many islands, one of which is home to a resident colony of herons. The greylag geese which breed around the Loch contribute to the resident population that remain in the Uists all year. Birds of prey hunting in the reserve include golden eagle, hen harriers, kestrel, peregrine and merlin.

5 **Kisimul Castle** is a sight to behold, situated in the bay of Castlebay Village on Barra. The stronghold of the MacNeils of Barra, this is the only surviving medieval castle in the Hebrides. Day tickets to visit the castle can be obtained at the local Tourist Information Centre.

7

ACTIVITIES

6 There are five **golf** courses in the Hebrides: Barra, Uist, Benbecula, Harris and Lewis. The 9-hole course at Scarista on Harris, in particular, is legendary for its stunning setting and challenging situation. The small greens, massive sand dunes and ever-present Atlantic winds combine for an enjoyable round!

7 The **surf** around the Hebrides is so good it has put the area on the map for international lovers of the sport. With over 70 beaches, it really is a surfer's paradise. The Isle of Lewis receives swells from almost every direction and is classed as having the most consistent surf in Europe. But with beaches on every coast you are sure to be guaranteed surf no matter what direction the swell is coming from.

8 With some of the most beautiful coastline in Britain, the Hebrides is the perfect wilderness to explore by **kayak**. See otters, dolphins and puffins as you glide through the crystal clear waters around the islands. The coastline is a labyrinth of complex bays, inlets, dramatic cliffs, secret coves, sandy beaches and offshore islands.... a sea paddler's paradise.

9 The Outer Hebrides is a game angler's dream location. Whether you are a solitary angler, form part of a larger group or are simply looking for a tranquil family vacation, the Outer Hebrides has it all - namely, some of the best summer salmon and trout **fishing** in Europe.

DON'T MISS

1 **Skara Brae**, 19 miles from Kirkwall, is an unrivalled example of life in Stone Age Orkney. Without doubt the best preserved village in western Europe, the houses contain stone beds, dressers, hearths and drains, giving a fantastic insight into how life was 5,000 years ago. Together with several other historical sites, it is part of a designated World Heritage Site.

2 Discovered in 1958, the **Tomb of the Eagles** is a 5,000 year old tomb containing ceremonial tools, beds, talons and other bones of the white-tailed eagle, pottery and working tools.

3 In the heart of Orkney's main town, Kirkwall, lies **St Magnus Cathedral**. It was built in 1137 by Earl Rognvald, in memory of his cousin Magnus who was earlier murdered by another cousin, Haakon, co-ruler at that time. Today the beautiful sandstone building continues to be a place of worship for the local people.

4 **The Pier Arts Centre** was reopened in 2007 and houses a remarkable collection of 20th century British art. The Collection charts the development of modern art in Britain and includes key work by Barbara Hepworth, Ben Nicholson and Naum Gabo amongst others.

5 Orkney is blessed with an abundance of birds and marine wildlife. Late spring sees the arrival of thousands of breeding seabirds including everybody's favourite the colourful, clown-like puffin. Grey seals breed in huge numbers around the coast in late autumn, while whales, dolphins and porpoise are a regular sight off-shore throughout the summer. **Wildlife** is everywhere, and with a diverse range of professional guiding services there is something to suit everyone.

3

6

9

HISTORY AND HERITAGE

6 The **Ring of Brodgar** and the **Standing Stones of Stenness** are also included within the World Heritage Site. Undeniably mystical, these spiritual places reward visitors with a real sense of ancient times.

7 **Maeshowe** is a central feature of the Neolithic Orkney World Heritage Site. A chambered cairn, it is considered to be one of the finest architectural achievements of its time, around 5,000 years ago. Timed ticketing is in operation, ensuring lots of room and allowing the informative guides to point out all the interesting aspects of the site.

8 The **Broch of Gurness** at Aikerness is a well-organised Iron Age village, giving fascinating insight into community life 2,000 years ago.

9 Travel across the first of the Churchill Barriers to see an artistic phenomenon at the **Italian Chapel**. Built by Italian POWs in WWII, using only the most modest of materials, the intricate interior is all the more impressive.

DON'T MISS

1 Shetland's **local produce** has a reputation for being fresh, natural and good quality. From succulent Shetland smoked salmon to delicious hill lamb, Shetland's food suppliers are at your service.

2 Take a late evening trip to see the **storm petrels**, abundant visitors during the summer. Very small and generally black with a white rump, they can be seen fluttering low over the water pausing momentarily to dip and feed from the surface. They are said to have taken their name from *St Peter* as they appear to be able to walk on water.

3 Shetland is famous amongst those in the know as the place to enjoy sensational **seabird colonies**. If you want close-up views of tens of thousands of breeding gannets, alongside guillemots, puffins, razorbills, kittiwakes, and fulmars, then head for Sumburgh Head, Noss or Hermaness Nature Reserves. These three large seabird colonies are easily accessible and you may well see the famously rare great skuas, or the equally feisty arctic skua.

4 Shetland offers some of the finest **walking** in Europe. The combination of spectacular coastal scenery, quiet inland lochs, and gentle heathery hills is unsurpassed. The walker has the rare opportunity to discover ancient historical sites, dating back to Neolithic times, and observe a wonderful array of wildlife.

5 Officially described as 'one of the most remarkable archaeological sites ever excavated in the British Isles', **Jarlshof** came to light 100 years ago when storms exposed stonework above the beach at the West Voe of Sumburgh. Take a walk through the millenia at this extraordinarily well preserved site, from a Stone Age hut through an Iron Age broch and wheelhouses to a sizeable Viking village and medieval farmstead.

6 Take a trip to **Foula** – one of Britain's most remote inhabited islands. Gaze at the breathtaking 1,200 ft sheer drop at the back of the Kame, said to be one of the highest sea-cliffs in Britain. The name means 'Bird Island' in Old Norse and Foula is designated as a Special Protection Area for birds, a National Scenic Area and a Site of Special Scientific Interest for its plants, birds and geology. This island leaves a lasting impression on everyone who visits.

3

ATTRACTIONS

7 The broch, or fortified Iron Age tower, on the little island of Mousa is the only one in the world to have survived almost complete for more than 2,000 years. Built as a refuge against raiding local tribes, **Mousa Broch** is one of the wonders of European archaeology - and also ornithology. Tiny storm petrels nest in its stone, visiting the broch only after dark - a night excursion to hear their eerie calls is an experience not to be missed.

8 One of the best places to enjoy the cliff scenery by road is **Eshaness** lighthouse, perched above a precipice of volcanic lava. A short walk away is an impressive collapsed cave, Da Hols o' Scraada (the Devil's Caves). Nearby is Da Grind o' da Navir (Gate of the Borer), a huge gateway in the cliffs where the sea has ripped out a chunk of rock and hurled it inland, and the Loch of Houlland, where the ruin of one of the parish's many brochs provides an excellent example of Iron Age architecture.

9 At **Old Scatness Broch**, next to Sumburgh Airport, a recent archaeological dig revealed one of Britain's most exciting Iron Age villages, with many buildings standing at or near roof height and some still even 'decorated' with yellow clay! Buried for nearly 2,000 years, the site is rich in artefacts and remarkably well preserved.

10 **St Ninian's Isle** became famous in 1958, when a schoolboy helping at an archaeological dig on the island discovered a hoard of silver bowls and ornaments believed to date from around 800AD. Now inhabited only by sheep St Ninian's Isle is a beautiful spot for swimming, picnics and walking. Visit the lovely beach and discover the ruins of the old Celtic chapel.

MAP

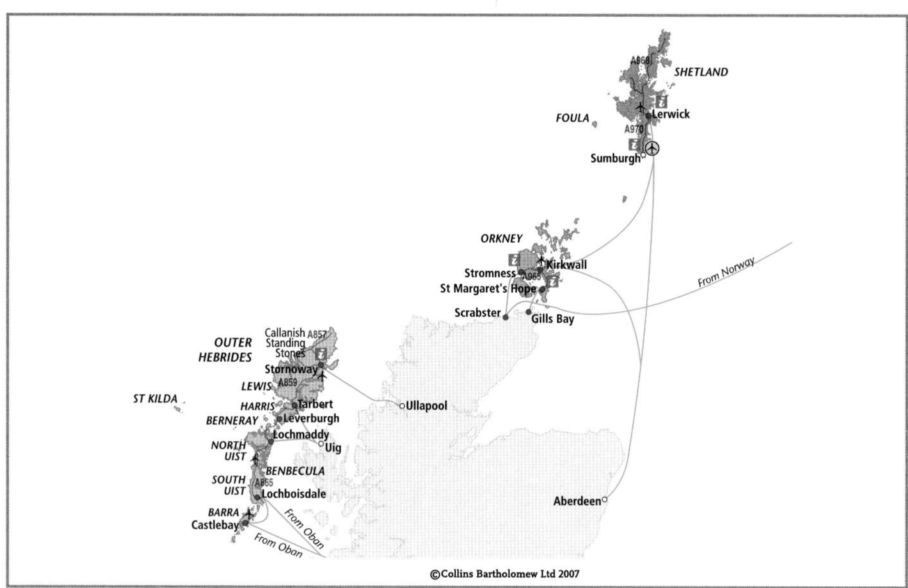

TOURIST INFORMATION CENTRES

Orkney	
Kirkwall	6 Broad Street, Kirkwall KW15 1DH
Stromness	Ferry Terminal Building, Pier Head, Stromness, Orkney KW16 3AA
Shetland	
Lerwick	Market Cross, Lerwick, Shetland ZE1 0LU
Sumburgh Airport	Wilshess Terminal, Sumburgh Airport, Shetland ZE3 9JP
Outer Hebrides	
Stornoway	26 Cromwell Street, Stornoway, Isle of Lewis HS1 2DD

Make the most of your stay in Scotland and make your first stop the Tourist Information Centre wherever you go.

Knowledgeable and friendly staff can help you with information and advice; they can answer your questions, book accommodation and you can even pick up some souvenirs to take home for friends and family.

For information and ideas about exploring Scotland in advance of your trip, call our booking and information service or go to **www.visitscotland.com**

Call 0845 22 55 121

or if calling from outside the UK call **+44 (0) 1506 832 121**

From Ireland call **1800 932 510**

A £4 booking fee applies to telephone bookings of accommodation.

53151

Scarista, Isle of Harris, Western Isles   Map Ref: 3C6

Scarista House

Scarista, Isle of Harris, HS3 3HX
Tel:01859 550238 Fax:01859 550277
Email:timandpatricia@scaristahouse.com
Web:www.scaristahouse.com

At Scarista House we offer traditional comfort in well-furnished guest rooms as well as natural, skilled cooking and good wines in the dining room. With stunning views: the ocean, heather-covered mountains, and a three-mile long shell sand beach, it is one of the most beautiful and remote places to stay in Britain.

5 rooms, All en-suite. Open Jan-Dec. B&B per room, single from £125.00, double from £170.00.

71531

Back, Isle of Lewis, Western Isles   Map Ref: 3E4

Broad Bay House

Back, Isle of Lewis, HS2 0LQ
Tel:01851 820990
Email:stay@broadbayhouse.co.uk
Web:www.broadbayhouse.co.uk

4 rooms
All en-suite
Open Jan-Dec
B&B per room, single from £105.00, double from £125.00.

66898

South Galson, Isle of Lewis, Western Isles   Map Ref: 3E3

Galson Farm Guest House

South Galson, Lewis, Western Isles, HS2 0SH
Tel/Fax:01851 850492
Email:galsonfarm@yahoo.com
Web:www.galsonfarm.co.uk

4 rooms
All en-suite
Open Jan-Dec
Room only rates, single from £44.00, double from £36.00 pp.
Evening meal £22.00.

17286

Stornoway, Isle of Lewis, Western Isles   Map Ref: 3D4

Cabarfeidh Hotel

Manor Park, Stornoway,, Isle of Lewis, HS1 2EU
Tel:01851 702604 Fax:01851 705567
Email:donnie@calahotels.com
Web:www.calahotels.com

46 rooms
All en-suite
Open Jan-Dec excl Xmas/New Year
B&B per person, single from £79.00, double from £59.00.

17507

Stornoway, Isle of Lewis, Western Isles   Map Ref: 3D4

Caladh Inn

James Street, Stornoway, Isle of Lewis, HS1 2QN
Tel:01851 702604 Fax:01851 703158
Email:caladhinn@calahotels.com
Web:www.calahotels.com

68 rooms
Open all year
B&B per person, single from £32.00, double/twin from £24.50.

52489 Stornoway, Isle of Lewis, Western Isles Map Ref: 3D4

Royal Hotel

Cromwell Street, Stornoway, Isle of Lewis, HS1 2DG
Tel:01851 702109 Fax:01851 702142
Email:royal@calahotels.com
Web:www.calahotels.com

24 rooms
All en-suite
Open Jan-Dec
Rates on application.

15808 Daliburgh, Isle of South Uist, Western Isles Map Ref: 3B10

Borrodale Hotel

Daliburgh, South Uist, Western Isles, HS8 5SS
Tel:01878 700444 Fax:01878 700446
Email:reception@borrodalehotel.co.uk
Web:www.witb.co.uk/links/isleshotels.htm

14 rooms
Open Jan-Dec excl Xmas/New Year
B&B per person, single from £38.00, double from £35.00.

48527 Lochcarnan, Isle of South Uist, Western Isles Map Ref: 3B9

Orasay Inn

Lochcarnan, South Uist, Outer Hebrides, HS8 5PD
Tel:01870 610298 Fax:01870 610267
Email:orasayinn@btinternet.com
Web:www.orasayinn.co.uk

Overlooking the coast and in quiet position. The Inn offers extensive menus including local seafood dishes. Conservatory dining area serving meals all day. Non-residents very welcome.

9 rooms, All en-suite. Open Jan-Dec. B&B per person, single from £50.00, double from £35.00, BB & Eve.Meal from £45.00.

64622

Evie, Orkney — Map Ref: 5B11

Woodwick House

Evie, Orkney, KW17 2PQ
Tel:01856 751330
Email:mail@woodwickhouse.co.uk
Web:www.woodwickhouse.co.uk

8 rooms
Some en-suite
Open Jan-Dec
B&B per person, single/double from £34.00.

76974

Kirkwall, Orkney — Map Ref: 5B12

Avalon House

Carness Road, Kirkwall, Orkney, KW15 1UE
Tel:01856 876665
Email:jane@avalon-house.co.uk
Web:www.avalon-house.co.uk

5 rooms
All en-suite
Open Jan-Dec
Room only per night, single from £40.00, double from £58.00.

Skara Brae, Orkney

VisitScotland, in conjunction with the English Tourism Council and Wales Tourist Board operates a national accessible scheme that identifies, acknowledges and promotes those accommodation establishments that meet the needs of visitors with disabilities.

The three categories of accessibility, drawn up in close consultation with specialist organisations concerned with the needs of people with disabilities are:

Category 1

Unassisted wheelchair access

Category 2

Assisted wheelchair access

Category 3

Access for visitors with mobility difficulties

CATEGORY 1

Aberdeen

Aberdeen Patio Hotel
Beach Boulevard
Aberdeen
Aberdeenshire
AB24 5EF
Tel: 01224 633339

Copthorne Hotel
122 Huntly Street
Aberdeen
AB10 1SU
Tel: 01224 630404

Express by Holiday Inn
Chapel Street
Aberdeen
AB10 1SQ
Tel: 01224 623500

King's Hall
University of Aberdeen
Aberdeen
AB24 3FX
Tel: 01224 272660

Thistle Aberdeen Airport Hotel
Argyll Road
Aberdeen
Aberdeenshire
AB21 0AF
Tel: 0870 333 9155

Thistle Aberdeen Altens
Souterhead Road
Altens, Aberdeen
Aberdeenshire
AB12 3LF
Tel: 01224 877000

Achnasheen

The Torridon
Torridon
Achnasheen
Ross-shire
IV22 2EY
Tel: 01445 791242

Alexandria

De Vere Cameron House
Loch Lomond
Alexandria
Dunbartonshire
G83 8QZ
Tel: 01389 755565

Auchencairn

Balcary Bay Hotel
Auchencairn, By Castle Douglas
Kirkcudbrightshire
DG7 1QZ
Tel: 01556 640217

Auchterarder

The Gleneagles Hotel
Auchterarder
Perthshire
PH3 1NF
Tel: 01764 662231

Auldearn

Covenanters' Inn
High Street
Auldearn
Nairn
IV12 5TG
Tel: 01667 452456

Ayr

Ramada Jarvis
Dalblair Road
Ayr
Ayrshire
KA7 1UG
Tel: 01292 269331

Ballater

Glenernan
37 Braemar Road
Ballater
Aberdeenshire
AB35 5RQ
Tel: 013397 53111

Brechin

Northern Hotel
2 Clerk Street
Brechin
Angus
DD9 6AE
Tel: 01356 625400

Brodick

Auchrannie Spa Resort
Brodick
Isle of Arran
KA27 8BZ
Tel: 01770 302234

Broughton, by Biggar

The Glenholm Centre
Broughton, by Biggar
Lanarkshire
ML12 6JF
Tel: 01899 830408

Burntisland

Kingswood Hotel
Kinghorn Road
Burntisland
Fife
KY3 9LL
Tel: 01592 872329

Carradale

Dunvalanree
Portrigh Bay
Carradale
Argyll
PA28 6SE
Tel: 01583 431226

Clydebank

The Beardmore Hotel & Conference Centre
Beardmore Street
Clydebank
Greater Glasgow
G81 4SA
Tel: 0141 951 6000

Connel, by Oban

Wide Mouthed Frog
Dunstaffnage Marina
Connel, by Oban
Argyll
PA37 1PX
Tel: 01631 567005

Daviot

The Lodge at Daviot Mains
Daviot
By Inverness
IV2 5ER
Tel: 01463 772215

Dumfries

Glenlossie Guest House
75 Annan Road
Dumfries
Dumfries-shire
DG1 3EG
Tel: 01387 254305

Category 1 continued

Dundee

West Park Centre
319 Perth Road
Dundee
Angus
DD2 1NN
Tel: 01382 573111

Dunfermline

Express By Holiday Inn Dunfermline
Halbeath
Dunfermline
Fife
KY11 8DY
Tel: 01383 748222/01383 748220

Edinburgh

Ardgarth Guest House
1 St Mary's Place, Portobello
Edinburgh
EH15 2QF
Tel: 0131 669 3021

Edinburgh City Centre (Morrison St) Premier Travel Inn
1 Morrison Link
Edinburgh
EH3 8DN
Tel: 01582 844266

Express By Holiday Inn
Britannia Way, Ocean Drive
Edinburgh
Lothian
EH6 6LA
Tel: 0131 5554422

Express By Holiday Inn
16-22 Picardy Place
Edinburgh
Lothian
EH1 3JT
Tel: 0131 5582300

Jurys Inn Edinburgh
43 Jeffrey Street
Edinburgh
Lothian
EH1 1DH
Tel: 0131 200 3300

Melville Guest House
2 Duddingston Crescent
Edinburgh
Lothian
EH15 3AS
Tel: 0131 6697856

Novotel Edinburgh Centre
80 Lauriston Place
Edinburgh
Lothian
EH3 9DE
Tel: 0131 656 3500

Ramada Mount Royal Hotel
53 Princes Street
Edinburgh
EH2 2DG
Tel: 0131 225 7161

Thistle Edinburgh
107 Leith Street
Edinburgh
EH1 3SW
Tel: 0141 3323311

Toby Carvery & Innkeepers Lodge Edin/West
114-116 St Johns Road
Edinburgh
EH12 8AX
Tel: 0131 334 8235

Forgandenny

Battledown Bed & Breakfast
Off Station Road
Forgandenny
Perthshire
PH2 9EL
Tel: 01738 812471

Fraserburgh

Findlays Hotel & Restaurant
Smiddyhill Road
Fraserburgh
Aberdeenshire
AB43 9WL
Tel: 01346 519547

Glasgow

Carlton George Hotel
44 West George Street
Glasgow
G2 1DH
Tel: 0141 353 6373

Glasgow Hilton
1 William Street
Glasgow
G3 8HT
Tel: 0141 204 5555

Glasgow Marriott
500 Argyle Street
Glasgow
G3 8RR
Tel: 0141 226 5577

Holiday Inn
161 West Nile Street
Glasgow
G1 2RL
Tel: 0141 352 8300

Jurys Inn Glasgow
Jamaica Street
Glasgow
G1 4QE
Tel: 0141 314 4800

Tulip Inn Glasgow
80 Ballater Street
Glasgow
G5 0TW
Tel: 0141 429 4233

Greenock

Express by Holiday Inn
Cartsburn
Greenock
PA15 4RT
Tel: 01475 786666

James Watt College
Waterfront Campus, Customhouse Way
Greenock
Renfrewshire
PA15 1EN
Tel: 01475 731360

Gretna

The Garden House Hotel
Sarkfoot Road
Gretna
Dumfriesshire
DG16 5EP
Tel: 01461 337621

Hunters Lodge Hotel
Annan Road
Gretna
Dumfriesshire
DG16 5DL
Tel: 01461 338214

Gretna Green

Days Inn
Welcome Break Service Area, M74
Gretna Green
Dumfriesshire
DG16 5HQ
Tel: 01461 337566

Smiths @ Gretna Green
Gretna Green
Dumfries & Galloway
DG16 5EA
Tel: 0845 3676768

Haddington

Maitlandfield House Hotel
24 Sidegate
Haddington
East Lothian
EH41 4BZ
Tel: 01620 826513

Invergordon

Delny House
Delny
Invergordon
Ross-shire
IV18 0NP
Tel: 01862 842678

Inverness

Inverness Marriott
Culcabock Road
Inverness
Inverness-shire
IV2 3LP
Tel: 01463 237166

Irvine

The Gailes Lodge
Marine Drive
Gailes
Irvine
KA11 5AE
Tel: 01294 204040

Thistle Irvine
46 Annick Road
Irvine
Ayrshire
KA11 4LD
Tel: 0141 332 3311

Kildonan

Kildonan Hotel
Kildonan
Isle of Arran
KA27 8SE
Tel: 0141 779 9205

Kilkenzie

Dalnaspidal Guest House
Tangy
Kilkenzie
Argyll
PA28 6QD
Tel: 01586 820466

Category 1 continued

Kilmarnock

Park Hotel
Rugby Park
Kilmarnock
Ayrshire
KA1 1UR
Tel: 01563 545999

Kingussie

Columba House Hotel & Garden Restaurant
Manse Road
Kingussie
Inverness-shire
PH21 1JF
Tel: 01540 661402

Kinlochleven

Tigh-Na-Cheo
Garbien Road
Kinlochleven
Argyll
PH50 4SE
Tel: 01855 831434

Kirkcudbright

Fludha Guest House
Tongland Road
Kirkcudbright
Dumfries & Galloway
DG6 4UU
Tel: 01557 331443

Isle of Lewis, Back

Broad Bay House
Back
Isle of Lewis
HS2 0LQ
Tel: 01851 820990

Livingston

Ramada Livingston
Almondview
Livingston
West Lothian
EH54 6QB
Tel: 01506 431222

Lochmaben

The Crown Hotel
8 Bruce Street
Lochmaben
Dumfriesshire
DG11 1PD
Tel: 01387 811750

Lossiemouth

Ceilidh B&B
34 Clifton Road
Lossiemouth
Moray
IV31 6DP
Tel: 01343 815848

Moffat

Lochhouse Farm Retreat Centre
Beattock
Moffat
Dumfries & Galloway
DG10 9SG
Tel: 01683 300451

Motherwell

Express By Holiday Inn
Strathclyde Park M74 Jct 5
Motherwell
Lanarkshire
ML1 3RB
Tel: 01698 858585

Motherwell College Stewart Hall
Dalzell Drive
Motherwell
Lanarkshire
ML1 2DD
Tel: 01698 261890

Isle of Mull, Salen

Ard Mhor House
Pier Road
Salen
Isle of Mull
PA72 6JL
Tel: 01680 300255

Nairn

Claymore House Hotel
45 Seabank Road
Nairn
Inverness-shire
IV12 4EY
Tel: 01667 453731

Newburgh

Mosspaul
Teviothead, Hawick
Newburgh
Roxburghshire
TD9 0LP
Tel: 01450 850245

by Newtonmore

Crubenbeg House
Falls of Truim
By Newtonmore
PH20 1BE
Tel: 01540 673300

Orkney, Kirkwall

Lav'rockha Guest House
Inganess Road
Kirkwall
Orkney
KW15 1SP
Tel: 01856 876103

Paisley

Express by Holiday Inn Glasgow Airport
St Andrews Drive
Paisley
PA3 2TJ
Tel: 0141 8421100

Travelodge Glasgow Airport
Marchburn Drive
Paisley
Glasgow
PA3 2AR
Tel: 0141 848 1359

Peebles

Cringletie House Hotel
Edinburgh Road
Peebles
Peeblesshire
EH45 8PL
Tel: 01721 725750

Peterhead

Invernettie Guest House
South Road, Burnhaven
Peterhead
Aberdeenshire
AB42 0YX
Tel: 01779 473530

Pitfodels, Aberdeen

Marcliffe at Pitfodels
North Deeside Road
Pitfodels, Aberdeen
AB15 9YA
Tel: 01224 861000

Portree

Cuillin Hills Hotel
Portree
Isle of Skye
IV51 9QU
Tel: 01478 612003

Viewfield House Hotel
Portree
Isle of Skye
IV51 9EU
Tel: 01478 612217

Rhu

Rosslea Hall Hotel
Ferry Road
Rhu
Dunbartonshire
G84 8NF
Tel: 0141 419 1919/
07920 597445

Shetland, Bressay

Northern Lights Holistic Spa
Sound View Uphouse
Bressay
Shetland
ZE2 9ES
Tel: 01595 820733

Shetland, Lerwick

Shetland Hotel
Holmsgarth Road
Lerwick
Shetland
ZE1 0PW
Tel: 01595 695515

Shetland, Walls

Burrastow House
Walls
Shetland
ZE2 9PD
Tel: 01595 809307

Category 1 continued

Spean Bridge

Old Pines Hotel and Restaurant
Gairlochy Road
Spean Bridge
Inverness-shire
PH34 4EG
Tel: 01397 712324

St Andrews

The Old Station, Country House
Stratvithie Bridge
St Andrews
Fife
KY16 8LR
Tel: 01334 880505

Stirling

Express by Holiday Inn - Stirling
Springkerse Business Park
Stirling
Stirlingshire
FK7 7XH
Tel: 01786 449922

Stirling Management Centre
University of Stirling
Stirling
FK9 4LA
Tel: 01786 451666

Swinton

The Wheatsheaf at Swinton
Main Street
Swinton
Berwickshire
TD11 3JJ
Tel: 01890 860257

Thurso

Park Hotel
Oldfield
Thurso
Caithness
KW14 8RE
Tel: 01847 893251

Turnberry

The Westin Turnberry Resort
Turnberry
Ayrshire
KA26 9LT
Tel: 01655 331000

Turriff

Deveron Lodge B&B Guesthouse
Bridgend Terrace
Turriff
Aberdeenshire
AB53 4ES
Tel: 01888 563613

Western Isles, South Uist

Crossroads
Stoneybridge
South Uist
Western Isles
HS8 5SD
Tel: 01870 620321

CATEGORY 2

Abbotsinch, Paisley

Ramada Glasgow Airport
Marchburn Drive
Abbotsinch, Paisley
Renfrewshire
PA3 2SJ
Tel: 0141 8402200

Aberdeen

Crombie House
University of Aberdeen
Aberdeen
AB24 3TS
Tel: 01224 272660

Aberfeldy

Tomvale
Tom of Cluny
Aberfeldy
Perthshire
PH15 2JT
Tel: 01887 820171

Aberfoyle

Crannaig House
Trossachs Road
Aberfoyle
Stirlingshire
FK8 3SR
Tel: 01877 382276

by Aberfoyle

Forest Hills Hotel
Kinlochard
By Aberfoyle
Stirlingshire
FK8 3TL
Tel: 08701 942105

Aviemore

Macdonald Academy
Aviemore Highland Resort
Aviemore
Inverness-shire
PH22 1PF
Tel: 01479 815100

Ayr

Horizon Hotel
Esplanade
Ayr
Ayrshire
KA7 1DT
Tel: 01292 264384

Western House Hotel
2 Whitletts Road
Ayr
Ayrshire
KA9 0JE
Tel: 0870 8505666

Ballantrae

Glenapp Castle
Ballantrae
Ayrshire
KA26 0NZ
Tel: 01465 831212

Benderloch

Isle of Eriska Hotel
Benderloch
Argyll
PA37 1SD
Tel: 01631 720371

Blairs, Aberdeen

Ardoe House Hotel
South Deeside Road
Blairs, Aberdeen
Aberdeenshire
AB12 5YP
Tel: 01224 867355

Bonnyrigg

The Retreat Castle
Cockpen Road
Bonnyrigg
Midlothian
EH19 3HS
Tel: 0131 660 3200

Bridge of Allan

The Queen's Hotel
24 Henderson Street
Bridge of Allan
Stirlingshire
FK9 4HP
Tel: 01786 833268

Brodick

Auchrannie Country House Hotel
Brodick
Isle of Arran
KA27 8BZ
Tel: 01770 302234

Brora

Glenaveron
Golf Road
Brora
Sutherland
KW9 6QS
Tel: 01408 621 601

Carrutherstown

Hetland Hall Hotel
Carrutherstown
Dumfriesshire
DG1 4JX
Tel: 01387 840201

Castle Douglas

Douglas House B&B
63 Queen Street
Castle Douglas
Dumfries
DG7 1HS
Tel: 01556 503262

Crieff

Comely Bank Guest House
32 Burrell Street
Crieff
Perthshire
PH7 4DT
Tel: 01764 653409

Category 2 continued

Murraypark Hotel
Connaught Terrace
Crieff
Perthshire
PH7 3DJ
Tel: 01764 653731

Drymen

Winnock Hotel
The Square
Drymen
Stirlingshire
G63 0BL
Tel: 01360 660245

Dumfries

Aston Hotel
The Crichton, Bankend Road
Dumfries
Dumfries and Galloway
DG1 4ZZ
Tel: 01325 329600

Dunfermline

Best Western Keavil House Hotel
Crossford
Dunfermline
Fife
KY12 8QW
Tel: 01383 736258

Garvock House Hotel
St John's Drive, Transy
Dunfermline
Fife
KY12 7TU
Tel: 01383 621067

Rooms at 29 Bruce Street
29-35 Bruce Street
Dunfermline
Fife
KY12 7AG
Tel: 01383 840041

Dunoon

Dhailling Lodge
155 Alexandra Parade
Dunoon
Argyll
PA23 8AW
Tel: 01369 701253

Dyce

Aberdeen Marriott Hotel
Riverview Drive
Farburn, Dyce
Aberdeenshire
AB21 7AZ
Tel: 0870 400 7291

Dyce Skean Dhu Hotel
Farburn Terrace
Dyce
Aberdeenshire
AB21 7DW
Tel: 01224 877000

Speedbird Inn
Argyll Road
Dyce, Aberdeen
Aberdeenshire
AB21 0AF
Tel: 01224 772884

Edinburgh

Caledonian Hilton Hotel
Princes Street
Edinburgh
EH1 2AB
Tel: 0131 222 8888

Edinburgh First
Chancellor Court, Pollock Halls
18 Holyrood Park Road
Edinburgh
EH10 5AY
Tel: 0131 651 2011

Edinburgh Marriott
111 Glasgow Road
Edinburgh
EH12 8NF
0870 400 7293

Gillis
100 Strathearn Road
Edinburgh
EH9 1BB
Tel: 0131 623 8933

Hilton Edinburgh Airport
Edinburgh International Airport
Edinburgh
EH28 8LL
Tel: 0131 519 4400

Hilton Edinburgh Grosvenor
7-21 Grosvenor Street
Edinburgh
EH12 5EF
Tel: 0131 527 1411

Holiday Inn Edinburgh
Corstorphine Road
Edinburgh
EH12 6UA
Tel: 0870 400 9026

Holiday Inn Edinburgh-North
107 Queensferry Road
Edinburgh
EH4 3HL
Tel: 8704009025

Salisbury Green Hotel Conference Centre
University of Edinburgh,
Pollock Halls
18 Holyrood Park Road
Edinburgh
EH16 5AY
Tel: 0131 6622000

Fort William

Clan MacDuff Hotel
Achintore Road
Fort William
Inverness-shire
PH33 6RW
Tel: 01397 702341

Glasgow

Campanile Glasgow
Tunnel Street
Glasgow
Scotland
G3 8HL
Tel: 0141 2877700

Crowne Plaza Hotel
Congress Road
Glasgow
G3 8QT
Tel: 0141 306 9988

Ibis Hotel Glasgow
220 West Regent Street
Glasgow
G2 4DQ
Tel: 0141 225 6000

Novotel Glasgow Centre
181 Pitt Street
Glasgow
G2 4DT
Tel: 0141 222 2775

Queen Margaret Hall
55 Bellshaugh Road
Glasgow
G12 0SQ
Tel: 0141 3303110

Wolfson Hall
Kelvin Campus,West Scotland
Science Park
Maryhill Road
Glasgow
G20 0TH
Tel: 0141 3303110

Gorebridge

Ivory House
14 Vogrie Road
Gorebridge
Midlothian
EH23 4HH
Tel: 01875 820755

Grangemouth

Leapark Hotel
130 Bo'ness Road
Grangemouth
Stirlingshire
FK3 9BX
Tel: 01324 486733

Grantown-on-spey

Muckrach Lodge Hotel
Dulnain Bridge
Grantown-on-spey
Moray
PH26 3LY
Tel: 01479 851257

Gretna

The Willows
Loanwath Road
Gretna
Dumfriesshire
DG16 5ES
Tel: 01461 337996

Hawick

Elm House Hotel
17 North Bridge Street
Hawick
Roxburghshire
TD9 9BD
Tel: 01450 372866

Whitchester Guest House
Hawick
Roxburghshire
TD9 7LN
Tel: 01450 377477

Category 2 continued

Hoy

Stromabank
Hoy
Orkney
KW16 3PA
Tel: 01856 701494

Inveraray

Loch Fyne Hotel
Newtown
Inveraray
Argyll
PA32 8XT
Tel: 0131 554 7173

Inverness

New Drumossie Hotel
Perth Road
Inverness
Inverness-shire
IV1 2BE
Tel: 01463 236451

Ramada Jarvis Inverness
Church Street
Inverness
Inverness-shire
IV1 1DX
Tel: 01463 235181

Inverurie

Grant Arms Hotel
Monymusk
Inverurie
Aberdeenshire
AB51 7HJ
Tel: 01467 651333

Kelso

Inglestone House
Abbey Row
Kelso
Roxburghshire
TD5 7HQ
Tel: 01573 225800/225315

Kinloch Rannoch

Dunalastair Hotel
The Square
Kinloch Rannoch
Perthshire
PH16 5PW
Tel: 01882 632323

Kirkmichael

The Log Cabin Hotel
Glen Derby
Kirkmichael, Blairgowrie
Perthshire
PH10 7NA
Tel: 01250 881288

Kirriemuir

Lochside Lodge & Roundhouse Restaurant
Bridgend of Lintrathen
Kirriemuir
Angus
DD8 5JJ
Tel: 01575 560340

Largs

Burnlea Hotel
Burnlea Road
Largs
Ayrshire
KA30 8BX
Tel: 01475 687235

Lochcarnan

Orasay Inn
Lochcarnan
South Uist, Outer Hebrides
HS8 5PD
Tel: 01870 610298

Lockerbie

Dryfesdale Country House Hotel
Dryfebridge
Lockerbie
Dumfriesshire
DG11 2SF
Tel: 01576 202427

Markinch

Balbirnie House Hotel
Balbirnie Park
Markinch, by Glenrothes
Fife
KY7 6NE
Tel: 01592 610066

Millport

The Cathedral of the Isles
The College
Millport
Isle of Cumbrae
KA28 0HE
Tel: 01475 530353

Minard

Minard Castle
Minard
Argyll
PA32 8YB
Tel: 01546 886272

Motherwell

The Alona Hotel
Strathclyde Country Park
Motherwell
North Lanarkshire
ML1 3RT
0870 112 3888/
01698 333777

Moorings Hotel
114 Hamilton Road
Motherwell
Lanarkshire
ML1 3DG
Tel: 01698 258131

Isle of Mull, Lochdon

Seilisdeir
Lochdon
Isle of Mull
PA64 6AP
Tel: 01680 812465

nr Peebles

Cardrona Hotel Golf & Country Club
Cardrona
Near Peebles
Peebles-shire
EH45 6LZ
Tel: 01896 831144

Nethybridge

Nethybridge Hotel
Nethybridge
Inverness-shire
PH25 3DP
Tel: 01479 821203

New Lanark

New Lanark Mill Hotel
New Lanark
Lanarkshire
ML11 9DB
Tel: 01555 667200

Orkney, North Ronaldsay

Observatory Guest House
North Ronaldsay
Orkney
KW17 2BE
Tel: 01857 633200

Perth

Huntingtower Hotel
Crieff Road
Perth
Perthshire
PH1 3JT
Tel: 01738 583771

by Perth

Glencarse Hotel
Glencarse
by Perth
Perthshire
PH2 7LX
Tel: 01382 737555

Polmont

Inchyra Grange Hotel
Grange Road
Polmont
Stirlingshire
FK2 0YB
Tel: 01324 711911

Portree

Auchendinny
Treaslane
Portree
Isle of Skye, Inverness-shire
IV51 9NX
Tel: 01470 532470

Prestwick

Parkstone Hotel
Esplanade
Prestwick
Ayrshire
KA9 1QN
Tel: 01292 477286

Roy Bridge

The Stronlossit Inn
Roy Bridge
Inverness-shire
PH31 4AG
Tel: 01397 712253

Category 2 continued

Sanquhar

Newark
Sanquhar
Dumfriesshire
DG4 6HN
Tel: 01659 50263

Shetland, Baltasound

The Baltasound Hotel
Baltasound, Unst
Shetland
ZE2 9DS
Tel: 01957 711334

St Andrews

Rufflets Country House Hotel
Strathkinness Low Road
St Andrews
Fife
KY16 9TX
Tel: 01334 472594

Talmine

Cloisters
Church Holme
Talmine
Sutherland
IV27 4YP
Tel: 01847 601286

by Taynuilt

Roineabhal Country House
Kilchrenan
by Taynuilt
Argyll
PA35 1HD
Tel: 01866 833207

Tobermory

Highland Cottage
Breadalbane Street
Tobermory
Isle of Mull
PA75 6PD
Tel: 01688 302030

Troon

Marine Hotel
Crosbie Road
Troon
Ayrshire
KA10 6HE
Tel: 01292 314444

South Beach Hotel
South Beach
Troon
Ayrshire
KA10 6EG
Tel: 01292 312033

Tummel Bridge

Kynachan Loch Tummel Hotel
Tummel Bridge
Perthshire
PH16 5SB
Tel: 01389 713713

West Linton

Drochil Castle Farm
West Linton
Peeblesshire
EH46 7DD
Tel: 01721 752249

Western Isles, North Uist

Tigh Dearg Hotel
Lochmaddy
Isle of North Uist
Western Isles
HS6 5AE
Tel: 01876 500700

Whitburn

Best Western Hilcroft Hotel
East Main Street
Whitburn
West Lothian
EH47 0JU
Tel: 01501 740818

CATEGORY 3

Aberdeen

Britannia Hotel
Malcolm Road
Aberdeen
Grampian
AB21 9LN
Tel: 01224 409988

Northern Hotel
1 Great Northern Road
Aberdeen
AB24 3PS
Tel: 01224 483342

Aberdour

Aberdour Hotel
38 High Street
Aberdour
Fife
KY3 0SW
Tel: 01383 860325

Aberfoyle

Rob Roy Hotel
Aberfoyle
Stirlingshire
FK8 3UX
Tel: 01877 382245

Aboyne

Chesterton House
Formaston Park
Aboyne
Aberdeenshire
AB34 5HF
Tel: 013398 86740

by Achmore

Soluis Mu Thuath
Braeintra
by Achmore
Lochalsh
IV53 8UP
Tel: 01599 577219

Annan

Rowanbank
20 St Johns Road
Annan
Dumfriesshire
DG12 5AW
Tel: 01461 204200

Arrochar

Village Inn
Main Street
Arrochar
Dunbartonshire
G83 7AX
Tel: 01301 702279

Auchterarder

Greystanes
Western Road
Auchterarder
Perthshire
PH3 1JJ
Tel: 01764 664239

Aviemore

Ravenscraig Guest House
141 Grampian Road
Aviemore
Inverness-shire
PH22 1RP
Tel: 01479 810278

Waverley
35 Strathspey Avenue
Aviemore
Inverness-shire
PH22 1SN
Tel: 01479 811226

Ayr

Fairfield House Hotel
12 Fairfield Road
Ayr
Ayrshire
KA7 2AS
Tel: 01292 267461

by Ayr

Alt-Na-Craig
Hollybush
by Ayr
KA6 7EB
Tel: 01292 560555

Enterkine Country House
Annbank
by Ayr
Ayrshire
KA6 5AL
Tel: 01292 520580

Ballater

Darroch Learg Hotel
Braemar Road
Ballater
Aberdeenshire
AB35 5UX
Tel: 01339 755443

Moorside Guest House
26 Braemar Road
Ballater
Aberdeenshire
AB35 5RL
Tel: 01339 755492

School House
Anderson Road
Ballater
Aberdeenshire
AB35 5QW
Tel: 013397 56333

Category 3 continued

Balloch

Barton Bed and Breakfast
12 Balloch Road
Balloch
West Dunbartonshire
G83 8SR
Tel: 01389 759653

Bellshill

Hilton Strathclyde
Pheonix Crescent
Bellshill
North Lanarkshire
ML4 3JQ
Tel: 01698 395500

Bishopton

Mar Hall
Mar Estate
Bishopton
Renfrewshire
PA7 5NW
Tel: 0141 812 9999

Blairgowrie

Bridge of Cally Hotel
Bridge of Cally
Blairgowrie
Perthshire
PH10 7JJ
Tel: 01250 886231

Holmrigg
Wester Essendy
Blairgowrie
Perthshire
PH10 6RD
Tel: 01250 884309

Bridge of Allan

Lynedoch
7 Mayne Avenue
Bridge of Allan
Stirlingshire
FK9 4QU
Tel: 01786 832178

Brodick

Belvedere Guest House
Alma Road
Brodick
Isle of Arran
KA27 8BZ
Tel: 01770 302234

Strathwhillan House
Strathwhillan Road
Brodick
Isle of Arran
KA27 8BQ
Tel: 01770 302331

Callander

Roman Camp Hotel
Main Street
Callander
Perthshire
FK17 8BG
Tel: 01877 330003

Canderside Toll

Shawlands Hotel
Ayr Road
Canderside Toll, by Larkhall
Lanarkshire
ML9 2TZ
Tel: 01698 791111

Coldingham

Dunlaverock
Coldingham Bay
Coldingham
Berwickshire
TD14 5PA
Tel: 01890 771450

Colvend

Clonyard House Hotel
Colvend, Dalbeattie
Kircudbrightshire
DG5 4QW
Tel: 01556 630372

Comrie

Drumearn Cottage
The Ross
Comrie
Perthshire
PH6 2JU
Tel: 01764 670030

Coupar Angus

Red House Hotel
Station Road
Coupar Angus
Perthshire
PH13 9AL
Tel: 01828 628500

Crieff

Achray House Hotel
St Fillans
Crieff
Perthshire
PH6 2NF
Tel: 01764 685 231

Crieff Hydro Hotel
Crieff
Perthshire
PH7 3LQ
Tel: 01764 655555

Fendoch Guest House
Sma' Glen
Crieff
Perthshire
PH7 3LW
Tel: 01764 653446

Dalmally

Glenorchy Lodge Hotel
Dalmally
Argyll
PA33 1AA
Tel: 018382 00312

Dalrymple

Kirkton Inn
1-3 Main Street
Dalrymple
Ayrshire
KA6 6DF
Tel: 01292 560241

Dirleton

Station House
Station Road
Dirleton
North Berwick
EH39 5LR
Tel: 01620 890512

Dornoch

Dornoch Castle Hotel
Castle Street
Dornoch
Sutherland
IV25 3SD
Tel: 01862 810216

Dumfries

Hazeldean Guest House
4 Moffat Road
Dumfries
DG1 1NJ
Tel: 01387 266178

Torbay Lodge
31 Lovers Walk
Dumfries
DG1 1LR
Tel: 01387 253922

Wallamhill House
Kirkton
Dumfries
Dumfriesshire
DG1 1SL
Tel: 01387 248249

Dundee

Hilton Dundee
Earl Grey Place
Dundee
Angus
DD1 4DE
Tel: 01382 229271

Dunfermline

Clarke Cottage Guest House
139 Halbeath Road
Dunfermline
Fife
KY11 4LA
Tel: 01383 735935

Pitbauchlie House Hotel
Aberdour Road
Dunfermline
Fife
KY11 4PB
Tel: 01383 722282

Duntocher

West Park Hotel
Great Western Road
Duntocher
Clydebank
G81 6DB
Tel: 01389 872333

Eastriggs

The Graham Arms Guest House
The Rand
Eastriggs
Dumfriesshire
DG12 6NL
Tel: 01461 40031

Category 3 continued

Edinburgh

Abbey Lodge Hotel
137 Drum Street
Gilmerton
Edinburgh
EH17 8RJ
Tel: 0131 6649548

Ben Craig House
3 Craigmillar Park
Edinburgh
EH16 5PG
Tel: 0131 667 2593

Brae Lodge Guest House
30 Liberton Brae
Edinburgh
Lothian
EH16 6AF
Tel: 0131 6722876

Holland House
18 Holyrood Park Road
Edinburgh
EH16 5AY
Tel: 0131 651 2011

Holyrood Hotel
Holyrood Road
Edinburgh
EH8 6AE
Tel: 0131 550 4500

Kelly's Guest House
3 Hillhouse Road
Edinburgh
Lothian
EH4 3QP
Tel: 0131 332 3894

The Laurels
320 Gilmerton Road
Edinburgh
Midlothian
EH17 7PR
Tel: 0131 666 2229

Lindsay Guest House
108 Polwarth Terrace
Edinburgh
Midlothian
EH11 1NN
Tel: 0131 337 1580

Masson House
18 Holyrood Park Road
Edinburgh
EH16 5AY
Tel: 0131 651 2011

Roxburghe Hotel
38 Charlotte Square
Edinburgh
EH2 4HG
Tel: 0131 240 5500

Edzell

Kelvingrove
Dunlappie Road
Edzell
Angus
DD9 7UB
Tel: 01356 648316

Erskine

Erskine Bridge Hotel
Erskine
Renfrewshire
PA8 6AN

Eskbank

Glenarch House
Melville Road
Eskbank
Dalkeith
EH22 3NJ
Tel: 0131 6631478

Fort William

Craig Nevis West
Belford Road
Fort William
Inverness-shire
PH33 6BU
Tel: 01397 702023

Lochan Cottage Guest House
Lochyside
Fort William
Inverness-shire
PH33 7NX
Tel: 01397 702695

by Fort William

The Inn at Ardgour
Ardgour
by Fort William
Inverness-shire
PH33 7AA
Tel: 01855 841225

Galashiels

Ettrickvale
33 Abbotsford Road
Galashiels
Selkirkshire
TD1 3HW
Tel: 01896 755224

Girvan

Garryloop
Penkill, Old Dailly
Girvan
South Ayrshire
KA26 9TG
Tel: 01465 871 393/
0788 4438 425

Gourock

Spinnaker Hotel
121 Albert Road
Gourock
Renfrewshire
PA19 1BU
Tel: 01475 633107

Grantown on Spey

Craiglynne Hotel
Woodlands Terrace
Grantown-on-Spey
Morayshire
PH26 3JX
Tel: 020 7403 8338

Holmhill House
Woodside Avenue
Grantown on Spey
Morayshire
PH26 3JR
Tel: 01479 873977

Kinross Guest House
Woodside Avenue
Grantown-on-Spey
Moray
PH26 3JR
Tel: 01479 872042

Willowbank
High Street
Grantown on Spey
Morayshire
PH26 3EN
Tel: 01479 872089

Greenock

Tontine Hotel
6 Ardgowan Square
Greenock
Renfrewshire
PA16 8NG
Tel: 01475 723316

Gretna

The Gables Hotel & Restaurant
1 Annan Road
Gretna
Dumfriesshire
DG16 5DQ
Tel: 01461 338300

Isle of Harris

Ardhasaig House
9 Ardhasaig
Isle of Harris
HS3 3AJ
Tel: 01859 502500

Carminish House
1a Strond
Isle of Harris
HS5 3UB
Tel: 01859 520400

Helensburgh

RSR Braeholm
31 East Montrose Street
Helensburgh
Argyll & Bute
G84 7HR
Tel: 01436 671880

Helmsdale

Kindale House
5 Lilleshall Street
Helmsdale
Sutherland
KW8 6JF
Tel: 01431 821415

Invergowrie

Swallow Hotel
Kingsway West
Invergowrie, Dundee
Angus
DD2 5JT
Tel: 01382 641122

Inverness

Avalon Guest House
79 Glenurquhart Road
Inverness
Inverness-shire
IV3 5PB
Tel: 01463 239075

Category 3 continued

Inverurie

Strathburn Hotel
Burghmuir Drive
Inverurie
Aberdeenshire
AB51 4GY
Tel: 01467 624422

Jedburgh

Allerton House
Oxnam Road
Jedburgh
Roxburghshire
TD8 6QQ
Tel: 01835 869633

Kelso

Craignethan House
Jedburgh Road
Kelso
Roxburghshire
TD5 8AZ
Tel: 01573 224818

Cross Keys Hotel
36-37 The Square
Kelso
Roxburghshire
TD5 7HL
Tel: 01573 223303

Edenmouth Farm
Kelso
Roxburghshire
TD5 7QB
Tel: 01890 830391

by Kilmarnock

Fenwick Hotel
Fenwick
by Kilmarnock
Ayrshire
KA3 6AU
Tel: 01560 600 478

Kinclaven, by Stanley

Ballathie House Hotel
Kinclaven, by Stanley
Perthshire
PH1 4QN
Tel: 01250 883268

Kingussie

The Hermitage Guest House
Spey Street
Kingussie
Inverness-shire
PH21 1HN
Tel: 01540 662137

Kintyre

Hunting Lodge Hotel
Bellochantuy
Kintyre
Argyll
PA28 6QE
Tel: 01583 421323

Kyle of Lochalsh

Isle of Raasay Hotel
Raasay
Kyle of Lochalsh
Ross-shire
IV40 8PB
Tel: 01478 660 222

by Lairg

Ruddyglow Park Country House
Loch Assynt
By Lairg
Sutherland
IV27 4HB
Tel: 01571 822216

Lamlash

Lilybank
Shore Road
Lamlash
Isle of Arran
KA27 8LS
Tel: 01770 600230

Linlithgow

Arden House
Belsyde
Linlithgow
West Lothian
EH49 6QE
Tel: 01506 670172

Loanhead

Aaron Glen Guest House
7 Nivensknowe Road
Loanhead
Midlothian
EH20 9AU
Tel: 0131 440 1293

Loch Lomond

Culag Lochside Guest House
Luss
Loch Lomond
Argyll and Bute
G83 8PD
Tel: 01436 860248

Lochmaben

Ardbeg Cottage
19 Castle Street
Lochmaben
Dumfries-shire
DG11 1NY
Tel: 01387 811855

Macmerry

Adniston Manor
West Adniston Farm
Macmerry
East Lothian
EH33 1EA
Tel: 01875 611190/

Melrose

Easter Cottage
Lilliesleaf
Melrose
Roxburghshire
TD6 9JD
Tel: 01835 870281

Milton

Milton Inn
Dumbarton Road
Milton
Dunbartonshire
G82 2DT
Tel: 01389 761401

Moffat

Black Bull Hotel
Churchgate
Moffat
Dumfriesshire
DG10 9EG
Tel: 01683 220206

Limetree House
Eastgate
Moffat
Dumfriesshire
DG10 9AE
Tel: 01683 220001

Monikie

Craigton House B&B
Craigton Road
Monikie
Angus
DD5 3QN
Tel: 01383 370570

Montrose

Best Western Links Hotel
Mid Links
Montrose
Angus
DD10 8RL
Tel: 01674 671000

Muir-of-Ord

Hillview Park
Muir-of-Ord
Ross-shire
IV6 7TU
Tel: 01463 870787

Isle of Mull, Lochdon

Birchgrove
Lochdon
Isle of Mull
PA64 4AP
Tel: 01680 812364

Isle of Mull, Tobermory

Tobermory Hotel
53 Main Street
Tobermory
Isle of Mull
PA75 6NT
Tel: 01688 302091

Musselburgh

Carberry Tower
Musselburgh
East Lothian
EH21 8PY
Tel: 0131 665 3135

Nairn

Napier
60 Seabank Road
Nairn
IV12 4HA
Tel: 01667 453330

Category 3 continued

New Cumnock

Lochside House Hotel
New Cumnock
Ayrshire
KA18 4PN
Tel: 01290 333000

Newton Stewart

East Culkae Farm House
Sorbie
Newton Stewart
Wigtownshire
DG8 8AS
Tel: 01988 850214

Category 3 continued

Oban

The Caledonian Hotel
Station Square
Oban
Argyll
PA34 5RT
Tel: 01631 563133

by Oban

Falls of Lora Hotel
Connel Ferry
by Oban
Argyll
PA37 1PB
Tel: 01631 710483

Orkney, Orphir

Houton Bay Lodge
Houton Bay
Orphir, Scapa Flow
Orkney
KW17 2RD
Tel: 01856 811320

Paisley

Ardgowan Town House Hotel
94 Renfrew Road
Paisley
Renfrewshire
PA3 4BJ
Tel: 0141 889 4763

Perth

Arisaig Guest House
4 Pitcullen Crescent
Perth
PH2 7HT
Tel: 01738 628240

Cherrybank Inn
210 Glasgow Road
Perth
PH2 0NA
Tel: 01738 624349

Petra's B&B
4 Albany Terrace
Perth
Perthshire
PH1 2BD
Tel: 01738 563050

Quality Hotel Perth
Leonard Street
Perth
Perthshire
PH2 8HE
Tel: 01738 624141

Sunbank House Hotel
50 Dundee Road
Perth
Perthshire
PH2 7BA
Tel: 01738 624882

by Peterhead

Greenbrae Farmhouse
Longside
By Peterhead
Aberdeenshire
AB42 4JX
Tel: 01779 821051

Pirnhall, Stirling

Barn Lodge
Croftside
Pirnhall, Stirling
Stirlingshire
FK7 8EX
Tel: 01786 813591

Pitlochry

The Atholl Palace
Atholl Road
Pitlochry
Perthshire
PH16 5LY
Tel: 01796 472400

Green Park Hotel
Clunie Bridge Road
Pitlochry
Perthshire
PH16 5JY
Tel: 01796 473248

The Poplars
27 Lower Oakfield
Pitlochry
Perthshire
PH16 5DS

The Well House
11 Toberargan Road
Pitlochry
Perthshire
PH16 5HG
Tel: 01796 472239
Tel: 01796 472129

by Pitlochry

East Haugh House Country Hotel & Restaurant
East Haugh
by Pitlochry
Perthshire
PH16 5TE
Tel: 01796 473121

Portpatrick

Braefield Guest House
Braefield Road
Portpatrick
Wigtownshire
DG9 8TA
Tel: 01776 810255

The Fernhill Hotel
Heugh Road
Portpatrick
Wigtownshire
DG9 8TD
Tel: 01776 810220

Portpatrick Hotel
Heugh Road
Portpatrick
Wigtownshire
DG9 8TQ
Tel: 01776 810333

Scone

Perth Airport Skylodge
Norwell Drive, Perth Airport
Scone
Perthshire
PH2 6PL
Tel: 01738 555700

Shetland, Gulberwick

Virdafjell
Shurton Brae
Gulberwick
Shetland
ZE2 9TX
Tel: 01595 694336

Shetland, Lerwick

Glen Orchy Guest House
20 Knab Road
Lerwick
Shetland
ZE1 0AX
Tel: 01595 692031

South Queensferry

Priory Lodge
8 The Loan
South Queensferry
West Lothian
EH30 9NS
Tel: 0131 331 4345

Spean Bridge

The Heathers
Invergloy Halt
Spean Bridge
Inverness-shire
PH34 4DY
Tel: 01397 712077

by Spean Bridge

Dreamweavers
Mucomir
By Spean Bridge
Inverness-shire
PH34 4EQ
Tel: 01397 712 548

St Andrews

Pitmilly West Lodge
Kingsbarns
St Andrews
Fife
KY16 8QA
Tel: 01334 880581

by Stranraer

Corsewall Lighthouse Hotel
Kirkcolm
by Stranraer
Wigtownshire
DG9 0QG
Tel: 01776 853220

Category 3 continued

Strathaven

Rissons At Springvale
18 Lethame Road
Strathaven
Lanarkshire
ML10 6AD
Tel: 01357 521131

Tarbet

Stewart House
Bemersyde
Tarbet
Dunbartonshire
G83 7DE
Tel: 01301 702230

by Thurso

Creag-Na-Mara
East Mey
by Thurso
Caithness
KW14 8XL
Tel: 01847 851850

Troon

Piersland House Hotel
15 Craigend Road
Troon
Ayrshire
KA10 6HD
Tel: 01292 314747

Ullapool

Dromnan Guest House
Garve Road
Ullapool
Ross-shire
IV26 2SX
Tel: 01854 612333

Upper Largo

Bayview
Drumeldrie
Upper Largo
Fife
KY8 6JD
Tel: 01333 360454

West Linton

Ingraston Farm B&B
Ingraston Farm
West Linton
Peebleshire
EH46 7AA
Tel: 01968 682219

Western Isles, Northbay

Airds Guest House
244 Bruernish
Northbay
Isle of Barra
HS9 5UY
Tel: 01871 890720

Western Isles, North Uist

Redburn House
Lochmaddy
Isle of North Uist
Western Isles
HS6 5AA
Tel: 01671 402554/
07860 600925

Western Isles, South Uist

Caloraidh
Milton
South Uist
HS8 5RY
Tel: 01878 710365

SOUTH OF SCOTLAND
Ayrshire and Arran, Dumfries and Galloway, Scottish Borders

AYRSHIRE AND ARRAN

Alloway

Belleisle Country House Hotel
Belleisle Park, Doonfoot, Ayr, Ayrshire, KA7 4DU
Tel: 01292 442331
★ Country House Hotel

The Wytchery
10 Doonvale Place, Alloway, Ayrshire, KA6 6FD
Tel: 01292 442070
Awaiting Inspection

Annbank

Enterkine Country House
Annbank, by Ayr, Ayrshire, KA6 5AL
Tel: 01292 520580
★★★★ Country House Hotel

Ayr

Abbotsford Hotel
14 Corsehill Road, Ayr, Ayrshire, KA7 2ST
Tel: 01292 261506
★★★ Small Hotel

Ayrshire & Galloway Hotel
1 Killoch Place, Ayr, Ayrshire, KA7 2EA
Tel: 01292 262626
★★★ Hotel

Belmont Guest House
15 Park Circus, Ayr, KA7 2DJ
Tel: 01292 265588
★★★ Guest House

Brig O' Doon Hotel
Alloway, Ayr, Ayrshire, KA7 4PQ
Tel: 01292 442466
★★★★ Small Hotel

Burnside Guest House
14 Queens Terrace, Ayr, Ayrshire, KA7 1DU
Tel: 01292 263912
★★★★ Guest House

Carrick Lodge Hotel
Carrick Road, Ayr, Ayrshire, KA7 2RE
Tel: 01292 262846
★★★ Small Hotel

Coila Guest House
10 Holmston Road, Ayr, Ayrshire, KA7 3BB
Tel: 01292 262642
★★★★ Guest House

Craggallan Guest House
8 Queens Terrace, Ayr, Ayrshire, KA7 1DU
Tel: 0192 264998
★★★★ Guest House

Daviot House
12 Queen's Terrace, Ayr, Ayrshire, KA7 1DU
Tel: 01292 269678
★★★★ Guest House

Dunlay House
1 Ailsa Place, Ayr, Ayrshire, KA7 1JG
Tel: 01292 610230
★★★★ Guest House

Ellisland
19 Racecourse Road, Ayr, Ayrshire, KA7 2TD
Tel: 01292 260111
★★★★ Small Hotel

Elms Court Hotel
21-23 Miller Road, Ayr, Ayrshire, KA7 2AX
Tel: 01292 264191
★★★ Small Hotel

Fairfield House Hotel
12 Fairfield Road, Ayr, Ayrshire, KA7 2AS
Tel: 01292 267461
★★★★ Hotel

Glenmore Guest House
35 Bellevue Crescent, Ayr, Ayrshire, KA7 2DP
Tel: 01292 269830
★★★ Guest House

Glenpark Hotel
5 Racecourse Road, Ayr, Ayrshire, KA7 2DG
Tel: 01292 263891
★★ Small Hotel

Horizon Hotel
Esplanade, Ayr, Ayrshire, KA7 1DT
Tel: 01292 264384
★★★ Hotel

Kilkerran Guest House
15 Prestwick Road, Ayr, Ayrshire, KA8 8LD
Tel: 01292 266477
★★ Guest House

Langley Bank Guest House
39 Carrick Road, Ayr, Ayrshire, KA7 2RD
Tel: 01292 264246
★★★★ Guest House

Miller House
36 Miller Road, Ayr, Ayrshire, KA7 2AY
Tel: 01292 282016
★★★ Guest House

No. 26 The Crescent
26 Bellevue Crescent, Ayr, Ayrshire, KA7 2DR
Tel: 01292 287329
★★★★★ Guest House

Queen's Guest House
10 Queen's Terrace, Ayr, Ayrshire, KA7 1DU
Tel: 01292 265618
★★★ Guest House

Ramada Jarvis
Dalblair Road, Ayr, Ayrshire, KA7 1UG
Tel: 01292 269331
★★★ Hotel

The Richmond
38 Park Circus, Ayr, KA7 2DL
Tel: 01292 265153
★★★ Guest House

Savoy Park Hotel
16 Racecourse Road, Ayr, Ayrshire, KA7 2UT
Tel: 01292 266112
★★★ Small Hotel

St Andrews Hotel
7 Prestwick Road, Ayr, Ayrshire, KA8 8LD
Tel: 01292 263211
Small Hotel

The Beechwood Guest House
37/39 Prestwick Road, Ayr, New Prestwick, Ayrshire, KA8 8LE
Tel: 01292 262093
★★★ Guest House

The Cariston Hotel
11 Miller Road, Ayr, Ayrshire, KA7 2AX
Tel: 01292 262474
★★ Small Hotel

The Windsor
6 Alloway Place, Ayr, Ayrshire, KA7 2AA
Tel: 01292 264689
★★ Guest House

Western House Hotel
2 Whitletts Road, Ayr, Ayrshire, KA9 0JE
Tel: 0870 8505666
★★★★ Hotel

Ballantrae

Glenapp Castle
Ballantrae, Ayrshire, KA26 0NZ
Tel: 01465 831212
★★★★★ Hotel

Barr, by Girvan

The King's Arms Hotel
1 Stinchar Road, Barr, Ayrshire, KA26 9TW
Tel: 01465 861230
Awaiting Inspection

Burnhouse, by Beith

The Burnhouse Manor Hotel
Burnhouse, by Beith, Ayrshire, KA15 1LJ
Tel: 01560 484006
★★★ Hotel

Cumnock

Royal Hotel
1 Glaisnock Street, Cumnock, Ayrshire, KA18 1BP
Tel: 01290 420822
★★★ Small Hotel

Dailly

Strathtalus
4 Brunston Wynd, Dailly, Ayrshire, KA26 9GA
Tel: 01465 811425
Awaiting Inspection

Darvel

Gowanbank House
Darvel, East Ayrshire, KA17 0LL
Tel: 01560 322538
Awaiting Inspection

Fenwick, by Kilmarnock

Fenwick Hotel
Fenwick, by Kilmarnock,
Ayrshire, KA3 6AU
Tel: 01560 600478
★★★ Hotel

Gatehead, by Kilmarnock

Old Rome Farmhouse B & B
Gatehead, Kilmarnock,
Ayrshire, KA2 9AJ
Tel: 01563 850265
★★★ Farmhouse

Girvan

Ardwell Farm
Girvan, Ayrshire, KA26 0HP
Tel: 01465 713389
★★ Farmhouse

Drumskeoch Farm
Pinwherry, Girvan, Ayrshire,
KA26 0QB
Tel: 01465 841172
★★★ Farmhouse

by Girvan

Glengennet Farm
Barr, Girvan, Ayrshire,
KA26 9TY
Tel: 01465 861220
★★★★ Farmhouse

Irvine

Annfield House Hotel
6 Castle Street, Irvine,
Ayrshire, KA12 8RJ
Tel: 01294 278903
★★ Small Hotel

Laurelbank Guest House
3 Kilwinning Road, Irvine,
Ayrshire, KA12 8RR
Tel: 01294 277153
★★★ Guest House

The Gailes Lodge
Marine Drive, Gailes, Irvine,
KA11 5AE
Tel: 01294 204040
★★★ Hotel

Thistle Irvine
46 Annick Road, Irvine,
Ayrshire, KA11 4LD
Tel: 01294 274272
★★★ Hotel

Isle of Arran

Blackwaterfoot

Kinloch Hotel
Blackwaterfoot, Isle of Arran,
KA27 8ET
Tel: 01770 860444
★★★ Hotel

Brodick

Auchrannie Country House Hotel
Brodick, Isle of Arran,
KA27 8BZ
Tel: 01770 302234
★★★★ Hotel

Auchrannie Spa Resort
Brodick, Isle of Arran,
KA27 8BZ
Tel: 01770 302234
★★★★ Hotel

Belvedere Guest House
Alma Road, Brodick,
Isle of Arran, KA27 8AZ
Tel: 01770 302397
★★★ Guest House

Carrick Lodge
Pier Lodge, Brodick,
Isle of Arran, KA27 8BH
Tel: 01770 302550
★★★ Guest House

Dunvegan House
Shore Road, Brodick,
Isle of Arran, KA27 8AJ
Tel: 01770 302811
★★★★ Guest House

Glenartney
Mayish Road, Brodick,
Isle of Arran, KA27 8BX
Tel: 01770 302220
★★★ Guest House

Glencloy Farm Guest House
Glen Cloy, Brodick,
Isle of Arran, KA27 8DA
Tel: 01770 302351
★★★ Guest House

Invercloy Hotel
Shore Road, Brodick,
Isle of Arran, KA27 8AJ
Tel: 01770 302225
★★★ Guest House

Kilmichael Country House Hotel
Brodick, Isle of Arran,
KA27 8BY
Tel: 01770 302219
★★★★ Country House Hotel

Ormidale Hotel
Brodick, Isle of Arran,
KA27 8BY
Tel: 01770 302293
★★ Small Hotel

Orwin House
Glengloy Road, Brodick,
Isle of Arran, KA27 8DW
Tel: 01770 302707
Awaiting Inspection

Strathwhillan House
Strathwhillan Road, Brodick,
Isle of Arran, KA27 8BQ
Tel: 01770 302331
★★ Guest House

Kildonan

Kildonan Hotel
Kildonan, Isle of Arran,
KA27 8SE
Tel: 01770 820207
★★★ Small Hotel

Lagg

Lagg Hotel
Lagg, Kilmory, Isle of Arran,
KA27 8PQ
Tel: 01770 870255
★★★ Small Hotel

Lamlash

Glenisle Hotel
Shore Road, Lamlash,
Isle of Arran, KA27 8LY
Tel: 01770 600559
★★★ Small Hotel

Lilybank
Shore Road, Lamlash,
Isle of Arran, KA27 8LS
Tel: 01770 600230
★★★★ Guest House

Lochranza

Apple Lodge
Lochranza, Isle of Arran,
KA27 8HJ
Tel: 01770 830229
★★★★ Guest House

Whiting Bay

Burlington Hotel
Shore Road, Whiting Bay,
Isle of Arran, KA27 8PZ
Tel: 01770 700255
★★★ Guest House

Invermay
Shore Road, Whiting Bay,
Isle of Arran, KA27 8PZ
Tel: 0770 00 431
★★ Guest House

The Royal Arran
Shore Road, Whiting Bay,
Isle of Arran, KA27 8PZ
Tel: 01770 700286
★★★★ Guest House

Viewbank House
Golf Course Road, Whiting
Bay, Isle of Arran, KA27 8QT
Tel: 01770 700326
★★★ Guest House

Isle of Cumbrae

Millport

The Millerston
29 West Bay Road, Millport,
Isle of Cumbrae, KA28 0HA
Tel: 01475 530480
★★★ Small Hotel

Kilbirnie

Moorpark House Hotel
School Road, Kilbirnie,
North Ayrshire, KA25 7LD
Tel: 07767 324879
★★★★ Country House Hotel

Kilmarnock

Dean Park Guest House
27 Wellington Street,
Kilmarnock, Ayrshire, KA3 1DZ
Tel: 01563 572794
★★★ Guest House

Eastlangton Farm
Dunlop, Kilmarnock, Ayrshire,
KA3 4DS
Tel: 01560 482978
Awaiting Inspection

Howard Park Hotel
136 Glasgow Road,
Kilmarnock, Ayrshire, KA3 1UT
Tel: 01563 531211
★★ Hotel

Kilmarnock (Cotton Mills) Premier Inn
Moorfield Roundabout,
Annadale, Kilmarnock,
Ayrshire, KA1 2RS
Tel: 08701 977148
Passed Budget Hotel

Park Hotel
Rugby Park, Kilmarnock,
Ayrshire, KA1 1UR
Tel: 01563 545999
★★★★ Hotel

Kilmarnock continued

Underwood House
Craigie, By Kilmarnock,
Ayrshire, KA1 5NG
Tel: 01563 830887
Awaiting Inspection

Kilmaurs

Aulton Farm
Kilmaurs, Ayrshire, KA3 2PQ
Tel: 01563 538208
★★★ Farmhouse

Kilwinning

High Smithstone Farmhouse
High Smithstone, Kilwinning,
Ayrshire, KA13 6PG
Tel: 01294 552361
★★★★ Farmhouse

Largs

Burnlea Hotel
Burnlea Road, Largs, Ayrshire,
KA30 8BX
Tel: 01475 687235
★★ Hotel

Haylie Hotel
108 Irvine Road, Largs,
Ayrshire, KA30 8EY
Tel: 01475 673207
★★ Small Hotel

Lilac Holm Guest House
14 Noddleburn Road, Largs,
Ayrshire, KA30 8PY
Tel: 01475 672020
★★★ Guest House

Tigh An Struan
29 Gogo Street, Largs,
North Ayrshire, KA30 8BU
Tel: 01475 670668
★★★ Guest House

Tigh-Na-Ligh
104 Brisbane Road, Largs,
Ayrshire, KA30 8NN
Tel: 01475 673975
★★★ Guest House

Whin-Park Guest House
16 Douglas Street, Largs,
Ayrshire, KA30 8PS
Tel: 01475 673437
★★★★ Guest House

Willowbank Hotel
96 Greenock Road, Largs,
North Ayrshire, KA30 8PG
Tel: 01475 672311
★★★ Hotel

Mauchline

Dykefield Farm
Mauchline, Ayrshire, KA5 6EY
Tel: 01290 553170
★★ Farmhouse

Monkton, by Prestwick

Ayr Premier Inn
Monkton Lodge,
Kilmarnock Road, Monkton,
Ayrshire, KA9 2RJ
Tel: 08701 977020
Passed Budget Hotel

nr New Cumnock

Lochside House Hotel
New Cumnock, Ayrshire,
KA18 4PN
Tel: 01290 333000
★★★ Hotel

Ochiltree

Laigh Tarbeg Farm
Ochiltree, Cumnock, Ayrshire,
KA18 2RL
Tel: 01290 700242
★★★★ Farmhouse

Prestwick

Fernbank Guest House
213 Main Street, Prestwick,
Ayrshire, KA9 1LH
Tel: 01292 475027
★★★ Guest House

Golf View
17 Links Road, Prestwick,
Ayrshire, KA9 1QG
Tel: 01292 671234
★★★★ Guest House

Kincraig Guest House
39 Ayr Road, Prestwick,
Ayrshire, KA9 1SY
Tel: 01292 479480
★★★ Guest House

North Beach Hotel
5-7 Link's Road, Prestwick,
Ayrshire, KA9 1QG
Tel: 01292 479069
Awaiting Inspection

Parkstone Hotel
Esplanade, Prestwick,
Ayrshire, KA9 1QN
Tel: 01292 477286
★★★ Hotel

Prestwick Old Course Hotel
13 Links Road, Prestwick,
Ayrshire, KA9 1QG
Tel: 01292 477446
Awaiting Inspection

Seamill

Seamill Hydro
39 Ardrossan Road, Seamill,
Ayrshire, KA23 9NB
Tel: 01294 822217
★★★ Hotel

Stevenston

Ardeer Steading
Ardeer Mains Farm,
Stevenston, Ayrshire,
KA20 3DD
Tel: 01294 465438
★★★★ Farmhouse

Troon

Hillhouse
Hillhouse, Troon, Ayrshire,
KA10 7HX
Tel: 01292 676400
★★★★★ Exclusive Use Venue

Lochgreen House
Monktonhill Road, Troon,
Ayrshire, KA10 7EN
Tel: 01292 313343
★★★★★ Hotel

Marine Hotel
Crosbie Road, Troon, Ayrshire,
KA10 6HE
Tel: 01292 314444
★★★★ Hotel

No 54
Spey Road, Troon, Ayrshire,
KA10 7DP
Tel: 01292 314134
Awaiting Inspection

Piersland House Hotel
15 Craigend Road, Troon,
Ayrshire, KA10 6HD
Tel: 01292 314747
★★★★ Hotel

South Beach Hotel
South Beach, Troon, Ayrshire,
KA10 6EG
Tel: 01292 312033
★★★ Hotel

Turnberry

Malin Court
Turnberry, Ayrshire, KA26 9PB
Tel: 01655 331457
★★★ Hotel

The Westin Turnberry Resort
Turnberry, Ayrshire, KA26 9LT
Tel: 01655 331000
★★★★★ Hotel

West Kilbride

Millstonford House Bed & Breakfast
Millstonford House,
West Kilbride, Ayrshire,
KA23 9PS
Tel: 01294 823430
Awaiting Inspection

DUMFRIES AND GALLOWAY

Annan

East Upper Priestside
Cummentrees, Annan,
Dumfries, DG12 5PX
Tel: 01387 259219
★★★ Farmhouse

Rowanbank
20 St Johns Road, Annan,
Dumfriesshire, DG12 5AW
Tel: 01461 204200
★★ Guest House

The Old Rectory Guest House
12 St Johns Road, Annan,
Dumfriesshire, DG12 6AW
Tel: 01461 202029
★★★ Guest House

Auchencairn, by Castle Douglas

Bluehill Farm
Auchencairn,
By Castle Douglas,
Dumfries & Galloway,
DG7 1QW
Tel: 01556 640228
★★★★ Farmhouse

Auldgirth

Friars Carse Hotel
Auldgirth, Dumfriesshire,
DG2 0SA
Tel: 01387 740388
★★★ Country House Hotel

Beattock

Marchbankwood House
Beattock, Moffat,
Dumfries & Galloway,
DG10 9RG
Tel: 01683 300118
★★★★ Guest House

Cairnryan

Cairnryan House
Main Street, Cairnryan,
Wigtownshire, DG9 8QX
Tel: 01581 200624
★★★ Guest House

Castle Douglas

Balcary Bay Hotel
Shore Road, Auchencairn, by Castle Douglas
Tel: 01556 640217
★★★ Country House Hotel

Craigadam
Castle Douglas, Dumfries & Galloway, DG7 3HU
Tel: 01556 650233
★★★★ Farmhouse

Crown Hotel
King Street, Castle Douglas, Kirkcudbrightshire, DG7 1AA
Tel: 01556 502031
Awaiting Inspection

Douglas Arms Hotel
200 - 206 King Street, Castle Douglas, Kirkcudbrightshire, DG7 1DB
Tel: 01556 502231
★★★ Hotel

Imperial Hotel
35 King Street, Castle Douglas, Kirkcudbrightshire, DG7 1AA
Tel: 01556 502086
★★★ Small Hotel

Kings Arms Hotel
St Andrew Street, Castle Douglas, Kirkcudbrightshire, DG7 1EL
Tel: 01556 502626
★★ Small Hotel

Station Hotel
1 Queen Street, Castle Douglas, Kirkcudbrightshire, DG7 1HX
Tel: 01556 502152
★★★ Small Hotel

The Urr Valley Hotel
Ernespie Road, Castle Douglas, Kirkcudbrightshire, DG7 3JG
Tel: 01556 502188
★★ Country House Hotel

by Castle Douglas

Meiklewood Farmhouse
Ringford, Castle Douglas, Kirkcudbrightshire, DG7 2AL
Tel: 01557 820226
Mobile: 07881 488087
★★★ Farmhouse

Colvend

Clonyard House Hotel
Colvend, Dalbeattie, Kirkcudbrightshire, DG5 4QW
Tel: 01556 630372
★★★ Country House Hotel

Crocketford, Dumfries

Galloway Arms Hotel
Crocketford, By Dumfries, Kirkcudbrightshire, DG2 8RA
Tel: 01556 690248
★★ Small Hotel

Dalry, by Castle Douglas

The Lochinvar Hotel
3 Main Street, Dalry, Kirkcudbrightshire, DG7 3UP
Tel: 01644 430107
★★ Small Hotel

Dumfries

Aberdour Hotel
16-20 Newall Terrace, Dumfries, Dumfries-shire, DG1 1LW
Tel: 01387 252060
★★★ Small Hotel

Alva House
Mainsriddle, Dumfries, Dumfries & Galloway, DG2 8AG
Tel: 07871 391104
Awaiting Inspection

Aston Hotel
The Crichton, Bankend Road, Dumfries, Dumfries and Galloway, DG1 4ZZ
Tel: 0845 6340205
★★★ Hotel

Cairndale Hotel & Leisure Club
English Street, Dumfries, Dumfriesshire, DG1 2DF
Tel: 01387 254111
★★★ Hotel

Dalston House Hotel
5 Laurieknowe, Dumfries, Dumfrieshire, DG2 7AH
Tel: 01387 254422
★★★ Small Hotel

Glenlossie Guest House
75 Annan Road, Dumfries, Dumfries-shire, DG1 3EG
Tel: 01387 254305
★★★★ Guest House

Hamilton House
12 Moffat Road, Dumfries, DG1 1NJ
Awaiting Inspection

Hazeldean Guest House
4 Moffat Road, Dumfries, DG1 1NJ
Tel: 01387 266178
★★★★ Guest House

Huntingdon House Hotel
18 St Marys Street, Dumfries, DG1 1LZ
Tel: 01387 254893
★★★ Small Hotel

Little Culmain (Bothy)
Crocketford Road, Near Milton, Dumfries, DG2 8QP
Tel: 01556 690 210
★★★ Farmhouse

Lochenlee Guest House
32 Ardwall Road, Dumfries, Dumfriesshire, DG1 3AQ
Tel: 01387 265153
★★★ Guest House

Moreig Hotel
67 Annan Road, Dumfries, DG1 3EG
Tel: 01387 255524
★★★ Small Hotel

Rivendell
105 Edinburgh Road, Dumfries, Dumfries-shire, DG1 1JX
Tel: 01387 252251
★★★★ Guest House

Station Hotel
49 Lovers Walk, Dumfries, Dumfries-shire, DG1 1LT
Tel: 01387 254316
★★★ Hotel

Torbay Lodge
31 Lovers Walk, Dumfries, DG1 1LR
Tel: 01387 253922
★★★★ Guest House

Woodland House Hotel
Newbridge, Dumfries, Dumfriesshire, DG2 0HZ
Tel: 01387 720233
Awaiting Inspection

by Dumfries

Comlongon Castle
Clarencefield, Dumfriesshire, DG1 4NA
Tel: 01387 870283
★★★ Country House Hotel

Dumfries Premier Inn
Solway Gate, Annan Road, Collin, Dumfries, DG1 3JX
Tel: 08701 977078
Passed Budget Hotel

Hetland Hall Hotel
Carrutherstown, Dumfriesshire, DG1 4JX
Tel: 01387 840201
★★★ Hotel

Nith Hotel
Glencaple, Dumfriesshire, DG1 4RE
Tel: 01387 770213
★★ Small Hotel

Dunscore, by Dumfries

Morrington House
Stepford Road, Dunscore, Dumfriesshire, DG2 0JN
Tel: 01387 820391
★★★★ Guest House

Eastriggs, by Annan

The Graham Arms Guest House
The Rand, Eastriggs, Dumfriesshire, DG12 6NL
Tel: 01461 40031
★★★ Guest House

Ecclefechan

Cressfield Country House Hotel
Townfoot, Ecclefechan, Dumfriesshire, DG11 3DR
Tel: 01576 300281
★★★ Small Hotel

Gatehouse of Fleet

Cally Palace Hotel
Gatehouse of Fleet, Kirkcudbrightshire, DG7 2DL
Tel: 01557 814341
★★★★ Hotel

Murray Arms Hotel
Ann Street, Gatehouse of Fleet, Kirkcudbrightshire, DG7 2HY
Tel: 01557 814207
★★★ Small Hotel

The Bank of Fleet Hotel
47 High Street, Gatehouse of Fleet, Kirkcudbrightshire, DG7 2HR
Tel: 01557 814302
★★★ Small Hotel

Gatehouse of Fleet continued

The Bobbin Guest House
36 High Street,
Gatehouse of Fleet,
Kirkcudbrightshire, DG7 2HP
Tel: 01557 814229
★★★ Guest House

Hunters Lodge Hotel
Annan Road, Gretna,
Dumfriesshire, DG16 5DL
Tel: 01461 338214
★★★ Small Hotel

Solway Lodge Hotel
97-99 Annan Road,
Gretna Green, Dumfriesshire,
DG16
Tel: 01461 338266
★★★ Small Hotel

The Gables Hotel & Restaurant
1 Annan Road, Gretna,
Dumfriesshire, DG16 5DQ
Tel: 01461 338300
★★★★ Hotel

The Garden House Hotel
Sarkfoot Road, Gretna,
Dumfriesshire, DG16 5EP
Tel: 01461 337621
★★★ Hotel

Gretna Hall Hotel
Gretna Green, Dumfriesshire,
DG16 5DY
Tel: 01461 338257
Awaiting Inspection

Smiths at Gretna Green
Gretna Green,
Dumfries & Galloway,
DG16 5EA
Tel: 0845 3676768
★★★★ Hotel

Dinwoodie Lodge Hotel
Johnstone Bridge,
by Lockerbie,
Dumfriesshire, DG11 2SL
Tel: 01576 470289
★★ Small Hotel

Rosemount
Kippford, Dalbeattie,
Kirkcudbrightshire, DG5 4LN
Tel: 01556 620214
★★★★ Guest House

Cavens
Kirkbean,by Dumfries,
By Dumfries, DG2 8AA
Tel: 01387 880234
★★★★ Country House Hotel

Fludha Guest House
Tongland Road, Kirkcudbright,
Dumfries & Galloway,
DG6 4UU
Tel: 01557 331443
★★★★★ Guest House

Gladstone House
48 High Street, Kirkcudbright,
DG6 4JX
Tel: 01557 331734
★★★★ Guest House

Gordon House Hotel
116 High Street,
Kirkcudbright,
Kirkcudbrightshire, DG6 4JQ
Tel: 01557 330670
★★★ Small Hotel

Sassoon House
3 High St, Kirkcudbright,
Dumfries & Galloway,
DG6 4JZ
Tel: 01557 330881
Awaiting Inspection

Selkirk Arms Hotel
High Street, Kirkcudbright,
Kirkcudbrightshire, DG6 4JG
Tel: 01557 330402
★★★ Small Hotel

Dryfesdale Country House Hotel
Dryfebridge, Lockerbie,
Dumfriesshire, DG11 2SF
Tel: 01576 202427
★★★★ Hotel

Lockerbie Manor
Boreland Road, Lockerbie,
Dumfriesshire, DG11 2RG
Tel: 01576 203939
★ Country House Hotel

Lockerbie Premier Inn (Annandale Water)
Annandale Water Motorway
Services, J16 M74,
Johnstonebridge, Lockerbie,
Dumfries & Galloway,
DG11 1HD
Tel: 08701977163

Passed Budget Hotel

Queens Hotel
Annan Road, Lockerbie,
Dumfriesshire, DG11 2RB
Tel: 01576 202415
★★★ Hotel

Ravenshill House Hotel
12 Dumfries Road,
Lockerbie, Dumfriesshire,
Tel: 01576 202882
★★ Small Hotel

Somerton House Hotel
35 Carlisle Road, Lockerbie,
Dumfries-shire, DG11 2DR
Tel: 01576 202583
★★★ Small Hotel

Castlehill Farm
Tundergarth, Lockerbie,
Dumfriesshire, DG11 2PX
Tel: 01576 710223
★★★ Farmhouse

Annandale Arms Hotel
High Street, Moffat,
Dumfriesshire, DG10 9HF
Tel: 01683 220013
★★★ Small Hotel

Black Bull Hotel
Churchgate, Moffat,
Dumfriesshire, DG10 9EG
Tel: 01683 220206
★★★ Small Hotel

Bridge House
Well Road, Moffat,
Dumfrieshire, DG10 9JT
Tel: 01683 220558
★★★★ Guest House

Buccleuch Arms Hotel
High Street, Moffat,
Dumfriesshire, DG10 9ET
Tel: 01683 220003
★★★ Small Hotel

Buchan Guest House
Beechgrove, Moffat,
Dumfriesshire, DG10 9RS
Tel: 01683 220378
★★★ Guest House

Limetree House
Eastgate, Moffat,
Dumfriesshire, DG10 9AE
Tel: 01683 220001
★★★★ Guest House

Moffat House Hotel
High Street, Moffat,
Dumfriesshire, DG10 9HL
Tel: 01683 220039
Awaiting Inspection

Rockhill Guest House
14 Beechgrove, Moffat,
Dumfriesshire, DG10 9RS
Tel: 01683 220283
★★★ Guest House

Seamore House
Academy Road, Moffat,
Dumfriesshire, DG10 9HW
Tel: 01683 220404
★★★ Guest House

Star Hotel
44 High Street, Moffat,
Dumfrieshire, DG10 9EF
Tel: 01683 220156
★★ Small Hotel

Auchen Castle Hotel
Beattock, Moffat,
Dumfriesshire, DG10 9SH
Tel: 01683 300407
★★★★ Country House Hotel

Leamington Hotel
High Street, New Galloway,
Kirkcudbrightshire, DG7 3RN
Tel: 01644 420327
★★ Guest House

The Bruce Hotel
88 Queen Street,
Newton Stewart,
Wigtownshire, DG8 6JL
Tel: 01671 402294
★★★ Hotel

Creebridge House Hotel
Minnigaff, Newton Stewart,
Dumfries & Galloway,
DG8 6NP
Tel: 01671 402121
★★★ Small Hotel

Crown Hotel
101 Queen Street,
Newton Stewart,
Wigtownshire, DG8 6EF
Tel: 01671 402727
★ Small Hotel

Newton Stewart continued

Flowerbank Guest House
Millcroft Road, Minnigaff,
Wigtownshire, DG8 6PJ
Tel: 01671 402629
★★★ Guest House

Kirroughtree House
Newton Stewart,
Wigtownshire, DG8 6AN
Tel: 01671 402141
★★★★ Country House Hotel

Rowallan
Corsbie Road,
Newton Stewart,
Wigtownshire, DG8 6JB
Tel: 01671 402520
★★★ Guest House

Stables Guest House
Corsbie Road,
Newton Stewart,
Wigtownshire, DG8 6JB
Tel: 01671 402157
★★★ Guest House

Portpatrick

Braefield Guest House
Braefield Road, Portpatrick,
Wigtownshire, DG9 8TA
Tel: 01776 810255
★★ Guest House

Dunskey Guest House
Heugh Road, Portpatrick,
Wigtownshire, DG9 8TD
Tel: 01776 810241
★★ Guest House

Knockinaam Lodge
Portpatrick, Wigtownshire,
DG9 9AD
Tel: 01776 810471
★★★★ Small Hotel

Portpatrick Hotel
Heugh Road, Portpatrick,
Wigtownshire, DG9 8TQ
Tel: 01776 810333
★★ Hotel

Rickwood House Hotel
Heugh Road, Portpatrick,
Wigtownshire, DG9 8TD
Tel: 01776 810270
★★★ Guest House

The Fernhill Hotel
Heugh Road, Portpatrick,
Wigtownshire, DG9 8TD
Tel: 01776 810220
★★★ Hotel

Torrs Warren Hotel
Stoneykirk, Stranraer,
Dumfries & Galloway,
DG9 9DH
Tel: 1776830204
★★★ Small Hotel

The Waterfront Hotel & Bistro
North Crescent, Portpatrick,
DG9 8SX
Tel: 01776 810800
★★★ Small Hotel

Port William

Monreith Arms Hotel
The Square, Port William,
Dumfries & Galloway,
DG8 9SE
Tel: 01988 700232
★★ Inn

Rockcliffe, by Dalbeattie

Baron's Craig Hotel
Rockcliffe, by Dalbeattie,
Kirkcudbrightshire, DG5 4QF
Tel: 01556 630225
★★ Hotel

Sandyhills, by Dalbeattie

Craigbittern House
Sandyhills, Dalbeattie,
Kirkcudbrightshire, DG5 4NZ
Tel: 0138778 247
★★★★ Guest House

Sanquhar

Blackaddie House Hotel
Blackaddie Road, Sanquhar,
Dumfriesshire, DG4 6JJ
Tel: 01659 50270
★★★ Small Hotel

nr Stranraer

Corsewall Lighthouse Hotel
Kirkcolm, by Stranraer,
Wigtownshire, DG9 0QG
Tel: 01776 853220
★★★ Small Hotel

Stranraer

George Hotel
49 George Street, Stranraer,
Wigtownshire, DG9 7RJ
Tel: 01776 702487
★ Guest Accommodation

Harbour Guest House
11 Market Street, Stranraer,
Wigtownshire, DG9 7RF
Tel: 01776 704626
★★★ Guest House

Harbour Lights Guest House
7 Agnew Crescent, Stranraer,
Wigtownshire, DG9 7JY
Tel: 01776 706261
★★★ Guest House

Hartforth Guest House
33 London Road, Stranraer,
Wigtownshire, DG9 8AF
Tel: 01776 704832
Awaiting Inspection

Neptunes Rest Guest House
25 Agnew Crescent, Stranraer,
Wigtownshire, DG9
Tel: 01776 704729
★★ Guest House

North West Castle Hotel
Royal Crescent, Stranraer,
Wigtownshire, DG9 8EH
Tel: 01776 704413
★★★★ Hotel

Thornhill

Buccleuch & Queensberry Hotel
112 Drumlanrig Street,
Thornhill, Dumfriesshire,
DG3 5LU
Tel: 01848 330215
★★★ Small Hotel

Gillbank House
8 East Morton Street,
Thornhill, Dumfriesshire,
DG3 5LZ
Tel: 01848 330597
★★★★ Guest House

The Thornhill Inn
103-106 Drumlanrig Street,
Thornhill, Dumfriesshire,
DG3 5LU
Tel: 01848 330326
★★★ Small Hotel

by Thornhill

Trigony House Hotel
Closeburn, Thornhill,
Dumfriesshire, DG3 5EZ
Tel: 01848 331211
★★★ Small Hotel

Torthorwald, by Dumfries

The Manor Country House Hotel
Lockerbie Road, Torthorwald,
Dumfries & Galloway,
DG1 3PT
Tel: 01387 750555
★★ Small Hotel

Wigtown

Fordbank Country House Hotel
Potato Mill Road, Bladnoch,
Dumfries & Galloway,
DG8 9BT
Tel: 01988 402346
★★★ Small Hotel

Hillcrest House
Maidland Place, Station Road,
Wigtown, Wigtownshire,
DG8 9EU
Tel: 01988 402018
★★★ Guest House

SCOTTISH BORDERS

Broughton, by Biggar

The Glenholm Centre
Broughton, by Biggar,
Lanarkshire, ML12 6JF
Tel: 01899 830408
★★★ Guest House

Chirnside, by Duns

Chirnside Hall Country House Hotel
Chirnside, By Duns,
Berwickshire, TD11 3LD
Tel: 01890 818219
★★★★ Country House Hotel

Coldingham

Priory View
Eyemouth Road, Coldingham,
Eyemouth, Berwickshire,
TD14 5NH
Tel: 01890 771525
★★★ Guest House

Coldstream

Calico House
44 High Street, Coldstream,
Berwickshire, TD12 4AS
Tel: 01890 885870
Awaiting Inspection

Duns

Duns Castle
Duns, Berwickshire,
TD11 3NW
Tel: 01361 883211
★★★★ Exclusive Use Venue

Duns continued

Ravelaw Farmhouse
Ravelaw, Duns, Berwickshire, TD11 3NQ
Tel: 01890 870207
★★★★ Farmhouse

Broomfield House
10 Thorn Street, Earlston, Berwickshire, TD4 6DR
Tel: 01896 848084
★★★ Guest House

Kings Hotel
56 Market Street, Galashiels, Selkirkshire, TD1 3AN
Tel: 01896 755497
★★ Guest House

Kingsknowes Hotel
Selkirk Road, Galashiels, Selkirkshire, TD1 3HY
Tel: 01896 758375
★★★ Small Hotel

Monorene
23 Stirling Street, Galashiels, Selkirkshire, TD1 1BY
Tel: 01896 753073
★★★ Guest House

Morven Guest House
12 Sime Place, Galashiels, Selkirkshire, TD1 1ST
Tel: 01896 756255
★★ Guest House

Watson Lodge Guest House
15/16 Bridge Street, Galashiels, Selkirkshire, TD1 1SW
Tel: 01896 750551
★★★ Guest House

Elm House Hotel
17 North Bridge Street, Hawick, Roxburghshire, TD9 9BD
Tel: 01450 372866
★★★ Small Hotel

Hizzy's Guest House
23 B&C North Bridge Street, Hawick, Roxburghshire, TD9 9DB
Tel: 01450 372101
Awaiting Inspection

Mansfield House Hotel
Weensland Road, Hawick, Roxburghshire, TD9 8LB
★★★ Small Hotel

Glenteviot Park Hotel
Hassendeanburn, by Hawick, Roxburghshire, TD9 8RU
Tel: 01450 870660
★★★★ Guest House

Whitchester Guest House
Hawick, Roxburghshire, TD9 7LN
Tel: 01450 377477
★★★ Guest House

Caddon View
14 Pirn Road, Innerleithen, Peeblesshire, EH44 6HH
Tel: 01896 830208
★★★★ Guest House

Allerton House
Oxnam Road, Jedburgh, Roxburghshire, TD8 6QQ
Tel: 01835 869633
★★★★ Guest House

Glenbank House Hotel
Castlegate, Jedburgh, Roxburghshire, TD8 6BD
Tel: 01835 862258
★ Small Hotel

Glenfriars House
The Friars, Jedburgh, Roxburghshire, TD8 6BN
Tel: 01835 862000
★★★ Guest House

Meadhon House
48 Castlegate, Jedburgh, Roxburghshire, TD8 6BB
Tel: 01835 862504
★★★ Guest House

The Spread Eagle Hotel
20 High Street, Jedburgh, Roxburghshire, TD8 6AG
Tel: 01835 862870
★ Small Hotel

Ferniehirst Mill Lodge
Jedburgh, Roxburghshire, TD8 6PQ
Tel: 01835 863279
★ Guest House

Bellevue House
Bowmont Street, Kelso, Roxburghshire, TD5 7DZ
Tel: 01573 224588
Awaiting Inspection

Cross Keys Hotel
36-37 The Square, Kelso, Roxburghshire, TD5 7HL
Tel: 01573 223303
★★★ Hotel

Ednam House Hotel
Bridge Street, Kelso, Roxburghshire, TD5 7HT
Tel: 01573 224168
★★★ Hotel

Inglestone House
Abbey Row, Kelso, Roxburghshire, TD5 7HQ
Tel: 01573 225800
★★★ Guest House

Crosshall Farm
Greenlaw, Duns, Berwickshire, TD10 6UL
Tel: 0189084 0220
★★★★ Farmhouse

Roxburghe Hotel and Golf Course
Heiton, Kelso, Roxburghshire, TD5 8JZ
Tel: 01573 450331
★★★★ Country House Hotel

The Lodge, Carfraemill
Lauder, Berwickshire, TD2 6RA
Tel: 01578 750750
★★★★ Restaurant with Rooms

No 16 Market Place
Market Place, Lauder, Berwickshire, TD2 6SR
Tel: 01578 718776
Awaiting Inspection

Braidwood
Buccleuch Street, Melrose, Roxburghshire, TD6 9LD
Tel: 01896 822488
★★★★ Guest House

Burts Hotel
Market Square, Melrose, Roxburghshire, TD6 9PL
Tel: 01896 822285
★★★ Small Hotel

Dryburgh Abbey Hotel
St Boswells, Melrose, Scottish Borders, TD6 0RQ
Tel: 01835 822261
Awaiting Inspection

George & Abbotsford Hotel
High Street, Melrose, Roxburghshire, TD6 9PD
Tel: 01896 822308
★★ Hotel

The Town House Hotel
3 Market Square, Melrose, Roxburghshire, TD6 9PQ
Tel: 01896 822645
★★★ Small Hotel

Waverley Castle Hotel
Melrose, Roxburghshire, TD6 9AA
Tel: 01896 436600
★★★ Hotel

Clint Lodge Country House
Clinthill, St Boswells, Melrose, Roxburghshire, TD6 0DZ
Tel: 01835 822027
★★★★ Guest House

Whitehouse
St Boswells, Roxburghshire, TD6 0ED
Tel: 01573 460343
★★★★★ Bed & Breakfast

Cardrona Hotel Golf & Country Club
Cardrona, Near Peebles, Peebles-shire, EH45 6LZ
Tel: 01896 831144
★★★★ Hotel

Castle Venlaw Hotel
Edinburgh Road, Peebles, Peeblesshire, EH45 8QG
Tel: 01721 720384
Awaiting Inspection

Lindores
60 Old Town, Peebles, Peebles-shire, EH45 8JE
Tel: 01721 722072
Awaiting Inspection

Peebles continued

Park Hotel
Innerleithen Road, Peebles,
EH45 8BA
Tel: 01721 720451
★★★ Hotel

Peebles Hotel Hydro
Innerleithen Road, Peebles,
Peebles-shire, EH45 8LX
Tel: 01721 720602
★★★★ Hotel

Tontine Hotel
High Street, Peebles,
Peeblesshire, EH45 8AJ
Tel: 01721 720892
★★★ Hotel

by Peebles

Cringletie House Hotel
Edinburgh Road, Peebles,
Peeblesshire, EH45 8PL
Tel: 01721 725750
★★★★ Country House Hotel

Glentress Hotel
Innerleithen Road, Peebles,
Peebles-shire, EH45 8NB
Tel: 01721 720100
★★ Small Hotel

St Boswells

Buccleuch Arms Hotel
The Green, St Boswells,
Roxburghshire, TD6 OEW
Tel: 01835 822243
★★★ Small Hotel

The Old Manse
Main Street, St Boswells,
Roxburghshire, TD6 0BB
Tel: 01835 822047
Awaiting Inspection

Selkirk

Heatherlie House Hotel
Heatherlie Park, Selkirk,
Selkirkshire, TD7 5AL
Tel: 01750 721200
★★★ Small Hotel

Philipburn Country House Hotel and Restaurant
Selkirk, Selkirkshire,
TD7 5LS
Tel: 01750 20747
★★★★ Country House Hotel

The County Hotel
Market Square,
3-5 High Street, Selkirk,
TD7 4BZ
Tel: 01750 721233
★★★ Small Hotel

The Glen Hotel
Yarrow Terrace, Selkirk,
Selkirkshire, TD7 5AS
Tel: 01750 20259
★★★ Small Hotel

Tower Street Guest House
29 Tower Street, Selkirk,
Scottsh Borders, TD7 4LR
Tel: 01750 23222
★★★ Guest House

by Skirling, by Biggar

Skirling House
Skirling, by Biggar,
Lanarkshire, ML12 6HD
★★★★★ Guest House

West Linton

Ingraston Farm B&B
Ingraston Farm, West Linton,
Peebleshire, EH46 7AA
Tel: 01968 682219
★★★ Farmhouse

Millburn House Bed & Breakfast
Dolphinton, West Linton,
Peebleshire, EH46 7AF
Tel: 01968 682252
Awaiting Inspection

EDINBURGH AND THE LOTHIANS

EDINBURGH AND LOTHIANS

Balerno

Haughhead Farm
Balerno, Midlothian, EH14 7JH
Tel: 0131 4493875
★★ Farmhouse

Bathgate

The Cairn Hotel
Blackburn Road, Bathgate,
West Lothian, EH48 2EL
Tel: 01506 633366
★★ Hotel

Bonnyrigg

The Retreat Castle
Cockpen Road, Bonnyrigg,
Midlothian, EH19 3HS
Tel: 0131 6603200
★★★ Small Hotel

Broxburn

Bankhead Farm
Dechmont, Broxburn,
West Lothian, EH52 6NB
Tel: 01506 811209
★★★★ Guest House

Dalkeith

Glenarch House
Melville Road, Eskbank,
Dalkeith, EH22 3NJ
Tel: 0131 6631478
★★★ Guest House

The County Hotel
152 High Street, Dalkeith,
Midlothian, EH22
Tel: 0131 663 3495
★★★ Hotel

The Guest House @ Eskbank
45 Eskbank Road,
Rathaonn House,
45 Eskbank Road, Midlothian,
Midlothian, EH22 3BH
Tel: 0131 663 3291
★★★★ Guest House

Dirleton

Open Arms Hotel
Dirleton, East Lothian,
EH39 5EG
Tel: 01620 850241
★★★ Small Hotel

Dunbar

Barns Ness Hotel
Station Road, Dunbar,
East Lothian, EH42 1JY
Tel: 01368 863231
★★★ Small Hotel

Broxmouth Park
Dunbar, East Lothian,
EH2 1QW
Tel: 01313 371180
Awaiting Inspection

Springfield Guest House
Belhaven Road, Dunbar,
East Lothian, EH42 1NH
Tel: 01368 862502
★★ Guest House

The Rossborough Hotel
Queens Road, Dunbar,
East Lothian, EH42 1LG
Tel: 01368 862356
★★ Small Hotel

East Linton

Robertson
1 Distillery Wynd, East Linton,
East Lothian, EH40 3EH
Tel: 01620 861864
Awaiting Inspection

Edinburgh

A'Abide'an'Abode
18 Moat Place, Edinburgh,
EH14 1PP
Tel: 0131 443 5668
★★★ Guest House

Aaran Lodge Guest House
30 Milton Road East,
Edinburgh, Midlothian,
EH15 2NW
Tel: 0131 657 5615
★★★★ Guest House

Aaron Lodge Guest House
128 Old Dalkeith Road,
Edinburgh, EH16 4SD
Tel: 0131 664 2755
★★★★ Guest House

Abbey Lodge Hotel
137 Drum Street, Gilmerton,
Edinburgh, EH17 8RJ
Tel: 0131 6649548
★★ Guest House

Abbotsford Guest House
36 Pilrig Street, Edinburgh,
EH6 5AL
Tel: 0131 554 2706
★★★ Guest House

Edinburgh continued

Abbotshead House
40 Minto Street, Edinburgh,
EH9 2BR
Tel: 0131 668 1658
Guest House

Abcorn Guest House
4 Mayfield Gardens,
Edinburgh, EH9 2BU
Tel: 0131 667 6548
★★★ Guest House

Abercorn Guest House
1 Abercorn Terrace,
Edinburgh, East Lothian,
EH15 2DD
Tel: 0131 6696139
★★★★ Guest House

Acer Lodge Guest house
425 Queensferry Road,
Edinburgh, Midlothian,
EH4 7NB
Tel: 0131 3362554
★★★★ Guest House

Adria House
11-12 Royal Terrace,
Edinburgh, EH7 5AB
Tel: 0131 556 7875
★★★ Guest House

Afton Guest House
1 Hartington Gardens,
Edinburgh, EH10 4LD
Tel: 0131 229 1019
★★★ Guest House

A Haven Townhouse
180 Ferry Road, Edinburgh,
EH6 4NS
Tel: 0131 554 6559
★★★ Metro Hotel

Airdenair Guest House
29 Kilmaurs Road, Edinburgh,
EH16 5DB
Tel: 0131 668 2336
★★★ Guest House

Airlie Guest House
29 Minto Street, Edinburgh,
EH9 1SB
Tel: 0131 667 3562
★★★ Guest House

Albyn Townhouse
16 Hartington Gardens,
Edinburgh, EH10 4LD
Tel: 0131 229 6459
★★★ Guest House

Allison House
17 Mayfield Gardens,
Edinburgh, EH9 2AX
Tel: 0131 667 8049
★★★★ Guest House

Alloway Guest House
96 Pilrig Street, Edinburgh,
EH6 5AY
Tel: 0131 554 1786
★★★ Guest House

Alness Guest House
27 Pilrig Street, Edinburgh,
EH6 5AN
Tel: 0131 554 1187
★★ Guest House

AmarAgua Guest House
10 Kilmaurs Terrace,
Edinburgh, Lothian,
EH16 5DR
Tel: 0131 667 6775
★★★★ Guest House

Aonach Mor Guesthouse
14 Kilmaurs Terrace,
Edinburgh, EH16 5DR
Tel: 0131 667 8694
★★★★ Guest House

Apex City
61 Grassmarket, Edinburgh,
EH1 2JF
Tel: 0131 300 3456
★★★★ Hotel

Apex European Hotel
90 Haymarket Terrace,
Edinburgh, EH12 5LQ
Tel: 0131 474 3456
★★★★ Hotel

Apex International Hotel
31/35 Grassmarket,
Edinburgh, EH1 2HY
Tel: 0131 300 3456
★★★★ Hotel

Appin House
4 Queens Crescent,
Edinburgh, Midlothian, EH9 2AZ
Tel: 0131 668 2947
★★ Guest House

Ard-Na-Said
5 Priestfield Road, Edinburgh,
Lothian, EH16 5HH
Tel: 0131 667 8754
★★★★ Guest House

Ardblair Guest House
1 Duddingston Crescent,
Milton Road, Edinburgh,
Lothian, EH15 3AS
Tel: 0131 6203081
★★★ Guest House

Arden Guest House
126 Old Dalkeith Road,
Edinburgh, Lothian, EH16 4SD
Tel: 0131 6643985
★★★ Guest House

Ardenlee Guest House
9 Eyre Place, Edinburgh,
EH3 5ES
Tel: 0131 556 2838
★★★ Guest House

Ardgarth Guest House
1 St Mary's Place,
Portobello, Edinburgh,
EH15 2QF
Tel: 0131 669 3021
★★★ Guest House

Ardgowan House
1 Lady Road, Edinburgh,
EH16 5PA
Tel: 0131 667 7774
★★ Guest House

Ardleigh Guest House
260 Ferry Road, Edinburgh,
EH5 3AN
Tel: 0131 552 1833
★★★ Guest House

Ardmillan Hotel
9-10 Ardmillan Terrace,
Edinburgh, EH11 2JW
Tel: 0131 337 9588
★★ Small Hotel

Ardmor House
74 Pilrig Street, Edinburgh,
Lothians, EH6 5AS
Tel: 0131 554 4944
★★★★ Guest House

Arrandale Guest House
28 Mayfield Gardens,
Edinburgh, Lothian, EH9 2BZ
Tel: 0131 622 2232
★★★ Guest House

Ascot Guest House
98 Dalkeith Road, Edinburgh,
EH16 5AF
Tel: 0131 667 1500
★ Guest House

Ashdene House
23 Fountainhall Road,
Edinburgh, EH9 2LN
Tel: 0131 6676026
★★★★ Guest House

Ashgrove House
12 Osborne Terrace,
Edinburgh, EH12 5HG
Tel: 0131 337 5014
★★★ Guest House

Ashlyn Guest House
42 Inverleith Row, Edinburgh,
EH3 5PY
Tel: 0131 552 2954
★★★ Guest House

Auld Reekie Guest House
16 Mayfield Gardens,
Edinburgh, EH9 2BZ
Tel: 0131 667 6177
★★★ Guest House

Ayden Guest House
70 Pilrig Street, Edinburgh,
EH6 5AS
Tel: 0131 554 2187
★★★★ Guest House

Aynetree Guest House
12 Duddingston Crescent,
Milton Road, Edinburgh,
EH15 3AS
Tel: 0131 258 2821
★★★ Guest House

Ballantrae Hotel
8 York Place, Edinburgh,
EH1 3EP
Tel: 0131 478 4748
★★★ Metro Hotel

Ballantrae-Albany Hotel
39/43 Albany Street,
Edinburgh, EH1 3QY
Tel: 0131 556 0397
Hotel

Ballantrae Apartments
12 York Place, Edinburgh,
Midlothian, EH1 3EP
Tel: 0131 4784748
★★★★ Serviced
Apartments

Ballantrae Hotel At The West End
6 Grosvenor Crescent,
Edinburgh, Midlothian,
EH12 5EP
Tel: 0131 225 7033
★★★ Small Hotel

Balmore House
34 Gilmore Place, Edinburgh,
Lothian, EH3 9NQ
Tel: 0131 2211331
★★★★ Guest House

Barony House
23 Mayfield Gardens,
Edinburgh, EH9 2BX
Tel: 0131 667 5806
★★★★ Guest House

Barossa Guest House
21 Pilrig Street, Edinburgh,
EH6 5AN
Tel: 0131 554 3700
★★ Guest House

Beechcroft House
46 Murrayfield Avenue, Edinburgh, Lothian, EH12 6AY
Tel: 0131 337 4009
★★★★ Guest House

Belford Guest House
13 Blacket Avenue, Edinburgh, EH9 1RR
Tel: 0131 667 2422
★★★ Guest House

Bellerose Guest House
36 Minto Street, Edinburgh, EH9 2BS
Tel: 0131 667 8933
★★ Guest House

Ben Cruachan
17 McDonald Road, Edinburgh, Midlothian, EH7 4LX
Tel: 0131 556 3709
★★★★ Guest House

Ben Doran
11 Mayfield Gardens, Edinburgh, Lothian, EH9 2AX
Tel: 0131 667 8488
★★★★ Guest House

Ben Craig House
3 Craigmillar Park, Edinburgh, EH16 5PG
Tel: 0131 667 2593
★★★ Guest House

Beresford Hotel
32 Coates Garden, Edinburgh, EH12 5LE
Tel: 0131 337 0850
★★ Guest House

Best Western Edinburgh City Hotel
79 Lauriston Place, Edinburgh, EH3 9HZ
Tel: 0131 622 7979
★★★ Hotel

Best Western Bruntsfield Hotel
69 Bruntsfield Place, Edinburgh, EH10 4HH
Tel: 0131 229 1393
★★★★ Hotel

Best Western Kings Manor Hotel
100 Milton Road East, Edinburgh, EH15 2NP
Tel: 0131 468 8003
★★★ Hotel

The Bonham
35 Drumsheugh Gardens, Edinburgh, EH3 7RN
Tel: 0131 274 7400
★★★★ Hotel

Bowmore Guest House
47 Gilmore Place, Edinburgh, Midlothian, EH3 9NG
Tel: 0131 221 1331
Awaiting Inspection

Brae Guest House
119 Willowbrae Road, Edinburgh, EH8 7HN
Tel: 0131 661 0170
★★★ Guest House

Brae Lodge Guest House
30 Liberton Brae, Edinburgh, Lothian, EH16 6AF
Tel: 0131 6722876
★★★ Guest House

Braid Hills Hotel
134 Braid Road, Edinburgh, EH10 6JD
Tel: 0131 447 8888
★★★ Hotel

Braveheart Guest House
26 Gilmore Place, Edinburgh, EH3 9NQ
Tel: 0131 221 9192
★ Guest House

Brig O'Doon Guest House
262 Ferry Road, Edinburgh, EH5 3AN
Tel: 0131 552 3953
★★★ Guest House

Briggend Guest House
19 Old Dalkeith Road, Edinburgh, EH16 4TE
Tel: 0131 258 0810
★★★ Guest House

Brodie's Guest House
22 East Claremont Street, Edinburgh, EH7 4JP
Tel: 0131 556 4032
★★★ Guest House

Brothaig House
18 Craigmillar Park, Edinburgh, EH16 5PS
Tel: 0131 667 2202
★★★ Guest House

The Broughton City Centre Hotel
37 Broughton Place, New Town, Edinburgh, Lothian, EH1 3RR
Tel: 0131 558 9792
★★★ Guest House

Caledonian Hilton Hotel
Princes Street, Edinburgh, EH1 2AB
Tel: 0131 222 8888
★★★★★ Hotel

Capital City Guest House
2 St Catherines Gardens, Edinburgh, EH12 7AZ
Tel: 0131 334 6159
★★ Guest House

Capital Guest House
7 Mayfield Road, Newington, Edinburgh, EH9 2NG
Tel: 0131 466 0717
★★★ Guest House

Caravel Guest House
30 London Street, Edinburgh, EH3 6NA
Tel: 0131 556 4444
★★ Guest House

Carlton Hotel
North Bridge, Edinburgh, EH1 1SD
Tel: 0131 472 3001
★★★★ Hotel

Carrington Guest House
38 Pilrig Street, Edinburgh, EH6 5AL
Tel: 0131 554 4769
★★★ Guest House

Casa Buzzo Guest House
8 Kilmaurs Road, Edinburgh, EH16 5DA
Tel: 0131 667 8998
★★★ Guest House

Castle View
30 Castle Street, Edinburgh, Lothian, EH2 3HT
Tel: 0131 226 5784
★★★ Guest House

Channings
12-16 South Learmonth Gardens, Edinburgh, EH4 1EZ
Tel: 0131 274 7401
★★★★ Hotel

Charleston House Guest House
38 Minto Street, Edinburgh, EH9 2BS
Tel: 0131 667 6589
★★★ Guest House

Cherry Tree Villa
9 East Mayfield, Edinburgh, Midlothian, EH9 1SD
Tel: 0131 258 0009
★★★ Guest House

Christopher North House Hotel
6 Gloucester Place, Edinburgh, EH3 6EF
Tel: 0131 225 2720
★★★ Small Hotel

Clan Walker Guest House
96 Dalkeith Road, Edinburgh, EH16 5AF
Tel: 0131 667 1244
★★★ Guest House

Claremont Hotel
14a/15 Claremont Crescent, Edinburgh, EH7 4HX
Tel: 0131 556 1487
★ Metro Hotel

Classic Guest House
50 Mayfield Road, Edinburgh, EH9 2NH
Tel: 0131 6675847
★★★ Guest House

Claymore Guest House
68 Pilrig Street, Edinburgh, EH6 5AS
Tel: 0131 554 2500
★★ Guest House

Cluaran House
47 Leamington Terrace, Edinburgh, EH10 4JS
Tel: 0131 221 0047
★★★★ Guest House

The Corstorphine Lodge
188 St Johns Road, Edinburgh, Lothians, EH12 8SG
Tel: 0131 5394237
★★★ Guest House

Craigellachie
21 Murrayfield Avenue, Edinburgh, EH12 6AU
Tel: 0131 337 4076
★★★★ Guest House

Craigmoss Guest House
62 Pilrig Street, Edinburgh, EH6 4HS
Tel: 0131 554 3885
★★★★ Guest House

Crioch Guest House
23 East Hermitage Place, Leith Links, Edinburgh
Tel: 0131 554 5494
★★★ Guest House

Cumberland Hotel
1-2 West Coates, Edinburgh, EH12 5JQ
Tel: 0131 337 1198
★★★ Metro Hotel

Edinburgh continued

Davenport House
58 Great King Street,
Edinburgh, Lothian, EH3 6QY
Tel: 0131 558 8495
★★★★ Guest House

Dene Guest House
7 Eyre Place,
off Dundas Street,
Edinburgh
Tel: 0131 556 2700
★★★ Guest House

Dorstan House
7 Priestfield Road, Edinburgh,
EH16 5HJ
Tel: 0131 667 6721
★★★ Guest House

Dunedin Guest House
8 Priestfield Road, Edinburgh,
Lothian, EH16 5HH
Tel: 0131 6681949
★★★★ Guest House

Dunstane City Hotel
5 Hampton Terrace,
Edinburgh, Lothian,
EH12 5JD
Tel: 0131 313 5500
Awaiting Inspection

Dunstane House Hotel
4 West Coates, Haymarket,
Edinburgh, EH12 5JQ
Tel: 0131 337 6169
★★★★ Small Hotel

Duthus Lodge
5 West Coates, Edinburgh,
EH12 5JG
Tel: 0131 337 6876
★★★ Guest House

Ecosse International
15 MacDonald Road,
Edinburgh, EH7 4LX
Tel: 0131 556 4967
★★★ Guest House

Edinburgh (Newcraighall) Premier Inn
Cuddie Brae,
91 Newcraighall Road,
Newcraighall, Edinburgh,
EH21 8RX
Tel: 0870 990 6336
Passed Budget Hotel

Edinburgh Agenda Hotel
92 St John's Road, Edinburgh,
EH12 8AT
Tel: 0131 316 4466
★★★ Hotel

Edinburgh Brunswick Hotel
7 Brunswick Street,
Edinburgh, EH7 5JB
Tel: 0131 556 1238
★★ Guest House

Edinburgh Capital Hotel
187 Clermiston Road,
Edinburgh, EH12 6UG
Tel: 0131 535 9988
★★★ Hotel

Edinburgh City Centre(Lauriston)Premier Inn
Laurison Place,
Lady Lawson Street,
Edinburgh, Lothian, EH3 9HZ
Tel: 0870 990 6610
Passed Budget Hotel

Edinburgh East Premier Inn
Lady Nairne,
228 Willowbrae Road,
Edinburgh, EH8 7NG
Tel: 08701 977091
Passed Budget Hotel

Edinburgh Marriott
111 Glasgow Road,
Edinburgh, EH12 8NF
Tel: 0870 400 7293
★★★★ Hotel

Edinburgh's Minto Hotel
16-18 Minto Street,
Edinburgh, EH9 9RQ
Tel: 0131 668 1234
Awaiting Inspection

Edinburgh City Centre (Morrison St) Premier Travel Inn
1 Morrison Link, Edinburgh,
EH3 8DN
Tel: 0870 238 3319
Passed Budget Hotel

Edinburgh House
11 McDonald Road,
Edinburgh, EH7 4LX
Tel: 0131 556 3434
★★★ Guest House

The Edinburgh Residence
7 Rothesay Terrace,
Edinburgh, EH3 7RY
Tel: 0131 274 7403
★★★★★ Townhouse Hotel

Elas Guest House
10 Claremont Crescent,
Edinburgh, EH7 4HX
Tel: 0131 556 1929
★ Guest House

Elder York Guest House
38 Elder Street, Edinburgh,
EH1 3DX
Tel: 0131 556 1926
★★★ Guest House

Ellersly House Hotel
Ellersly Road, Edinburgh,
EH12 6HZ
Tel: 0131 337 6888
★★ Hotel

Ellesmere Guest House
11 Glengyle Terrace,
Edinburgh, EH3 9LN
Tel: 0131 229 4823
★★★★ Guest House

Express By Holiday Inn
Britannia Way, Ocean Drive,
Edinburgh, Lothian, EH6 6LA
Tel: 0131 555 4422
★★★ Hotel

Fairholme
13 Moston Terrace,
Edinburgh, EH9 2DE
Tel: 0131 667 8645
★★★ Guest House

Falcon Crest Guest House
70 South Trinity Road,
Edinburgh, EH5 3NX
Tel: 0131 552 5294
★ Guest House

Four Twenty Guest House
420 Ferry Road, Edinburgh,
EH5 2AD
Tel: 0131 552 2167
★ Guest House

Four Hill Street
4 Hill Street, Edinburgh,
EH2 3JZ
Tel: 0131 225 8884
★★★★ Guest House

Frederick House Hotel
42 Frederick Street,
Edinburgh, EH2 1EX
Tel: 0131 226 1999
★★★ Lodge

Galloway Guest House
22 Dean Park Crescent,
Edinburgh, EH4 1PH
Tel: 0131 332 3672
★★★ Guest House

George Hotel
19 / 21 George St.,
Edinburgh, EH2 2PB
Tel: 0131 225 1251
★★★★ Hotel

Gifford House
103 Dalkeith Road,
Edinburgh, EH16 5AJ
Tel: 0131 667 4688
★★★★ Guest House

Gildun Guest House
9 Spence Street, Edinburgh,
EH16 5AG
Tel: 0131 667 1368
★★★★ Guest House

Gillis
100 Strathearn Road,
Edinburgh, EH9 1BB
Tel: 0131 623 8933
★★★ Guest House

Gladstone Guest House
90 Dalkeith Road, Edinburgh,
EH16 5AF
Tel: 0131 6674708
★★★ Guest House

The Glasshouse
2 Greenside Place,
Edinburgh, EH1 3AA
Tel: 0131 5258200
★★★★★ Metro Hotel

Glenalmond House
25 Mayfield Gardens,
Edinburgh, EH9 2BX
Tel: 0131 668 2392
★★★★ Guest House

The Glenora
14 Rosebery Crescent,
Edinburgh, EH12 5JY
Tel: 0131 337 1186
★★★★ Guest House

The Globetrotter Inn Edinburgh Limited
Cramond Foreshore,
Marine Drive, Edinburgh,
Lothian, EH4 5EP
Tel: 0131 3361030
★★★★ Hostel

Granville Guest House
13 Granville Terrace,
Edinburgh, EH10 4PQ
Tel: 0131 229 1676
★★ Guest House

Greenside Hotel
9 Royal Terrace, Edinburgh,
EH7 5AB
Tel: 0131 557 0121
★★★ Metro Hotel

Grosvenor Gardens Hotel
1 Grosvenor Gardens,
Edinburgh, EH12 5JU
Tel: 0131 313 3415
★★★ Guest House

Halcyon Hotel
8 Royal Terrace, Edinburgh, EH7 5AB
Tel: 0131 556 1033
★★ Guest House

Hampton Hotel
14 Corstorphine Road, Edinburgh, EH12 6HN
Tel: 0131 337 1130
★★★ Small Hotel

Harvest Guest House
33, Straiton Place, Edinburgh, EH15 2BA
Tel: 0131 657 3160
★ Guest House

Haymarket Hotel
1-3 Coates Gardens, Edinburgh, Lothian, EH12 5LG
Tel: 0131 337 1045
★★★ Metro Hotel

Herald House Hotel
70/72 Grove Street, Edinburgh, EH3 8AP
Tel: 0131 228 2323
★★ Metro Hotel

Heriott Park Guest House
254/256 Ferry Road, Edinburgh, EH5 3AN
Tel: 0131 552 3456
★★★ Guest House

Highfield Guest House
83 Mayfield Road, Edinburgh, EH9 3AE
Tel: 0131 667 8717
★★★★ Guest House

Hilton Edinburgh Airport
Edinburgh International Airport, Edinburgh, EH28 8LL
Tel: 0131 519 4400
★★★★ Hotel

Hilton Edinburgh Grosvenor
7-21 Grosvenor Street, Edinburgh, EH12 5EF
Tel: 0131 226 6001
★★★ Hotel

Holiday Inn Edinburgh
Corstorphine Road, Edinburgh, EH12 6UA
Tel: 0870 400 9026
★★★★ Hotel

Holiday Inn Edinburgh-North
107 Queensferry Road, Edinburgh, EH4 3HL
Tel: 08704009025
★★★ Hotel

Holyrood Hotel
Holyrood Road, Edinburgh, EH8 6AE
Tel: 0131 550 4500
★★★★ Hotel

Hotel Ceilidh-Donia
14-16 Marchhall Crescent, Edinburgh, EH16 5HL
Tel: 0131 667 2743
★★★ Small Hotel

Hotel Ibis Edinburgh
6 Hunter Square, Edinburgh, EH1 1QW
Tel: 0131 240 7000
★★ Hotel

The Howard
34 Great King Street, Edinburgh, EH3 6QH
Tel: 0131 274 7402
★★★★★ Townhouse Hotel

The Inverleith Hotel
5 Inverleith Terrace, Edinburgh, EH3 5NS
Tel: 0131 556 2745
★★★ Metro Hotel

Ivy House Guest House
7 Mayfield Gardens, Edinburgh, EH9 2AX
Tel: 0131 667 3411
★★ Guest House

Joppa Turrets Guest House
1 Lower Joppa (at Beech end of Morton St), Edinburgh, EH15 2ER
Tel: 0131 669 5806
★★★ Guest House

Jurys Inn Edinburgh
43 Jeffrey Street, Edinburgh, Lothian, EH1 1DH
Tel: 0131 200 3300
★★★ Hotel

Kaimes Guest House
12 Granville Terrace, Edinburgh, EH10 4PQ
Tel: 0131 478 2779
★★ Guest House

Kariba Guest House
10 Granville Terrace, Edinburgh, EH10 4PQ
Tel: 0131 229 3773
★★★ Guest House

Kelly's Guest House
3 Hillhouse Road, Edinburgh, Lothian, EH4 3QP
Tel: 0131 3323894
★★★ Guest House

Kenvie Guest House
16 Kilmaurs Road, Edinburgh, EH16 5DA
Tel: 0131 668 1964
★★★ Guest House

Kew House
1 Kew Terrace, Murrayfield, Edinburgh, EH12 5JE
Tel: 0131 313 0700
★★★★★ Guest House

Kildonan Lodge Hotel
27 Craigmillar Park, Edinburgh, EH16 5PE
Tel: 0131 667 2793
★★★★ Small Hotel

Kilmaurs House
9 Kilmaurs Road, Edinburgh, EH16 5DA
Tel: 0131 667 8315
★★★ Guest House

Kingsburgh House
2 Corstorphine Road, Murrayfield, Edinburgh, Midlothian, EH12 6HN
Tel: 0131 313 1679
★★★★★ Guest House

Kingsley Guest House
30 Craigmillar Park, Edinburgh, EH16 5PS
Tel: 0131 667 3177
★★★ Guest House

Kingsview Guest House
28 Gilmore Place, Edinburgh, EH3 9NQ
Tel: 0131 229 8004
★★ Guest House

Kirklea Guest House
11 Harrison Road, Edinburgh, EH11 1EG
Tel: 0131 337 1129
★★★ Guest House

Lauderville House
52 Mayfield Road, Edinburgh, EH9 2NH
Tel: 0131 667 7788
★★★★ Guest House

The Laurels
320 Gilmerton Road, Edinburgh, Midlothian, EH17 7PR
Tel: 0131 666 2229
★★★ Guest House

Le Monde Hotel
16 George Street, Edinburgh, EH3 6EE, EH3 6EE
Tel: 0131 270 3900
★★★★ Hotel

Ms Teresa Legg
115 Lauriston Place, Edinburgh, EH3 9JG
Tel: 0131 622 6677
★★★★ Serviced Apartments

Lindsay Guest House
108 Polwarth Terrace, Edinburgh, Midlothian, EH11 1NN
Tel: 0131 337 1580
★★★ Guest House

Links Hotel and Bar
4 Alvanley Terrace, Whitehouse Loan, Edinburgh, Lothian, EH9 1DU
Tel: 0131 622 6800
★★ Hotel

The Lodge Hotel
6 Hampton Terrace, Edinburgh, EH12 5JD
Tel: 0131 3373682
★★★★ Guest House

MacIntosh Guest House
21 Downie Terrace, Edinburgh, Lothian, EH12 7AU
Tel: 0131 334
Awaiting Inspection

Mackenzie Guest House
2 East Hermitage Place, Edinburgh, EH6 8AA
Tel: 0131 554 3763
★★★★ Guest House

Clarendon Hotel
25-33 Shandwick Place, Edinburgh, EH2 4RG
Tel: 0131 229 1467
★★★ Hotel

Malmaison Hotel et Brasserie
1 Tower Place, Leith, Edinburgh, EH6 7DB
Tel: 0131 4685000
★★★★ Hotel

Mayfield Lodge
75 Mayfield Road, Edinburgh, EH9 3AA
Tel: 0131 6628899
★★★ Guest House

Melville Castle Hotel
Melville Gate, Gilmerton Road, Midlothian, EH18 1AP
Tel: 0131 6540088
★★★★ Hotel

Edinburgh continued

Melville Guest House
2 Duddingston Crescent,
Edinburgh, Lothian, EH15 3AS
Tel: 0131 669 7856
★★★ Guest House

Melvin House Hotel
3 Rothesay Terrace,
Edinburgh, EH3 7RY
Tel: 0131 225 5084
★★★ Hotel

Menzies Belford Hotel
69 Belford Road, Edinburgh,
EH4 3DG
Tel: 0131 332 2545
★★★★ Hotel

Menzies Guest House
33 Leamington Terrace,
Edinburgh, EH10 4JS
Tel: 0131 229 4629
★★ Guest House

Mingalar
2 East Claremont Street,
Edinburgh, Midlothian,
EH7 4JP
Tel: 0131 556 7000
★★★ Guest House

Murrayfield Park Hotel
89 Corstorphine Road,
Edinburgh, EH12 5QE
Tel: 0131 337 5370
★★★ Guest House

MW Guesthouse
94 Dalkeith Road, Edinburgh,
Mid Lothian, EH16 5AF
Tel: 0131 662 9265
★★★★ Guest House

MW Town House
11 Spence Street, Edinburgh,
Mid Lothian, EH16 5AG
Tel: 0131 662 9265
★★★★ Guest House

No. 13 Jean Armour Avenue
13 Jean Armour Avenue,
Edinburgh, Lothian, EH16 6XB
Tel: 0131 6648951
Awaiting Inspection

No. 322 Leith Walk
322 Leith Walk, Edinburgh,
Lothian, EH6 5BU
Tel: 0774 764
Awaiting Inspection

Novotel Edinburgh Centre
80 Lauriston Place,
Edinburgh, Lothian, EH3 9DE
Tel: 0131 656 3500
★★★★ Hotel

Old Waverley Hotel
43 Princes Street, Edinburgh,
EH2 2BY
Tel: 0131 556 4648
★★★ Hotel

One Royal Circus
1 Royal Circus, Edinburgh,
EH3 6TL
Tel: 0131 225 5854
★★★★★ Exclusive Use Venue

Osbourne Hotel
51-59 York Place, Edinburgh,
EH1 3JD
Tel: 0131 556 5577
★ Hotel

Parklands Guest House
20 Mayfield Gardens,
Edinburgh, EH9 2BZ
Tel: 0131 667 7184
★★★ Guest House

Parliament House Hotel
15 Calton Hill, Edinburgh,
EH1 3BJ
Tel: 0131 478 4000
★★★ Hotel

Piries Hotel
4-8 Coates Gardens,
Haymarket, Edinburgh,
EH12 5LB
Tel: 0131 337 1108
Awaiting Inspection

The Point Hotel
34 Bread Street, Edinburgh,
EH3 9AF
Tel: 0131 221 5555
★★★ Hotel

Premier Inn Edinburgh Leith
Newhaven Quay,
51/53 Newhaven Place,
Edinburgh, EH6 4LX
Tel: 08701 977093
Passed Budget Hotel

Prestonfield
Priestfield Road, Edinburgh,
Lothian, EH16 5UT
Tel: 0131 668 3346
★★★★★ Hotel

Radisson SAS Hotel
80 High Street, Edinburgh,
EH1 1TH
Tel: 0131 557 9797
★★★★ Hotel

Ramada Mount Royal Hotel
53 Princes Street, Edinburgh,
EH2 2DG
Tel: 0131 225 7161
★★★ Hotel

Ravensdown Guest House
248 Ferry Road, Edinburgh,
Midlothian, EH5 3AN
Tel: 0131 552 5438
★★★ Guest House

Regent House Hotel
3-5 Forth Street, Edinburgh,
EH1 3JX
Tel: 0131 556 1616
★ Metro Hotel

Relax Guest House
11 Eyre Place, Edinburgh,
Scotland, EH3 5ES
Tel: 0131 5561433
★★ Guest House

Ritz Hotel
14-18 Grosvenor Street,
Edinburgh, EH12 5EG
Tel: 0131 337 4315
★★ Hotel

Robb's Guest House
5 Granville Terrace,
Edinburgh, EH10 4PQ
Tel: 0131 229 2086
★★ Guest House

Robertson Guest House
5 Hartington Gardens,
Edinburgh, EH10 4LD
Tel: 0131 229 2652
★★★ Guest House

Rosehall Hotel
101 Dalkeith Road,
Newington, Edinburgh,
EH16 5AJ
Tel: 0131 667 9372
★★★ Metro Hotel

Rosevale House
15 Kilmaurs Road, Edinburgh,
EH16 5DA
Tel: 0131 667 4781
★★ Guest House

Rowan Guest House
13 Glenorchy Terrace,
Edinburgh, EH9 2DQ
Tel: 0131 667 2463
★★★ Guest House

Roxburghe Hotel
38 Charlotte Square,
Edinburgh, EH2 4HG
Tel: 0131 240 5500
★★★★ Hotel

Royal British Hotel
20 Princes Street, Edinburgh,
EH2 2AN
Tel: 0131 556 4901
★★★ Hotel

Royal Terrace Hotel
18 Royal Terrace, Edinburgh,
EH7 5AQ
Tel: 0131 557 3222
★★★★ Hotel

The St Valery
36 Coates Gardens,
Edinburgh, EH12 5LE
Tel: 0131 337 1893
★★★ Guest House

Sakura House
18 West Preston Street,
Edinburgh, EH8 9PU
Tel: 0131 668 1204
★ Guest House

The Salisbury Hotel
43-45 Salisbury Road,
Edinburgh, EH16 5AA
Tel: 0131 667 1264
★★★★ Small Hotel

Salisbury Green Hotel
Conference Centre
University of Edinburgh,
Pollock Halls,
18 Holyrood Park Road,
Edinburgh, EH16 5AY
Tel:
★★★ Metro Hotel

San Marco
24 Mayfield Gardens,
Edinburgh, EH9 2BZ
Tel: 0131 667 8982
★★★★ Guest House

Sandaig Guest House
5 East Hermitage Place,
Leith Links, Edinburgh
Tel: 0131 554 7357
★★★★ Guest House

Sandilands House
25 Queensferry Road,
Edinburgh, EH4 3HB
Tel: 0131 332 2057
★★★ Guest House

Shalimar Guest House
20 Newington Road,
Edinburgh, EH9 1QS
Tel: 0131 6672827/0789
★★ Guest House

Sheraton Grand Hotel & Spa, Edinburgh
1 Festival Square, Edinburgh, EH3 9SR
Tel: 0131 229 9131
★★★★★ Hotel

Sheridan Guest House
1 Bonnington Terrace, Edinburgh, EH6 4BP
Tel: 0131 554 4107
★★★ Guest House

Sherwood Guest House
42 Minto Street, Edinburgh, EH9 2BR
Tel: 0131 667 1200
★★★★ Guest House

Six Marys Place Guest House
Raeburn Place, Stockbridge, Edinburgh, EH4 1JH
Tel: 0131 332 8965
★★★ Guest House

Sonas Guest House
3 East Mayfield, Edinburgh, EH9 1SD
Tel: 0131 667 2781
★★★ Guest House

Southside
8 Newington Road, Edinburgh, EH9 1QS
★★★★ Guest House

St Conan's Guest House
30 Minto Street, Edinburgh, EH9 1SB
Tel: 0131 667 8393
★★★ Guest House

Star Villa
36 Gilmore Place, Edinburgh, EH3 9NQ
Tel: 0131 229 4991
★★★ Guest House

St Bernards Guest House
22 St Bernards Crescent, Edinburgh, EH4 1NS
Tel: 0131 332 2339
★★ Guest House

Strathallan Guest House
44 Minto Street, Edinburgh, Lothian, EH9 2BR
Tel: 0131 667 6678
★★★ Guest House

Straven Guest House
3 Brunstane Road North, Edinburgh, EH15 2DL
Tel: 0131 669 5580
★★★ Guest House

Tania Guest House
19 Minto Street, Edinburgh, EH9 1RQ
Tel: 0131 667 4144
★ Guest House

Tankard Guest House
40 East Claremont Street, Edinburgh, EH7 4JR
Tel: 0131 556 4218
★ Guest House

Ten Hill Place Hotel
10 Hill Place, Edinburgh, EH8 9DS
Tel: 0131 668 9243
★★★ Metro Hotel

Terrace Hotel
37 Royal Terrace, Edinburgh, EH7 5AH
Tel: 0131 556 3423
★★ Guest House

Teviotdale House
53 Grange Loan, Edinburgh, EH9 2ER
Tel: 0131 667 4376
★★★★ Guest House

The Alexander Guest House
35 Mayfield Gardens, Edinburgh, EH9 2BX
Tel: 0131 258 4028
★★★★ Guest House

The Armadillo Guest House
12 Gilmore Place, Edinburgh, EH3 9NQ
Tel: 0131 229 6457
★★★ Guest House

The Balmoral Hotel
Princes Street, Edinburgh, EH2 2EQ
Tel: 0131 556 2414
★★★★★ Hotel

The Beverley
40 Murrayfield Avenue, Edinburgh, EH12 6AY
Tel: 0131 337 1128
★★★★ Guest House

The Boisdale
9 Coates Gardens, Edinburgh, EH12 5LG
Tel: 0131 337 1134
★★★ Guest House

The Lairg
11 Coates Gardens, Edinburgh, EH12 5LG
Tel: 0131 3371050
★★★ Guest House

The Lodge Bed & Breakfast
35 Glasgow Road, Corstorphine, Edinburgh, Midlothian, EH12 8HW
Tel: 0131 334 0773
Awaiting Inspection

The McDonald Guest House
5 McDonald Road, Edinburgh, Midlothian, EH7 4LX
Tel: 0131 557 5935
★★★ Guest House

The Quality Hotel Edinburgh Airport
Ingliston, by Edinburgh, Midlothian, EH28 8AU
Tel: 0131 333 4331
★★★ Hotel

The Rosebery Hotel
13 Rosebery Crescent, Edinburgh, EH12 5JY
Tel: 0131 337 1085
★ Guest House

The Royal Over-Seas League
100 Princes Street, Edinburgh, EH2 3AB
Tel: 0131 225 1501
★★★ Small Hotel

The Royal Scots Club
30 Abercromby Place, Edinburgh, Lothian, EH3 6QE
Tel: 0131 556 4270
★★★ Hotel

The Royal Scotsman
Edinburgh Waverley Station, Edinburgh
★★★★★ Train

The Scotsman Hotel
20 North Bridge, Edinburgh, EH1 1YT
Tel: 0131 556 5565
★★★★★ Townhouse Hotel

The Town House
65 Gilmore place, Edinburgh, EH3 9NU
Tel: 0131 229 1985
★★★★ Guest House

Thistle Edinburgh
107 Leith Street, Edinburgh, EH1 3SW
Tel: 0870 3339153
★★★ Hotel

Thistle Hotel
59 Manor Place, Edinburgh, EH3 7EG
Tel: 0131 225 6144
★★★ Metro Hotel

Thistle House
1 Kilmaurs Terrace, Edinburgh, EH16 5BZ
Tel: 0131 667 2002
★★ Guest House

Thrums Hotel
14-15 Minto Street, Edinburgh, EH9 1RQ
Tel: 0131 667 5545
★★★ Guest House

Tigerlily
125 George Street, Edinburgh, EH7 4GG
Tel: 0131 2255005
★★★★ Hotel

The Turret Guest House
8 Kilmaurs Terrace, Edinburgh, EH16 5DR
Tel: 0131 667 6704
★★★★ Guest House

Victoria Park Hotel
221 Ferry Road, Edinburgh, EH6 4NN
Tel: 0131 4777033
★★★ Small Hotel

The Walton
79 Dundas Street, Edinburgh, EH3 6SD
Tel: 0131 556 1137
★★★★ Guest House

Western Manor House
92 Corstorphine Road, Edinburgh, EH12 6JG
Tel: 0131 538 7490
★★★ Guest House

by Edinburgh

Dalhousie Castle & Spa
Cockpen Road, Bonnyrigg, Edinburgh, Midlothian, EH19 3JB
Tel: 01875 820153
★★★★ Hotel

nr Edinburgh

The Laird & Dog Hotel
5 High Street, Lasswade, Midlothian, EH18 1NA
Tel: 0131 663 9219
★★ Inn

Fauldhouse

East Badallan Farm
Fauldhouse, by Bathgate, West Lothian, EH47 9AG
Tel: 01501 770251
★★★ Farmhouse

Old Farmhouse B&B
O[DRedskill Farm, Gifford,
Haddington, East Lothian,
EH41 4JN
Tel: 01620 810406
Awaiting Inspection

Ivory House
14 Vogrie Road, Gorebridge,
Midlothian, EH23 4HH
Tel: 01875 820755
★★★★ Guest House

Greywalls
Muirfield, Gullane,
East Lothian, EH31 2EG
Tel: 01620 842144
★★★★ Country House Hotel

Mallard Hotel
East Links Road, Gullane,
East Lothian, EH31 2AF
Tel: 01620 843288
★★ Small Hotel

Saltcoats Farmhouse
Saltcoats Farm, Gullane,
EH31 2AG
Tel: 01620 842204
★★ Farmhouse

Abbey Mains
Haddington, East Lothian,
EH41 3SB
Tel: 01620 823286
★★★★ Farmhouse

Maitlandfield House Hotel
24 Sidegate, Haddington,
East Lothian, EH41 4BZ
Tel: 01620 826513
★★★★ Hotel

Norton House Hotel
Ingliston, Edinburgh,
EH28 8LX
Tel: 0131 333 1275
★★★★ Hotel

The Marriott Dalmahoy Hotel
and Country Club, Kirknewton,
Midlothian, EH27 8EP
Tel: 0131 3331845
★★★★ Hotel

The Bonsyde House Hotel
Bonsyde, By Linlithgow,
West Lothian, EH49 7NU
Tel: 01506 842229
★★★ Small Hotel

West Port Hotel
West Port, Linlithgow,
West Lothian, EH49 7AZ
Tel: 01506 847456
★★ Small Hotel

Livingston Premier Inn
Deer Park Avenue, Deer Park,
Livingston, Lothian, EH54 8AD
Tel: 0870 1977161
Passed Budget Hotel

Ramada Livingston
Almondview, Livingston,
West Lothian, EH54 6QB
Tel: 01506 431222
★★★ Hotel

Aaron Glen Guest House
7 Nivensknowe Road,
Loanhead, Midlothian,
EH20 9AU
Tel: 0131 440 1293
★★★ Guest House

Adniston Manor
West Adniston Farm,
Macmerry, East Lothian,
EH33 1EA
Tel: 01875 611190
★★★★ Guest House

Arden House
26 Linkfield Road,
Musselburgh, East Lothian,
EH21 7LL
Tel: 0131 665 0663
★★★★ Guest House

Carberry Tower
Musselburgh, East Lothian,
EH21 8PY
Tel: 0131 665 3135/3488
★★ Guest House

Edinburgh Inveresk Premier Inn
Craig House,Carbery Road,
Musselburgh, Edinburgh,
EH21 8PT
Tel: 08701 977092
Passed Budget Hotel

Fenton Tower
Kingston, North Berwick,
East Lothian, EH39 5JH
Tel: 01620 890089
★★★★★ Exclusive Use Venue

Glentruim
53 Dirleton Avenue,
North Berwick, East Lothian,
EH39 4BL
Tel: 01620 890064
Awaiting Inspection

MacDonald Marine Hotel & Spa
Cromwell Road,
North Berwick, East Lothian,
EH39 4LZ
Tel: 0870 400 8129
★★★★ Hotel

Nether Abbey Hotel
20 Dirleton Avenue,
North Berwick, EH39 4BQ
Tel: 01620 892802
★★★ Small Hotel

Borthwick Castle Hotel
North Middleton,
Gorebridge, Midlothian,
EH23 4QY
Tel: 01875 820514
★★★ Small Hotel

Braidwood Farm
Penicuik, Midlothian,
EH26 9LP
Tel: 01968 679959
★★★ Bed & Breakfast

Peggyslea Farm
Nine Mile Burn, Penicuik,
Midlothian, EH26 9LX
Tel: 01968 660930/
07740288662
★★★★ Guest House

Patieshill Farm
Carlops,by Penicuik,
Midlothian, EH26 9ND
Tel: 01968 660551
★★★ Farmhouse

Dundas Castle
South Queensferry, Edinburgh,
EH30 9SP
Tel: 0131 3192039
★★★★★ Exclusive Use Venue

Edinburgh South Queensferry Premier Inn
Queens Crossing, Builyeon
Road, South Queensferry,
Edinburgh, EH30 9YJ
Tel: 08701 977
Passed Budget Hotel

Priory Lodge
8 The Loan,
South Queensferry,
West Lothian
Tel: 0131 331 4345
★★★★ Guest House

Rosebank Guest House
161 High Street, Tranent,
East Lothian, EH33 1LP
Tel: 01875 610967
★★★ Guest House

Macdonald Houstoun House Hotel
Uphall, West Lothian,
EH52 6JS
Tel: 01506 853831
★★★ Hotel

Limefield House
West Calder, West Lothian,
EH55 8QL
Tel: 01506 871237
★★★ Guest Accommodation

Best Western Hilcroft Hotel
East Main Street, Whitburn,
West Lothian, EH47 0JU
Tel: 01501 740818
★★★ Hotel

GREATER GLASGOW AND CLYDE VALLEY

GREATER GLASGOW AND CLYDE VALLEY

Abington

Abington Hotel
Carlisle Road, Abington,
Lanarkshire, ML12 6SD
Tel: 01864 502467
★★★ Hotel

Airdrie

Easter Glentore Farm
Slamannan Road, Greengairs,
Airdrie, Lanarkshire, ML6 7TJ
Tel: 01236 830243
★★★★ Farmhouse

Knight's Rest
150 Clark Street, Airdrie,
Lanarkshire, ML6 6DZ
Tel: 01236 606193
★★★ Guest House

Barrhead, Glasgow

Dalmeny Park Hotel
Lochlibo Road, Barrhead,
Renfrewshire, G78 1LG
Tel: 0141 881 9211
★★★★ Small Hotel

Bellshill

Glasgow Bellsill Premier Inn
Bellzielhill Farm, New
Edinburgh Road, Bellshill,
Glasgow, Lanarkshire, ML4 3HH
Tel: 08701 977106
Passed Budget Hotel

Biggar

Cornhill House
Cornhill Road, Coulter, Biggar,
Lanarkshire, ML12 6QE
Tel: 01899 220001
★★★ Country House Hotel

Shieldhill Hotel
Quothquan, Biggar,
Lanarkshire, ML12 6NA
Tel: 01899 220035
★★★★ Country House Hotel

Bishopton

Mar Hall
Mar Estate, Bishopton,
Renfrewshire, PA7 5NW
Tel: 0141 812 9999
★★★★★ Hotel

Bridge of Weir

The Sycamores
20 Kilmacolm Road,
Bridge of Weir, Renfrewshire,
PA11 3PU
Tel: 01505 613137
Awaiting Inspection

Calderbank, By Airdrie

Calder Guest House
13 Main Street, Calderbank,
by Airdrie, Lanarkshire,
ML6 9SG
Tel: 01236 769077
★★★ Guest House

Cambuslang, Glasgow

Glasgow Cambuslang Premier Inn
Orion Way,
Cambuslang Investment Park,
off London Road, Glasgow,
G32 8EY, G32 8EY
Tel: 08701 977
Passed Budget Hotel

Chryston, by Glasgow

Crowwood House Hotel
Cumbernauld Road, Muirhead,
Glasgow, G69 9BJ
Tel: 0141 779 3861
★★★ Hotel

by Coatbridge

Auchenlea
153 Langmuir Road,
Bargeddie, Lanarkshire,
G69 7RT
Tel: 0141 771 6870
★★★ Guest House

Coatbridge

Georgian Hotel
26 Lefroy Street, Coatbridge,
Lanarkshire, ML5 1LZ
Tel: 01236 421888
★★ Small Hotel

Cumbernauld

Glasgow Cumbernauld Premier Inn
4 South Muirhead Road,
Cumbernauld, Glasgow,
G67 1AX
Tel: 08701 977108
Passed Budget Hotel

Westerwood Hotel
1 St Andrews Drive,
Cumbernauld,
North Lanarkshire, G68 0EW
Tel: 01236 457171
★★★ Hotel

East Kilbride

Crutherland House Hotel
Strathaven Road, East
Kilbride, Lanarkshire, G75 0QJ
Tel: 01355 577000
★★★★ Hotel

Glasgow East Kilbride Central Premier Inn
Crooked Lum, Brunel Way,
The Murray, East Kilbride,
Glasgow, G75 0JY
Tel: 08701 977110
Passed Budget Hotel

Glasgow East Kilbride Premier Inn
Kingway East, Meadow Place,
Nerston, East Kildbride,
G74 3AW
Tel: 08708 506324
Passed Budget Hotel

Glasgow East Kilbride Premier Inn
Eaglesham Road,
East Kilbride, Glasgow,
G75 8LW
Tel: 0870 9906542
Passed Budget Hotel

The Bruce Hotel
35 Cornwall Street,
East Kilbride, G74 1AF
Tel: 01355 229771
★★★ Hotel

Torrance Hotel
135 Main Street, East Kilbride,
Lanarkshire, G74 4LN
Tel: 013552 25241
★★ Small Hotel

Erskine

Erskine Bridge Hotel
Erskine, Renfrewshire,
PA8 6AN
Tel: 0141 812 0123
★★★ Hotel

Giffnock, Glasgow

Redhurst Hotel Glasgow
27 Eastwoodmains Road,
Giffnock, Glasgow, G46 6QE
Tel: 0141 638
★★ Small Hotel

Glasgow

Acorn Hotel
140 Elderslie Street, Glasgow,
G3 7AW
Tel: 0141 3326556
Awaiting Inspection

Adelaides
209 Bath Street, Glasgow,
G2 4HZ
Tel: 0141 248 4970
★★ Guest House

Albion Hotel
405 North Woodside Road,
Glasgow, G20 6NN
Tel: 0141 339 8620
★★★ Metro Hotel

Alison Guest House
26 Circus Drive, Glasgow,
G31 2JH
Tel: 0141 556 1431
★★ Guest House

Amadeus Guest House
411 North Woodside Road,
Glasgow, G20 6NN
Tel: 0141 3398257
★★ Guest House

Ambassador Hotel
7 Kelvin Drive, Glasgow,
G20 8QG
Tel: 0141 946 1018
★★★ Metro Hotel

Argyll Hotel
973 Sauchiehall Street,
Glasgow, G3 7TQ
Tel: 0141 337 3313
★★★ Hotel

Bearsden Guest House
6 New Kirk Road, Bearsden,
Glasgow, G61 3SL
Tel: 0141 9422424
Awaiting Inspection

Belgrave Guest House
2 Belgrave Terrace,
Hillhead, Glasgow, G12 8JD
Tel: 0141 337 1850
★★ Guest House

Glasgow continued

Best Western Glasgow City Hotel
25/27 Elmbank Street, Glasgow, G2 4PB
Tel: 0141 227 2772
★★★ Metro Hotel

Botanic Hotel
1 Alfred Terrace, Glasgow, G12 8RF
Tel: 01413 377007
★★★ Guest House

Bothwell Bridge Hotel
89 Main Street, Bothwell, Glasgow, G71 8EU
Tel: 01698 852246
★★★ Hotel

Buchanan Hotel
185 Buchanan Street, Glasgow, G1 2JY
Tel: 0141 332 7284
★ Hotel

Burnside Hotel
East Kilbride Road, Rutherglen, Glasgow, G73 5EA
Tel: 0141 634 1276
★★ Small Hotel

Busby Hotel
Field Road, Clarkston, Glasgow, G76 8RX
Tel: 0141 6442661/ 07717204903
★★ Hotel

Caledonian Court
Dobbies Loan, Glasgow, G4 0JF
Tel: 0141 3313980
Awaiting Inspection

Campanile Hotel Glasgow
Tunnel Street, Glasgow, G3 8HL
Tel: 0141 287 7700
★★★ Hotel

Carlton George Hotel
44 West George Street, Glasgow, G2 1DH
Tel: 0141 353 6373
★★★★ Hotel

City Inn Glasgow
Finnieston Quay, Glasgow, G3 8HN
★★★ Hotel

Clifton Hotel
27 Buckingham Terrace, Glasgow, G12 8ED
Tel: 0141 3348080
★★ Guest House

Craigpark Guest House
33 Circus Drive, Glasgow, G31 2JG
Tel: 0141 554 4160
★★ Guest House

Crowne Plaza Hotel
Congress Road, Glasgow, G3 8QT
Tel: 0870 443 4691
★★★★ Hotel

Devoncove Hotel
931 Sauchiehall Street, Glasgow, G3 7TQ
Tel: 0141 334 4000
★★ Hotel

Euro Hostels - Glasgow's Only City Centre Hostel.
318 Clyde Street, Glasgow, G1 4NR
Tel: 0141 222 2828
★★★ Hostel

Ewington Hotel
32 Balmoral Terrace, 132 Queen's Drive, Glasgow, G42 8QW
Tel: 0141 423 1152
Hotel

Express by Holiday Inn
Theatreland, 165 West Nile Street, Glasgow, Lanarkshire, G1 2RL
Tel: 0141 331 6800
★★★ Hotel

Express by Holiday Inn Glasgow
122 Stockwell Street, Glasgow, G1 4LT
Tel: 0141 548 5000
★★★ Hotel

Garfield House Hotel
Cumbernauld Road, Stepps, Glasgow, Lanarkshire, G33 6HW
Tel: 0141 779 2111
★★★ Hotel

Glasgow Bearsden Premier Inn
Milngavie Road, Glasgow, G61 3TA
Tel: 0870 9906532
Passed Budget Hotel

Glasgow City Centre George Square Premier Inn
Slice, 187 George Street, Glasgow, G1 1YU
Tel: 0870 2383320
Passed Budget Hotel

Glasgow City Centre Premier Inn (Argyle Street)
377 Argyle Street, Glasgow, G2 4PP, G2 4PP
Tel: 0870 9906312
Passed Budget Hotel

Glasgow City Centre (Charing Cross) Premier Inn
10 Elmbank Gardens, Glasgow, G2 4PP
Tel: 0870 9906312
Passed Budget Hotel

Glasgow Hilton
1 William Street, Glasgow, G3 8HT
Tel: 0141 204 5555
★★★★★ Hotel

Glasgow Marriott
500 Argyle Street, Glasgow, G3 8RR
Tel: 0141 226 5577
★★★★ Hotel

Glasgow North East Stepps Premier Inn
Buchanan Gate, Crowood Roundabout, Cumbernauld Road, Stepps, Glasgow, G33 6HT
Tel: 08701 977111
Passed Budget Hotel

Glasgow Pond Hotel
Great Western Road, Glasgow, G12 0XP
Tel: 0141 334 8161
★★★ Hotel

Hampton Court Hotel
230 Renfrew Street, Glasgow, G3 6TX
Tel: 0141 332 6623
★★ Guest House

Heritage Hotel
4-5 Alfred Terrace, Glasgow, Strathclyde, G12 8RF
Tel: 0141 339 6955
★★★ Guest House

Hilton Glasgow Grosvenor
Grosvenor Terrace, Glasgow, G12 0TA
Tel: 0141 339 8811
★★★★ Hotel

Hilton Strathclyde
Pheonix Crescent, Bellshill, North Lanarkshire, ML4 3JQ
Tel: 01698 395500
★★★★ Hotel

Holiday Inn
161 West Nile Street, Glasgow, G1 2RL
Tel: 0141 352 8300
★★★★ Hotel

Hotel Du Vin at One Devonshire Gardens
1 Devonshire Gardens, Glasgow, Lanarkshire, G12 0UX
Tel: 0141 339 2001
★★★★★ Townhouse Hotel

Ibis Hotel Glasgow
220 West Regent Street, Glasgow, G2 4DQ
Tel: 0141 225 6000
★★ Hotel

Jurys Inn Glasgow
Jamaica Street, Glasgow, G1 4QE
Tel: 0141 314 4800
★★★ Hotel

Kelvingrove Hotel
944 Sauchiehall Street, Glasgow, G3 7TH
Tel: 0141 339 5011
★★★ Guest House

Kelvin Hotel
15 Buckingham Terrace, Glasgow, G12 8EB
Tel: 0141 339 7143
★★ Guest House

Kings Park Hotel
250 Mill Street, Rutherglen, Glasgow, South Lanarkshire, G73 2LX
Tel: 0141 647 5491
Awaiting Inspection

Lomond Hotel
6 Buckingham Terrace, Glasgow, G12 8EB
Tel: 0141 339 2339
★★ Guest House

The Malmaison
278 West George Street, Glasgow, G2 4LL
Tel: 0141 5721000
★★★★ Hotel

Manor Park Hotel
28 Balshagray Drive, Glasgow, G11 7DD
Tel: 0141 339 2143
★★★ Guest House

Marks Hotel
110 Bath Street, Glasgow, G2 2EN
Tel: 0141 353 0800
Awaiting Inspection

McLays Guest House
268 Renfrew Street, Glasgow, G3 6TT
Tel: 0141 332 4796
★ Guest House

Menzies Glasgow
27 Washington Street, Glasgow, G3 8AZ
Tel: 0141 2222929
★★★★ Hotel

Newton House Hotel
248-252 Bath Street, Glasgow, G2 4JW
Tel: 0141 3321666
★★★ Guest House

Novotel Glasgow Centre
181 Pitt Street, Glasgow, G2 4DT
Tel: 0141 222 2775
★★★ Hotel

Park Inn, Glasgow City Centre
2 Port Dundas Place, Glasgow, G2 3LB
Tel: 0141 333 1500
★★★★ Hotel

Quality Hotel Central
99 Gordon Street, Glasgow, G1 3SF
Tel: 0141 2219680
★★ Hotel

Radisson SAS Hotel Glasgow
301 Argyle Street, Glasgow, G2 8DL
Tel: 0141 204 3333
★★★★★ Hotel

The Sandyford Hotel
904 Sauchiehall Street, Glasgow, G3 7TF
Tel: 0141 334 0000
★★ Lodge

Seton Guest House
6 Seton Terrace, Dennistoun, Glasgow, G31 2HU
Tel: 0141 556 7654
★★ Guest House

Sherbrooke Castle Hotel
11 Sherbrooke Avenue, Glasgow, G41 4PG
Tel: 0141 427 4227
★★★ Hotel

Smiths Hotel
3 David Donnelly Place, Kirkintilloch, Glasgow, G66 1DD
Tel: 0141 775 0398
★★★ Hotel

Swallow Hotel
517 Paisley Road West, Glasgow, G51 1RW
Tel: 0141 427 3146
Awaiting Inspection

The Alamo Guest House Ltd
46 Gray Street, Glasgow, G3 7SE
Tel: 0141 339 2395
★★★ Guest House

The Arthouse Glasgow Ltd
129 Bath Street, Glasgow, G2 2SZ
Tel: 0141 2216789
★★★★ Hotel

The Belhaven Hotel
15 Belhaven Terrace, Glasgow, G12 0TG
Tel: 0141 339 3222
★★★ Guest House

The Kirklee
11 Kensington Gate, Glasgow, G12 9LG
Tel: 0141 334 5555
★★★ Guest House

The Millennium Glasgow Hotel
George Square, Glasgow, G2 1DS
Tel: 0141 332 6711
★★★★ Hotel

The Ramada Glasgow City
201 Ingram Street, Glasgow, G1 1DQ
Tel: 0141 248 4401
Hotel

The Town House
4 Hughenden Terrace, Glasgow, G12 9XR
Tel: 0141 3570862
★★★ Guest House

Thistle Glasgow
36 Cambridge Street, Glasgow, G2 3HN
Tel: 0141 332 3311
★★★★ Hotel

The Townhouse Hotel
21 Royal Crescent, Glasgow, G3 7SL
Tel: 0141 332 9009
★★ Lodge

Tulip Inn Glasgow
80 Ballater Street, Glasgow, G5 0TW
Tel: 0141 429 4233
★★★ Hotel

Willow Hotel
228 Renfrew Street, Glasgow, G3 6TX
Tel: 0141 332 2332
★★ Guest House

nr Glasgow

Uplawmoor Hotel
Neilston Road, Uplawmoor, Glasgow, G78 4AF
Tel: 01505 850565
★★★ Small Hotel

Glasgow Airport

Holiday Inn Glasgow Airport
Abbotsinch, Paisley, Glasgow, Renfrewshire, PA3 2TR
Tel: 0870 4009031
★★★ Hotel

Gourock

Ramada Jarvis Gourock
Cloch Road, Gourock, Renfrewshire, PA15 1AR
Tel: 01475 634671
Hotel

Spinnaker Hotel
121 Albert Road, Gourock, Renfrewshire, PA19 1BU
Tel: 01475 633107
★★ Small Hotel

Greenock

Express by Holiday Inn
Cartsburn, Greenock, PA15 4RT
Tel: 01475 786666
★★★ Hotel

Greenock Premier Inn
Garvel Point, James Watt Way, Greenock, Renfrewshire, PA15 2AJ
Tel: 08701 977
Passed Budget Hotel

Tontine Hotel
6 Ardgowan Square, Greenock, Renfrewshire, PA16 8NG
Tel: 01475 723316
★★★ Hotel

Hamilton

Avonbridge Hotel
Carlisle Road, Hamilton, Lanarkshire, ML3 7DG
Tel: 01698 420525
★★★ Hotel

Clydesdale Hotel
12 Clydesdale Street, Hamilton, Lanarkshire, ML3 0DP
Tel: 01698 891897
★★★ Small Hotel

Glasgow Hamilton Premier Inn
Hamilton Motorway Service(M74 N), Hamilton, Lanarkshire, ML3 6JW
Tel: 08701 977124
Passed Budget Hotel

The Villa Hotel
49/51 Burnbank Road, Hamilton, Lanarkshire, ML3 9AQ
Tel: 01698 891777
★★★ Small Hotel

Harthill, by Shotts

Blairmains Guest House
Harthill, Shotts, Lanarkshire, ML7 5TJ
Tel: 01501 751278
★★ Guest House

Howwood

Bowfield Hotel & Country Club
Howwood, Renfrewshire, PA9 1DZ
Tel: 01505 705225
★★★ Hotel

Johnstone

Lynnhurst Hotel
Park Road, Johnstone, Renfrewshire, PA5 8LS
Tel: 01505 324331
★★★ Hotel

Kilsyth

Allanfauld Farm
Kilsyth, North Lanarkshire, G65 9DF
Tel: 01236 822155
★★★ Farmhouse

Twechar Farm B&B
Twechar Farm, Kilsyth, East Dunbartonshire, G65 9LH
Tel: 01236 823216
★★★ Farmhouse

Clarkston Farm
Kirkfieldbank, Lanark,
ML11 9UN
Tel: 01555 663751
★★★ Farmhouse

Cartland Bridge Country House Hotel
Glasgow Road, Lanark,
ML11 9UE
Tel: 01555 664426
★★★ Country House Hotel

Corehouse Farm
Lanark, ML11 9TQ
Tel: 01555 661377
★★★ Farmhouse

Glasgow Milngavie Premier Inn
West Highland Gate,
Main Street, Milngavie,
Glasgow, G62 6JJ
Tel: 08701 977112
Passed Budget Hotel

Kincaid House Hotel
Milton of Campsie, Glasgow,
GG6 8BZ
Tel: 0141 776 2226
★★★ Small Hotel

Dakota Hotel
Eurocentral Business Park,
Motherwell,
North Lanarkshire, ML1 4UD
Tel: 01698 835444
★★★ Hotel

Moorings Hotel
114 Hamilton Road,
Motherwell, Lanarkshire,
ML1 3DG
Tel: 01698 258131
★★★ Hotel

The Alona Hotel
Strathclyde Country Park,
Motherwell,
North Lanarkshire, ML1 3RT
Tel: 0870 112 3888
★★★★ Hotel

Glasgow Motherwell Premier Inn
Edinburgh Road, Newhouse,
by Motherwell, Lanarkshire,
ML1 5SY
Tel: 08701 977164
Passed Budget Hotel

New Lanark Mill Hotel
New Lanark, Lanarkshire,
ML11 9DB
Tel: 01555 667200
★★★ Hotel

Ardgowan Town House Hotel
94 Renfrew Road, Paisley,
Renfrewshire, PA3 4BJ
Tel: 0141 889 4763
★★★ Guest House

Ashtree House
9 Orr Square, Paisley,
Renfrewshire, PA1 2DL
Tel: 0141 8486411
★★★★ Guest House

Dryesdale Guest House
37 Inchinnan Road, Paisley,
Renfrewshire, PA3 2PR
Tel: 0141 889 7178
★★ Guest House

Express by Holiday Inn Glasgow Airport
St Andrews Drive, Paisley,
PA3 2TJ
Tel: 0141 842 1100
★★★ Hotel

Glasgow Airport Premier Inn
Whitecart Road, Glasgow
Airport, Paisley, Renfrewshire,
PA3 2TH
Tel: 0870 2383321
Passed Budget Hotel

Glasgow Paisley Premier Inn
Phoenix Retail Park, Paisley,
Glasgow, Renfrewshire,
PA1 2BH
Tel: 08701 97713
Passed Budget Hotel

Ramada Glasgow Airport
Marchburn Drive, Abbotsinch,
Paisley, Renfrewshire,
PA3 2SJ
Tel: 0141 840 2200
★★★ Hotel

Watermill Hotel
1 Lonend, Paisley,
Renfrewshire, PA1 1SR
Tel: 0141 889 3201
★★ Hotel

Glynhill Hotel
169 Paisley Road, Renfrew,
Near Glasgow Airport,
Renfrewshire, PA4 8XB
Tel: 0141 886 5555
★★★ Hotel

The Normandy Hotel
Inchinnan Road, Renfrew,
Renfrewshire, PA4 5EJ
Tel: 0141 886 4100
★★★ Hotel

Popinjay Hotel
Lanark Road, Rosebank,
Lanarkshire, ML8 5QB
Tel: 01555 860441
★★★ Hotel

Strathaven Hotel
Hamilton Road, Strathaven,
Lanarkshire, ML10 6SZ
Tel: 01357 521778
★★★ Hotel

Glasgow East Premier Inn
Black Bear, Glasgow Zoo,
601 Hamilton Road,
Uddingston, Glasgow,
G75 0JY
Tel: 08701 977109
Passed Budget Hotel

Herdshill Guest House
224 Main Street, Bogside,
Wishaw, Lanarkshire,
ML2 8HA
Tel: 01698 381579
★★★ Guest House

WEST HIGHLANDS AND ISLANDS, LOCH LOMOND, STIRLING AND TROSSACHS

WEST HIGHLANDS AND ISLANDS

Ardrishaig, by Lochgilphead

Allt-Na-Craig House
Tarbert Road, Ardrishaig,
Argyll, PA30 8EP
Tel: 01546 603245
★★★★ Guest House

Dalriada
Glenburn Road, Ardrishaig,
Argyll, PA30 8EU
Tel: 01546 603345
Awaiting Inspection

Arduaine

Loch Melfort Hotel
Arduaine, Argyll, PA34 4XG
Tel: 01852 200233
★★★★ Hotel

Bellochantuy, by Campbeltown

Hunting Lodge Hotel
Bellochantuy, Kintyre, Argyll,
PA28 6QE
Tel: 01583 421323
★★ Small Hotel

Cairndow

Cairndow Stagecoach Inn
Cairndow, Argyll, PA26 8BN
Tel: 01499 600286
★★ Inn

Campbeltown

Ardshiel Hotel
Kilkerran Road, Campbeltown,
Argyll, PA28 6JL
Tel: 01586 552133
★★ Small Hotel

Craigard House
Low Askomil, Campbeltown,
Argyll, PA28 6EP
Tel: 01586 554242
★★★ Small Hotel

Dellwood Hotel
Drumore, Campbeltown,
Argyll, PA28 6HD
Tel: 01586 552465
★★ Small Hotel

Westbank Guest House
Dell Road, Campbeltown,
Argyll, PA28 6JG
Tel: 01586 553660
★★★ Guest House

Carradale

Carradale Hotel
Carradale, Nr Campbeltown,
Argyll, PA28 6RY
Tel: 01583 431223
★★★ Small Hotel

Dunvalanree
Portrigh Bay, Carradale,
Argyll, PA28 6SE
Tel: 01583 431226
★★★★ Guest House

Kiloran Guest House
Carradale, Argyll, PA28 6QG
Tel: 01583 431795
★★ Guest House

Clachan, by Tarbert

Balinakill Country House Hotel
Clachan, by Tarbert, Argyll,
PA29 6XL
Tel: 01880 740206
★★★ Country House Hotel

Colintraive

Colintraive Hotel
Colintraive, Argyll, PA22 3AS
Tel: 01700 841207
★★★ Small Hotel

Isle of Coll

Coll Hotel
Arinagour, Isle of Coll,
Argyll, PA78 6SZ
Tel: 01879 230334
★★★ Inn

Isle of Colonsay

The Colonsay
Isle of Colonsay, Argyll,
PA61 7YP
Tel: 01951 200316
★★★ Small Hotel

Connel

Greenacre
Connel, by Oban, Argyll,
PA31 1PJ
Tel: 01631 710756
★★★ Guest House

Ronebhal Guest House
Connel, by Oban, Argyll,
PA37 1PJ
Tel: 01631 710310
★★★★ Guest House

Crinan, by Lochgilphead

Crinan Hotel
Crinan, Argyll, PA31 8SR
Tel: 01546 830261
★★★★ Small Hotel

Dalmally

Dalmally Hotel
Dalmally, Argyll, PA33 1AY
Tel: 01838 200444
★★★ Hotel

Glenorchy Lodge Hotel
Dalmally, Argyll, PA33 1AA
Tel: 018382 00312
★★★ Small Hotel

Dunoon

Abbot's Brae Hotel
West Bay, Dunoon, Argyll,
PA23 7QJ
Tel: 01369 705021
★★★★ Small Hotel

Ardtully Guest House
297 Marine Parade,
Hunters Quay, Dunoon, Argyll,
PA23 3HN
Tel: 01369 702478
★★★ Guest House

Argyll Hotel
Argyll Street, Dunoon, Argyll,
PA23 7NE
Tel: 01369 702059
★ Hotel

Bay House
West Bay Promenade,
Dunoon, Argyll, PA23 7HU
Tel: 01369 704832/702348
★★★ Guest House

Craigen Hotel
85 Argyll Street, Dunoon,
PA23 7DH
Tel: 01369 702307
★★ Guest House

Craigieburn
Alexandra Parade, East Bay,
Dunoon, Argyll, PA23 8AN
Tel: 01369 702048
★★ Guest House

Dhailling Lodge
155 Alexandra Parade,
Dunoon, Argyll, PA23 8AW
Tel: 01369 701253
★★★★ Guest House

Eileagan
47 Kilbride Road, Dunoon,
Argyll, PA23 7LN
Tel: 01369 707047
Awaiting Inspection

Enmore Hotel
Marine Parade, Kirn,
Dunoon, Argyll, PA23 8HH
Tel: 01369 702230
★★★★ Small Hotel

Esplanade Hotel
West Bay, Dunoon, Argyll,
PA23 7HU
Tel: 01369 704070
★★★ Hotel

Hunters Quay Hotel
Marine Parade, Dunoon,
Argyll, PA23 8HJ
Tel: 01369 707070
★★★★ Small Hotel

Mayfair Hotel
7 Clyde Street, Kirn,
Dunoon, Argyll, PA23 8DX
Tel: 01369 703803
★★★ Guest House

Milton Tower Hotel
West Bay, Dunoon, Argyll,
PA23 7LD
Tel: 01369 705785
★★★ Guest House

Park Hotel
3 Glenmorag Avenue,
Dunoon, Argyll, PA23 7LG
Tel: 01369 702383
★★★ Hotel

Royal Marine Hotel
Hunter's Quay, Dunoon, Argyll,
PA23 8HJ
Tel: 01369 705810
★★★ Hotel

Sebright
41A Alexandra Parade,
Dunoon, Argyll, PA23 8AF
Tel: 01369 702099
★★ Guest House

St Ives Hotel
West Bay, Dunoon, Argyll,
PA23 7HU
Tel: 01369 702400/704825
★★★ Small Hotel

Dunoon continued

The Cedars
51 Alexandra Parade,
East Bay, Dunoon, Argyll,
PA23 8AF
Tel: 01369 702425
★★★★ Guest House

The Watermill
Glendaruel Colintraive,
Dunoon, Argyll, PA22 3AB
Tel: 01369 820203
Awaiting Inspection

Undercliff Bed and Breakfast
275 Marine Parade,
Hunters Quay, Dunoon, Argyll,
PA23 8HN
Tel: 01369 704688
★★★ Guest House

West End Hotel
54 Victoria Parade, Dunoon,
Argyll, PA23 7HU
Tel: 01369 702907
★★ Small Hotel

Stewart Hotel
Glen Duror, Appin, Argyll,
PA38 4BW
Tel: 01631 740268
★★ Hotel

Ford House
Ford, By Lochgilphead, Argyll,
PA31 8RH
Tel: 01546 810273
★★★ Guest House

Gigha Hotel
Isle of Gigha, Argyll, PA41 7AA
Tel: 01583 505254
★★★ Small Hotel

The Glendaruel Hotel
Clachan of Glendaruel,
Argyll, PA22 3AA
Tel: 01369 820274
Awaiting Inspection

The Osborne Hotel
44 Shore Road, Innellan,
By Dunoon, Argyll, PA23 7TJ
Tel: 01369 830445
★★ Small Hotel

Creag Dhubh
Inveraray, Argyll, PA32 8XT
Tel: 01499 302430
★★★★ Guest House

Killean Farm House
Inveraray, Argyll, PA32 8XT
Tel: 01499 302474
★★★ Guest House

Loch Fyne Hotel
Newtown, Inveraray, Argyll,
PA32 8XT
Tel: 01499 302148
★★★ Hotel

St Columba Hotel
Isle of Iona, Argyll, PA76 6SL
Tel: 01681 700304
★★★ Hotel

St Blane's Hotel
Kilchattan Bay, Isle of Bute,
PA20 9NW
Tel: 01700 831224
★★ Small Hotel

The Ardyne
(Hotel and Restaurant)
38 Mountstuart Road,
Rothesay, Isle of Bute,
PA20 9EB
Tel: 01700 502052
★★★ Guest House

Argyle House
3 Argyle Place, Rothesay,
Isle of Bute, PA20 0AZ
Tel: 01700 502424
★★ Guest House

Bayview Hotel
21-22 Mountstuart Road,
Rothesay, Isle of Bute,
PA20 9EB
Tel: 01700 505411
★★★★ Guest House

Bute House Hotel
4 West Princess Street,
Rothesay, Isle of Bute,
PA20 9AF
Tel: 01700 502481
★★★ Guest House

Glenburn Hotel
Mount Stewart Road,
Rothesay, Isle of Bute,
PA20 9JB
Tel: 01700 502500
★★★ Hotel

Glendale Guest House
20 Battery Place, Rothesay,
Isle of Bute, PA20 9DU
Tel: 01700 502329
★★★★ Guest House

The Regent Hotel
23 Battery Place, Rothesay,
Isle of Bute, PA20 9DU
Tel: 01700 502006
★★★ Guest House

The Commodore
12 Battery Place, Rothesay,
Isle of Bute, PA20 9DP
Tel: 01700 502178
Awaiting Inspection

The Victoria Hotel
55 Victoria Street, Rothesay,
Isle of Bute, PA20 0AP
Tel: 01700 500016
★★★ Small Hotel

Kilmeny
Ballygrant, Isle of Islay,
PA45 7QW
Tel: 01496 840668
★★★★★ Guest House

The Harbour Inn and Restaurant
Bowmore, Isle of Islay,
Argyll, PA43 7JR
Tel: 01496 810330
★★★★ Restaurant with Rooms

Lambeth Guest House
Jamieson Street, Bowmore,
Isle of Islay, Argyll, PA43 7HL
Tel: 01496 810597
★★ Guest House

Lochside Hotel
Shore Street, Bowmore,
Isle of Islay, PA43 7LB
Tel: 01496 810244
★★★ Small Hotel

Bridgend Hotel
Bridgend, Isle of Islay,
PA44 7PJ
Tel: 01496 810212
★★★ Small Hotel

Port Charlotte Hotel
Main Street, Port Charlotte,
Isle of Islay, Argyll, PA48 7TU
Tel: 01496 850360
★★★★ Small Hotel

Glenegedale House
Glenegedale, Port Ellen,
Isle of Islay, Argyll, PA42 7AS
Tel: 01496 300400
★★★★★ Guest House

Machrie Hotel
Port Ellen, Islay, Argyll,
PA42 7AN
Tel: 01496 302310
★★★ Small Hotel

Arle Lodge Ltd
Arle Lodge, Aros, Isle of Mull,
PA72 6JS
Tel: 01680 300299
★★ Guest House

Newcrofts
Bunessan, Isle of Mull, Argyll,
PA67 6DS
Tel: 01681 700471
★★★ Farmhouse

Isle of Mull Hotel
Craignure, Isle of Mull, Argyll,
PA65 6BB
Tel: 08709 506267
★★★ Hotel

Pennygate Lodge
Craignure, Isle of Mull, Argyll,
PA65 6AY
Tel: 01680 812333
★★★ Guest House

by Dervaig

The Calgary Hotel
by Dervaig, Isle of Mull, Argyll, PA75 6QW
Tel: 01688 400256
★★★ Restaurant with Rooms

Dervaig

Druimnacroish
Dervaig, Isle of Mull, PA75 6QW
Tel: 01688 400274
★★★ Guest House

Fionnphort

Achaban House
Fionnphort, Isle of Mull, Argyll, PA66 6BL
Tel: 01681 700205
★★★ Guest House

Seaview
Fionnphort, Isle of Mull, PA66 6BL
Tel: 01681 700235
★★★ Guest House

Pennyghael

Pennyghael Hotel
Pennyghael, Isle of Mull, Argyll, PA70 6HB
Tel: 01681 704288
Awaiting Inspection

Salen, Aros

Ard Mhor House
Pier Road, Salen, Isle of Mull, PA72 6JL
Tel: 01680 300255
★★★ Guest House

Salen Hotel
Salen, Isle of Mull, Argyll, PA72 6JE
Tel: 01680 300324
★★ Small Hotel

Tiroran

Tiroran House
Tiroran, Isle of Mull, Argyll, PA69 6ES
Tel: 01681 705232
★★★★ Country House Hotel

Tobermory

Baliscate Guest House
Salen Road, Tobermory, Isle of Mull, Argyll, PA75 6QA
Tel: 01688 302048
★★★ Guest House

Carnaburg
55 Main Street, Tobermory, Isle of Mull, PA75 6NT
Tel: 01688 302479
★★ Guest House

Failte Guest House
Main Street, Tobermory, Isle of Mull, Argyll, PA75 6NU
Tel: 01688 302495
★★★ Guest House

Fairways Lodge
Erray Road, Tobermory, Isle of Mull, Argyll, PA75 6PS
Tel: 01688 302792
★★★★ Guest House

Highland Cottage
Breadalbane Street, Tobermory, Isle of Mull
Tel: 01688 302030
★★★★ Small Hotel

Killoran House
Dervaig, Isle of Mull, PA75 6QR
Tel: 01688 400362
Awaiting Inspection

Park Lodge Hotel
Western Road, Tobermory, Isle of Mull, Argyll, PA75 6PR
Tel: 01688 302430
★★ Small Hotel

Tobermory Hotel
53 Main Street, Tobermory, Isle of Mull, PA75 6NT
Tel: 01688 302091
★★★ Small Hotel

Uisken, by Bunessan

Ardachy House Hotel
Uisken, Bunessan, Isle of Mull, Argyll, PA67 6DS
Tel: 01681 700505
★★★ Small Hotel

Isle of Seil

Clachan Seil, by Oban

Willowburn Hotel
Clachan Seil, By Oban, Argyll, PA34 4TS
Tel: 01852 300276
★★ Small Hotel

Isle of Tiree

Gott Bay

Kirkapol Guest House
Gott Bay, Isle of Tiree, Argyll, PA77 6TW
Tel: 01879 220729
★★★ Guest House

Isle of Jura

Jura Hotel
Isle of Jura, Argyll, PA60 7XU
Tel: 01496 820243
★★ Small Hotel

Kilchrenan

Ardanaiseig Hotel
Kilchrenan, by Taynuilt, Argyll, PA35 1HE
Tel: 01866 833333
★★★★ Country House Hotel

Taychreggan Hotel
Kilchrenan,by Taynuilt, Argyll, PA35 1HQ
Tel: 01866 833211
★★★ Hotel

Kilfinan

Kilfinan Hotel
Kilfinan, Nr Tighnabruaich, Argyll, PA21 2EP
Tel: 01700 821201
★★★ Small Hotel

Kilkenzie, by Campbeltown

Dalnaspidal Guest House
Tangy, Kilkenzie, Argyll, PA28 6QD
Tel: 01586 820466
★★★★★ Guest House

Kilninver, by Oban

Knipoch Hotel
Knipoch, Argyll, PA34 4QT
Tel: 01852 316251
★★★★ Hotel

Ledaig, by Oban

Isle of Eriska Hotel
Benderloch, Argyll, PA37 1SD
Tel: 01631 720371
★★★★★ Country House Hotel

Lerags, by Oban

Foxholes Hotel
Cologin, Lerags, by Oban, Argyll, PA34 4SE
Tel: 01631 564982
★★★★ Guest House

Lochawe

Loch Awe Hotel
Loch Awe, Dalmally, Argyll, PA33 1AQ
Tel: 01838 200261
★★★ Hotel

Lochaweside

Loch Awe House
East Lochaweside, Near Inverary, Argyll, PA33 1BW
Tel: 01200 447507
Awaiting Inspection

by Lochgilphead

Cairnbaan Hotel
Cairnbaan, by Lochgilphead, Argyll, PA31 8SJ
Tel: 01546 603668
★★★ Small Hotel

Lochgilphead

The Stag Hotel
Argyll Street, Lochgilphead, Argyll, PA31 8NE
Awaiting Inspection

Lochgoilhead

Drimsynie House Hotel
Lochgoilhead, Argyll, PA24 8AD
Tel: 01301 703247
★★ Small Hotel

Lochgoilhead Hotel
Lochgoilhead, Argyll, PA24 8AA
Tel: 01301 703 247
★★ Small Hotel

The Lodge
Lochgoilhead, Argyll, PA24 8AE
Tel: 01301 703193
★★★★★ Exclusive Use Venue

North Connel

Lochnell Arms Hotel
North Connel, Argyll, PA37 1RP
Tel: 01631 710239
★★★ Inn

Alexandra Hotel
The Esplanade, Oban, Argyll, PA34 5AA
Tel: 01838 200444
★★★ Hotel

Alltavona
Corran Esplanade, Oban, Argyll, PA34 5AQ
Tel: 01631 565067
★★★★ Guest House

Arbour Guest House
Dunollie Road, Oban, Argyll, PA34 5PJ
Tel: 01631 564394
Awaiting Inspection

Ayres Guest House
3 Victoria Crescent, Corran Esplanade, Oban, Argyll, PA34 5JL
Tel: 01631 562 260
★★ Guest House

The Barriemore
Corran Esplanade, Oban, Argyll, PA34 5AQ
Tel: 01631 566356
★★★★ Guest House

Beech Grove Guest House
Croft Road, Oban, Argyll, PA34 5JL
Tel: 01631 66111
★★★★ Guest House

Columba Hotel
North Pier, Oban, Argyll, PA34 5QD
Tel: 01631 562183
★★ Hotel

Corriemar House
6 Corran Esplanade, Oban, Argyll, PA34 5AQ
Tel: 01631 562476
★★★★ Guest House

Dungallan Country House
Gallanach Road, Oban, Argyll, PA34 4PD
Tel: 01631 563799
★★★★★ Guest House

Dunheanish Guest House
Ardconnel Road, Oban, Argyll, PA34 5DW
Tel: 01631 566556
★★★ Guest House

Glenbervie Guest House
Dalriach Road, Oban, Argyll, PA34 5JD
Tel: 01631 564770
★★★★ Guest House

Glenburnie
Esplanade, Oban, Argyll, PA34 5AQ
Tel: 01631 562089
★★★★ Guest House

Glengorm
Dunollie Road, Oban, Argyll, PA34 5PH
Tel: 01631 564386
★★★ Guest House

Glenrigh Guest House
The Esplanade, Oban, Argyll, PA34 5AQ
Tel: 01631 562991
★★★★ Guest House

Glenroy Guest House
Rockfield Road, Oban, Argyll, PA34 5DQ
Tel: 01631 562 585
★★★ Guest House

Gramarvin Guest House
Breadalbane Street, Oban, Argyll, PA34 5PE
Tel: 01631 564622
★★★ Guest House

Great Western Hotel
Corran Esplanade, Oban, Argyll, PA34 5PP
Tel: 01631 563101
★★★ Hotel

Greencourt Guest House
Benvoullin Road, Oban, Argyll, PA34 5EF
Tel: 01631 563987
★★★★ Guest House

Heatherfield House
Albert Road, Oban, Argyll, PA34 5EY
Tel: 01631 562806
Awaiting Inspection

Herbridean Princess
South Pier, Oban
★★★★★ Cruise Ship

Kathmore Guest House
Soroba Road, Oban, Argyll, PA34 4JF
Tel: 01631 562104
★★★ Guest House

Kelvin Hotel
Shore Street, Oban, Argyll, PA34 4LQ
Tel: 01631 562150
★ Guest House

Kilchrenan House
Corran Esplanade, Oban, Argyll, PA34 5AQ
Tel: 01631 562663
★★★★ Guest House

Kings Knoll Hotel
Dunollie Road, Oban, PA34 5JH
Tel: 01631 562536
★★★ Small Hotel

Lagganbeg Guest House
Dunollie Road, Oban, PA34 5PH
Tel: 01631 563151
★★★ Guest House

The Manor House
Gallanoch Road, Oban, Argyll, PA34 4LS
Tel: 01631 562087
★★★★ Small Hotel

Maridon House
Dunuaran Road, Oban, Argyll, PA34 4NE
Tel: 01631 562670
★★★ Guest House

Oban Bay Hotel
Esplanade, Oban, Argyll, PA34 5AE
Tel: 0870 950 6273
★★★ Hotel

Roseneath Guest House
Dalriach Road, Oban, Argyll, PA34 5EQ
Tel: 01631 562929
★★★ Guest House

Royal Hotel
Argyll Square, Oban, Argyll, PA34 4BE
Tel: 01631 563021
★★★ Hotel

Sgeir Mhaol Guest House
Soroba Road, Oban, Argyll, PA34 4JF
Tel: 01631 562650
★★★ Guest House

St Anne's Guest House
Dunollie Road, Oban, Argyll, PA34 5PH
Tel: 01631 562743
★★★ Guest House

Strathnaver Guest House
Dunollie Road, Oban, Argyll, PA34 5JQ
Tel: 01631 63305
★★★ Guest House

Sutherland Hotel
Corran Esplanade, Oban, Argyll, PA34 5PN
Tel: 01631 562539
Awaiting Inspection

The Caledonian Hotel
Station Square, Oban, Argyll, PA34 5RT
Tel: 01631 563133
★★★★ Hotel

The Kimberley Hotel
Dalriach Road, Oban, Argyll, PA34 5EQ
Tel: 01631 571115
Awaiting Inspection

The Old Manse
Dalriach Road, Oban, Argyll, PA34 5JE
Tel: 01631 564886
★★★★ Guest House

The Town House
George Street, Oban, Argyll, PA34 5NX
Tel: 01631 562954
★★ Guest House

Thornlea
Laurel Road, Oban, Argyll, PA34 5EA
Tel: 01631 562792
Awaiting Inspection

Thornloe Guest House
Albert Road, Oban, Argyll, PA34 5JD
Tel: 01631 562879
★★★★ Guest House

Ulva Villa
Soroba Road, Oban, Argyll, PA34 4JF
Tel: 01631 563042
★★★ Guest House

Wellpark House
Esplanade, Oban, Argyll, PA34 5AQ
Tel: 01631 562948
★★★ Guest House

Ards House
Connel, Oban, Argyll, PA37 1PT
Tel: 01631 710255
★★★★ Guest House

by Oban continued

Braeside Guest House
Kilmore, by Oban, Argyll,
PA34 4QR
Tel: 01631 770243
★★★ Guest House

Falls of Lora Hotel
Connel Ferry, by Oban,
Argyll, PA37 1PB
Tel: 01631 710483
★★★ Hotel

Port Appin

The Airds Hotel
Port Appin, Appin, Argyll,
PA38 4DF
Tel: 01631 730236
★★★★ Small Hotel

Linnhe House
Port Appin, Appin, Argyll,
PA38 4DE
Tel: 01631 730245
Awaiting Inspection

The Pierhouse Hotel
Port Appin, Appin, Argyll,
PA38 4DE
Tel: 01631 730302
★★★ Small Hotel

St Catherines

Thistle House
St Catherines, Argyll,
PA25 8AZ
Tel: 01499 302209
★★★★ Guest House

Southend, by Campbeltown

Low Cattadale Farm
Southend, Campbeltown,
Argyll, PA28 6RN
Tel: 01586 830205
★★★ Farmhouse

Ormsary Farm
Southend, by Campbeltown,
Argyll, PA28 6RN
Tel: 01586 830665
★★★ Farmhouse

Strachur

The Creggans Inn
Strachur, Argyll, PA27 8BX
Tel: 01369 860279
★★★ Small Hotel

Strontian

Ben View Hotel
Strontian, Acharacle, Argyll,
PH36 4HY
Tel: 01967 402333
★★ Small Hotel

Heatherbank
Upper Scotstown, Strontian,
Argyll, PH36 4JB
Tel: 01967 402201
★★★★ Guest House

Kilcamb Lodge Hotel
Strontian, Argyll, PH36 4HY
Tel: 01967 402257
★★★★ Country House Hotel

Tighnabruaich

An Lochan
Shore Road, Tighnabruaich,
Argyll, PA21 2BE
Tel: 01700 811239
★★★★ Small Hotel

LOCH LOMOND AND THE TROSSACHS

Aberfoyle

Crannaig House
Trossachs Road, Aberfoyle,
Stirlingshire, FK8 3SR
Tel: 01877 382276
★★★ Guest House

Forest Hills Hotel
Kinlochard, By Aberfoyle,
Stirlingshire, FK8 3TL
Tel: 08701 942105
★★★★ Hotel

The Forth Inn
Main Street, Aberfoyle,
Perthshire, FK8 3UQ
Tel: 01877 382372
★★★ Inn

Inverard Lodge B&B
Lochard Road, Aberfoyle,
Stirlingshire, FK8 3TD
Tel: 01877 389113
Awaiting Inspection

Mrs A Jennings
The Bield, Trossachs Road,
Aberfoyle, Perthshire, FK8 3SX
Tel: 01877 382351
Awaiting Inspection

Rob Roy Hotel
Aberfoyle, Stirlingshire,
FK8 3UX
Tel: 01877 382245
★★ Hotel

Stoneypark
Lochard Road, Aberfoyle,
Stirling, FK8 3SZ
Tel: 01877 382208
Awaiting Inspection

Alexandria, Loch Lomond

De Vere Cameron House
Loch Lomond, Alexandria,
Dunbartonshire, G83 8QZ
Tel: 01389 755565
★★★★★ Hotel

Arden, Loch Lomond

Duck Bay Hotel & Marina
Loch Lomond, Arden,
by Alexandria,
Dunbartonshire, G83 8QZ
Tel: 01389 751234
★★★ Small Hotel

Polnaberoch
Arden, By Luss, Loch Lomond,
G83 8RQ
Tel: 01389 850615
Awaiting Inspection

Ardeonaig, by Killin

The Ardeonaig Hotel
South Loch Tay, Killin,
Perthshire, FK21 8SU
★★★ Small Hotel

Ardlui

Ardlui Hotel
Ardlui, Loch Lomond, Argyll,
G83 7EB
Tel: 01301 704269
★★★ Small Hotel

Arrochar

Claymore Hotel
Arrochar, Argyll & Bute,
G83 7BB
Tel: 01301 702238
★★ Hotel

Loch Long Hotel
Arrochar, Dunbartonshire,
G83 7AA
Tel: 01301 702434
★★★ Hotel

Village Inn
Main Street, Arrochar,
Dunbartonshire, G83 7AX
Tel: 01301 702279
★★★ Inn

Balloch

Gowanlea
Drymen Road, Balloch,
Dunbartonshire, G83 8HS
Tel: 01389 752456
Awaiting Inspection

Norwood Guest House
60 Balloch Road, Balloch,
Dunbartonshire, G83 8LE
Tel: 01389 750309
★★★ Guest House

Time Out
24 Balloch Road, Balloch,
Dunbartonshire, G83 8LE
Tel: 07957 436731
★★★ Guest House

Tullie Inn
Balloch Road, Balloch,
Dunbartonshire, G83 8SW
Tel: 01389 752052
★★★ Inn

Balquhidder

King's House Hotel
Balquhidder, Perthshire,
FK19 8NY
Tel: 0877 384646
★★ Small Hotel

Monachyle Mhor
Balquhidder, Lochearnhead,
Perthshire, FK19 8PQ
Tel: 0877 384622
★★★★ Small Hotel

Bridge of Orchy

Bridge of Orchy Hotel
Bridge of Orchy, Argyll,
PA36 4AD
Tel: 01838 400208
★★★★ Inn

Callander

Abbotsford Lodge Guest House
Stirling Road, Callander,
Perthshire, FK17 8DA
Tel: 0877 330066
★★★ Guest House

Annfield Guest House
18 North Church Street,
Callander, Perthshire,
Tel: 01877 330204
★★★★ Guest House

Arden House
Bracklinn Road, Callander,
Perthshire, FK17 8EQ
Tel: 01877 330235
★★★★ Guest House

Callander continued

Auchenlaich Farmhouse Guest House
Auchenlaich Farmhouse, Keltie Bridge, Callander, Perthshire, FK17 8LQ
Tel: 01877 331683
★★★★ Guest House

The Crags Hotel
101 Main Street, Callander, Perthshire, FK17 8BQ
Tel: 01877 330257
Awaiting Inspection

Dalgair House Hotel
115 Main Street, Callander, Perthshire, FK17 8BQ
Tel: 01877 330283
★★ Small Hotel

Dunmor House
Leny Road, Callander, FK17 8AL
Tel: 01877 330756
★★★★ Guest House

Lubnaig House
Leny Feus, Callander, Perthshire, FK17 8AS
Tel: 01877 330376
★★★★ Guest House

Poppies Hotel and Restaurant
Leny Road, Callander, Perthshire, FK17 8AL
Tel: 01877 330329
★★★ Small Hotel

Riverview Guest House
Leny Road, Callander, Perthshire, FK17 8AL
Tel: 01877 330635
★★★ Guest House

Roman Camp Hotel
Main Street, Callander, Perthshire, FK17 8BG
Tel: 01877 330003
★★★★ Small Hotel

Southfork Villa
25 Cross Street, Callander, Perthshire, FK17 8EA
Tel: 01877 330831
★★★★ Guest House

The Coppice
Leny Road, Callander, Perthshire, FK17 8AL
Tel: 01877 330188
Awaiting Inspection

The Knowe
Ancaster Road, Callander, Perthshire, FK17 8EL
Tel: 01877 330076
★★★★ Guest House

The Old Rectory Guest House
Leny Road, Callander, Perthshire, FK17 8AL
Tel: 01877 339215
★★★ Guest House

The Beardmore Hotel & Conference Centre
Beardmore Street, Clydebank, Greater Glasgow, G81 4SA
Tel: 0141 9516000
★★★★ Hotel

Knockderry Hotel
Shore Road, Cove, Helensburgh, G84 0NX
Tel: 01436 842283
★★★★ Country House Hotel

Ewich House
Strathfillan, Crianlarich, Perthshire, FK20 8RU
Tel: 01838 300300
★★★ Guest House

Glenardran
Crianlarich, Perthshire, FK20 8QS
Tel: 01838 300236
★★★ Guest House

Highland Hotel
Crianlarich, Perthshire, FK20 8RW
Tel: 01838 300272
★★★ Hotel

Inverardran House
A85, Crianlarich, Perthshire, FK20 8QS
Tel: 01838 300240
★★★ Guest House

Riverside Guest House
Tigh Na Struith, Crianlarich, Perthshire, FK20 8RU
Tel: 01838 300235
★★ Guest House

Suie Lodge Hotel
Glendochart, Crianlarich, Perthshire, FK20 8QT
Tel: 01567 820417
Awaiting Inspection

The Lodge House
Crianlarich, Perthshire, FK20 8RU
Tel: 01838 300276
Awaiting Inspection

West Highland Lodge
Crianlarich, Perthshire, FK20 8RU
Tel: 01838 300283
★★★ Guest House

Buchanan Arms Hotel & Leisure Club
Main Street, Drymen, Stirlingshire, G63 0BQ
Tel: 01360 660588
★★ Hotel

Kilmaronock House
Loch Lomond, Near Drymen, West Dumbartonshire, G83 8SB
Tel: 01360 660351
Awaiting Inspection

Winnock Hotel
The Square, Drymen, Stirlingshire, G63 0BL
★★★ Hotel

Dumbuck House Hotel
Glasgow Road, Dumbarton, Dunbartonshire, G82 1EG
Tel: 01389 734336
★★★ Hotel

Milton Inn
Dumbarton Road, Milton, Dunbartonshire, G82 2DT
Tel: 01389 761401
★★★ Inn

The Abbotsford Hotel
Stirling Road, Dumbarton, G82 2PJ
Tel: 01389 733304
★★★ Hotel

West Park Hotel
Great Western Road, Duntocher, Clydebank, G81 6DB
Tel: 01389 872333
★★ Hotel

Rock House
Garelochhead, Argyll & Bute, G84 0AN
Tel: 01436 810082
★★ Guest House

Gartmore House
Gartmore, Stirling, FK8 3SZ
Tel: 01877 382991
Guest House

Bellfield
199 East Clyde Street, Helensburgh, Dunbartonshire, G84 7AJ
Tel: 01436 673361
★★★ Bed & Breakfast

No 28 Campbell Street
28 Campbell Street, Helensburgh, Argyll & Bute, G84 8BQ
Tel: 01436 675372
Awaiting Inspection

Sinclair House
91/93 Sinclair Street, Helensburgh, Argyll & Bute, G84 8TR
Tel: 01436 676301
★★★★ Guest House

The Inverbeg Inn
Luss, Alexandria, Loch Lomand, Argyll, G83 8PD
Tel: 01436 860678
Awaiting Inspection

Inversnaid Hotel
Inversnaid, by Aberfoyle, Stirlingshire, FK8 3TU
Tel: 01877 386223
★★★ Hotel

Breadalbane House
Main Street, Killin, Perthshire, FK21 8UT
Tel: 01567 820134
★★★ Guest House

Craigbuie Guest House
Main Street, Killin, Perthshire, FK21 8UH
Tel: 01567 820439
★★★ Guest House

Killin continued

Drumfinn Country Guest House
Manse Road, Killin, Perthshire, FK21 8UY
Tel: 01567 820900
★★★ Guest House

Fairview House
Main Street, Killin, Perthshire, FK21 8UT
Tel: 01567 820667
★★★ Guest House

Invertay House
Main Road, Killin, Perthshire, FK21 8TN
Tel: 01567 820492
★★★ Guest House

Killin Hotel
Main Street, Killin, Perthshire, FK21 8TP
Tel: 01567 820296
★★ Hotel

Lochearnhead

Lochearnhead Hotel
Lochside, Lochearnhead, Perthshire, FK19 8PU
Tel: 01567 830229
★★ Small Hotel

Mansewood Country House
Lochearnhead, Stirlingshire, FK19 8NS
Tel: 01567 830213
★★★★ Guest House

Luss

Colquhoun Arms Hotel
Luss,by Alexandria, Dunbartonshire, G83 8NY
Tel: 01436 860282
★★ Small Hotel

Culag Lochside Guest House
Luss, Loch Lomond, G83 8PD
Tel: 01436 860248
★★★★ Guest House

The Lodge on Loch Lomond
Luss, Dunbartonshire, G83 8NT
Tel: 01436 860201
★★★★ Hotel

Rhu

Rosslea Hall Hotel
Ferry Road, Rhu, Dunbartonshire, G84 8NF
Tel: 01436 439955
★★★ Hotel

Rowardennan

Rowardennan Hotel
Rowardennan, By Drymen, Stirlingshire, G63 0AR
Tel: 01360 870273
★★★ Small Hotel

Strathyre

Creagan House Restaurant with Accommodation
Strathyre, Callander, Perthshire, FK18 8ND
Tel: 01877 384638
★★★★ Restaurant with Rooms

Tarbet, by Arrochar

Tarbet Hotel
Loch Lomond, Arrochar, Dunbartonshire, G83 7DE
Tel: 01301 702346
★★ Hotel

Trossachs, by Callander

Loch Achray Hotel
by Callander, Stirlingshire, FK17 8HZ
Tel: 01877 376229
★★★ Hotel

Tyndrum, by Crianlarich

Ben Doran Hotel
Tyndrum, Perthshire, FK20
Tel: 01838 400373
★★★ Hotel

Dalkell Cottages
Lower Station Road, Tyndrum, Perthshire, FK20 8RY
Tel: 01838 400285
★★★ Guest House

Glengarry House
Tyndrum, Perthshire, FK20 8RY
Tel: 01838 400224
★★★ Guest House

Invervey Hotel
Tyndrum, by Crianlarich, Perthshire, FK20 8RY
Tel: 01838 400219
★★ Small Hotel

Royal Hotel
Tyndrum,by Crianlarich, Perthshire, FK20 8RZ
Tel: 01838 400272
★★★ Hotel

STIRLING AND FORTH VALLEY

Airth, by Falkirk

Airth Castle Hotel & Spa Resort
Airth, By Falkirk, Stirlingshire, FK2 8JF
Tel: 01324 831411
★★★★ Country House Hotel

Bridgend Farm Country B&B
Moss Road, Near Airth, Falkirk, Stirlingshire, FK2 8RT
Tel: 01324 832060
Awaiting Inspection

Falkirk North Premier Inn
Kincardine Way, Bowtreees Roundabout, Hough of Airth, Falkirk, FK2 8PJ
Tel: 08701 977099
Passed Budget Hotel

Bo'ness

Carriden House
Carriden Brae, Bo'ness, West Lothian, EH51 9SN
Tel: 01506 829811
★★★ Guest House

Bridge of Allan

Knockhill Guest House
Bridge of Allan, Stirling, FK9 4ND
Tel: 01786 833123
Awaiting Inspection

The Queen's Hotel
24 Henderson Street, Bridge of Allan, Stirlingshire, FK9 4HP
Tel: 01786 833268
★★★★ Small Hotel

Royal Hotel
55 Henderson Street, Bridge of Allan, Stirlingshire, FK9 4HG
Tel: 01786 832284
Awaiting Inspection

Castlecary Village, by Cumbernauld

Castlecary House Hotel
Castlecary Road, Castlecary, Cumbernauld, G68 0HD
Tel: 01324 840233
★★★ Hotel

Dollar

Castle Campbell Hotel
Bridge Street, Dollar, Clackmannanshire, FK14 7DE
Tel: 01259 742519
★★★ Small Hotel

by Dunblane

Cromlix House
Kinbuck, Dunblane, Perthshire, FK15 9JT
Tel: 01786 822125
★★★★ Country House Hotel

Dunblane

Dunblane Hydro
Perth Road, Dunblane, Perthshire, FK15 0HG
Tel: 01786 822551
★★★★ Hotel

Falkirk

Cladhan Hotel
Kemper Avenue, Falkirk, Stirlingshire, FK1 1UF
Tel: 01324 627421
★★★ Hotel

Falkirk West Pemier Inn
Glenbervie Business Park, Bellsdyke Rd, Larbert, Falkirk, Stirlingshire, FK5 4EG
Tel: 0870 9906550
Passed Budget Hotel

Park Hotel Falkirk
Camelon Road, Falkirk, Stirlingshire, FK1 5RY
Tel: 01324 628331
★★★ Hotel

Grangemouth

Grangeburn House
55 Bo'ness Road, Grangemouth, Stirlingshire, FK3 9BJ
Tel: 01324 471301
★★★★ Guest House

Leapark Hotel
130 Bo'ness Road, Grangemouth, Stirlingshire, FK3 9BX
Tel: 01324 486733
★★★ Hotel

The Grange Manor
Glensburgh, Grangemouth, Stirlingshire, FK3 8XJ
Tel: 01324 474836
★★★★ Hotel

Lismore House
Wester Bowhouse Farm,
Maddiston, Falkirk,
Stirlingshire, FK2 0BX
Tel: 01324 720929
★★★★ Farmhouse

Broomhall Castle
Long Row, Menstrie,
Clackmannanshire,
FK11 7EA
Tel: 01259 760396
★★ Hotel

Falkirk East Premier Inn
Cadger's Brae,
Beancross Road, Polmont,
Falkirk, FK2 0YS
Tel: 08701 977098
Passed Budget Hotel

Inchyra Grange Hotel
Grange Road, Polmont,
Stirlingshire, FK2 0YB
Tel: 01324 711911
★★★★ Hotel

Allan Park Hotel
20 Allan Park, Stirling,
Stirlingshire, FK8 2QG
Tel: 01786 473598
★★ Metro Hotel

Burns View
1 Albert Place, Stirling,
Stirlingshire, FK8 2QL
Tel: 01786 451002
★★★ Guest House

Calsay House
64 Causewayhead Road,
Stirling, FK9 5EZ
Tel: 01786 472636
Awaiting Inspection

Craigquarter Farm
Stirling, FK7 9QP
Tel: 01786 812668
★★★★ Farmhouse

Express by Holiday Inn - Stirling
Springkerse Business Park,
Stirling, Stirlingshire, FK7 7XH
Tel: 01786 449922
★★★ Hotel

Forth Guest House
23 Forth Place, Riverside,
Stirling, Stirlingshire, FK8 1UD
Tel: 01786 471020
★★★★ Guest House

Harviestoun Country Hotel & Restaurant
Dollar Road, Tillicoultry,
Clackmannanshire
Tel: 01259 752522
★★★ Small Hotel

King Robert Hotel
Glasgow Road,
Bannockburn, Stirling,
FK7 0LJ
Tel: 01786 811666
★★★ Hotel

Linden Guest House
22 Linden Avenue, Stirling,
Stirlingshire, FK7 7PQ
Tel: 01786 448850
★★★★ Guest House

Munro Guest House
14 Princes Street, Stirling,
FK8 1HQ
Tel: 01786 472685
★★★ Guest House

No 31 Kenningknowes Road
Kenningknowes Road, Stirling,
Stirlingshire, FK7 9JF
Tel: 01786 475511
Awaiting Inspection

Park Lodge Hotel
32 Park Terrace, Stirling,
FK8 2JS
Tel: 01786 474862
★★★ Small Hotel

St Alma
37 Causewayhead Road,
Stirling, FK9 5EG
Tel: 01786 465795
★ Guest House

Stillrovin In Scotland
Stillrovin, Bannockburn Road,
Cowie, Stirlingshire, FK7 7BG
Tel: 01786 818899
Awaiting Inspection

Stirling Highland Hotel
Spittal Street, Stirling,
FK8 1DU
Tel: 01786 272727
★★★★ Hotel

Stirling Management Centre
University of Stirling, Stirling,
FK9 4LA
Tel: 01786 451666
★★★ Hotel

Stirling Premier Inn
Pirnhall Inn, Whins of Milton,
Glasgow Road, Stirling,
FK7 8EX
Tel: 08701 977241
Passed Budget Hotel

Terraces Hotel
4 Melville Terrace, Stirling,
Stirlingshire, FK8 2ND
Tel: 01786 472268
★★★ Small Hotel

The Golden Lion Hotel
8-10 King Street, Stirling,
Stirlingshire, FK8 1BD
Tel: 01786 475351
Awaiting Inspection

The Haven
24 Causewayhead Road,
Stirling, Stirlingshire, FK9 5EU
Tel: 01786 464060
Awaiting Inspection

The Whitehouse
13 Glasgow Road, Stirling,
Stirlingshire, FK7 0PA
Tel: 01786 462636
★★★ Guest House

PERTHSHIRE, ANGUS AND DUNDEE AND THE KINGDOM OF FIFE

PERTHSHIRE

by Aberfeldy

Aberfeldy Weem Hotel
Weem, By Aberfeldy,
Perthshire, PH15 2LD
Tel: 01887 820381
★★★ Small Hotel

Coshieville House
By Keltneyburn, Aberfeldy,
Perthshire, PH15 2NE
Tel: 01887 830319
★★★ Guest House

Aberfeldy

Ardtalnaig Lodge
Ardtalnaig, Aberfeldy,
Perthshire, PH15 2HX
Tel: 01567 820771
Awaiting Inspection

Balnearn House
Crieff Road, Aberfeldy,
Perthshire, PH15 2BJ
Tel: 01887 820431
★★★ Guest House

Fortingall Hotel
Fortingall, Aberfeldy,
Perthshire, PH15 2NQ
★★★★ Small Hotel

The Moness House Hotel & Country Club
Crieff Road, Aberfeldy,
Perthshire, PH15 2DY
Tel: 0870 4431460
★★★ Small Hotel

Tomvale
Tom of Cluny, Aberfeldy,
Perthshire, PH15 2JT
Tel: 01887 820171
★★★ Farmhouse

Alyth

Alyth Hotel
6 Commercial Street, Alyth,
Perthshire, PH11 8AT
Tel: 01828 632447
★★★ Inn

Lands of Loyal Hotel
Loyal Road, Alyth,
Blairgowrie, PH11 8JQ
Tel: 01828 633151
★★★★ Country House Hotel

Tigh Na Leigh
22-24 Airlie Street, Alyth,
Perthshire, PH11 8AD
Tel: 01828 632372
★★★★★ Guest House

Amulree

Amulree
Amulree, Dunkeld, Perthshire,
PH8 0EF
★★ Guest House

Auchterarder

Cairn Lodge Hotel
Orchil Road, Auchterarder,
Perthshire, PH3 1LX
Tel: 01764 662634
★★★ Small Hotel

Collearn House Hotel
High Street, Auchterarder,
Perthshire, PH3 1DF
Tel: 01764 663553
★★★★ Small Hotel

Duchally Country Estate
Duchally Country Estate,
Duchally, Auchterarder,
Perthshire, PH3 1PN
Tel: 01764 663071
★★★ Country House Hotel

The Gleneagles Hotel
Auchterarder, Perthshire,
PH3 1NF
Tel: 01764 662231
★★★★★ Hotel

Ballinluig, by Pitlochry

Cuil -an- Daraich Guest House
2 Cuil -an- Daraich, Logierait,
Pitlochry, Perthshire, PH9 0LH
Tel: 01796 482750
★★★ Guest House

Blackford

Blackford Hotel
Moray Street, Blackford,
Perthshire, PH4 1QF
Tel: 01764 682497
★★★ Small Hotel

Blair Atholl

Atholl Arms Hotel
Old North Road, Blair Atholl,
by Pitlochry,
Tel: 01796 481205
★★★ Hotel

Bridge of Tilt Hotel
Bridge of Tilt, Blair Atholl,
Perthshire, PH18 5SU
Tel: 01796 481333
★★ Hotel

Blairgowrie

Altamount Country House Hotel
Rosemount, Blairgowrie,
Perthshire, PH10 6JN
Tel: 01250 873512
★★★ Country House Hotel

Angus Hotel
Wellmeadow, Blairgowrie,
Perthshire, PH10 6NQ
Tel: 01250 872455
★★★ Hotel

Broadmyre Motel
Carsie, Blairgowrie,
Perthshire, PH10 6QW
Tel: 01250 873262
★★ Guest House

Glensheiling House
Hatton Road, Blairgowrie,
Perthshire, PH10 7HZ
Tel: 01250 874605
★★★★ Guest House

Ivybank Guest House
Boat Brae, Blairgowrie,
Perthshire, PH10 7BH
Tel: 01250 873056
★★★★ Guest House

Rosebank House
Balmoral Road, Blairgowrie,
Perthshire, PH10 7AF
Tel: 01250 872912
★★★ Guest House

Royal Hotel
53 Allan Street, Blairgowrie,
Perthshire, PH10 6AB
Tel: 01250 872226
Hotel

The Laurels Guest House
Golf Course Road, Rosemount,
Blairgowrie, Perthshire,
PH10 6LH
Tel: 01250 874920
★★★ Guest House

by Blairgowrie

Kinloch House Hotel
Blairgowrie, Perthshire,
PH10 6SG
Tel: 01250 884237
★★★★ Country House Hotel

Bridge of Cally

Bridge of Cally Hotel
Bridge of Cally, Blairgowrie,
Perthshire, PH10 7JJ
Tel: 01250 886231
★★★ Small Hotel

Bridge of Earn

The Last Cast
Main Street, Bridge of Earn,
Perthshire, PH2 9PL
Tel: 01738 812578
★★ Guest House

Comrie

Royal Hotel
Melville Square, Comrie,
Perthshire, PH6 2DN
Tel: 01764 679200
★★★ Small Hotel

Crieff

Arduthie House
Perth Road, Crieff, Perthshire,
PH7 3EQ
Tel: 01764 653113
★★★★ Guest House

Comely Bank Guest House
32 Burrell Street, Crieff,
Perthshire, PH7 4DT
Tel: 01764 653409
★★★ Guest House

Crieff Hydro Hotel
Crieff, Perthshire, PH7 3LQ
Tel: 01764 655555
★★★★ Hotel

Fendoch Guest House
Sma' Glen, Crieff,
Perthshire, PH7 3LW
Tel: 01764 653446
★★★ Guest House

Glenearn House
Perth Road, Crieff, Perthshire,
PH7 3EQ
Tel: 01764 650000
★★★★ Guest House

Crieff continued

Kingarth
Perth Road, Crieff,
Perthshire, PH7 3EQ
Tel: 01764 652060
★★★ Guest House

Murraypark Hotel
Connaught Terrace, Crieff,
Perthshire, PH7 3DJ
Tel: 01764 653731
★★★ Hotel

Roundelwood Health Spa
Drummond Terrace, Crieff,
Perthshire, PH7 4AN
Tel: 01764 653806
★★★ Small Hotel

Cultoquhey House
Gilmerton, by Crieff,
Perthshire, PH7 3NE
Tel: 01764 653253
★ Guest House

Westacre Bed & Breakfast
New Fowlis, by Crieff,
Perthshire, PH7 3NH
Tel: 01764 683365
Awaiting Inspection

Atholl Arms Hotel
Tay Street, Bridgehead,
Dunkeld, Perthshire, PH8 0AQ
Tel: 01350 727219
Awaiting Inspection

Hilton Dunkeld
Dunkeld, Perthshire, PH8 0HX
Tel: 01350 727771
★★★★ Hotel

Royal Dunkeld Hotel
Atholl Street, Dunkeld,
PH8 0AR
Tel: 01350 727322
★★★ Hotel

The Birnam Guest House
4 Murthly Terrace, Birnam,
By Dunkeld, Perthshire,
PH8 0BG
Tel: 01350 727201
★★★ Guest House

Waterbury Guest House
Murthly Terrace, Birnam,
by Dunkeld, Perthshire,
PH8 0BG
Tel: 01350 727324
★★★★ Guest House

Kinnaird
Kinnaird Estate, Dalguise,
by Dunkeld, Perthshire,
PH8 0LB
Tel: 01796 482440
★★★★★ Country House Hotel

The Famous Bein Inn
Glenfarg, Perthshire, PH2 9PY
Tel: 01577 830216
Awaiting Inspection

Dalmunzie
Spittal of Glenshee,
Blairgowrie, Perthshire
Tel: 01250 885224
★★★ Country House Hotel

Kenmore Hotel
The Square, Kenmore,
Perthshire, PH15 2NU
Tel: 01887 830205
★★★ Hotel

Killiecrankie House Hotel
Killiecrankie, Perthshire,
PH16 5LG
Tel: 01796 473220
★★★★ Country House Hotel

Dunalastair Hotel
The Square, Kinloch
Rannoch, Perthshire,
PH16 5PW
Tel: 01882 632218
★★★ Hotel

Loch Rannoch Hotel
Kinloch Rannoch, Perthshire,
PH16 5PS
Tel: 01882 632201
★★★ Hotel

The Green Hotel
2 The Muirs, Kinross,
KY13 8AS
Tel: 01577 863467
★★★★ Hotel

Kirklands Hotel
20 High Street, Kinross,
Perthshire, KY13 8AN
Tel: 01577 863313
★★★ Small Hotel

Roxburghe Guest House
126 High Street, Kinross,
Perthshire, KY13 8DA
Tel: 01577 862498
★★ Guest House

Windlestrae Hotel
The Muirs, Kinross,
Perthshire, KY13 8AS
Tel: 01577 863217
★★★ Hotel

Mawcarse House
Mawcarse House, Milnathort,
Kinross-shire, KY13 9SJ
Tel: 01577 862220
★★★★ Farmhouse

The Log Cabin Hotel
Glen Derby, Kirkmichael,
Blairgowrie, Perthshire,
PH10 7NA
Tel: 01250 881288
★★ Small Hotel

Achray House Hotel
St Fillans, Perthshire,
PH6 2NF
Tel: 01764 685231
★★★ Small Hotel

The Four Seasons Hotel
St Fillans, Perthshire,
PH6 2NF
Tel: 01764 685333
★★★ Small Hotel

Talladh-a-Bheithe Lodge
Loch Rannoch,by Pitlochry,
Perthshire, PH17 2QW
Tel: 01882 633203
★★★ Guest House

Aberdeen Guest House
13 Pitcullen Terrace, Perth,
Perthshire, PH2 7HT
Tel: 01738 633183
★★★★ Guest House

Achnacarry Guest House
3 Pitcullen Crescent, Perth,
PH2 7HT
Tel: 01738 621421
★★★★ Guest House

Ackinnoull Guest House
5 Pitcullen Crescent, Perth,
PH2 7HT
Tel: 01738 634165
★★★★ Guest House

Adam Guest House
6 Pitcullen Crescent, Perth,
PH2 7HT
Tel: 01738 627179
★★★ Guest House

Almond Villa Guest House
51 Dunkeld Road, Perth,
PH1 5RP
Tel: 01738 629356
★★★★ Guest House

Ardfern House
15 Pitcullen Crescent, Perth,
Perthshire, PH2 7HT
Tel: 01738 637031
★★★★ Guest House

Arisaig Guest House
4 Pitcullen Crescent, Perth,
PH2 7HT
Tel: 01738 628240
★★★★ Guest House

Beechgrove Guest House
Dundee Road, Perth,
PH2 7AQ
Tel: 01738 636147
★★★★ Guest House

Best Western Queens Hotel
105 Leonard Street, Perth,
Perthshire, PH2 8HB
Tel: 01738 442222
★★★ Hotel

Cherrybank B&B
217 Glasgow Road, Perth,
Perthshire, PH2 0NB
Tel: 01738 451982
★★★★ Guest House

Clifton House
36 Glasgow Road, Perth,
Perthshire, PH2 0PB
Tel: 01738 621997
★★★★ Guest House

Dunallan Guest House
10 Pitcullen Crescent, Perth,
Perthshire, PH2 7TH
Tel: 01738 622551
Awaiting Inspection

Perth continued

Express by Holiday Inn
200 Dunkeld Road, Inveralmond, Perth, Perthshire, PH1 3AQ
Tel: 01738 636666
★★★ Lodge

Grampian Hotel
37 York Place, Perth, Perthshire, PH2 8EH
Tel: 01738 621057
★★★ Small Hotel

Hazeldene Guest House
Strathmore Street, Perth, Perthshire, PH2 7HP
Tel: 01738 623550
★★★★ Guest House

Heidl Guest House
43 York Place, Perth, Perthshire, PH2 8EH
Tel: 01738 635031
★★★ Guest House

Huntingtower Hotel
Crieff Road, Perth, Perthshire, PH1 3JT
Tel: 01738 583771
★★★ Hotel

Kinnaird Guest House
5 Marshall Place, Perth, Perthshire, PH2 8AH
Tel: 01738 628021
★★★ Guest House

Lorne Villa Guest House
65 Dunkeld Road, Perth, Perthshire, PH1 5RP
Tel: 01738 628043
★★★ Guest House

Luncarty Inn and Grill
Marshall Way, Luncarty, Perth, PH1 3UX
Tel: 01738 827777
Awaiting Inspection

The New County Hotel
22-30 County Place, Perth, PH2 8EE
Tel: 01738 623355
★★★ Hotel

Northlees Farm
Kingfauns, Perth, Perthshire, PH2 7LJ
Tel: 01738 860852
★★ Farmhouse

Parklands Hotel
2 St Leonards Bank, Perth, Perthshire, PH2 8EB
Tel: 01738 622451
★★★★ Small Hotel

Pitcullen Guest House
17 Pitcullen Crescent, Perth, Perthshire, PH2 7HT
Tel: 01738 626506
Awaiting Inspection

Quality Hotel Perth
Leonard Street, Perth, Perthshire, PH2 8HE
Tel: 01738 624141
Hotel

Ramada Hotel
West Mill Street, Perth, Perthshire, PH1 5QP
Tel: 01738 628281
★★★ Hotel

The Royal George
Tay Street, Perth, PH1 5LD
Tel: 01738 624455
★★★ Hotel

Salutation Hotel
34 South Street, Perth, PH2 8PH
Tel: 01738 630066
★★ Hotel

Sunbank House Hotel
50 Dundee Road, Perth, Perthshire, PH2 7BA
Tel: 01738 624882
★★★★ Small Hotel

Symphony Lovat Hotel
Glasgow Road, Perth, Perthshire, PH2 0LT
Tel: 01738 636555
★★★ Hotel

The Gables Guest House
24 Dunkeld Road, Perth, Perthshire, PH1 5RW
Tel: 01738 624717
★★★ Guest House

Westview Bed & Breakfast
49 Dunkeld Road, Perth, PH1 5RP
Tel: 01738 627787
★★★★ Bed & Breakfast

WoodLea Hotel
23 York Place, Perth, Perthshire, PH2 8EP
Tel: 01738 621744
★★★ Small Hotel

by Perth

Ballathie House Hotel
Kinclaven, by Stanley, Perthshire, PH1 4QN
Tel: 01250 883268
★★★★ Country House Hotel

Murrayshall Hotel
Scone, Perth, Perthshire, PH2 7PH
Tel: 01738 551171
★★★★ Country House Hotel

Newmill Farm
Stanley, Perth, Perthshire, PH1 4PS
Tel: 01738 828281
★★★ Farmhouse

Tayside Hotel
51 Mill Street, Stanley, Perth, Perthshire, PH1 4NL
Tel: 01738 828249
★★★ Small Hotel

Pitlochry

Acarsaid Hotel and Lodge
8 Atholl Road, Pitlochry, Perthshire, PH16 5BX
Tel: 01796 472389
★★★ Hotel

Annslea Guest House
164 Atholl Road, Pitlochry, Perthshire, PH16 5AR
Tel: 01796 472430
★★★ Guest House

Atholl Villa Guest House
29/31 Atholl Road, Pitlochry, Perthshire, PH16 5BX
Tel: 01796 473820
★★★ Guest House

Atholl Palace Hotel
Pitlochry, Perthshire, PH16 5LY
Tel: 01796 472400
★★★★ Hotel

Beinn Bhracaigh
Higher Oakfield, Pitlochry, Perthshire, PH16 5HT
Tel: 01796 470355
Awaiting Inspection

Bendarroch House
Strathtay, Perthshire, PH9 0PG
Tel: 01887 840420
★★★ Guest House

Birchwood Hotel
2 East Moulin Road, Pitlochry, Perthshire, PH16 5DW
Tel: 01796 472477
★★★ Small Hotel

Buttonboss Lodge
27 Atholl Road, Pitlochry, Perthshire, PH16 5BX
Tel: 01796 472065
★★★ Guest House

Claymore Hotel
162 Atholl Road, Pitlochry, Perthshire, PH16 5AR
Tel: 01796 472888
★★★ Small Hotel

Craigatin House & Courtyard
165 Atholl Road, Pitlochry, Perthshire, PH16 5QL
Tel: 01796 472478
Awaiting Inspection

Craigmhor Lodge
27 West Moulin Road, Pitlochry, Perthshire, PH16 5EF
Tel: 01796 472123
★★★★ Guest House

Craigvrack Hotel
38 West Moulin Road, Pitlochry, Perthshire, PH16 5EQ
Tel: 01796 472399
★★★ Small Hotel

Dalshian House
Old Perth Road, Pitlochry, Perthshire, PH16 5TD
Tel: 01796 472173
Awaiting Inspection

Dundarach Hotel
Perth Road, Pitlochry, Perthshire, PH16 5DJ
Tel: 01796 472862
★★★ Hotel

Dunmurray Lodge Guest House
72 Bonnethill Road, Pitlochry, Perthshire, PH16 5ED
Tel: 01796 473624
★★★★ Guest House

East Haugh House Country Hotel & Res
East Haugh, by Pitlochry, Perthshire, PH16 5TE
Tel: 01796 473121
★★★★ Small Hotel

Easter Croftinloan Farmhouse
Croftloan Farm, Pitlochry, Perthshire, PH16 5TA
Tel: 01796 473454
★★★★ Guest House

Fasganeoin Country House
Perth Road, Pitlochry, PH16 5DJ
Tel: 01796 472387
★★★ Guest House

Pitlochry continued

Fishers Hotel
75-79 Atholl Road, Pitlochry, Perthshire, PH16 5BN
Tel: 01796 472000
Awaiting Inspection

The Green Park Hotel
Clunie Bridge Road, Pitlochry, Perthshire,
Tel: 01796 473248
★★★★ Country House Hotel

Knockendarroch House Hotel
Higher Oakfield, Pitlochry, Perthshire, PH16 5HT
Tel: 01796 473473
★★★★ Small Hotel

Loch Tummel Inn
Queens View, Strathtummel, Pitlochry, Perthshire,
Tel: 01882 634272
★★★ Inn

Macdonald's Restaurant & Guest House
140 Atholl Road, Pitlochry, Perthshire, PH16 5AG
Tel: 01796 472170
★★★ Guest House

Moulin Hotel
Moulin Hotel,
11-13 Kirkmichael Road, Pitlochry, Perthshire, PH16 5EW
Tel: 0796 47 2196
★★★ Hotel

Pine Trees Hotel
Strathview Terrace, Pitlochry, Perthshire,
Tel: 01796 472121
★★★★ Country House Hotel

Pitlochry Hydro Hotel
Knockard Road, Pitlochry, Perthshire, PH16 5JH
Tel: 01796 472666
★★★ Hotel

Rosehill
47 Atholl Road, Pitlochry, Perthshire, PH16 5BX
Tel: 01796 472958
★★★ Guest House

Rosemount Hotel
12 Higher Oakfield, Pitlochry, PH16 5HT
Tel: 01796 472302
★★★ Hotel

Scotlands Hotel
40 Bonnethill Road, Pitlochry, Perthshire, PH16 5BT
Tel: 01796 472292
★★★ Hotel

The Poplars
27 Lower Oakfield, Pitlochry, Perthshire, PH16 5DS
Tel: 01796 472911
★★★ Guest House

Tigh Na Cloich Hotel
Larchwood Road, Pitlochry, Perthshire, PH16 5AS
Tel: 01796 472216
★★★ Small Hotel

Tir Aluinn
10 Higher Oakfield, Pitlochry, Perthshire, PH16 5HT
Tel: 01796 473811
★★★ Guest House

Torrdarach House
Golf Course Road, Pitlochry, Perthshire, PH16 5AU
Tel: 01796 472136
★★★★ Guest House

The Well House
11 Toberargan Road, Pitlochry, Perthshire,
Tel: 01796 472239
★★★★ Guest House

Wellwood House
13 West Moulin Road, Pitlochry, Perthshire, PH16 5EA
Tel: 01796 474288
★★★★ Guest House

Westlands Hotel
160 Atholl Road, Pitlochry, Perthshire, PH16 5AR
Tel: 01796 472266
★★★ Small Hotel

Kynachan Loch Tummel Hotel
Tummel Bridge, Perthshire, PH16 5SB
Tel: 01796 484848
★★★ Hotel

Blairdene Guest House
216 High Street, Arbroath, Angus, DD11 1HY
Tel: 01241 872380
★★ Guest House

Cliffburn Hotel
Cliffburn Road, Arbroath, Angus, DD11 5BT
Tel: 01241 873432
★ Small Hotel

Harbour Nights Guest House
4 Shore, Arbroath, Angus, DD11 1PB
Tel: 01241 434343
★★★★ Guest House

Rosely Country House Hotel
Forfar Road, Arbroath, Angus, DD11 3RB
Tel: 01241 876828
★★ Small Hotel

Towerbank Guest House
9 James Street, Arbroath, Angus, DD11 1JP
Tel: 01241 431343
★★★ Guest House

Northern Hotel
2 Clerk Street, Brechin, Angus, DD9 6AE
Tel: 01356 625400
★★★ Small Hotel

Dundee East Premier Inn
Bell Tree,
115-117 Lawers Drive, Broughty Ferry, Dundee, DD5 3UP
Tel: 0870 9906324
Passed Budget Hotel

No 1 Kerrington Crescent
Broughty Ferry, Dundee, DD5 2TS
Tel: 01382 480489
Awaiting Inspection

Redwood Guest House
89 Monifieth Road, Broughty Ferry, Dundee, DD5 2SB
Tel: 01382 736550
★★★★ Guest House

Aboukir Hotel
38 Ireland Street, Carnoustie, Angus, DD7 6AT
Tel: 01241 852149
★★ Small Hotel

Carnoustie Coach House B&B
Carlogie Road, Carnoustie, Angus, DD7 6LD
Tel: 01241 857319
Awaiting Inspection

Old Downie Farmhouse
Old Downie Farm, Carnoustie, Angus, DD7 7SG
Tel: 01382 370863
Awaiting Inspection

Seaview Private Hotel
29 Ireland Street, Carnoustie, Angus, DD7 6AS
Tel: 01241 851092
★★★ Small Hotel

Station Hotel
Station Road, Carnoustie, Angus, DD7 6AR
Tel: 01241 852447
★★ Small Hotel

Aberlaw Guest House
230 Broughty Ferry Road, Dundee, Angus, DD4 7JP
Tel: 01382 456929
★★★ Guest House

Alcorn Guest House
5 Hyndford Street, Dundee, Angus, DD2 1HQ
Tel: 01382 668433
★★★ Guest House

Anderson's Guest House
285 Perth Road, Dundee, Tayside, DD2 1JS
Tel: 01382 668585
★★★ Guest House

Apex City Quay Hotel & Spa
1 West Victoria Dock Road, Dundee, DD1 3JP
Tel: 01382 202402
★★★★ Hotel

Cullaig Guest House
1 Rosemount Terrace, Dundee, Tayside, DD3 6JQ
Tel: 01382 322154
★★★ Guest House

Dundee continued

Dundee North Premier Inn
Outside Inn,
Camperdown Leisure Park,
Dayton Drive, Kingsway,
Dundee, DD2 3SQ
Tel: 0870 9906420
Passed Budget Hotel

Dundee West Premier Inn
Gourdie House,
Kingsway West, Dundee,
Angus, DD2 5JU
Tel: 08701 977081
Passed Budget Hotel

Dunlaw House Hotel
10 Union Terrace, Dundee,
Angus, DD3 6JD
Tel: 01382 221703
★★ Small Hotel

Errolbank Guest House
9 Dalgleish Road, Dundee,
Angus, DD4 7JN
Tel: 01382 462118
★★★ Guest House

Grosvenor Hotel
1 Grosvenor Road, Dundee,
Angus, DD2 1LF
Tel: 01382 642991
★★★ Guest House

Hilton Dundee
Earl Grey Place, Dundee,
Angus, DD1 4DE
Tel: 01382 229271
★★★★ Hotel

Hotel Broughty Ferry
16 West Queen Street,
Broughty Ferry, Dundee,
DD5 1AR
Tel: 01382 480027
★★★★ Small Hotel

Invercarse Hotel
371 Perth Road, Dundee,
Angus, DD2 1PG
Tel: 01382 669231
★★★ Hotel

Kemback Guest House
8 McGill Street, Dundee,
Angus, DD4 6PH
Tel: 01382 461273/
07776380650/07766145211
Awaiting Inspection

Park House Hotel
40 Coupar Angus Road,
Dundee, Angus, DD2 3HY
Tel: 01382 611151
★★★ Small Hotel

Premier Inn Dundee Centre
Discovery Quay,
Riverside Drive, Dundee,
Angus, DD1 4XA
Tel: 08701 977079
Passed Budget Hotel

Premier Inn Dundee Monifeith
Monifeith Farm,
Ethiebeaton Park, Monifeith,
Dundee, Angus, DD5 4HB
Tel: 08701 977080
Passed Budget Hotel

Queens Hotel
160 Nethergate, Dundee,
Angus, DD1 4DU
Tel: 01382 322515
★★★ Hotel

Shaftesbury Hotel
1 Hyndford Street, Dundee,
Angus, DD2 1HQ
Tel: 01382 669216
★★★ Small Hotel

St Leonard B&B
22 Albany Terrace, Dundee,
Angus, DD3 6HR
Tel: 01382 227146/227461
★ Guest House

Strathdon Guest House
277 Perth Road, Dundee,
Angus, DD2 1JS
Tel: 01382 665648
★★★ Guest House

Swallow Hotel
Kingsway West, Invergowrie,
Dundee, Angus, DD2 5JT
Tel: 01382 641122
Awaiting Inspection

Taychreggan Hotel
4 Ellieslea Road,
Broughty Ferry, Dundee,
Angus, DD5 1JG
Tel: 01382 778626
★★★ Small Hotel

The Craigtay Hotel
101 Broughty Ferry Road,
Dundee, Angus, DD4 6JE
Tel: 01382 451142
★★ Small Hotel

The Fisherman's Tavern Hotel
10-16 Fort Street,
Broughty Ferry, Dundee,
Angus, DD5 2AD
Tel: 01382 775941
Awaiting Inspection

The Fort Hotel
58-60 Fort Street,
Broughty Ferry, Dundee,
Angus, DD5 2AB
Tel: 01382 737999
★★ Small Hotel

The Grampian
295 Perth Road, Dundee,
DD2 1JS
Tel: 01382 667785
★★★ Guest House

West Adamston Farmhouse
West Adamston Farm,
Muirhead, Dundee, DD2 5QX
Tel: 01382 580215
Awaiting Inspection

Woodlands Hotel
13 Panmure Terrace, Barnhill,
Dundee, Angus, DD5 2QL
Tel: 01382 480033
★★★ Hotel

Edzell

Glenesk Hotel
High Street, Edzell, Tayside,
DD9 7TF
Tel: 01356 648319
★★★ Hotel

Panmure Arms Hotel
52 High Street, Edzell,
Angus, DD9 7TA
Tel: 01356 648950
★★★ Small Hotel

Glamis

Castleton House Hotel
Glamis, Angus, DD8 1SJ
Tel: 01307 840340
★★★★ Country House Hotel

Glen Clova, by Kirriemuir

Glen Clova Hotel
Glen Clova, by Kirriemuir,
Angus, DD8 4QS
Tel: 01575 550350
★★★ Small Hotel

Glenisla

Glenisla Hotel
Kirkton of Glenisla, Glenisla,
by Blairgowrie, Perthshire,
PH11 8PH
Tel: 01575 582223
Awaiting Inspection

Kirriemuir

Thrums Hotel
25 Bank Street, Kirriemuir,
Angus, DD8 4BE
Tel: 01575 572758
★★★ Small Hotel

Monifieth, by Dundee

Milton Hotel
Grange Road, Monifieth,
DD5 4LU
Tel: 01382 539016
★★★ Small Hotel

Montrose

Best Western Links Hotel
Mid Links, Montrose, Angus,
DD10 8RL
Tel: 01674 671000
★★★★ Hotel

Oaklands
10 Rossie Island Road,
Montrose, Angus, DD10 9NN
Tel: 01674 672018
★★★ Guest House

Park Hotel
61 John Street, Montrose,
Angus, DD10
Tel: 01674 663400
★★★ Hotel

FIFE

Aberdour

Aberdour Hotel
38 High Street, Aberdour, Fife,
KY3 0SW
Tel: 01383 860325
★★★ Small Hotel

The Cedar Inn
20 Shore Road, Aberdour, Fife,
KY3 0TR
Tel: 01383 860310
Awaiting Inspection

The Woodside Hotel
High Street, Aberdour, Fife,
KY3 0SW
Tel: 01383 860328
★★★ Hotel

Anstruther

The Spindrift
Pittenween Road,
Anstruther, Fife, KY10 3DT
Tel: 01333 310573
★★★★ Guest House

Anstruther continued

Symphony Craws Nest Hotel
Bankwell Road, Anstruther,
Fife, KY10 3DA
Tel: 01333 310691
★★★ Hotel

Myres Castle
Auchtermuchty, Fife,
KY14 7EW
Tel: 01337 828350
★★★★★ Exclusive Use Venue

Burntisland Sands Hotel
Lochies Road, Burntisland,
Fife, KY3 9JX
Tel: 01592 872230
★★★ Small Hotel

Kingswood Hotel
Kinghorn Road, Burntisland,
Fife, KY3 9LL
Tel: 01592 872329
★★★ Small Hotel

No 6 Urquhart Wynd
Cellardyke, Anstruther, Fife,
KY10 3BN
Tel: 01333 310939
Awaiting Inspection

Meldrums Hotel
56 Main Street, Ceres, Fife,
KY15 5NA
Tel: 01334 828286
★★ Inn

Balcomie Links Hotel
Balcomie Road, Crail, Fife,
KY10 3TN
Tel: 01333 450237
★★ Small Hotel

Caiplie House
53 High Street, Crail, Fife,
KY10 3RA
Tel: 01333 450564
★★★ Guest House

Marine Hotel
54 Nethergate, Crail, Fife,
KY10 3TZ
Tel: 01333 450207
★★★ Guest House

The Hazelton
29 Marketgate, Crail, Fife,
KY10 3TH
Tel: 01333 450250
★★★ Guest House

The Honeypot Guest House
6 High Street South, Crail,
Fife, KY10 3TD
Tel: 01333 450935
★★★ Guest House

Craigsanquhar Country House Hotel
Logie, Cupar, Fife, KY15 4PZ
Tel: 01334 653426
★★★ Country House Hotel

Best Western Keavil House Hotel
Crossford, Fife, KY12 8QW
Tel: 01383 736258
★★★ Hotel

Carneil Farm
Carnock, Dunfermline, Fife,
KY12 9JJ
Tel: 01383 850285
★★★★ Farmhouse

Clarke Cottage Guest House
139 Halbeath Road,
Dunfermline, Fife, KY11 4LA
Tel: 01383 735935
★★★ Guest House

Davaar House Hotel
126 Grieve Street,
Dunfermline, Fife,
KY12 8DW
Tel: 01383 721886
★★★ Small Hotel

Express By Holiday Inn Dunfermline
Halbeath, Dunfermline, Fife,
KY11 8DY
Tel: 01383 748220
★★★ Lodge

Garvock House Hotel
St Johns Drive,
Dunfermline, KY12 7TU
Tel: 01383 621067
★★★★ Hotel

King Malcolm Hotel
Queensferry Road,
Dunfermline, Fife, KY11 8DS
Tel: 01383 722611
★★★ Hotel

Pitbauchlie House Hotel
Aberdour Road,
Dunfermline, KY11 4PB
Tel: 01383 722282
★★★ Hotel

Pitreavie Guest House
3 Aberdour Road,
Dunfermline, Fife, KY11 4PB
Tel: 01383 724244
★★★ Guest House

Premier Inn Dunfermline
Crooked Glen,
Fife Leisure Park,
Whimbrel Place, Dunfermline,
Fife, KY11 8EX
Tel: 0870 600 1486
Passed Budget Hotel

Rooms at 29 Bruce Street
29-35 Bruce Street,
Dunfermline, Fife, KY12 7AG
Tel: 01383 840041
★★★ Small Hotel

Roscobie Farmhouse
Dunfermline, Fife, KY12 0SG
Tel: 01383 731571
★★★★ Farmhouse

Lomond Hills Hotel and Leisure Centre
Parliament Square,
Freuchie, Cupar, Fife,
KY15 7EY
Tel: 01337 857329
★★★ Hotel

Balgeddie House Hotel
Balgeddie Way, Glenrothes,
Fife, KY6 3ET
Tel: 01592 742511
★★★ Hotel

Express by Holiday Inn
Leslie Road, Glenrothes,
KY7 6XX
Tel: 01592 745509
★★★ Hotel

The Gilvenbank Hotel
Huntsmans Road,
Glenrothes, Fife, KY7 6NT
Tel: 01592 742077
★★★ Hotel

Glenrothes Premier Inn
Bankhead Gate,
Beaufort Drive,
Bankhead Roundabout,
Glenrothes, Fife, KY7 4UJ
Tel: 08701 977114
Passed Budget Hotel

Bay Hotel
Burntisland Road, Kinghorn,
Fife, KY3 9YE
Tel: 01592 892222
Awaiting Inspection

Dean Park Hotel
Chapel Level, Kirkcaldy, Fife,
KY2 6QW
Tel: 01592 261635
★★★ Hotel

Dunnikier House Hotel
Dunnikier Park, Kirkcaldy, Fife,
KY1 3LP
Tel: 01592 268393
★★★ Hotel

Mintella
38 Bennochy Road, Kirkcaldy,
Fife, KY2 5RB
Tel: 01592 593446
★★ Guest House

The Belvedere Hotel
Coxstool, West Wemyss, Fife,
KY1 4SL
Tel: 01592 654167
★★★ Small Hotel

Rescobie House Hotel
6 Valley Drive, Leslie, Fife,
KY6 3BQ
Tel: 01592 749555
★★★ Small Hotel

St Michaels Inn
St Michaels, Leuchars,
by St Andrews, Fife,
KY16 0DU
Tel: 01334 839220
Awaiting Inspection

Caledonian Hotel
81 High Street, Leven, Fife,
KY8 4NG
Tel: 01333 424101
Awaiting Inspection

Leven continued

Craigdene
20 Main Street, Colinsburgh, Leven, KY9 1LR
Tel: 01333 340408
Awaiting Inspection

Dunclutha
16 Victoria Road, Leven, Fife, KY8 4EX
Tel: 01333 425515
★★★★ Guest House

Lomond Guest House
6 Church Road, Leven, Fife, KY8 4JE
Tel: 01333 300930
Awaiting Inspection

Lower Largo

Crusoe Hotel
2 Main Street, Lower Largo, Fife, KY8 6BT
Tel: 01333 320759
★★★ Small Hotel

Lundin Links

Lundin Links Hotel
Leven Road, Lundin Links, Fife, KY8 6AP
Tel: 01333 320207
★★★ Hotel

Swallow Old Manor Hotel
55 Leven Road, Lundin Links, Fife, KY8 6AJ
Tel: 01333 320368
Awaiting Inspection

Markinch

Balbirnie House Hotel
Balbirnie Park, Markinch, by Glenrothes, Fife, KY7 6NE
Tel: 01592 610066
★★★★ Hotel

Laurel Bank Hotel
1 Balbirnie Street, Markinch, Fife, KY7 6DB
Tel: 01592 611205
★★ Small Hotel

by North Queensferry

Queensferry Hotel
St Margarets Head, North Queensferry, Fife, KY11 1HP
Tel: 01383 410000
★★★ Hotel

St Andrews

Albany Hotel
56-58 North Street, St Andrews, Fife, KY16 9AH
Tel: 01334 477737
★★★ Small Hotel

Amberside
4 Murray Park, St Andrews, Fife, KY16 9AW
Tel: 01334 474644
★★★ Guest House

Annandale Guest House
23 Murray Park, St Andrews, Fife, KY16 9AW
Tel: 01334 475310
★★★ Guest House

Ardgowan Hotel
2 Playfair Terrace, St Andrews, Fife, KY16 9HX
Tel: 01334 472970
★★★ Small Hotel

Arran House
5 Murray Park, St Andrews, Fife, KY16 9AW
Tel: 01334 474 724
★★★ Guest House

Aslar House
120 North Street, St Andrews, Fife, KY16 9AF
Tel: 01334 473460
★★★★ Guest House

Bell Craig
8 Murray Park, St Andrews, Fife, KY16 9AW
Tel: 01334 472962
★★★ Guest House

Brooksby House
Queens Terrace, St Andrews, Fife, KY16 9ER
Tel: 01334 470723
★★★★★ Guest House

Brownlees
7 Murray Place, St Andrews, Fife, KY16 9AP
Tel: 01334 473868
★★★★ Guest House

Burness House
1 Murray Park, St Andrews, Fife, KY16 9AW
Tel: 01334 474314
★★★★ Guest House

Cameron House
11 Murray Park, St Andrews, Fife, KY16 9AW
Tel: 01334 72306
★★★★ Guest House

Charlesworth House
9 Murray Place, St Andrews, Fife, KY16 9AP
Tel: 01334 476528
★★★★ Guest House

Cleveden Guest House
3 Murray Place, St Andrews, Fife, KY16 9AP
Tel: 01334 474212
★★★ Guest House

Craigmore Guest House
3 Murray Park, St Andrews, Fife, KY16 9AW
Tel: 01334 472142
★★★★ Guest House

Deveron House
64 North Street, St Andrews, Fife, KY16 9AH
Tel: 01334 473513
★★★ Guest House

Doune House
5 Murray Place, St Andrews, Fife, KY16 9AP
Tel: 01334 475195
★★★★ Guest House

Dunvegan Hotel
7 Pilmour Place, North Street, St Andrews, Fife, KY16 9HZ
Tel: 01334 473105
★★★ Small Hotel

Five Pilmour Place
North Street, St Andrews, Fife, KY16 9HZ
Tel: 01334 478665
★★★★ Guest House

Glenderran Guest House
9 Murray Park, St Andrews, Fife, KY16 9AW
Tel: 01334 477951
★★★★ Guest House

Greyfriars Hotel
129 North Street, St Andrews, Fife, KY16 9AG
Tel: 01334 474906
★★★ Small Hotel

Hazelbank Hotel
28 The Scores, St Andrews, Fife, KY16 9AS
Tel: 01334 472466
★★★ Metro Hotel

Lorimer House
19 Murray Park, St Andrews, Fife, KY16 9AW
Tel: 01334 476599
★★★★ Guest House

Macdonald Rusacks Hotel
Pilmour Links, St Andrews, Fife, KY16 9JQ
Tel: 0870 4008128
★★★★ Hotel

Montague House
21 Murray Park, St Andrews, Fife, KY16 9AW
Tel: 01334 479 287
★★★ Guest House

Nethan House
17 Murray Park, St Andrews, Fife, KY16 9AW
Tel: 01334 472104
★★★★ Guest House

New Hall, University of St Andrews
North Haugh, St Andrews, Fife,
Tel: 01334 467000
★★★ Hotel

Old Course Hotel, Golf Resort & Spa
St Andrews, Fife, KY16 9SP
Tel: 01334 474371
★★★★★ International Resort

Rufflets Country House Hotel
Strathkinness Low Road, St Andrews, Fife, KY16 9TX
Tel: 01334 472594
★★★★★ Hotel

Scores Hotel
76 The Scores, St Andrews, Fife, KY16 9BB
Tel: 01334 472451
★★★ Hotel

Shandon House
10 Murray Place, St Andrews, Fife, KY16 9AP
Tel: 01334 472412
★★★ Guest House

Fairmont St Andrews, Scotland
St Andrews, Fife, KY16 8PN
Tel: 01334 837000
★★★★★ International Resort

St Andrews Golf Hotel
40 The Scores, St Andrews, Fife, KY16 9AS
Tel: 01334 472611
★★★★ Hotel

St Andrews continued

The Old Station, Country House
Stratvithie Bridge, St Andrews, Fife, KY16 8LR
Tel: 01334 880505
★★★★ Guest House

The Russell Hotel
26 The Scores, St Andrews, Fife, KY16 9AS
Tel: 01334 473447
★★★ Small Hotel

West Bar & Kitchen
170 South Street, St Andrews, Fife, KY16 9EG
Tel: 01334 473186
★★★ Inn

Whitecroft Guest House
33 Strathkinness High Road, St Andrews, Fife, KY16 9UA
Tel: 01334 474448
★★★★ Guest House

Yorkston Guest House
68-70 Argyle Street, St Andrews, Fife, KY16 9BU
Tel: 01334 472019
★★★ Guest House

Edenside House
Edenside, By St Andrews, Fife, KY16 9QS
Tel: 0133483 8108
★★★ Guest House

The Inn At Lathones
By Largoward, St Andrews, Fife, KY9 1JE
Tel: 01334 840494
★★★★ Inn

Pinewood Country House
Tayport Road, St Michaels, Fife, KY16 0DU
Tel: 01334 839860
★★★★ Guest House

Riverview Guest House
Edenside, St Andrews, Fife, KY16 9SQ
Tel: 01334 838009
★★★ Guest House

ABERDEEN AND GRAMPIAN HIGHLANDS:
Scotland's Castle and Whisky Country

376 Great Western Road
Aberdeen, Aberdeenshire, AB10 6PH
Tel: 01224 313678
★★★ Guest House

Abbotswell Guest House
28 Abbotswell Crescent, Aberdeen, AB12 5AR
Tel: 01224 871788
★★★ Guest House

Aberdeen Allan Guest House
56 Polmuir Road, Aberdeen, Aberdeenshire, AB11 7RT
Tel: 01224 584484
★★★★ Guest House

Aberdeen Central West Premier Inn
Cocket Hat, North Anderson Drive, Aberdeen, Aberdeenshire, AB15 6DW
Tel: 0870 9906430
Passed Budget Hotel

Aberdeen City Centre Premier Inn
Invelair House, West North Street, Aberdeen, Aberdeenshire, AB24 5AR
Tel: 0870 9906300
Passed Budget Hotel

Aberdeen Douglas Hotel
43-45 Market Street, Aberdeen, AB11 5EL
Tel: 01224 582255
★★★ Hotel

Aberdeen Guest House
218 Great Western Road, Aberdeen, AB10 6PD
Tel: 01224 211733
★★★ Guest House

Aberdeen Marriott Hotel
Riverview Drive, Farburn, Dyce, Aberdeenshire, AB21 7AZ
Tel: 0870 400 7291
★★★★ Hotel

Aberdeen Patio Hotel
Beach Boulevard, Aberdeen, Aberdeenshire, AB24 5EF
Tel: 01224 633339
★★★★ Hotel

Adelphi Guest House
8 Whinhill Road, Aberdeen, AB11 7XH
Tel: 01224 583078
★★★ Guest House

Aldersyde Guest House
138 Bon Accord Street, Aberdeen, AB11 6TX
Tel: 01224 580012
★★ Guest House

Aldridge
60 Hilton Drive, Aberdeen, Aberdeenshire, AB24 4NP
Tel: 01224 485651
Awaiting Inspection

Antrim Guest House
157 Crown Street, Aberdeen, AB11 6HT
Tel: 01224 590987
★★ Guest House

Arden Guest House
61 Dee Street, Aberdeen, Aberdeenshire, AB10 2EE
Tel: 01224 580700
★★★ Guest House

Ardoe House Hotel
South Deeside Road, Blairs, Aberdeen, Aberdeenshire, AB12 5YP
Tel: 01224 867355
★★★★ Hotel

Arkaig Guest House
43 Powis Terrace, Aberdeen, AB25 3PP
Tel: 01224 638872
★★★ Guest House

Armadale Guest House
605 Holburn Street, Aberdeen, AB10 7JN
Tel: 01224 580636
★★★ Guest House

Ashgrove Guest House
34 Ashgrove Road, Aberdeen, AB25 3AD
Tel: 01224 484861
★★★ Guest House

Atholl Hotel
54 Kings Gate, Aberdeen, AB15 4DA
Tel: 01224 323505
★★★★ Hotel

Beeches
193 Great Western Road, Aberdeen, AB10 6PS
Tel: 01224 586413
★★★ Guest House

Bimini Guest House
69 Constitution Street, Aberdeen, AB24 5ET
Tel: 01224 646912
★★★ Guest House

Braeside Guest House
68 Bon-Accord Street, Aberdeen, Scotland, AB11 6EL
Tel: 01224 571471
★★ Guest House

Brentwood Hotel
101 Crown Street, Aberdeen, AB11 6HH
Tel: 01224 595440
★★★ Hotel

Brentwood Villa
560 King Street, Aberdeen, Grampian, AB24 5SR
Tel: 01224 480633
★★★ Guest House

Britannia Hotel
Malcolm Road, Aberdeen, Grampian, AB21 9LN
Tel: 01224 409988
★★★ Hotel

Burnett Guest House
75 Constitution Street, Aberdeen, AB24 5ET
Tel: 01224 647995
★★★ Guest House

Aberdeen continued

Butler's Islander Guest House
122 Crown Street, Aberdeen, Aberdeenshire, AB11 6HJ
Tel: 01224 212411
★★★ Guest House

Cedars Guest House
339 Great Western Road, Aberdeen, AB10 6NW
Tel: 01224 583225
★★★ Guest House

Cloverleaf Hotel
Kepplehills Road, Bucksburn, Aberdeen, AB21 9DG
Tel: 01224 714294
★ Hotel

Copthorne Hotel
122 Huntly Street, Aberdeen, AB10 1SU
Tel: 01224 630404
★★★★ Hotel

Craighaar Hotel
Waterton Road, Bucksburn, Aberdeen, AB21 9HS
Tel: 01224 712275
★★★ Hotel

Cults Hotel
The Square, Aberdeen, AB15 9SE
Tel: 01224 867632
★★★ Hotel

Dunrovin Guest House
168 Bon-Accord Street, Aberdeen, AB11 6TX
Tel: 01224 586081
Awaiting Inspection

Dyce Skean Dhu Hotel
Farburn Terrace, Dyce, Aberdeenshire, AB21 7DW
Tel: 01224 723101
★★★ Hotel

Ellenville Guest House
50 Springbank Terrace, Aberdeen, AB11 6LR
Tel: 01224 213334
★★★ Guest House

Furain Guest House
92 North Deeside Road, Peterculter, Aberdeen,
Tel: 01224 732189
★★★ Guest House

Granville Guest House
401 Great Western Road, Aberdeen, AB10 6NY
Tel: 01224 313043
★★★ Guest House

Greyholme
35 Springbank Terrace, Aberdeen, AB10 2LR
Tel: 01224 587081
★★★ Guest House

Hilton Aberdeen Treetops
161 Springfield Road, Aberdeen, AB15 7AQ
Tel: 01224 313377
★★★★ Hotel

Holiday Inn
Claymore Drive, Aberdeen, AB23 8GP
Tel: 08704 009046
★★★ Hotel

Kildonan Guest House
410 Great Western Road, Aberdeen, AB10 6NR
Tel: 01224 316115
★★★ Guest House

Marcliffe Hotel and Spa
North Deeside Road, Pitfodels, Aberdeen, AB15 9YA
Tel: 01224 861000
★★★★★ Hotel

Mariner Hotel
349 Great Western Road, Aberdeen, AB10 6NW
Tel: 01224 588901
★★★ Hotel

Merkland Guest House
12 Merkland Road East, Aberdeen, AB24 5PR
Tel: 01224 634451
★★ Guest House

Northern Hotel
1 Great Northern Road, Aberdeen, AB24 3PS
Tel: 01224 483342
★★★ Hotel

Norwood Hall Hotel
Garthdee Road, Aberdeen, AB15 9NX
Tel: 01224 868951
★★★★ Hotel

Open Hearth Guest House
349 Holburn Street, Aberdeen, AB10 7FQ
Tel: 01224 591675
★ Guest House

Palm Court Hotel
81 Seafield Road, Aberdeen, AB15 7YX
Tel: 01224 310351
★★★ Hotel

Penny Meadow
189 Great Western Road, Aberdeen, Aberdeenshire, AB10 6PS
Tel: 01224 588037
★★★★ Guest House

Roselea House
12 Springbank Terrace, Aberdeen, AB10 2LS
Tel: 01224 583060
★★★ Guest House

Royal Crown Guest House
111 Crown Street, Aberdeen, AB11 2HN
Tel: 01224 586461
★★★ Guest House

Royal Hotel
1-3 Bath Street, Aberdeen, AB11 6BJ
Tel: 01224 585152
★★ Hotel

Simpson's Hotel
59 Queens Road, Aberdeen, Aberdeen-shire, AB15 4YP
Tel: 01224 327777
★★★★ Hotel

Skene House HotelSuites
96 Rosemount Viaduct, Aberdeen, AB25 1NX
Tel: 01224 645971
★★★★ Serviced Apartments

Speedbird Inn
Argyll Road, Dyce, Aberdeen, Aberdeenshire, AB21 0AF
Tel: 01224 772883
★★★ Hotel

St Elmo
64 Hilton Drive, Aberdeen, AB24 4NP
Tel: 01224 483065
★★★★ Guest House

The Jays Guest House
422 King Street, Aberdeen, AB24 3BR
Tel: 01224 638295
★★★★ Guest House

Thistle Aberdeen Airport Hotel
Argyll Road, Aberdeen, Aberdeenshire, AB21 0AF
Tel: 01224 725252
★★★★ Hotel

Thistle Aberdeen Altens
Souterhead Road, Altens, Aberdeen, Aberdeenshire, AB12 3LF
Tel: 01224 877000
★★★ Hotel

Thistle Aberdeen Caledonian
10-14 Union Terrace, Aberdeen, Aberdeenshire, AB10 1WE
Tel: 01224 640233
★★★★ Hotel

University of Aberdeen, King's Hall
College Bounds, Aberdeen, AB24 3TT
Tel: 01224 273444
★★ Lodge

Water Wheel Toby Hotel
203 North Deeside Rd, Bieldside, Aberdeen, AB15 9EQ
Tel: 01224 861659
Awaiting Inspection

by Aberdeen

Maryculter Country House Hotel
Maryculter, Kincardineshire, AB12 5GB
Tel: 01224 732124
★★★ Country House Hotel

nr Aberdeen

Old Mill Inn
South Deeside Road, Maryculter, Aberdeen, AB12 5FX
Tel: 01224 733212
★★★ Inn

Strathburn Hotel
Burghmuir Drive, Inverurie, Aberdeenshire,
Tel: 01467 624422
★★★ Hotel

Aberlour

Dowans Hotel
Aberlour, Banffshire, AB38 9LS
Tel: 01340 871488
Awaiting Inspection

by Alford

Forbes Arms Hotel
Alford, Aberdeenshire, AB33 8QJ
Tel: 01975 562108
★★★ Small Hotel

Archiestown Hotel
The Square, Archiestown,
Morayshire, AB38 7QL
Tel: 01340 810218
★★★ Small Hotel

Alexandra Hotel
12 Bridge Square, Ballater,
Aberdeenshire, AB35 5QJ
Tel: 01339 755376
★★★ Small Hotel

Balgonie Country House
Braemar Place, Ballater,
Aberdeenshire, AB35 5NQ
Tel: 013397 55482
★★★★ Country House Hotel

Cambus O'May Hotel
nr Ballater, Aberdeenshire,
AB35 5SE
Tel: 013397 55428
★★★ Country House Hotel

Darroch Learg Hotel
Braemar Road, Ballater,
Aberdeenshire, AB35 5UX
Tel: 013397 55443
★★★★ Small Hotel

Deeside Hotel
Braemar Road, Ballater,
Aberdeenshire, AB35 5RQ
Tel: 013397 55420
★★★ Small Hotel

Glen Lui Hotel
14 Invercauld Road, Ballater,
Aberdeenshire, AB35 5PP
Tel: 01339 755402
★★★ Small Hotel

Glenernan Guest House
37 Braemar Road, Ballater,
Aberdeenshire, AB35 5RQ
Tel: 013397 53111
★★★ Guest House

The Gordon Guest House
Station Square, Ballater,
Aberdeenshire, AB35 5QB
Tel: 013397 55996
★★★★ Guest House

Hilton Craigendarroch Hotel
Braemar Road, Ballater,
Aberdeenshire, AB35 5RQ
Tel: 013397 55858
★★★ Hotel

Moorside Guest House
26 Braemar Road, Ballater,
Aberdeenshire, AB35 5RL
Tel: 01339 755492
★★★★ Guest House

Morvada House
28 Braemar Road, Ballater,
Deeside, AB35 5RL
Tel: 013397 56334
★★★★ Guest House

Netherley Guest House
2 Netherley Place, Ballater,
Aberdeenshire, AB35 5QE
Tel: 013397 55792
★★★★ Guest House

Loch Kinord Hotel
Ballater Road, Dinnet,
Royal Deeside,
Tel: 013398 85229
★★★ Hotel

Banchory Lodge Country House Hotel
Off Dee Street, Banchory,
Kincardineshire, AB31 5HS
Tel: 01330 822625
★★★ Country House Hotel

The Burnett Arms Hotel
25 High Street, Banchory,
Aberdeenshire,
Tel: 01330 824944
★★★ Small Hotel

Lochton
Durris, Banchory,
Kincardineshire, AB31 6DB
Tel: 01330 844543
★★★ Guest House

Raemoir Country House Hotel
Raemoir, Banchory,
Kincardineshire, AB31 4ED
Tel: 01330 824884
★★★ Country House Hotel

Learney Arms Hotel
The Square, Torphins,
Kincardineshire, AB31 4GP
Tel: 01339 882202
★★ Small Hotel

Carmelite House Hotel
Low Street, Banff, Banffshire,
AB45 1AY
Tel: 01261 812152
★★ Small Hotel

Fife Lodge Hotel
Sandyhill Road, Banff,
AB45 1BE
Tel: 01261 812436
★★★ Small Hotel

Gardenia House
19 Castle Street, Banff,
Banff & Buchan, AB45 1DH
Tel: 01261 812675
★★★ Guest House

The Trinity and Alvah Manse
21 Castle Street, Banff,
Aberdeen-shire, AB45 1DH
Tel: 01261 812244
★★★ Guest House

Braemar Lodge Hotel
Glenshee Road, Braemar,
Aberdeenshire, AB35 5YQ
Tel: 013397 41627
★★★ Small Hotel

Callater Lodge Guest House
9 Glenshee Road, Braemar,
Aberdeenshire, AB35 5YQ
Tel: 013397 41275
★★★★ Guest House

Craiglea
Hillside Road, Braemar,
Aberdeenshire, AB35 5YU
Tel: 013397 41641
★★★ Guest House

Cranford Guest House
15 Glenshee Road, Braemar,
Aberdeenshire, AB35 5YQ
Tel: 01339 741675
★★★ Guest House

Schiehallion Guest House
10 Glenshee Road, Braemar,
Aberdeenshire, AB35 5YQ
Tel: 013397 41679
★★★ Guest House

The Invercauld Arms Hotel
Invercauld Road, Braemar,
Aberdeenshire, AB35 5YR
Tel: 01339 741605
★★★ Hotel

Premier Inn Aberdeen North (Murcar)
Mill Of Mundurno, Murcar,
Bridge of Don, Aberdeen,
AB23 8BP
Tel: 08701 977012
Passed Budget Hotel

Marine Hotel
Marine Place, Buckie,
Banffshire, AB56 1UT
Tel: 01542 832249
★★★ Small Hotel

The Old Coach House Hotel
26 High Street, Buckie,
Banffshire, AB56 1AR
Tel: 01542 836266
★★★ Hotel

Kilmarnock Arms Hotel
Bridge Street, Cruden Bay,
by Peterhead, AB42 0HD
Tel: 01779 812213
★★★ Small Hotel

Norwood House
11 Seafield Place, Cullen,
Banffshire, AB56 4TE
Tel: 01542 840314
★★★ Guest House

Seafield Arms Hotel
19 Seafield Street, Cullen,
Moray, AB56 4SG
Tel: 01542 840791
★★★ Hotel

Fernbank House
Parkmore, Dufftown, Keith,
Banffshire, AB55 4DL
Tel: 01340 820136
Awaiting Inspection

Gowan Brae
19 Church Street, Dufftown,
Banffshire, AB55 4AR
Tel: 01340 821344
★★★ Guest House

Tannochbrae Guest House & Restaurant
22 Fife Street, Dufftown,
Banffshire, AB55 4AL
Tel: 01340 820541
★★★ Guest House

Auchmillan
12 Reidhaven Street, Elgin,
IV30 1QG
Tel: 01343 549077
★★★ Guest House

Elgin continued

Eight Acres Hotel & Leisure Club
Morriston Road, Elgin, Moray, IV30 6UL
Tel: 01343 543077
★★★ Hotel

Elgin Premier Inn
Linkwood Loddge
15 Linkwood Way, Elgin, Morayshire, IV30 1HY
Tel: 08701 977 095
Passed Budget Hotel

Laichmoray Hotel
Maisondieu Road, Elgin, Moray, IV30 1QR
Tel: 01343 540045
★★★ Hotel

Moraydale
276 High Street, Elgin, Morayshire, IV30 1AG
Tel: 01343 546381
★★★ Guest House

Royal Hotel
Station Road, Elgin, Moray, IV30 1QW
Tel: 01343 542320
★★★ Small Hotel

Southbank Guest House
36 Academy Street, Elgin, Moray, IV30 1LP
Tel: 01343 547132
★★★ Guest House

Sunninghill Hotel
Hay Street, Elgin, Moray, IV30 1NH
Tel: 01343 547799
★★★ Small Hotel

The Lodge
Duff Avenue, Elgin, Moray, IV30 1QS
Tel: 01343 549981
★★★★ Guest House

The Mansefield Hotel
Mayne Road, Elgin, Moray, IV30 1NY
Tel: 01343 540883
★★★★ Hotel

The Mansion House Hotel
The Haugh, Elgin, Moray, IV30 1AW
Tel: 01343 548811
★★★ Hotel

The Pines Guest House
East Road, Elgin, Moray, IV30 1XG
Tel: 01343 552495
★★★★ Guest House

West End Guest House
282 High Street, Elgin, Moray, IV30 1AQ
Tel: 01343 549629
★★★ Guest House

Ellon

Station Hotel
Station Brae, Ellon, Aberdeenshire, AB41 9BD
Tel: 01358 720209
★★ Small Hotel

Forres

Cluny Bank Hotel
St Leonards Road, Forres, Morayshire, IV36 1DW
Tel: 01309 674304
★★★★ Small Hotel

Ramnee Hotel
Victoria Road, Forres, Moray, IV36 3BN
Tel: 01309 672410
★★★★ Hotel

by Forres

Knockomie Hotel
Grantown Road, Forres, Morayshire, IV36 0SG
Tel: 01309 673146
★★★★ Country House Hotel

Milton of Grange Farm
Forres, Moray, IV36 2TR
Tel: 01309 676360
★★★★ Farmhouse

Glenlivet

Minmore House Hotel
Glenlivet, Ballindalloch, Banffshire, AB37 9DB
Tel: 01807 590378
★★★ Country House Hotel

Huntly

Castle Hotel
Huntly, Aberdeenshire, AB54 4SH
Tel: 01466 792696
★★★★ Country House Hotel

Dunedin Guest House
17 Bogie Street, Huntly, Aberdeenshire, AB5 5DX
Tel: 01466 794162
★★ Guest House

Gordon Arms Hotel
The Square, Huntly, Aberdeenshire, AB54 8AF
Tel: 01466 792288
★★ Small Hotel

Huntly Hotel
No 18, The Square, Huntly, Aberdeenshire, AB54 8BR
Tel: 01466 792703
★★ Small Hotel

by Huntly

Drumdelgie House
Drumdelgie, by Huntly, Aberdeenshire, AB5 4TH
Tel: 01466 760368
Awaiting Inspection

Inverurie

Ardennan House Hotel
Kemnay Road, Port Elphinstone, Inverurie, Aberdeenshire, AB51 3XD
Tel: 01467 621502
★★ Small Hotel

Breaslann Guest House
Old Chapel Road, Inverurie, Aberdeenshire, AB51 4QN
Tel: 01467 621608
★★★ Guest House

Grant Arms Hotel
Monymusk, Inverurie, Aberdeenshire, AB51 7HJ
Tel: 01467 651226
★★★ Inn

Swallow Thainstone House Hotel
Thainstone Estate, Inverurie Road, Inverurie, Aberdeenshire, AB51 5NT
Tel: 01467 621643
Awaiting Inspection

by Inverurie

Pittodrie House Hotel
Chapel of Garioch, by Inverurie, Aberdeen
Tel: 01467 681444
★★★ Country House Hotel

by Keith

Chapelhill Croft
Grange, Keith, Banffshire, AB55 6LQ
Tel: 01542 870302
★★★ Farmhouse

The Haughs
Keith, Banffshire, AB55 3QN
Tel: 01542 882238
★★★ Farmhouse

Kemnay

Bennachie Lodge Hotel
Victoria Terrace, Kemnay, Aberdeenshire, AB51 5RL
Tel: 01467 642789
★★ Small Hotel

Burnett Arms Hotel
Bridge Street, Kemnay, Aberdeenshire, AB51 5QT
Tel: 01467 642208
★★ Small Hotel

Kildrummy

Kildrummy Castle Hotel
Kildrummy,by Alford, Aberdeenshire, AB36 8RA
Tel: 019755 71288
★★★★ Hotel

Kintore

Torryburn Hotel
School Road, Kintore, Aberdeenshire, AB51 0XP
Tel: 01467 632269
★★ Small Hotel

Lossiemouth

Ardivot House B&B
Ardivot Farm, Lossiemouth, Moray, IV31 6RY
Tel: 01343 811076
★★★ Farmhouse

Norland
Stotfield Road, Lossiemouth, Moray, IV31 6QP
Tel: 01343 813570
Awaiting Inspection

Skerry Brae Hotel
Stotfield Road, Lossiemouth, Moray, IV31 6QS
Tel: 01343 812040
★★★ Small Hotel

Macduff

Knowes Hotel
78 Market Street, Macduff, Banffshire, AB44 1LL
Awaiting Inspection

The Park Hotel
Fife Street, Macduff, Banffshire, AB44 1YA
Tel: 01261 832265
★★★ Guest House

Macduff continued

Waterfront Hotel
25 Union Road, MacDuff,
Aberdeen-shire, AB44 1UD
Tel: 01261 831661
★★★ Small Hotel

Mrs Karen Berry
Main Street, Newburgh,
Aberdeenshire, AB41 6BP
Tel: 01358 789257
★★★ Small Hotel

Saplinbrae House Hotel
Old Deer, Mintlaw,
Aberdeenshire, AB42 4LP
Tel: 01771 623 515
★★ Small Hotel

Meldrum House Hotel Golf Country Estate
Old Meldrum, Aberdeenshire,
AB51 0AE
Tel: 01651 872294
★★★ Country House Hotel

The Redgarth
Kirk Brae, Oldmeldrum,
Aberdeenshire, AB51 0DJ
Tel: 01651 872353
★★★★ Inn

The Lodge Hotel
Old Rayne, Insch,
Aberdeenshire, AB52 6RY
Tel: 01464 851205
★★ Small Hotel

Carrick Guest House
16 Merchant Street,
Peterhead, Aberdeenshire,
Tel: 01779 470610
★★ Guest House

Invernettie Guest House
South Road, Burnhaven,
Peterhead, Aberdeenshire,
AB42 0YX
Tel: 01779 473530
★★★ Guest House

Palace Hotel
Prince Street, Peterhead,
Aberdeenshire, AB42 6PL
Tel: 01779 474821
★★★ Hotel

Waterside Inn
Fraserburgh Road, Peterhead,
Aberdeenshire, AB42 3BN
Tel: 0779 471121
Awaiting Inspection

Ashdon Guest House
Old Kemney Road,
Port Elphinstone, Inverurie,
Aberdeenshire, AB51 5XJ
Tel: 01467 620980
★★★ Guest House

Aberdeen South Premier Inn
Mains of Balquham,
Portlethen, Aberdeenshire,
AB12 4QS
Tel: 08701 977013
Passed Budget Hotel

Station Hotel
Seafield Street, Portsoy,
Aberdeenshire, AB45 2QT
Tel: 01261 842327
★★ Small Hotel

Rothie Inn
Main Street, Rothienorman,
Aberdeenshire, AB51 8UD
Tel: 01651 821206
★★★ Inn

The Tufted Duck Hotel
Corsekelly Place, St Combs,
Fraserburgh, Aberdeenshire,
AB43 8ZS
Tel: 01346 582481
★★★ Small Hotel

Arduthie Guest House
Ann Street, Stonehaven,
Kincardineshire, AB39
Tel: 01569 762381
★★★★ Guest House

Dunnottar Mains Farm
Stonehaven, Kincardineshire,
AB39 2TL
Tel: 01569 762621
★★★★ Farmhouse

Heugh Hotel
Westfield Road, Stonehaven,
Aberdeenshire, AB39 2EE
Tel: 01569 762379
★★★ Small Hotel

The Ship Inn
5 Shore Head, Stonehaven,
Aberdeen-Shire, AB39 2JY
Tel: 01569 762 617
★★ Inn

The Belvedere Hotel
41 Evan Street, Stonehaven,
Aberdeenshire, AB39 2ET
Tel: 01569 762672
Awaiting Inspection

Woodside of Glasslaw
Stonehaven, Aberdeenshire,
AB39 3XQ
Tel: 01569 763799
★★★ Guest House

The Colquhonnie House Hotel
Strathdon, Aberdeenshire,
AB36 8UN
Tel: 01975 651210
★★★ Inn

Findron Farm
Braemar Road,
Tomintoul,Ballindalloch,
Morayshire, AB37 9ER
Tel: 01807 580382
Awaiting Inspection

Richmond Hotel
The Square, Tomintoul,
Aberdeenshire, AB37 9ET
Tel: 01807 580777
★ Hotel

The Gordon Hotel
The Square, Tomintoul,
Aberdeenshire, AB37 9ET
Tel: 01807 580206
★★★ Hotel

Aberdeen Westhill Premier Inn
Shepherds Rest, Stakis Road,
Westhill, Aberdeenshire,
AB32 6HF
Tel: 0870 9906348
Passed Budget Hotel

Holiday Inn Aberdeen West
Westhill Drive, Westhill,
Aberdeen, Aberdeenshire,
AB32 6TT
Tel: 01224 270300
★★★★ Hotel

THE HIGHLANDS AND SKYE

NORTHERN HIGHLANDS, INVERNESS, LOCH NESS AND NAIRN

Abriachan

Angelshare
Abriachan, Inverness,
Inverness-shire, IV3 8LB
Tel: 01463 861410
Awaiting Inspection

Achnasheen

Ledgowan Lodge Hotel
Ledgowan, Achnasheen,
Ross-shire, IV22 2EJ
Tel: 01445 720252
★★★ Small Hotel

Ardross

Kildermorie Estate
Ardross, Easter Ross,
IV17 0YH
Tel: 020 7352 6248
Awaiting Inspection

Aultbea

Cartmel Guest House
Birchburn Road, Aultbea,
Ross-shire, IV22 2HZ
Tel: 01445 731375
★★★★ Guest House

Mellondale Guest House
47 Mellon Charles, Aultbea,
Ross-shire, IV22 2JL
Tel: 01445 731326
★★★★ Guest House

Beauly

Archdale Guest House
High Street, Beauly,
Inverness-shire, IV4 7BT
Tel: 01463 783043
★★ Guest House

Priory Hotel
The Square, Beauly,
Inverness-shire, IV4 7BX
Tel: 01463 782309
★★★ Hotel

Brackla, Loch Ness-side

Loch Ness Clansman Hotel
Brackla, Loch Ness Side,
Inverness-shire, IV3 8LA
Tel: 01456 450326
★★★ Hotel

Brora

Royal Marine Hotel
Golf Road, Brora, Sutherland,
KW9 6GS
Tel: 01408 621252
★★★★ Hotel

Castletown, by Thurso

Greenland House
Main Street, Castletown,
Caithness, KW14 8TU
Tel: 01847 821694
★★★ Guest House

St Clair Arms Hotel
Main Street, Castletown,
Thurso, Caithness, KW14 8TP
Tel: 01847 821656
Awaiting Inspection

by Dingwall

Kinkell Country House
Easter Kinkell,
by Conon Bridge,
Ross-shire, IV7 8HY
Tel: 01349 861270
★★★ Small Hotel

Dornoch

Burghfield House Hotel
Dornoch, Sutherland,
IV25 3HN
Tel: 01862 810212
Hotel

Dornoch Hotel
Dornoch, Sutherland,
IV25 3LD
Tel: 01862 810351
★★ Hotel

Dornoch Castle Hotel
Castle Street, Dornoch,
Sutherland, IV25 3SD
Tel: 01862 810216
★★★ Hotel

Eagle Hotel
Dornoch, Sutherland,
IV25 3SR
Tel: 01862 810008
★★★ Small Hotel

Drumnadrochit

Clunebeg Lodge Guest House
Clunebeg Estate,
Drumnadrochit,
Inverness-shire, IV63 6US
Tel: 01456 450387
★★★ Guest House

Loch Ness Inn
Lewiston, Drumnadrochit,
Inverness-shire, IV63 6UW
Tel: 07889 496092
Awaiting Inspection

Loch Ness Lodge Hotel
Drumnadrochit,
Inverness-shire, IV63 6TU
Tel: 01456 450342
★★★ Hotel

Durness

MacKays
Durness, Sutherland,
IV27 4PN
Tel: 01971 511209
★★★★ Guest House

Wild Orchid Guest House
Durine, Durness,
Sutherland, IV27 4PN
Tel: 01971 511280
Awaiting Inspection

Evanton

Assynt House
Evanton, Ross-shire,
IV16 9XW
Tel: 01349 832923
★★★★★ Exclusive Use Venue

by Evanton

Kiltearn House
Kiltearn House, Kiltearn,
by Evanton, Ross-shire, IV16 9UY
Tel: 01349 830 617
★★★★ Guest House

Farr, by Inverness

Grouse & Trout at The Steadings
Flichity, Farr, Inverness-shire,
IV2 6XD
Tel: 01808 521314
★★★ Small Hotel

Fearn

Fearn Hotel
Hill of Fearn, Fearn,
Ross-shire, IV20 1TJ
Tel: 0186283 2234
★★★ Restaurant with Rooms

Forss, by Thurso

Forss House Hotel
Forss, by Thurso, Caithness,
KW14 7XY
Tel: 01847 861201
★★★★ Country House Hotel

Fort Augustus

Caledonian Hotel
Fort Augustus,
Inverness-shire, PH32 4BQ
Tel: 01320 366256
★★★ Small Hotel

Hillside
1 The Steadings, Auchterawe,
Fort Augustus,
Inverness-shire, PH32 4BT
Tel: 01320 366253
Awaiting Inspection

Inchnacardoch Hotel
Fort Augustus,
Inverness-shire, PH32 4BL
Tel: 01456 450900
★★★ Country House Hotel

The Lovat Arms Hotel
Fort William Road,
Fort Augustus,
Inverness-shire, PH32 4DU
Tel: 01320 366366
★★★ Hotel

Gairloch

Gairloch Hotel
Gairloch, Ross-shire, IV21 2BL
Tel: 01445 712001
★★★ Hotel

Millcroft Hotel
Strath, Gairloch, Ross-shire,
IV21 2BT
Tel: 01445 712376
★★ Small Hotel

Shieldaig Lodge Hotel
Gairloch, Wester Ross,
IV21 2AW
Tel: 01445 741250
★★★ Country House Hotel

Glen Urquhart

Glenurquhart House
Glenurquhart,
Drumnadrochit,
Inverness-shire,
Tel: 01456 476234
★★★ Small Hotel

Golspie

The Golf Links Hotel
Church Street, Golspie,
Sutherland, KW10 6TT
Tel: 01408 633 408
★★ Small Hotel

Helmsdale

Kindale House
5 Lilleshall Street, Helmsdale,
Sutherland, KW8 6JF
Tel: 01431 821415
★★★★ Guest House

Invergarry

Forest Lodge
South Laggan, Invergarry,
Inverness-shire, PH34 4EA
Tel: 01809 501219
★★★ Guest House

Glengarry Castle Hotel
Invergarry, Inverness-shire,
PH35 4HW
Tel: 01809 501254
★★★ Country House Hotel

Invergordon

Kincraig House Hotel
Invergordon, Ross-shire,
IV18 0LF
Tel: 01349 852587
★★★★ Hotel

Inverness

Aberfeldy Lodge Guest House
11 Southside Road, Inverness,
Inverness-shire, IV2 3BG
Tel: 01463 231120
★★★ Guest House

Ach Aluinn Guest House
27 Fairfield Road, Inverness,
IV3 5QD
Tel: 01463 230127
★★★★ Guest House

Acorn House
Bruce Gardens, Inverness,
Inverness-shire, IV3 5ED
Tel: 01463 717021
★★★ Guest House

Anchor and Chain
Coulmore Bay,
North Kessock,
Inverness-shire, IV1 3XB
Tel: 01463 731313
★★★ Restaurant with Rooms

Ardconnel House
21 Arconnel Street, Inverness,
Inverness-shire, IV2 3EU
Tel: 01463 240455
★★★★ Guest House

Avalon
46 Brookfield, Culloden Moor,
Inverness, Inverness-shire,
IV2 5GL
Tel: 01463 798072
Awaiting Inspection

Avalon Guest House
79 Glenurquhart Road,
Inverness, Inverness-shire,
IV3 5PB
Tel: 01463 239075
★★★★ Guest House

Ballifeary Guest House
10 Ballifeary Road,
Inverness, IV3 5PJ
Tel: 01463 235572
★★★★ Guest House

Beaufort Hotel
11 Culduthel Road, Inverness,
IV2 4AG
Tel: 01463 222897
★★★ Hotel

Bunchrew House Hotel
Bunchrew, by Inverness,
Inverness-shire, IV3 6TA
Tel: 01463 234917
★★★★ Country House Hotel

Castle View Guest House
2A Ness Walk, Inverness,
IV3 5NE
Tel: 01463 241443
★★★ Guest House

Craigmonie Hotel
9 Annfield Road, Inverness,
Inverness-shire, IV2 3HX
Tel: 01463 231649
★★★ Hotel

Craignay House
16 Ardross Street, Inverness,
IV3 5NS
Tel: 01463 226563
Awaiting Inspection

Crown Guest House
19 Ardconnel Street,
Inverness, Inverness-shire,
IV2 3EU
Tel: 01463 231135
★★★ Guest House

Culloden House Hotel
Milton of Culloden,
Inverness, IV1 2NZ
Tel: 01463 792181
★★★★ Hotel

Daisy Cottage
111 Ballifeary Road,
Inverness, Inverness-shire,
IV3 5PE
Tel: 01463 234273
Awaiting Inspection

Dalmore Guest House
101 Kenneth Street,
Inverness, IV3 5QQ
Tel: 01463 237224
★★★ Guest House

Dunain Park Hotel
Inverness, IV3 8JN
Tel: 01463 230512
Awaiting Inspection

Dunhallin House
164 Culduthel Road,
Inverness, IV2 4BH
Tel: 01463 220824
★★★ Guest House

Eden House
8 Ballifeary Road, Inverness,
Inverness-shire, IV3 5PJ
Tel: 01463 230278
★★★★ Guest House

Eildon Guest House
29 Old Edinburgh Road,
Inverness, Inverness-shire,
IV2 3HJ
Tel: 01463 231969
★★★ Guest House

Eskdale House
41 Greig Street, Inverness,
IV3 5PX
Tel: 01463 240933
★★★ Guest House

Express by Holiday Inn
Stoneyfield, Inverness,
IV2 7PA
Tel: 01463 732700
★★★ Lodge

Furan Cottage
100 Old Edinburgh Road,
Inverness, IV2 3HT
Tel: 01463 712094
★★ Guest House

Glen Mhor Hotel
9-12 Ness Bank, Inverness,
Inverness-shire, IV2 4SG
Tel: 01463 234308
★★★ Hotel

Glencairn and Ardross House
18-19 Ardross Street,
Inverness, IV3 5NS
Tel: 01463 232965
★★★ Guest House

Glenmoriston Town House
20 Ness Bank, Inverness,
Inverness-shire, IV2 4SF
Tel: 01463 223777
★★★★ Hotel

Heathcote B&B
59 Glenurquhart Road,
Inverness, Inverness-shire,
IV3 5PB
Tel: 01463 243650
Awaiting Inspection

Inverglen
7 Abertarff Road, Inverness,
IV2 3NW
Tel: 01463 236281
★★★ Guest House

Inverness Centre Premier Inn
Millburn Road, Inverness,
IV2 3QX
Tel: 08701 977141
Passed Budget Hotel

Inverness East Premier Inn
Inshes Gate, Beechwood
Business Park, Inverness,
IV2 3BW
Tel: 08701 977142
Passed Budget Hotel

Ivanhoe Guest House
68 Lochalsh Road, Inverness,
IV3 8HW
Tel: 01463 223020
★★ Guest House

Kessock Hotel
North Kessock, Ross-shire,
IV1 1XN
Tel: 01463 731208
★★★ Small Hotel

Kingsmills Hotel, Inverness
Culcabock Road, Inverness,
IV2 3LP
Tel: 01463 237166
★★★★ Hotel

Inverness continued

Loch Ness Lodge
Brachla, Loch Ness-side,
Inverness-shire, IV3 8LA
Tel: 01456 459469
Awaiting Inspection

Lochardil House Hotel
Stratherrick Road, Inverness,
Inverness-shire, IV2 4LF
Tel: 01463 235995
★★★★ Hotel

Loch Ness House Hotel
Glenurquhart Road,
Inverness, Inverness-shire,
IV3 8JL
Tel: 01463 231248
★★★ Hotel

MacDonald House
1 Ardross Terrace, Inverness,
IV3 5NQ
Tel: 01463 232878
★★★ Guest House

MacDougall Clansman Hotel
103 Church Street,
Inverness, IV1 1ES
Tel: 01463 713702
★★ Metro Hotel

Malvern
54 Kenneth Street, Inverness,
Inverness-shire, IV3 5PZ
Tel: 01463 242251
★★★ Guest House

Maple Court Hotel
Ness Walk, Inverness, IV3 5SQ
Tel: 01463 230330
★★★ Small Hotel

Moray Park Guest House
1 Island Bank Road,
Inverness, IV2 4SX
Tel: 01463 233528
★★★ Guest House

Ness Bank Guest House
7 Ness Bank, Inverness,
Inverness-shire, IV2 4SF
Tel: 01463 232939
★★★ Guest House

Drumossie Hotel
Old Perth Road, Inverness,
Inverness-shire, IV2 5BE
Tel: 01463 236451
★★★★ Hotel

Palace Hotel
Ness Walk, Inverness,
Inverness-shire, IV3 5NG
Tel: 01463 223243
★★★ Hotel

Park Hill Guest House
17 Ardconnel Street,
Inverness, Inverness-shire,
IV2 3EU
Tel: 01463 223300
★★★ Guest House

Pitfaranne
57 Crown Street, Inverness,
IV2 3AY
Tel: 01463 239338
★★★ Guest House

Ramada Jarvis Inverness
Church Street, Inverness,
Inverness-shire, IV1 1DX
Tel: 01463 235181
★★★ Hotel

Redcliffe Hotel
1 Gordon Terrace, Inverness,
IV2 3HD
Tel: 01463 232767
★★★ Small Hotel

Riverview Guest House
2 Moray Park,
Island Bank Road, Inverness,
Inverness-shire, IV2 4SX
Tel: 01463 235557
★★★ Guest House

Rocpool Reserve Hotel
14 Culduthel Road, Inverness,
Inverness-shire, IV2 4AG
Tel: 01463 240089
★★★★★ Small Hotel

Roseneath Guest House
39 Greig Street, Inverness,
IV3 5PX
Tel: 01463 220201
★★★ Guest House

Royston Guest House
16 Millburn Road, Inverness,
IV2 3PS
Tel: 01463 231243
★★★ Guest House

St Ann's House
37 Harrowden Road,
Inverness, Inverness-shire,
IV3 5QN
Tel: 01463 236157
★★★ Guest House

Strathness Guest House
4 Ardross Terrace,
Inverness, IV3 5NQ
Tel: 01463 232765
★★★ Guest House

Talisker House
25 Ness Bank, Inverness,
Inverness-shire, IV2 4SF
Tel: 01463 236221
★★★ Guest House

The Alexander
16 Ness Bank, Inverness,
Inverness-shire, IV2 4SF
Tel: 01463 231151
★★★ Guest House

Thistle Inverness
Millburn Road, Inverness,
Inverness-shire, IV2 3TR
Tel: 0870 333 9155
★★★ Hotel

Waterside Hotel
Ness Bank, Inverness,
Inverness-shire, IV2 4SF
Tel: 01463 233065
★★★ Hotel

Whinpark Guest House
17 Ardross Street,
Inverness, Inverness-shire,
IV3 5NS
Tel: 01463 232549
★★★ Guest House

White Lodge
15 Bishops Road, Inverness,
IV3 5SB
Tel: 01463 230693
★★★★ Guest House

Winston Guest House
10 Ardross Terrace,
Inverness, Inverness-shire,
IV3 5NQ
Tel: 01463 234477
★★★ Guest House

John o'Groats

Caber Feidh Guest House
John O'Groats, Caithness,
KW1 4YR
Tel: 01955 611219
★★ Guest House

Seaview Hotel
John O'Groats, Caithness,
KW1 4YR
Tel: 01955 611220
★★ Small Hotel

Kiltarlity

Cherry Trees
Kiltarlity, Inverness-shire,
IV4 7JQ
Tel: 01463 741368
★★★★ Farmhouse

Kinlochbervie

The Kinlochbervie Hotel
Kinlochbervie, Sutherland,
IV27 4RP
Tel: 01971 521275
★★ Small Hotel

Kinlochewe

Kinlochewe Hotel
Kinlochewe, By Achnasheen,
Wester Ross, IV22 2PA
Tel: 01445 760253
★★ Small Hotel

Kylesku

Newton Lodge
Kylesku, Sutherland,
IV27 4HW
Tel: 01971 502070
★★★★ Guest House

Lairg

The Nip Inn
Main Street, Lairg, Sutherland,
IV27 4DB
Tel: 01549 402243
★★★ Small Hotel

by Lairg

The Overscaig House Hotel
Loch Shin, Sutherland,
IV27 4NY
Tel: 01549 431203
★★★ Small Hotel

Lochcarron

Lochcarron Hotel
Main Street, Lochcarron,
Rosshire, IV54 8YS
Tel: 01520 722226
Awaiting Inspection

Lochend, Loch Ness-side

Kimcraigan B&B
Kimcraigan, Lochend,
Inverness-shire, IV3 8LA
Tel: 01463 861474
Awaiting Inspection

Lochinver

Inver Lodge Hotel
Lochinver, Sutherland,
IV27 4LU
Tel: 01571 844496
★★★★ Hotel

Polcraig Guest House
Lochinver, Sutherland,
IV27 4LD
Tel: 01571 844429
★★★★ Guest House

Lochinver continued

The Albannach
Baddidarroch, Lochinver,
Sutherland, IV27 4LP
Tel: 01571 844407
★★★★ Small Hotel

Loch Ness

Craigdarroch House Hotel
South Loch Ness Side, Foyers,
Inverness, Inverness-shire,
IV2 6XU
Tel: 01456 486400
Awaiting Inspection

Melvich

Bighouse Lodge
Melvich, by Thurso,
Sutherland, KW14 7YJ
Tel: 01641 531207
★★★★ Small Hotel

Mey

Castle Arms Hotel
Mey,by Thurso, Caithness,
KW14 8XH
Tel: 01847 851244
★★ Small Hotel

Muir of Ord

Ord House Hotel
Muir of Ord, Ross-shire,
IV6 7UH
Tel: 01463 870492
★★ Small Hotel

Nairn

Aurora Hotel
2 Academy Street, Nairn,
Nairn-shire, IV12 4RJ
Tel: 01667 453551
★★ Small Hotel

Bracadale House
Albert Street, Nairn, IV12 4HF
Tel: 01667 452547
★★★★ Guest House

Brackla Farmhouse
Cawdor, Nairn,
Inverness-shire, IV12 5QY
Tel: 01667 404223
★★★★ Farmhouse

Braeval Hotel
Crescent Road, Nairn,
Inverness-shire, IV12 4NB
Tel: 01667 452341
★★★ Small Hotel

Cawdor House
7 Cawdor Street, Nairn,
Inverness-shire, IV12 4QD
Tel: 01667 455855
★★★ Guest House

Claymore House Hotel
Seabank Road, Nairn,
IV12 4EY
Tel: 01667 453731
★★★★ Small Hotel

Glen Lyon Lodge
19 Waverley Road, Nairn,
Nairnshire, IV12 4RH
Tel: 01667 452780
★★★ Guest House

Golf View Hotel
Seabank Road, Nairn,
Inverness-shire, IV12 4HD
Tel: 01667 452301
Awaiting Inspection

Invernairne Guest House
Thurlow Road, Nairn,
Inverness-shire, IV12 4EZ
Tel: 01667 452039
★★★ Guest House

Sunny Brae Hotel
Marine Road, Nairn,
Inverness-shire, IV12 4AE
Tel: 01667 452309
★★★★ Small Hotel

Windsor Hotel
16 Albert Street, Nairn,
Inverness-shire, IV12 4HP
Tel: 01667 453108
Awaiting Inspection

Plockton

Duncraig Castle
By Plockton, Ross-shire,
IV52 8TZ
Tel: 01599 544295
Awaiting Inspection

The Haven Hotel
Innes Street, Plockton,
Ross-shire, IV52 8TW
Tel: 01599 544223
★★ Small Hotel

Poolewe

Corriness House
Poolewe, Wester Ross,
IV22 2JU
Tel: 01445 781785
★★★★ Guest House

Pool House
Poolewe, Rosshire, IV22 2LD
Tel: 01445 781272
★★★★ Small Hotel

Poolewe Hotel
Main Street, Poolewe,
IV22 2JX
Tel: 01445 781241
Awaiting Inspection

Reay

The Old Inn
Reay, Thurso, Caithness,
KW14 7RE
Tel: 01847 811554
Awaiting Inspection

Rhiconich

Rhiconich Hotel
Rhiconich, Sutherland,
IV27 4RN
Tel: 01971 521224
★★★ Small Hotel

Rosehall, by Lairg

Woodland Guest House
Woodland, Rosehall, by Lairg,
Sutherland, IV27 4BD
Tel: 01549 441715
Awaiting Inspection

Scourie

Eddrachilles Hotel
Badcall Bay, Scourie,
Sutherland, IV27 4TH
Tel: 01971 502080
★★★ Small Hotel

Scourie Guest House
55 Scourie Village, By Lairg,
Sutherland, IV27 4TE
Tel: 01971 502001
★★★ Guest House

Scourie Hotel
Scourie, Sutherland,
IV27 4SX
Tel: 01971 502396
★★★ Small Hotel

Stoer

Cruachan Guest House
Stoer, by Lochinver,
Sutherland, IV27 4JE
Tel: 01571 855303
★★★★ Guest House

Strathpeffer

Ben Wyvis Hotel
Strathpeffer, Ross-shire,
IV14 9DN
Tel: 01997 421323
★★★ Hotel

Coul House Hotel
Contin, By Strathpeffer,
Ross-shire, IV14 9ES
Tel: 01997 421487
★★★ Hotel

Garden House
Garden House Brae,
Strathpeffer, Ross-shire,
IV14 9BJ
Tel: 01997 421242
★★★ Guest House

Highland Hotel
Strathpeffer, Ross-shire,
IV14 9AS
Tel: 01997 421457
★★ Hotel

Struy, by Beauly

Cnoc Hotel
Struy, By Beauly,
Inverness-shire, IV4 7JU
Tel: 01463 761 264
★★★ Small Hotel

Tain

Dunbius Guest House
Morangie Road, Tain,
Ross-shire, IV19 1HP
Tel: 01862 894902
★★★ Guest House

Golf View Guest House
13 Knockbreck Road, Tain,
Ross-shire, IV19 1BN
Tel: 01862 892856
★★★★ Guest House

Mansefield Castle Hotel
Scotsburn Road, Tain,
Ross-shire, IV19 1PR
Tel: 01862 892052
★★★ Hotel

Morangie House Hotel
Morangie Road, Tain,
Ross-shire, IV19 1PY
Tel: 01862 892281
★★★ Hotel

Pitcalzean House
Pitcalnie, Nr Tain, Ross-shire,
IV19 1QT
★★★ Guest House

Thurso

Park Hotel
Thurso, KW14 8RE
Tel: 01847 893251
★★★ Small Hotel

Pentland Hotel
Princes Street, Thurso,
Caithness, KW14 7AA
Tel: 01847 893202
★★★ Hotel

Pentland Lodge House
Granville Street, Thurso,
Caithness, KW14 7LG
Tel: 01847 8611206
★★★★ Guest House

St Clair Hotel
Sinclair Street, Thurso,
Caithness, KW14 7AJ
Tel: 01847 896481
★★★ Hotel

Thurso continued

Station Hotel and Apartments
54-58 Princes Street, Thurso, Caithness, KW14 7DH
Tel: 01847 892003
★★★ Hotel

Weigh Inn Hotel
Burnside, Thurso, Caithness, KW14 7UG
Tel: 01847 893722
★★★ Hotel

Tomich

Tomich Hotel
Tomich, by Cannich, near Beauly, Inverness-shire, IV4 7LY
Tel: 01456 415399
★★★ Small Hotel

Tongue

Ben Loyal Hotel
Main Street, Tongue, Sutherland, IV27 4XE
Tel: 01847 611216
★★★ Small Hotel

Borgie Lodge Hotel
Skerray, By Tongue, Sutherland, KW14 7TH
Tel: 01641 521332
★★ Small Hotel

Tongue Hotel
Tongue, Sutherland, V27 4XD
Tel: 01847 611206
★★★★ Small Hotel

Torridon

The Torridon
Torridon, Achnasheen, Ross-shire, IV22 2EY
Tel: 01445 791242
★★★★ Country House Hotel

Ullapool

Ardvreck House
North Road, Morefield, Ullapool, IV26 2TH
Tel: 01854 612028
★★★★ Guest House

Dromnan Guest House
Garve Road, Ullapool, Ross-shire, IV26 2SX
Tel: 01854 612333
★★★★ Guest House

Eilean Donan Guest House
14 Market Street, Ullapool, Ross-shire, IV26 2XE
Tel: 01854 612524
★★★ Guest House

Harbour Lights Hotel
Garve Road, Ullapool, Ross-shire, IV26 2SX
Tel: 01854 612222
★★ Small Hotel

Riverside
Quay Street, Ullapool, Ross-shire, IV26 2UE
Tel: 01854 612239
★★★ Guest House

Strathmore Guest House
Morefield, Ullapool, Ross-shire, IV26 2TH
Tel: 01854 612423
★★★ Guest House

The Argyll Hotel
18 Argyle Street, Ullapool, IV26 2UB
Tel: 01854 612422
★★ Small Hotel

Westlea Guest House
2 Market Street, Ullapool, Ross-shire, IV26 2XE
Tel: 01854 612594
★★★★ Guest House

Whitebridge

Kinbrylie
Whitebridge, Inverness-shire, IV2 6UN
Tel: 01456 486658
Awaiting Inspection

Whitebridge Hotel
Whitebridge, Inverness-shire, IV2 6UN
Tel: 01456 486226
★★ Small Hotel

Wick

Impala Craigie Highland Home
Broadhaven Road, Wick, Caithness, KW1 4RF
Tel: 01955 602194
★★★ Guest House

Mackays Hotel
46 Union Street, Wick, Caithness, KW1 5ED
Tel: 01955 602323
★★★ Hotel

Nethercliffe Hotel
Louisburgh Street, Wick, Caithness, KW1 4NS
Tel: 01955 602044
★★★ Small Hotel

Queens Hotel
16 Francis Street, Wick, Caithness, KW1 5PZ
Tel: 01955 602992
★★ Small Hotel

FORT WILLIAM AND LOCHABER, SKYE AND LOCHALSH

Ardelve, by Dornie

Caberfeidh House
Caberfeidh House, Upper Ardelve, by Kyle of Lochalsh, Ross-shire, IV40 8DY
Tel: 01599 555293
★★★ Guest House

Conchra House
Sallachy Road, Ardelve, by Kyle, Ross-shire, IV40 8DZ
Tel: 01599 555233
★★★ Guest House

Arisaig

Cnoc-Na-Faire
Back of Keppoch, Arisaig, Inverness-shire, PH39 4NS
Tel: 01687 450249
★★★★ Small Hotel

The Arisaig Hotel
Arisaig, Inverness-shire, PH39 4NH
Tel: 01687 450210
★★ Small Hotel

Ballachulish

Ballachulish House
Ballachulish, Argyll, PH49 4JX
Tel: 01855 811266
★★★★★ Guest Accommodation

Craiglinnhe House
Lettermore, Ballachulish, Argyll, PH49 4JD
Tel: 01855 811270
★★★★ Guest House

Fern Villa Guest House
Loan Fern, Ballachulish, Argyll, PH49 4JE
Tel: 01855 811393
★★★ Guest House

Isles of Glencoe Hotel & Leisure Centre
Ballachulish, Argyll, PH49 4HL
Tel: 01855 811602
★★★ Hotel

Lyn Leven Guest House
Ballachulish, Argyll, PH49 4JP
Tel: 01855 811392
★★★★ Guest House

The Ballachulish Hotel
Ballachulish, Argyll, PH49 4JY
Tel: 01855 811606
★★★ Hotel

Corpach, by Fort William

Braeburn
Badabrie, Fort William, Inverness-shire, PH33 7LX
Tel: 01397 77 772047
★★★★ Guest House

Dornie, by Kyle of Lochalsh

Dornie Hotel
Francis Street, Dornie, Ross-shire, IV40 8DT
Tel: 01599 555205
★★★ Small Hotel

Eilean A-Cheo
Dornie, by Kyle of Lochalsh, Ross-shire, IV40 8DY
Tel: 01599 555485
★★★ Guest House

Loch Duich Hotel & Seafood Restaurant
Ardelve, By Kyle of Lochalsh, Ross-shire, IV40 8DY
Tel: 01599 555213
★★ Small Hotel

Fort William

Alexandra Hotel
The Parade, Fort William, Inverness-shire, PH33 6AZ
Tel: 01397 702241
★★ Hotel

Ben Nevis Hotel & Leisure Club
North Road, Fort William, Inverness-shire, PH33 6TG
Tel: 01397 702331
★★ Hotel

Berkeley House
Belford Road, Fort William, Inverness-shire, PH33 6BT
Tel: 01397 701185
★★★ Guest House

Fort William continued

Caledonian Hotel
Achintore Road, Fort William,
Inverness-shire, PH33 6RW
Tel: 01397 703117
★★ Hotel

Clan MacDuff Hotel
Achintore Road,
Fort William,
Inverness-shire, PH33 6RW.
Tel: 01397 702341
★★★ Hotel

Constantia House
Fassifern Road, Fort William,
Inverness-shire, PH33 6BD
Tel: 01397 702893
★★ Guest House

Craig Nevis West
Belford Road, Fort William,
Inverness-shire, PH33 6BU
Tel: 01397 702023
★★ Guest House

Cruachan Hotel
Achintore Road,
Fort William,
Inverness-shire,
Tel: 01397 702022
★★ Hotel

Distillery Guest House
Nevis Bridge, Fort William,
Inverness-shire,
Tel: 01397 700103
★★★★ Guest House

Fortwilliam Loch Iall Premier Inn
An Aird, Fort William,
Inverness-shire, PH33 6AN
Tel: 08701 977104
Passed Budget Hotel

Gara-Ni
Fassifern Road, Fort William,
Invernes-shire, PH33 6BD
Tel: 01397 701724
Awaiting Inspection

Glenlochy Guest House
Nevis Bridge, Fort William,
Inverness-shire, PH33 6LP
Tel: 01397 702909
★★★ Guest House

Glentower Lower Observatory
Achintore Road, Fort William,
Inverness Shire, PH33 6PQ
Tel: 01397 704007
★★★★ Guest House

Guisachan Guest House
Alma Road, Fort William,
Inverness-shire, PH33 6HA
Tel: 01397 703797
★★★ Guest House

Inverlochy Castle Hotel
Torlundy, Fort William,
Inverness-shire, PH33 6SN
Tel: 01397 702177
★★★★★ Country House Hotel

Lawriestone Guest House
Achintore Road,
Fort William,
Inverness-shire, PH33 6RQ
Tel: 01397 700777
★★★★ Bed & Breakfast

Lime Tree An Ealdhain
Achintore Road,
Fort William,
Inverness-shire, PH33 6RQ
Tel: 01397 701806
★★★ Small Hotel

Lochan Cottage Guest House
Lochyside, Fort William,
Inverness-shire, PH33 7NX
Tel: 01397 702695
★★★★ Guest House

Lochiel Villa Guest House
Achintore Road, Fort William,
Inverness-shire, PH33 6RQ
Tel: 01397 703616
★★★ Guest House

Lochview House
Heathercroft, off Argyll
Terrace, Fort William,
Inverness-shire, PH33 6RE
Tel: 01397 703149
★★★ Guest House

Mansefield Guest House
Corpach, Fort William,
Inverness-shire, PH33 7LT
Tel: 01397 772262
★★★★ Guest House

Nevis Bank Hotel
Belford Road, Fort William,
Inverness-shire, PH33 6BY
Tel: 01397 705721
★ Hotel

Stronchreggan View Guest House
Achintore Road, Fort William,
Inverness-shire, PH33 6RW
Tel: 01397 704644
★★★ Guest House

The Imperial Hotel
Fraser Square, Fort William,
Inverness-shire, PH33 6DW
Tel: 01397 702040
★★★ Hotel

The Moorings Hotel
Banavie, by Fort William,
Inverness-shire, PH33 7LY
Tel: 01397 772797
★★★★ Hotel

West End Hotel
Achintore Road,
Fort William, PH33 6ED
Tel: 01397 702614
★★★ Hotel

by Fort William

Carinbrook
Banavie, Fort William,
Inverness-shire, PH33 7LX
Tel: 01397 772318
★★★ Guest House

Glen Loy Lodge
Banavie, Fort William,
Inverness-shire, PH33 7PD
Tel: 01397 712 700
★★★ Guest House

Old Pines Hotel & Restaurant
Spean Bridge,
by Fort William, PH34 4EG
Tel: 01397 712324
★★★ Small Hotel

nr Fort William

The Tailrace Inn
Riverside Road,
Kinlochleven, Argyll,
PH50 4QH
Tel: 01855 831777
★★★ Inn

Glencoe

Clachaig Inn
Glencoe, Argyll, PH49 4HX
Tel: 01855 811252
★★ Inn

Dorrington Lodge
6 Tigh Phuirst, Glencoe, Argyll,
PH49 4HN
Tel: 01855 811653
★★★ Guest House

MacDonald Hotel
Fort William Road,
Kinlochleven, Argyll,
PH50 4QL
Tel: 01855 831539
★★★ Small Hotel

Scorrybreac Guest House
Glencoe, Argyll, PH49 4HT
Tel: 01855 811354
★★★★ Guest House

Strathassynt Guest House
Loan Fern, Ballachulish,
Argyll, PH49 4JB
Tel: 01855 811261
★★★ Guest House

Glenfinnan

The Princes' House Hotel
Glenfinnan, Inverness-shire,
PH37 4LT
Tel: 01397 722246
★★★ Small Hotel

Glen Nevis, by Fort William

Ben Nevis Guest House
Glen Nevis, Fort William,
Inverness-shire, PH33 6PF
Tel: 01397 708817
★★★ Guest House

Glenshiel, by Kyle of Lochalsh

Kintail Lodge Hotel
Glenshiel, Ross-shire,
IV40 8HL
Tel: 01599 511275
★★★ Small Hotel

Isle of Skye

Ardvasar, Sleat

Ardvasar Hotel
Ardvasar, Isle of Skye,
IV45 8RS
Tel: 01471 844223
★★★ Small Hotel

Broadford

Benview
6 Black Park, Broadford,
Isle of Skye, IV49 9AE
Tel: 01471 822445
Awaiting Inspection

Broadford Hotel
Broadford, Isle of Skye,
Inverness-shire, IV49 9AB
Tel: 01471 822414
★★★★ Hotel

Seaview
Main Street, Broadford,
Isle of Skye, IV49 9AB
Tel: 01471 820308
★★★ Guest House

Slapin View
Torrin, Broadford, Isle of Skye,
IV49 9BA
Tel: 01471 822672
★★ Farmhouse

Carbost

Fineviews
11B Portnalong, Carbost,
Isle of Skye, IV47 8SL
Tel: 07810 710485
Awaiting Inspection

Phoenix House Bed & Breakfast
Phoenix House, Carbost,
Isle of Skye, IV47 8SR
Tel: 01478 640775
Awaiting Inspection

Colbost, by Dunvegan

The Three Chimneys and The House Over-By
Colbost, by Dunvegan,
Isle of Skye, IV55 8ZT
Tel: 01470 511258
★★★★★ Restaurant with Rooms

Dunvegan

Dunorin House Hotel
2 Herebost, Dunvegan,
Isle of Skye,
Inverness-shire, IV55 8GZ
Tel: 01470 521488
★★★★ Small Hotel

Dunvegan Hotel
Main Street, Dunvegan,
Isle of Skye, IV55 8WA
Tel: 01470 521497
★★★ Small Hotel

The Tables Hotel
Main Street, Dunvegan,
Isle of Skye, Inverness-shire,
IV55 8WA
Tel: 01470 521404
★★ Small Hotel

Edinbane

Tir Alainn - Kildonan
2A Kildonan, Edinbane,
Portree, Isle of Skye, IV51 9PU
Tel: 01470 582335
Awaiting Inspection

Glendale

Carter's Rest
8/9 Upper Milovaig, Glendale,
Isle of Skye, IV55 8WY
Tel: 01470 511272
★★★★ Guest House

Isleornsay

Kinloch Lodge
Sleat, Isle of Skye, IV43 8QY
Tel: 01471 833214
★★★★ Country House Hotel

Kensaleyre, by Portree

Corran Guest House
Eyre, Kensaleyre, Portree,
Isle of Skye, Inverness-shire,
IV51 9XE
Tel: 01470 532311
★★★★ Guest House

Kyleakin

Glenarroch
Main Street, Kyleakin,
Isle of Skye, IV41 8PH
Tel: 01599 534845
★★★ Guest House

Mackinnon Country House Hotel
Old Farm Road, Kyleakin,
Isle of Skye, Inverness-shire,
IV41 8PQ
Tel: 01599 534180
★★★ Small Hotel

Portree

25 Urquhart Place
Portree, Isle of Skye,
Inverness-shire, IV51 9HJ
Tel: 01478 612374
Awaiting Inspection

Almondbank
Viewfield Road, Portree,
Isle of Skye, IV51 9EU
Tel: 01478 612696
★★★★ Guest House

An Airidh
6 Fisherfield, Portree,
Isle of Skye, IV51 9EU
Tel: 01478 612250
★★★ Guest House

Balloch
Viewfield Road, Portree,
Isle of Skye, Inverness-shire,
IV51 9ES
Tel: 01478 612093
★★★★ Guest House

Coolin View Guest House
Bosville Terrace, Portree,
Isle of Skye, Inverness-shire,
IV51 9DG
Tel: 01478 611280
Awaiting Inspection

Cuillin Hills Hotel
Portree, Isle of Skye,
IV51 9QU
Tel: 01478 612003
★★★★ Country House Hotel

Givendale Guest House
Heron Place, Portree,
Isle of Skye, IV51 9GU
Tel: 01478 612183
★★★ Guest House

Green Acres Guest House
Viewfield Road, Portree,
Isle of Skye, IV51 9EU
Tel: 01478 613175
★★★★ Guest House

Marmalade
Home Farm Road, Portree,
Isle of Skye, IV51 9LX
Tel: 01478 611711
★★★ Small Hotel

Meadowbank House
Seafield Place, Portree,
Isle of Skye, IV51 9ES
Tel: 01478 612059
★★★ Guest House

Quiraing Guest House
Viewfield Road, Portree,
Isle of Skye, Inverness-shire,
IV51 9ES
Tel: 01478 612870
★★★★ Guest House

Rosebank House
Springfield Road, Portree,
Isle of Skye, Inverness-shire,
IV51 9QX
Tel: 01478 612282
★★★ Guest House

Rosedale Hotel
Beaumont Crescent,
Portree, Isle of Skye,
IV51 9DB
Tel: 01478 613131
★★★ Hotel

Royal Hotel
Bank Street, Portree,
Isle of Skye,
Inverness-shire, IV51 9BU
Tel: 01478 61 2525
★★★ Hotel

The Bosville Hotel
10 Bosville Terrace, Portree,
Isle of Skye, Inverness-shire,
IV51 9DG
Tel: 01478 612846
★★★★ Hotel

Viewfield House Hotel
Portree, Isle of Skye, IV51 9EU
Tel: 01478 612217
★★★★ Guest House

br Portree

Greshornish House Hotel
Edinbane, By Portree,
Isle of Skye, IV51 9PN
Tel: 01470 582266
★★★ Country House Hotel

Sleat

Duisdale Hotel
Isle Ornsay, Sleat,
Isle of Skye, IV43 8QW
Tel: 01471 833202
Awaiting Inspection

Eilean Iarmain
Camus Cross, Sleat,
Isle of Skye, IV43 8QR
Tel: 01471 833332
★★★ Small Hotel

Toravaig House Hotel & Iona Restaurant
Knock Bay, Sleat,
Isle of Skye, IV44 8RE
Tel: 01471 833231
★★★★ Small Hotel

Staffin

Flodigarry Country House Hotel
Flodigarry, Staffin,
Isle of Skye, IV51 9HZ
Tel: 01470 552203
★★★ Small Hotel

Glenview Hotel
Culnacnoc, Staffin,
Isle of Skye, IV51 9JH
Tel: 01470 562248
Awaiting Inspection

Treaslane

Auchendinny
Treaslane, Portree,
Isle of Skye, Inverness-shire,
IV51 9NX
Tel: 01470 532470
★★★ Guest House

Uig

Uig Hotel
Uig, Isle of Skye,
Inverness-shire, IV51 9YE
Tel: 01470 542205
★★★ Small Hotel

Kentallen, by Appin

Holly Tree Hotel
Kentallen, Appin, Argyll,
PA38 4BY
Tel: 01631 740292
★★★ Hotel

Kinlochleven

Mamore Lodge Hotel
Kinlochleven, Argyll,
PH50 4QN
Tel: 01855 831 213
★ Small Hotel

Knoydart

Doune-Knoydart
Doune, Knoydart, Mallaig,
Inverness-shire, PH41 4PU
Tel: 01687 462667
★★★ Restaurant with Rooms

Kyle of Lochalsh

Tingle Creek Hotel
Erbusaig, Kyle, Ross-shire,
IV40 8BB
Tel: 01599 534430
★★ Small Hotel

Mallaig

Garramore House
South Morar, Mallaig,
Inverness-shire, PH40 4PD
Tel: 01687 450268
★★ Guest House

Seaview
Mallaig, Inverness-shire,
PH41 4QS
Tel: 01687 462059
★★★ Guest House

The Moorings
East Bay, Mallaig,
Inverness-shire, PH41 4PQ
Tel: 01687 462225
★★★ Guest House

Western Isles Guest House
East Bay, Mallaig,
Inverness-shire, PH41 4QG
Tel: 01687 462320
★★★ Guest House

West Highland Hotel
Mallaig, Inverness-shire,
PH41 4QZ
Tel: 01687 462210
★★★ Hotel

Morar

Morar Hotel
Morar, By Mallaig,
Inverness-shire, PH40 4PA
Tel: 01687 462346
★★ Hotel

Onich, by Fort William

Camus House
Lochside Lodge, Onich,
Inverness-shire, PH33 6RY
Tel: 01855 821200
★★★ Guest House

The Lodge on the Loch Hotel
Onich, North Ballachulish,
Fort William, PH33 6RY
Awaiting Inspection

Onich Hotel
Onich, Inverness-shire,
PH33 6RY
Tel: 01855 821214
★★★ Hotel

Isle of Raasay

Isle of Raasay Hotel
Raasay, Kyle of Lochalsh,
Ross-shire, IV40 8PB
Tel: 01478 660222
★★★ Small Hotel

Roy Bridge

Glenspean Lodge Hotel
Roy Bridge, Inverness-shire,
PH31 4AW
Tel: 01397 712223
Awaiting Inspection

The Stronlossit Inn
Roy Bridge, Inverness-shire,
PH31 4AG
Tel: 01397 712253
★★★ Small Hotel

Spean Bridge

Achnabobane Farmhouse
Spean Bridge,
Inverness-shire, PH34 4EX
Tel: 01397 712919
★★★ Farmhouse

Coire Glas Guest House
Roybridge Road,
Spean Bridge,
Inverness-shire, PH34 4EU
Tel: 01397 712272
★★★ Guest House

Corriegour Lodge Hotel
Loch Lochy,
by Spean Bridge,
Inverness-shire
Tel: 01397 712685
★★★★ Small Hotel

Distant Hills Guest House
Roybridge Road,
Spean Bridge,
Inverness-shire, PH34 4EU
Tel: 01397 712452
★★★★ Guest House

Inverour Guest House
Roy Bridge Road,
Spean Bridge,
Inverness-shire, PH34 4EU
Tel: 01397 712218
★★★ Guest House

Spean Bridge Hotel
Main Road, Spean Bridge,
Inverness-shire, PH34 4ES
Tel: 01397 712250
★★ Hotel

The Braes Guest House
Spean Bridge,
Inverness-shire, PH34 4EU
Tel: 01397 71243
★★★ Guest House

The Heathers
Invergloy Halt, Spean Bridge,
Inverness-shire, PH34 4DY
Tel: 01397 712077
★★★★ Guest House

Torlundy

Aonach Mor House
Torlundy, Fort William,
Lochaber, PH33 6SW
Tel: 01397 704525
Awaiting Inspection

AVIEMORE AND THE CAIRNGORMS

Aviemore

Aviemore Four Seasons
Aviemore, Inverness-shire,
PH22 1PJ
Tel: 01479 815100
★★★ Hotel

Cairngorm Guest House
Grampian Road, Aviemore,
Inverness-shire, PH22 1RP
Tel: 01479 810630
★★★ Guest House

Cairngorm Hotel
Grampian Road, Aviemore,
PH22 1PE
Tel: 01479 810233
★★★ Hotel

Corrour House
Inverdruie, Aviemore,
Inverness-shire, PH22 1QH
Tel: 01479 810220
★★★★ Guest House

Hilton Coylumbridge Hotel
Coylumbridge, by Aviemore,
Inverness-shire, PH22 1QN
Tel: 01479 810661
Hotel

Junipers
5 Dellmhor, Aviemore,
Inverness-shire, PH22 1QW
Tel: 01479 810405
★★★ Guest House

Kinapol Guest House
Dalfaber Road, Aviemore,
Inverness-shire, PH22 1PY
Tel: 01479 810513
★★★ Guest House

Macdonald Highlands Hotel
Aviemore Centre, Aviemore,
Inverness-shire, PH22 1PJ
★★★★ Hotel

Mackenzies
12S Grampian Road,
Aviemore, Inverness-shire,
PH22 1RL
Tel: 01479 810672
Awaiting Inspection

Ravenscraig Guest House
Grampian Road, Aviemore,
Inverness-shire, PH22 1RP
Tel: 01479 810278
★★★★ Guest House

The Rowan Tree Country Hotel
Loch Alvie, Aviemore,
Inverness-shire, PH22 1QB
Tel: 01479 810207
★★★ Small Hotel

Boat of Garten

The Boat Hotel
Boat of Garten,
Inverness-shire, PH24 3BH
Tel: 01479 831258
Awaiting Inspection

Boat of Garten

Granlea House
Deshar Road, Boat of Garten,
Inverness-shire, PH24 3BN
Tel: 01479 831601
★★★ Guest House

Heathbank House
Drumuillie Road,
Boat of Garten,
Inverness-shire, PH24 3BD
Tel: 01479 831234
★★★ Guest House

Moorfield House
Deshar Road,
Boat of Garten,
Inverness-shire,
Tel: 01479 831646
★★★★ Guest House

Carrbridge

The Cairn Hotel
Main Road, Carrbridge,
Inverness-shire, PH23 3AS
Tel: 01479 841212
★★★ Inn

Carrbridge Hotel
Main Street, Carrbridge,
Inverness-shire, PH23 3AS
Tel: 01479 841202
Awaiting Inspection

Carrmoor Guest House
Carr Road, Carrbridge,
Inverness-shire, PH23 3AD
Tel: 01479 841244
★★★ Guest House

Craigellachie House
Main Street, Carrbridge,
Inverness-shire, PH23 3AS
Tel: 01479 841641
★★★★ Guest House

Dalrachney Lodge Hotel
Carrbridge, Inverness-shire,
PH23 3AT
Tel: 01479 841252
★★★ Country House Hotel

Fairwinds Hotel
Carrbridge, Inverness-shire,
PH23 3AA
Tel: 01479 841240
★★★ Small Hotel

Dulnain Bridge, by Grantown-on-Spey

Muckrach Lodge Hotel
Dulnain Bridge,
Grantown-on-spey, Moray,
PH26 3LY
Tel: 01479 851257
★★★ Country House Hotel

Rosegrove Guest House
Skye of Curr Road,
Dulnain Bridge,
Grantown on Spey, PH26 3PA
Tel: 01479 851335
★★★ Guest House

Grantown-on-Spey

An Cala Guest House
Woodlands Terrace,
Grantown on Spey, Moray,
PH26 3JU
Tel: 01479 873293
★★★★★ Guest House

Ben Mhor Hotel
53-57 High Street,
Grantown on Spey, Moray,
PH26 3EG
Tel: 01479 872056
Awaiting Inspection

Brooklynn
Grant Road,
Grantown on Spey,
Morayshire, PH26 3LA
Tel: 01479 873113
★★★★ Guest House

Craiglynne Hotel
Woodlands Terrace,
Grantown-on-Spey,
Morayshire, PH26 3JX
Tel: 01479 872597
Awaiting Inspection

Culdearn House
Woodland Terrace,
Grantown-on-Spey,
Morayshire, PH26 3JU
Tel: 01479 872106
★★★★★ Guest House

Dunallan House
Woodside Avenue,
Grantown-on-Spey, Moray,
PH26 3JN
Tel: 01479 872140
★★★★ Guest House

Gaich Farm
Balnacruie, Boat of Garten,
Grantown-on-Spey,
Inverness-shire, PH26 3NT
Tel: 01479 851381
★★ Farmhouse

Garden Park Guest House
Woodside Avenue,
Grantown-on-Spey, Moray,
PH26 3JN
Tel: 01479 873235
★★★ Guest House

Garth Hotel
The Square,
Grantown-on-Spey, Moray,
PH26 3HN
Tel: 01479 872836
★★★ Small Hotel

Holmhill House
Woodside Avenue,
Grantown on Spey,
Morayshire, PH26 3JR
Tel: 01479 873977
★★★★ Guest House

Kinross Guest House
Woodside Avenue,
Grantown-on-Spey, Moray,
PH26 3JR
Tel: 01479 872042
★★★★ Guest House

Parkburn Guest House
High Street,
Grantown-on-Spey, Moray,
PH26 3EN
Tel: 01479 873116
★★★ Guest House

Ravenscourt House Hotel
Seafield Avenue,
Grantown-on-Spey,
Morayshire, PH26 3JG
Tel: 01479 872286
★★★★ Small Hotel

Rosehall Guest House
13 The Square,
Grantown On Spey,
Morayshire, PH26 3HG
Tel: 01479 872721
★★★★ Guest House

Rossmor Guest House
Woodlands Terrace,
Grantown on Spey, Moray,
PH26 3JU
Tel: 01479 872201
★★★★ Guest House

Seafield Lodge Hotel
Woodside Avenue,
Grantown-on-Spey,
Morayshire, PH26 3JN
Tel: 01479 872152
★★★ Small Hotel

Strathallan House
Grant Road,
Grantown-on-Spey, Moray,
PH26 3LD
Tel: 01479 872165
★★★★ Guest House

The Pines
Woodside Avenue,
Grantown-on-Spey, Moray,
PH26 3JR
Tel: 01479 872092
★★★★★ Guest Accommodation

Willowbank
High Street,
Grantown on Spey,
Morayshire, PH26 3EN
Tel: 01479 872089
★★★ Guest House

by Grantown-on-Spey

Haugh Hotel
Cromdale, Grantown-on-Spey,
Morayshire, PH26 3LW
Tel: 01479 872583
Awaiting Inspection

Kincraig, by Kingussie

Suie Hotel
Kincraig, Inverness-shire,
PH21 1NA
Tel: 01540 651 344
★★★ Guest House

Kingussie

Allt Gynack Guest House
Gynack Villa, 1 High Street,
Kingussie, Inverness-shire,
PH21 1HS
Tel: 01540 661081
★★★ Guest House

Arden House
Newtonmore Road,
Kingussie, Inverness-shire,
PH21 1HE
Tel: 01540 661369
★★★★ Guest House

Columba House Hotel & Garden Restaurant
Manse Road, Kingussie,
Inverness-shire, PH21 1JF
Tel: 01540 661402
★★★ Small Hotel

Duke of Gordon Hotel
Kingussie, Inverness-shire,
PH21 1HE
Tel: 01540 661302
★★★ Hotel

The Scot House Hotel
Newtonmore Road,
Kingussie, Inverness-shire,
PH21 1HE
Tel: 01540 661351
★★★ Small Hotel

Sonnhalde Guest House
East Terrace, Kingussie,
Inverness-shire, PH21 1JS
Tel: 015401 661266
★★★ Guest House

The Hermitage Guest House
Spey Street, Kingussie,
Inverness-shire, PH21 1HN
Tel: 01540 662137
★★★★ Guest House

West Wing of Clifton
Clifton, Middle Terrace,
Kingussie, Inverness-shire,
PH21 1EY
Tel: 01540 661248
Awaiting Inspection

Laggan Bridge, by Newtonmore

Laggan Country Hotel
Laggan, Inverness-shire,
PH20 1BS
Tel: 01528 544250
★★ Hotel

Monadhliath Hotel
Laggan Bridge,
nr Newtonmore,
Inverness-shire
Tel: 01528 544276
★★★ Small Hotel

Nethy Bridge

Mount View Hotel
Nethy Bridge, Inverness-shire,
PH25 3EB
Tel: 01479 821 248
★★★ Small Hotel

Nethybridge Hotel
Nethybridge,
Inverness-shire, PH25 3DP
Tel: 01479 821203
★★★ Hotel

Newtonmore

Alvey House
Golf Course Road,
Newtonmore,
Inverness-shire,
Tel: 01540 673260
★★★ Guest House

Ard-Na-Coille
Kingussie Road, Newtonmore,
Inverness-shire, PH20 1AY
Tel: 01450 673214
Awaiting Inspection

Balavil Sport Hotel
Main Street, Newtonmore,
Inverness-shire, PH20 1DL
Tel: 01540 673220
★★ Hotel

Coig Na Shee
Fort William Road,
Newtonmore,
Inverness-shire, PH20 1DG
Tel: 01540 670109
★★★★ Guest House

Crubenbeg House
Falls of Truim,
By Newtonmore, PH20 1BE
Tel: 01540 673300
★★★★ Guest House

Greenways
Golf Course Road,
Newtonmore, Inverness-shire,
PH20 1AT
Tel: 01540 670136
Awaiting Inspection

Rothiemurchus

The Old Ministers House
Rothiemurchus, Aviemore,
Inverness-shire, PH22 1QH
Tel: 01479 812181
★★★★ Guest House

THE OUTER ISLANDS:
Outer Hebrides, Orkney, Shetland

OUTER HEBRIDES

Isle of Barra

Castlebay

Castlebay Hotel
Castlebay, Isle of Barra,
HS9 5XD
Tel: 01871 810223
Awaiting Inspection

Craigard Hotel
Castlebay, Barra,
Outer Hebrides, HS9 5XD
Tel: 01871 810200
★★★ Small Hotel

Isle of Benbecula

Creagorry

The Isle of Benbecula House Hotel
Creagorry, Benbecula,
Western Isles, HS7 5PG
Tel: 01870 602024
★★★ Hotel

Liniclate

Dark Island Hotel
Liniclate, Isle of Benbecula,
Western Isles, HS7 5PJ
Tel: 0870 602414
★★ Hotel

Torlum

Borve Guest House
5 Torlum, Benbecula,
Western Isles, HS7 5PP
Tel: 01870 602685
★★★★ Guest House

Isle of Benbecula

Isle of Benbecula

Lionacleit Guest House
27 Liniclate, Benbecula,
Western Isles, HS7 5PY
Tel: 01870 602176
★★★ Guest House

Isle of Harris

Amhuinnsuidhe

Amhuinnsuidhe Castle
Isle of Harris, Western Isles,
HS3 3AS
Tel: 01859 560200
★★★★ Exclusive Use Venue

Kyles Harris

Rodel Hotel
Rodel, Isle of Harris, HS5 3TW
Tel: 01859 520 210
★★★ Small Hotel

Leverburgh

Grimisdale
Leverburgh, Isle of Harris,
Western Isles, HS5 3TS
Tel: 01859 520460
★★★★ Guest House

Scarista

Scarista House
Scarista, Isle of Harris, HS3 3HX
Tel: 01859 550238
★★★★ Guest House

Tarbert

Ceol Na Mara Guest House
7 Direclete, Tarbert,
Isle of Harris, HS3 3DP
Tel: 01859 502464
★★★★ Guest House

Harris Hotel
Tarbert, Isle of Harris,
Western Isles, HS3 3DL
Tel: 01859 502154
★★ Hotel

Isle of Lewis

Achmore

Cleascro House
Achmore,, Isle of Lewis,
HS2 9DU
Tel: 01851 860302
★★★★ Guest House

Back

Broad Bay House
Back, Isle of Lewis, HS2 0LQ
Tel: 01851 820990
★★★★★ Guest House

Crowberry
43 Vatisker, Back,
Isle of Lewis, HS2 0LF
Tel: 01851 605004
Awaiting Inspection

Breasclete

Eshcol Guest House
21 Breasclete, Callanish,
Lewis, Outer Hebrides,
HS2 9DY
Tel: 01851 621357
★★★★ Guest House

Breasclete continued

Loch Roag Guest House
22A Breasclete, Isle of Lewis, Western Isles, HS2 9EF
Tel: 01851 621357
★★★★ Guest House

Callanish

Leumadair Guest House
7 Callanish, HS2 9DY
Tel: 01857 621706
★★★★ Guest House

South Galson

Galson Farm Guest House
South Galson, Lewis, Western Isles, HS2 0SH
Tel: 01851 850492
★★★★ Guest House

Stornoway

Braighe House
20 Braighe Road, Stornoway, Isle Of Lewis, HS2 0BQ
Tel: 01851 705287
★★★★ Guest House

Cabarfeidh Hotel
Manor Park, Stornoway, Isle of Lewis, HS1 2EU
Tel: 01851 702604
★★★ Hotel

Caladh Inn
James Street, Stornoway, Isle of Lewis, HS1 2QN
Tel: 01851 702604
★★ Hotel

Greenacres
8 Smith Avenue, Stornoway, Isle of Lewis, Western Isles, HS1 2PY
Tel: 01851 706383
★★★ Guest House

Hal-O The Wynd
2 Newton Street, Stornoway, Isle of Lewis, HS1 2RE
Tel: 01851 706073
★★★ Guest House

Hebridean Guest House
61 Bayhead, Stornoway, Isle of Lewis, HS1 2DZ
Tel: 01851 702268
★★★ Guest House

Holm View Guest House
18 Bhraighe Road, Branahuie, Stornoway, Isle of Lewis, HS2 0BQ
Tel: 01851 706826
★★★★ Guest House

Park Guest House
30 James Street, Stornoway, Isle of Lewis, HS1 2QN
Tel: 01851 702485
★★★★ Guest House

Royal Hotel
Cromwell Street, Stornoway, Isle of Lewis, HS1 2DG
Tel: 01851 702109
★★ Hotel

Timsgarry

Baile-Na-Cille
Timsgarry, Uig, Isle of Lewis, HS2 9SD
Tel: 01851 672242
★★ Guest House

Isle of Uist

Carinish

Temple View Hotel
Carinish, North Uist, Western Isles, HS6 5EJ
Tel: 01876 580676
★★★★ Small Hotel

Lochmaddy

Lochmaddy Hotel
Lochmaddy, North Uist, Western Isles, HS6 5AA
Tel: 01876 500331
★★ Hotel

Tigh Dearg Hotel
Lochmaddy, Isle of North Uist, Western Isles, HS6 5AE
Tel: 01876 500700
★★★★ Small Hotel

Daliburgh

Borrodale Hotel
Daliburgh, South Uist, Western Isles, HS8 5SS
Tel: 01878 700444
★★★ Small Hotel

Eochdar

Anglers Retreat
1 Ardmore, Iochdar, South Uist, HS8 5QY
Tel: 01870 610325
★★★ Guest House

Lochboisdale

Brae Lea House
Lasgair, Lochboisdale, Isle of South Uist, HS8 5TH
Tel: 01878 700497
★★★ Guest House

Lochboisdale Hotel
Lochboisdale, South Uist, HS8 5TH
Tel: 01878 700332
★★ Small Hotel

Lochcarnan

Orasay Inn
Lochcarnan, South Uist, Outer Hebrides, HS8 5PD
Tel: 01870 610298
★★★ Small Hotel

ORKNEY

Birsay

Barony Hotel
Birsay, Orkney, KW17 2LS
Tel: 01856 721327
★★ Small Hotel

Burray

Sands Hotel
Burray, Orkney, KW17 2SS
Tel: 01856 731298
★★★★ Small Hotel

Evie

Woodwick House
Evie, Orkney, KW17 2PQ
Tel: 01856 751330
★★★ Guest House

Harray

Merkister Hotel
Loch Harray, Orkney, KW17 2LF
Tel: 01856 771366
★★★ Country House Hotel

Hoy

Stromabank
Hoy, Orkney, KW16 3PA
Tel: 01856 701494
★★★ Small Hotel

Kirkwall

Albert Hotel
Mounthoolie Lane, Kirkwall, Orkney, KW15 1JZ
Tel: 01856 876000
★★★ Small Hotel

Avalon House
Carness Road, Kirkwall, Orkney, KW15 1UE
Tel: 01856 876665
★★★★ Guest House

Ayre Hotel
Ayre Road, aberfeid, Orkney, KW15 1QX
Tel: 01856 873001
★★★ Hotel

Bellavista
Carness Road, Kirkwall, Orkney, KW15 1UE
Tel: 01856 872306
Awaiting Inspection

Brekkness Guest House
Muddisdale Road, Kirkwall, Orkney, KW15 1RS
Tel: 01856 874317
★★★ Guest House

Foveran Hotel
St Ola, Kirkwall, Orkney, KW15 1SF
Tel: 01856 872389
★★★ Small Hotel

Kirkwall Hotel
Harbour Street, Kirkwall, Orkney, KW15 1LF
Tel: 01856 872232
★★★ Hotel

Lav'rockha Guest House
Inganess Road, Kirkwall, Orkney, KW15 1SP
Tel: 01856 876103
★★★★ Guest House

Lynnfield Hotel
Holm Road, Kirkwall, Orkney, KW15 1SU
Tel: 01856 872505
★★★★ Small Hotel

No 5 Ingale
Kirkwall, Orkney, KW15 1UY
Tel: 01856 875721
Awaiting Inspection

Orkney Hotel
Victoria Street, Kirkwall, Orkney, KW15
Tel: 01856 873477
★★★ Hotel

Polrudden Guest House
Peerie Sea Loan, Kirkwall, Orkney, KW15 1UH
Tel: 01856 874761
★★★ Guest House

Royal Oak Guest House
Holm Road, Kirkwall, Orkney, KW15 1PY
Tel: 01856 873487
★★★ Guest House

Kirkwall continued

Sanderlay Guest House
2 Viewfield Drive, Kirkwall,
Orkney, KW15 1RB
Tel: 01856 875587
★★★ Guest House

St Ola Hotel
Harbour Street, Kirkwall,
Orkney, KW15 1LE
Tel: 01856 875090
★★★ Guest House

The Inn B&B
St Marys, Holm, Kirkwall,
Orkney, KW17 2RU
Tel: 01856 781786
Awaiting Inspection

Observatory Guest House
North Ronaldsay, Orkney,
KW17 2BE
Tel: 01857 633200
★★★ Guest House

Beltane House
Papay Community
Cooperative Ltd,
Papa Westray, Orkney,
KW17 2BU
Tel: 01857 644321
★★ Guest House

Hyval Farm B&B
North Dyke Road, Quoyloo,
Orkney, KW16 3LS
Tel: 01856 841522
★★★ Farmhouse

Commodore Chalets
St Mary's, Holm, Orkney, W17 2RU
Tel: 01856 781319
★★★ Guest House

Balfour Castle
Balfour Village, Shapinsay,
Orkney, KW17 2DY
Tel: 01856 711282
★★★ Country House Hotel

Hilton Farmhouse
Shapinsay, Balfour, Orkney,
KW17 2EA
Tel: 01856 711239
★★★★ Farmhouse

Standing Stones Hotel
Stenness, Stromness, Orkney,
KW16 3JX
Tel: 01856 850449
★★★ Small Hotel

**Millers House &
Harbourside B&B**
7 & 13 John Street,
Stromness, Orkney, KW16 3AD
Tel: 01856 851969
★★★ Guest House

Orca Guest House
76 Victoria Street, Stromness,
Orkney, KW16 3BS
Tel: 01856 850447
★★ Guest House

Royal Hotel
55-57 Victoria Street,
Stromness, Orkney, KW16 3BS
Tel: 01856 850342
★★ Small Hotel

Stromness Hotel
Victoria Street, Stromness,
Orkney, KW16 3AA
Tel: 01856 850298
★★★ Hotel

The Ferry Lodge
15 John Street, Stromness,
Orkney, KW16 3AD
Tel: 01856 850109
★★ Guest Accommodation

Cleaton House
Cleaton, Westray, Orkney,
KW17 2DB
Tel: 01857 677508
★★★★ Small Hotel

Buness House
Balta Sound, Unst, Shetland,
ZE2 9DS
Tel: 01957 711315
★★★★ Guest House

Brae Hotel
Brae, Shetland, ZE2 9QJ
Tel: 01806 522026
★ Hotel

Busta House Hotel
Busta, North Mainland,
Shetland, ZE2 9QN
Tel: 01806 522506
★★★ Hotel

Northern Lights Holistic Spa
Sound View Uphouse,
Bressay, Shetland, ZE2 9ES
Tel: 01595 820733
★★★★ Guest House

**Fair Isle Bird Observatory
Lodge**
Fair Isle, Shetland, ZE2 9JU
Tel: 01595 760258
★★ Guest House

Alderlodge Guest House
6 Clairmont Place, Lerwick,
Shetland, ZE1 0BR
Tel: 01595 695705
★★★ Guest House

Bonavista Guest House
26 Church Road, Lerwick,
Shetland, ZE1 0AE
Tel: 01595 692269
★★★ Guest House

Breiview
43 Kanterstead Road,
Lerwick, Shetland, ZE1 0RJ
Tel: 01595 695956
★★★ Guest House

Brentham House
7 Harbour Street, Lerwick,
Shetland, ZE1 0LR
Tel: 01950 460201
**★★★★ Guest
Accommodation**

Eddlewood Guest House
8 Clairmont Place, Lerwick,
Shetland, ZE1 0BR
Tel: 01595 692772
★★★ Guest House

Fort Charlotte Guest House
1 Charlotte Street, Lerwick,
Shetland, ZE1 0JL
Tel: 01595 692140
★★★ Guest House

Glen Orchy Guest House
20 Knab Road, Lerwick,
Shetland, ZE1 0AX
Tel: 01595 692031
★★★ Guest House

Grand Hotel
Commercial Street, Lerwick,
Shetland, ZE1 0HX
Tel: 01595 692826
★★★ Hotel

Kveldsro House Hotel
Greenfield Place, Lerwick,
Shetland, ZE1 0AN
Tel: 01595 692195
★★★ Small Hotel

Lerwick Hotel
15 South Road, Lerwick,
Shetland, ZE1 0RB
Tel: 01595 692166
★★★ Hotel

Queen's Hotel
Commercial Street, Lerwick,
Shetland, ZE1 0AB
Tel: 01595 692826
★★★ Hotel

Shetland Hotel
Holmsgarth Road, Lerwick,
Shetland, ZE1 0PW
Tel: 01595 695515
★★★ Hotel

Solheim Guest House
34 King Harald Street,
Lerwick, Shetland, ZE1 0EQ
Tel: 01595 695275
★★★ Guest House

Spiggie Hotel
Scouseburgh, Shetland Isles,
ZE2 9JE
Tel: 01950 460409
★★★ Small Hotel

Sumburgh Hotel
Sumburgh, Virkie, Shetland,
ZE3 9JN
Tel: 01950 60201
★★★ Hotel

The Baltasound Hotel
Baltasound, Unst, Shetland,
ZE2 9DS
Tel: 01957 711334
★★ Hotel

Burrastow House
Walls, Shetland, ZE2 9PD
Tel: 01595 809307
★★★★ Guest House

INDEX BY LOCATION